Scottish Literature in English and Scots

AMERICAN LITERATURE, ENGLISH LITERATURE, AND WORLD LITERATURES IN ENGLISH: AN INFORMATION GUIDE SERIES

Series Editor: Theodore Grieder, Curator, Division of Special Collections, Fales Library, New York University

Associate Editor: Duane DeVries, Associate Professor, Polytechnic Institute of New York, Brooklyn

Other books on world literatures in this series:

BLACK AFRICAN LITERATURE IN ENGLISH—*Edited by Bernth Lindfors*

ASIAN LITERATURE IN ENGLISH—*Edited by G.L. Anderson*

AUSTRALIAN LITERATURE TO 1900—*Edited by Barry G. Andrews and William H. Wilde*

MODERN AUSTRALIAN POETRY, 1920-1970—*Edited by Herbert C. Jaffa*

MODERN AUSTRALIAN PROSE, 1901-1975—*Edited by A. Grove Day*

ENGLISH-CANADIAN LITERATURE TO 1900—*Edited by R.G. Moyles*

MODERN ENGLISH-CANADIAN POETRY—*Edited by Peter Stevens*

MODERN ENGLISH-CANADIAN PROSE—*Edited by Helen Hoy**

INDIAN LITERATURE IN ENGLISH, 1827-1979—*Edited by Amritjit Singh, Rajiva Verma, and Irene Joshi*

IRISH LITERATURE, 1800-1875—*Edited by Brian McKenna*

NEW ZEALAND LITERATURE TO 1977—*Edited by John Thomson*

AUTHOR NEWSLETTERS AND JOURNALS—*Edited by Margaret Patterson*

*in preparation

The above series is part of the
GALE INFORMATION GUIDE LIBRARY

The Library consists of a number of separate series of guides covering major areas in the social sciences, humanities, and current affairs.

General Editor: Paul Wasserman, Professor and former Dean, School of Library and Information Services, University of Maryland

Managing Editor: Denise Allard Adzigian, Gale Research Company

Scottish Literature in English and Scots

A GUIDE TO INFORMATION SOURCES

Volume 37 in the American Literature, English Literature, and World Literatures in English Information Guide Series

W.R. Aitken

*formerly Reader
Department of Librarianship
University of Strathclyde
Glasgow*

Gale Research Company
Book Tower, Detroit, Michigan 48226

Library of Congress Cataloging in Publication Data

Aitken, William Russell.
   Scottish literature in English and Scots.

   (American literature, English literature, and world
literatures in English information guide series ; v. 37)
(Gale information guide library)
     Includes indexes.
    1. Scottish literature—History and criticism—
Bibliography. 2. English literature—Scottish authors—
History and criticism—Bibliography. 3. Authors,
Scottish—Biography—Bibliography. 4. Bibliography—
Bibliography—Scottish literature. 5. Scotland—
Bibliography. I. Title. II. Series: Gale information
guide library. American literature, English literature,
and world literatures in English ; v. 37.
Z2057.A35 [PR8511] 016.82'09'9411   82-2997
ISBN 0-8103-1249-2   AACR2

To my daughter
CHRISTINE
and her daughters
MARION and ALISON
to whose generation the future belongs

VITA

W.R. Aitken retired in 1978 from his post as reader in the department of librarianship, University of Strathclyde, Glasgow, where he had taught bibliographical studies for sixteen years; but in his retirement, he still teaches each spring term a course in bibliography for postgraduate students in the department of English literature, University of Edinburgh.

Aitken received his M.A. and Ph.D. degrees from the University of Edinburgh. His Ph.D. thesis, A HISTORY OF THE PUBLIC LIBRARY MOVEMENT IN SCOTLAND, was published by the Scottish Library Association in 1971 as the first of its series of Scottish Library Studies. He was president of the Scottish Library Association in 1965, and edited the quarterly LIBRARY REVIEW for thirteen years, from 1964 to 1976.

He first wrote on Scottish literature in 1948, an essay, "The Scottish Literary Renaissance," submitted as part of the qualification for his Fellowship of Library Association; and he has since published many bibliographical notes and checklists on various modern Scottish authors. He has edited William Soutar's POEMS IN SCOTS AND ENGLISH (1961, 1975) and, with the poet's son, the COMPLETE POEMS OF HUGH MacDIARMID (1978).

CONTENTS

Contents

Contents

Contents

Contents

Contents

Contents

ACKNOWLEDGMENTS

This guide is the outcome of an interest in Scottish literature which was first aroused by an inspiring teacher during my last year at Dunfermline High School and then quickened and confirmed in my years in Edinburgh when I was a student under Professor Herbert Grierson and first met "Scotland's vortex maker," Hugh MacDiarmid. It is the end-product of a long involvement with the bibliography of Scottish literature in which I have had the pleasure of working with many friends and colleagues, some of whom must have had an influence, conscious or unconscious, on my shaping of this guide.

One in particular I must name: Professor David Buchan of St. John's, Newfoundland, whose help and advice in connection with the section on "Popular and Folk Literature" I gratefully acknowledge. I should make it clear, nevertheless, that Professor Buchan is not to be held accountable for any deficiencies in that section, for which I accept full responsibility.

Finally, I would put on record my thanks to Betsy, my wife, for her constant help and encouragement while this work was in progress.

W.R. Aitken
Dunblane, Perthsire

INTRODUCTION

Scottish literature is difficult to define satisfactorily. It will include writing by Scots in Scots ("braid Lallans" or "Lallan," as Burns and Stevenson called it),[1] in English, and in every degree of Scots and English in combination; it should also include writing in Gaelic, and some would say in Latin, for in George Buchanan and Arthur Johnston and many others, Scotland produced Latin poetry which (in Dr. Johnson's phrase) "would have done honour to any nation." Here we are concerned with Scottish literature in Scots and English.

There is a tendency for the Scots writer's nationality to make itself felt, even when writing in English. The English prose of Thomas Carlyle is inherently Scottish; there are Scottish characteristics in Byron, who was only partly Scots, but spent his formative years in Aberdeen; and there are other Scots who write "profoundly Scottish poems in English" (as David Daiches says of W.S. Graham).

Thirty years ago, Harvey Wood offered a tentative definition: "One can only say, perhaps, that Scottish literature is literature, whether in Scots or English, written by Scotsmen to whom the Scottish habit of mind and Scottish literary conventions were more natural than English."[2] An understanding of that habit of mind and these literary conventions will emerge only from a study of all the literature which such a definition may possibly circumscribe.

The work of at least the major Scottish writers is frequently treated as part of English literature, but the scattered attention Scottish writers are given in histories and bibliographies of English literature is doubly unsatisfactory. It obscures the possibility that an independent Scottish tradition exists, and it fails to provide for a true assessment of the writers in a Scottish context or perspective. English literary criticism cannot be expected to recognize how a Scottish community may produce and influence its authors, nor explain what these authors have meant to Scots and can still mean to them.

T.S. Eliot was aware of the problem: "I suspect Arnold of helping to fix the wholly mistaken notion of Burns as a singular untutored English dialect poet, instead of as a decadent representative of a great alien tradition." That there is something that can be called the Scottish literary tradition is now becoming recognized, even if there is still no great agreement on what that tradition is nor on which writers belong to it.

Some of the characteristics of Scots literature were identified in a lecture delivered seventy years ago by J.C. Smith, at the time president of the Scottish branch of the English Association;[3] others have been suggested by another Smith, in the book which made such a mark on Hugh MacDiarmid.[4] Gregory Smith's concept of the "Caledonian antisyzygy"--the zigzag of contradictions; the two aspects the Scot presents which appear contradictory, yet intermingle; "the absolute propriety of a gargoyle's grinning at the elbow of a kneeling saint"--is now part of Scotland's literary mythology; and the Scot's "freedom in passing from one mood to another," which Gregory Smith also noted, is certainly a very real characteristic. Read, for example, Norman MacCaig's memorial tribute to Sydney Goodsir Smith.[5]

This freedom of movement manifests itself in an interest in language, and an openness to other literatures. Scots have provided a goodly number of translators, from Gavin Douglas and his AENEID to Edwin Morgan's translations into Scots from Mayakovsky: among them Sir Thomas Urquhart's Rabelais, Carlyle's Goethe, William Archer's Ibsen, C.K. Scott Moncrieff's Stendhal and Proust, Edwin and Willa Muir's Kafka, and Douglas Young's Aristophanes. Hugh Mac-Diarmid's CONTEMPORARY SCOTTISH STUDIES could well have been paralleled by a companion volume of contemporary European studies, if his essays in the NEW AGE had been collected.

As to the authors who may be considered to belong to the Scottish tradition, there is no final agreement; and there is never likely to be. Harvey Wood, in the study already quoted, would seem to exclude the poet John Davidson; yet a two-volume edition of his poetry was one of the early publications of the Association for Scottish Literary Studies. There are those who would dispute that Norman Douglas is in any sense a Scottish writer, although Hugh MacDiarmid, writing in 1926, had no doubt about either Douglas' Scottishness or his stature.

SCOPE

This bibliographic guide is selective: first, in the choice of authors to be included; second, in the listing of their work and the critical studies of that work.

As to the first, I have tried to throw my net widely, including authors not with the intention of claiming them as essentially and uniquely Scottish, but because they are Scottish writers whose work should be of interest to those who wish to comprehend what Scottish literature is--or is not.

In the twentieth-century section I have been less rigorously exclusive, partly because time has not yet passed its sentence on the authors' reputations, partly because even minor writers have an intrinsic interest when they are of our age and are writing of the world around us. Throughout I have concentrated on literary writers in the stricter sense, excluding, for example, the philosophers and the historians of the eighteenth century; but I have not been pedantically consistent in these exclusions. Later I have included the author of THE GOLD-EN BOUGH because of the particular importance of that work; but with some regret I have omitted as "extra-literary" that "most unsettling person," Sir Patrick Geddes, despite the pervasive influence of his ideas. I was tempted to include Sir Ronald Ross, the Scots physician who discovered the malaria parasite, and Ronald Campbell Macfie; they share an essay in MacDiarmid's CONTEMPORARY SCOTTISH STUDIES, but their poetry is largely forgotten nowadays.

In listing an author's work I have concentrated on his original writing, including only exceptionally his translations or editions of books by other authors. To the end of the nineteenth century, section 4, this bibliography of an author's own writing, the primary material, is in the form of a checklist giving only a work's title and year of publication; thereafter, place of publication and publisher are also given. Where a work has been published elsewhere with a different title, this is noted. Collections and selections, and modern critical editions of individual works, are cited in full, where they exist.

For biographical and critical studies, the secondary material, both standard and recent works are listed, with the emphasis on books rather than articles.

ARRANGEMENT

The bibliography is presented in six main sections. The first deals with Scottish literature in general: bibliographies and reference works, literary history and criticism, anthologies, language and dictionaries, collective biography, and background studies.

For the four sections which follow I have adhered to the period divisions already familiar to users of the NEW CAMBRIDGE BIBLIOGRAPHY OF ENGLISH LITERATURE: to 1660, 1660-1800, 1800-1900, and from 1900 on. In this I am following the precedent of both the ANNUAL BIBLIOGRAPHY OF SCOTTISH LITERATURE and the YEAR'S WORK IN SCOTTISH LITERARY AND LINGUISTIC STUDIES, where the same period divisions are adopted.

The sixth section deals with Scotland's popular and folk literature, including the ballads, also given separate treatment in both the ANNUAL BIBLIOGRAPHY and the YEAR'S WORK.

Each of the period sections, 2 to 5, begins with a selection of general works dealing with that period and its literature, and following (with any necessary variation) the groupings already adopted in section 1, "General Works." Within these subdivisions the arrangement of individual works under each heading or subheading is normally chronological by year of publication. Any exceptions are noted.

Introduction

Within each period the individual writers of that period are arranged in sequence by their year of birth, rather than alphabetically, as in the ANNUAL BIBLIOGRAPHY OF SCOTTISH LITERATURE, for although (as F.W. Bateson points out in his admirable GUIDE TO ENGLISH AND AMERICAN LITERATURE) "an alphabetical order is easier no doubt for the casual enquirer to use, . . . to learn that [two authors] were born in the same year is, on the other hand, to acquire a fact of considerable critical importance." An author whose year of birth is doubtful or cannot be ascertained or revealed is included in the chronological sequence of authors at an appropriate place, as are the early anonymous works in section 2.

There is with this arrangement a problem at both the beginning and the end of the nineteenth-century period, a problem also encountered in the NEW CAMBRIDGE BIBLIOGRAPHY. Some nineteenth-century authors were born earlier than the later-born authors of the eighteenth century, and some authors whom we rightly consider to belong to the twentieth century were born before the later-born nineteenth-century authors. In every instance where there is a departure from the strict chronological sequence by year of birth, a cross-reference is provided. "The sceptic and the incurably unchronological" (to use Bateson's phrase) will, of course, resort to the alphabetical index of authors.

The bibliographies of individual authors follow a standard pattern. First, there is a chronological checklist of the author's separate works, with details of any modern critical editions. This is followed by chronological lists of collections and selections, and of letters and journals, if any. The secondary bibliography of biographical and critical studies follows, again in chronological order, and there is a final group for bibliographies and reference works, if there are publications of that kind to be included.

Since the listings in this guide are selective, and therefore by implication every book or article listed is recommended, it has been thought unnecessary to annotate each entry, particularly where the title is self-explanatory. Annotations are given, however, when a particular point is to be underlined.

NOTES TO THE INTRODUCTION

1.   "They . . . spak their thoughts in plain, braid Lallans."
Burns: "To W.S*****n, Ochiltree."

   "No bein' fit to write in Greek,/ I wrote in Lallan."
R.L.S.: "The Maker To Posterity."

2.   Henry Harvey Wood, SCOTTISH LITERATURE (London: Longmans, Green, for the British Council, 1952), p. 7.

3.   James C. Smith, SOME CHARACTERISTICS OF SCOTS LITERATURE (Oxford: OUP, for the English Association, 1912).

4.   George Gregory Smith, SCOTTISH LITERATURE: CHARACTER AND INFLUENCE (London: Macmillan, 1919).

5.   FOR SYDNEY GOODSIR SMITH (Loanhead: Macdonald, 1975), pp. 7-10.

ABBREVIATIONS

ASLS   Association for Scottish Literary Studies

CA   CONTEMPORARY AUTHORS. Vol. 1-- . Detroit: Gale Research Co., 1962-- .

CAP   CONTEMPORARY AUTHORS. Permanent series. Vol. 1-- . Detroit: Gale Research Co., 1975-- .

CD   CONTEMPORARY DRAMATISTS. Ed. James Vinson. 2nd ed. London: St. James Press, 1977.

CN   CONTEMPORARY NOVELISTS. Ed. James Vinson. London: St. James Press, 1972.

CP   CONTEMPORARY POETS. Ed. James Vinson. 2nd ed. London: St. James Press, 1975.

CSS   CONTEMPORARY SCOTTISH STUDIES. By Hugh MacDiarmid. 1926; new ed., Edinburgh: Scottish Educational Journal, 1976.

D   Daiches, David. THE PRESENT AGE: AFTER 1920. London: Cresset Press, 1958.

EETS   Early English Text Society

ELH   JOURNAL OF ENGLISH LITERARY HISTORY

ELT   ENGLISH LITERATURE IN TRANSITION

EUSPB   Edinburgh University Student Publications Board

H   Hart, Francis R. THE SCOTTISH NOVEL: A CRITICAL SURVEY. London: John Murray, 1978.

HMSO   Her (His) Majesty's Stationery Office

MLR   MODERN LANGUAGE REVIEW

NCBEL   NEW CAMBRIDGE BIBLIOGRAPHY OF ENGLISH LITERATURE. Ed. George Watson and I.R. Willison. 5 vols. Cambridge: Cambridge University Press, 1969-77.

OUP   Oxford University Press

Abbreviations

P	PENGUIN COMPANION TO LITERATURE: BRITAIN AND THE COMMONWEALTH. Ed. David Daiches. London: Allen Lane, Penguin Press, 1971.
RES	REVIEW OF ENGLISH STUDIES
SHR	SCOTTISH HISTORICAL REVIEW
SLJ	SCOTTISH LITERARY JOURNAL
SLN	SCOTTISH LITERARY NEWS
SSL	STUDIES IN SCOTTISH LITERATURE
STS	Scottish Text Society
T	Temple, Ruth Z., and Martin Tucker, eds. TWENTIETH-CENTURY BRITISH LITERATURE: A REFERENCE GUIDE AND BIBLIOGRAPHY. New York: Ungar, 1968.
TCA	TWENTIETH CENTURY AUTHORS. Ed. Stanley J. Kunitz and Howard Haycraft. New York: H.W. Wilson, 1942.
TCA-1	TWENTIETH CENTURY AUTHORS. First supplement. Ed. Stanley J. Kunitz. New York: H.W. Wilson, 1955.
W	WHO'S WHO IN TWENTIETH-CENTURY LITERATURE. Ed. Martin Seymour-Smith. London: Weidenfeld and Nicolson, 1976.
WA-50	WORLD AUTHORS: 1950-1970. Ed. John Wakeman. New York: H.W. Wilson, 1975.
WA-70	WORLD AUTHORS: 1970-1975. Ed. John Wakeman. New York: H.W. Wilson, 1980.

Section 1

GENERAL WORKS

The general works listed here are grouped under eight headings:

A. Bibliographies and Reference Works
B. Literary History and Criticism
C. Current Scottish Literary Periodicals
D. Anthologies
E. Language
F. Dictionaries
G. Collective Biography
H. Background Studies

Under each heading or subheading the works are arranged in chronological order by the year of publication.

A ninth heading, I. Societies and Organizations, provides notes on societies and organizations operating in the field of Scottish literature.

A. BIBLIOGRAPHIES AND REFERENCE WORKS

English Literature

1   THE NEW CAMBRIDGE BIBLIOGRAPHY OF ENGLISH LITERATURE. Ed.
    George Watson and Ian Roy Willison. 5 vols. Cambridge: Cambridge
    University Press, 1969-77.

    Volume 1, 600-1660; volume 2, 1660-1800; volume 3, 1800-
    1900; volume 4, 1900-1950; volume 5, INDEX. The most ela-
    borate of the general bibliographies. There are separate sec-
    tions for Scottish literature in volume 1 (by Priscilla J. Baw-
    cutt and James Craigie) and in volume 2 (by G. Ross Roy). In
    volumes 3 and 4 there are no such separate sections, Scottish
    writers being included along with their English contemporaries.
    Nevertheless, the NCBEL is a prime bibliographical source for
    the study of Scottish literature.

2   Howard-Hill, Trevor Howard. BIBLIOGRAPHY OF BRITISH LITERARY
    BIBLIOGRAPHIES. Index to British Literary Bibliography, 1. Oxford:
    Clarendon Press, 1969. Supplement in SHAKESPEARIAN BIBLIOGRAPHY
    AND TEXTUAL CRITICISM, Index to British Literary Bibliography, 2
    (Oxford: Clarendon Press, 1971), pp. 181-322.

3   Myers, Robin. A DICTIONARY OF LITERATURE IN THE ENGLISH LAN-
    GUAGE, FROM CHAUCER TO 1940. 2 vols. Oxford: Pergamon, 1970.

    A comprehensive checklist arranged alphabetically by author.
    A sequel continues the DICTIONARY from 1940 to 1970 (Oxford:
    Pergamon, 1978).

4   Bateson, Frederick W., and Harrison T. Meserole. A GUIDE TO ENGLISH
    AND AMERICAN LITERATURE. 3rd ed. London: Longman, 1976.

    A convenient one-volume guide, which includes unfortunately
    few Scottish writers. Its general advice is excellent.

Annual lists and surveys of each year's publications in the field of English literature are also of value to the student of Scottish literature.

5   THE YEAR'S WORK IN ENGLISH STUDIES. London: John Murray, for
    the English Association, 1919-- .

6   ANNUAL BIBLIOGRAPHY OF ENGLISH LANGUAGE AND LITERATURE.
    Cambridge [later London]: Modern Humanities Research Association,
    1921-- .

7   MLA INTERNATIONAL BIBLIOGRAPHY. New York: New York Univer-
    sity Press, for the Modern Language Association of America, 1964-- .
    Annual.

2

8   ABSTRACTS OF ENGLISH STUDIES. Boulder, Colo.: National Council
     of Teachers of English, 1958-80. Ten issues a year. Vol. 24-- .
     Calgary, Alta.: University of Calgary, English Department, 1981-- .
     Four issues a year.

9   STUDIES IN ENGLISH LITERATURE, 1500-1900. Houston: Rice Univer-
     sity, 1961-- . Quarterly.

Scottish Literature

10   National Library of Scotland. Edinburgh. BIBLIOGRAPHY OF SCOTLAND:
     A CATALOGUE OF BOOKS PUBLISHED IN SCOTLAND AND OF BOOKS
     PUBLISHED ELSEWHERE OF SCOTTISH RELEVANCE. 1976-77. Edin-
     burgh: HMSO, 1978.

     This first volume, covering two years, is continued in annual
     volumes. The first of these (for 1978) was published in 1979,
     1979 was published in 1980, and 1980 was published in 1981.

Since 1969, the pattern of annual lists and critical surveys, familiar in the field
of English literature, has been paralleled for Scottish literature.

11   ANNUAL BIBLIOGRAPHY OF SCOTTISH LITERATURE. 1969-- .

     Issued annually as a supplement to THE BIBLIOTHECK (see no. 45).

12   THE YEAR'S WORK IN SCOTTISH LITERARY STUDIES. 1969-- . Since
     1973 with the title THE YEAR'S WORK IN SCOTTISH LITERARY AND
     LINGUISTIC STUDIES. Published regularly in SCOTTISH LITERARY NEWS
     and its successor, SCOTTISH LITERARY JOURNAL (or its supplements).

13   Bell, Alan. "Accessions of Scottish Literary Manuscripts, National Library
     of Scotland, 1973." SLJ, 1 (July 1974), 61-63.

     The first of a series of annual notes that has continued in the
     same journal (or its supplements). Full lists are published in the
     National Library's ANNUAL REPORTS.

At least one older general bibliography is still valuable:

14   Black, George F. LIST OF WORKS RELATING TO SCOTLAND. New
     York: New York Public Library, 1916.

There are useful sections on Scottish language and literature in two introductory
bibliographies for the general reader:

15   SCOTTISH BOOKS: A BRIEF BIBLIOGRAPHY FOR TEACHERS AND GEN-
     ERAL READERS. Edinburgh: Saltire Society, 1963.

16   READER'S GUIDE TO SCOTLAND: A BIBLIOGRAPHY. London: National Book League, 1968.

There is interest too in the recent report of the Scottish Education Department's Scottish Central Committee on English:

17   SCOTTISH LITERATURE IN THE SECONDARY SCHOOL: A REPORT ON THE STUDY OF SCOTTISH LITERATURE IN SCHOOLS. Edinburgh: HMSO, 1976.

Also relevant here is an excellent two-volume survey:

18   Craigie, James. A BIBLIOGRAPHY OF SCOTTISH EDUCATION BEFORE 1872. London: University of London Press, 1970.

19   _____. A BIBLIOGRAPHY OF SCOTTISH EDUCATION, 1872-1972. London: University of London Press, 1974.

Notes on many Scottish authors--biographical and critical, as well as bibliographical--are to be found in the wide range of companions, dictionaries, guides, and encyclopedias now available. The following are specially helpful:

20   THE PENGUIN COMPANION TO LITERATURE: BRITAIN AND THE COMMONWEALTH. Ed. David Daiches. London: Allen Lane, The Penguin Press, 1971.

21   CASSELL'S ENCYCLOPAEDIA OF WORLD LITERATURE. Ed. John Buchanan-Brown. Rev. and enl. ed. 3 vols. London: Cassell, 1973.

There are, as one would expect, large collections of books of Scottish interest in all the major libraries of Scotland: the National Library of Scotland in Edinburgh (the only Scottish library to have the right of legal deposit under the Copyright Acts), the university libraries, and the great public libraries in Glasgow (The Mitchell Library) and Edinburgh; but there are liable to be special collections, some of unique value, even in the smaller libraries. There is, however, a comprehensive directory, revised as required from time to time:

22   LIBRARY RESOURCES IN SCOTLAND. 4th ed. Ed. James A. Tait and Heather F.C. Tait. Glasgow: Scottish Library Association, 1981.

B. LITERARY HISTORY AND CRITICISM

23   Millar, John Hepburn. A LITERARY HISTORY OF SCOTLAND. London: T. Fisher Unwin, 1903.

        Still the standard history.

24   Henderson, Thomas F. SCOTTISH VERNACULAR LITERATURE: A SUC-
      CINCT HISTORY. 3rd rev. ed. Edinburgh: John Grant, 1910.

25   Smith, George Gregory. SCOTTISH LITERATURE: CHARACTER AND IN-
      FLUENCE. London: Macmillan, 1919; rpt. Folcroft, Pa.: Folcroft Library
      Editions, 1972.

      A brilliant essay.

26   EDINBURGH ESSAYS ON SCOTS LITERATURE. Preface by Sir Herbert
      Grierson. Edinburgh: Oliver and Boyd, 1933.

27   Power, William. LITERATURE AND OATMEAL: WHAT LITERATURE HAS
      MEANT TO SCOTLAND. London: Routledge, 1935.

      A short popular account.

28   Muir, Edwin. SCOTT AND SCOTLAND: THE PREDICAMENT OF THE
      SCOTTISH WRITER. London: Routledge, 1936.

      Important.

29   Murray, John, ed. ESSAYS IN LITERATURE. Edinburgh: Oliver and
      Boyd, 1936.

      Essays by various contributors on Gavin Douglas, Fergusson,
      Burns, James Thomson, and Lewis Grassic Gibbon.

30   Smith, Sydney Goodsir. A SHORT INTRODUCTION TO SCOTTISH LITERA-
      TURE. Edinburgh: Serif Books, 1951.

      A modern Scottish poet's brief survey, with a good "Book List,"
      particularly on the modern period.

31   Wood, Henry Harvey. SCOTTISH LITERATURE. London: Longmans,
      Green, for the British Council, 1952.

      A short introduction.

32   Kinsley, James, ed. SCOTTISH POETRY: A CRITICAL SURVEY. Lon-
      don: Cassell, 1955; rpt. Folcroft, Pa.: Folcroft Library Editions, 1973.

      The ten essays provide a history of Scottish poetry from the
      medieval makars (poets) to the present day.

33   Wittig, Kurt. THE SCOTTISH TRADITION IN LITERATURE. Edinburgh:
      Oliver and Boyd, 1958; rpt. Westport, Conn.: Greenwood Press, 1972;
      rpt. Edinburgh: James Thin, Mercat Press, 1978.

      Not a history of Scottish literature, although it is chronologically
      arranged, but a sympathetic foreigner's view of the characteristics
      of the Scottish tradition.

34   Craig, David. SCOTTISH LITERATURE AND THE SCOTTISH PEOPLE,
      1680-1830. London: Chatto and Windus, 1961.

      An interesting examination of Scottish literature in relation to
      the society from which it emerged.

35   Speirs, John. THE SCOTS LITERARY TRADITION: AN ESSAY IN
      CRITICISM. 2nd rev. ed. London: Faber, 1962.

      Much of this book first appeared in F.R. Leavis' periodical,
      SCRUTINY.

36   Lindsay, Maurice. HISTORY OF SCOTTISH LITERATURE. London:
      Robert Hale, 1977.

      The first comprehensive history to appear since Millar's (no. 23).

37   Hart, Francis R. THE SCOTTISH NOVEL: A CRITICAL SURVEY. Lon-
      don: John Murray, 1978.

      Two centuries of Scottish fiction reviewed.

38   Caird, James B. "Random Reflections on the Scottish Novel." BRUN-
      TON'S MISCELLANY, 1 (Winter 1979), 3-6.

The case for a new literary history of Scotland has been well presented in three
articles: "The Writing of Scottish Literary History," by David Daiches, reprinted in his LITERARY ESSAYS (Edinburgh: Oliver and Boyd, 1966), pp.
132-53; "Towards a Literary History of Scotland," by Edwin Morgan (SLN, 1
[1971], 37-40); and by Matthew P. McDiarmid (SLN, 1 [1971], 59-65), in an
essay which announces a collaborative seven-volume history to replace the history by J.H. Millar (no. 23) published in 1903.

Histories of English Literature

Since the work of many Scottish writers can be considered to form part of English literature, histories of that literature should also be consulted.

39   THE CAMBRIDGE HISTORY OF ENGLISH LITERATURE. Ed. Adolphus W.
      Ward and Alfred R. Waller. 14 vols. Cambridge: Cambridge University
      Press, 1907-16. Vol. 15: GENERAL INDEX, 1927. Rpt. without bib-
      liographies, 1932.

      The separate chapters are by individual scholars, and a number
      deal with Scottish writers.

40   Sampson, George. THE CONCISE CAMBRIDGE HISTORY OF ENGLISH
      LITERATURE. 1941. 3rd ed. rev. by R.C. Churchill. Cambridge:
      Cambridge University Press, 1970.

A summary of the larger CAMBRIDGE HISTORY (no. 39), revised throughout and with additional chapters.

41   THE OXFORD HISTORY OF ENGLISH LITERATURE. Ed. Frank P. Wilson and Bonamy Dobrée. 12 vols. Oxford: Clarendon Press, 1945-- .

In progress.

42   Daiches, David. A CRITICAL HISTORY OF ENGLISH LITERATURE. 2nd ed. 4 vols. London: Secker and Warburg, 1969. 2 vols. New York: Ryerson Press, 1970.

C. CURRENT SCOTTISH LITERARY PERIODICALS

The more important current periodicals which deal wholly or mainly with Scottish literature are listed here, but a glance at any issue of the ANNUAL BIBLIOGRAPHY OF SCOTTISH LITERATURE will confirm that articles of interest on Scottish literary topics will be found scattered over a wide range of journals.

43   NEW SHETLANDER. Lerwick: Shetland Council of Social Service, 1946-- . Originally monthly, now quarterly.

44   LINES REVIEW. Edinburgh [later Loanhead]: Macdonald, 1952-- . Quarterly.

45   THE BIBLIOTHECK. Edinburgh: Library Association (University, College, and Research Section: Scottish Group), 1956-- . Three issues a year, with annual supplement.

46   STUDIES IN SCOTTISH LITERATURE. Columbia: University of South Carolina Press, 1963-- . Volumes 1-12, quarterly; volume 13-- , annual.

47   AKROS. Preston [later Nottingham]: Akros Publications, 1965-- . Three issues a year.

48   NEW EDINBURGH REVIEW. Edinburgh: EUSPB, 1969-- . Originally monthly, now quarterly.

49   CHAPMAN. Hamilton [later Edinburgh], 1970-- . Irregular.

50   LALLANS. Dunfermline: Scots Language Society, 1973-- . Two issues a year.

51   SCOTTISH LITERARY JOURNAL. Aberdeen: ASLS, 1974-- . Two issues a year, with two or three supplements.

General Works

73 Reid, James M., ed. SCOTTISH SHORT STORIES. London: OUP, 1963.

74 Hendry, James Findlay, ed. THE PENGUIN BOOK OF SCOTTISH SHORT STORIES. Harmondsworth: Penguin, 1970.

E. LANGUAGE

75 Murray, James A.H. THE DIALECT OF THE SOUTHERN COUNTIES OF SCOTLAND. London: Philological Society, 1873.

76 Smith, George Gregory. SPECIMENS OF MIDDLE SCOTS. Edinburgh: Blackwood, 1902.

77 Wilson, Sir James. LOWLAND SCOTCH. London: OUP, 1915.

78 Grant, William, and James Main Dixon. MANUAL OF MODERN SCOTS. Cambridge: Cambridge University Press, 1920.

79 Watson, George. THE ROXBURGHSHIRE WORD-BOOK. Cambridge: Cambridge University Press, 1923.

80 Wilson, Sir James. THE DIALECT OF ROBERT BURNS. London: OUP, 1923.

81 _____. THE DIALECTS OF CENTRAL SCOTLAND. London: OUP, 1926.

82 _____. OLD SCOTCH SONGS AND POEMS, PHONETICALLY SPELT AND TRANSLATED. London: OUP, 1927.

83 Marwick, Hugh. THE ORKNEY NORN. London: OUP, 1929.

84 Young, Douglas. "PLASTIC SCOTS" AND THE SCOTTISH LITERARY TRADITION: AN AUTHORITATIVE INTRODUCTION TO A CONTROVERSY. Glasgow: Maclennan, 1948.
    A spirited defense of the modern revival of Braid Scots or Lallans.

85 Robertson, Thomas Alexander, and John James Graham. GRAMMAR AND USAGE OF THE SHETLAND DIALECT. Lerwick: Shetland Times, 1952.

86 EDINBURGH STUDIES IN ENGLISH AND SCOTS. Ed. Adam Jack Aitken et al. London: Longman, 1971.

87   Aitken, Adam Jack, ed. LOWLAND SCOTS: PAPERS PRESENTED TO
      AN EDINBURGH CONFERENCE, MAY 1972. Aberdeen: ASLS, 1973.

88   Glauser, Beat. THE SCOTTISH-ENGLISH LINGUISTIC BORDER: LEXI-
      CAL ASPECTS. Bern: Francke, 1974.

89   McClure, J. Derrick, ed. THE SCOTS LANGUAGE IN EDUCATION.
      Aberdeen: ASLS, 1975.

90   _____. "The English Speech of Scotland." ABERDEEN UNIVERSITY
      REVIEW, 46 (1975), 173-89.

91   Mather, James Y., and H.H. Speitel. THE LINGUISTIC ATLAS OF
      SCOTLAND. Scots section. 2 vols. London: Croom Helm, 1975-77.
      A third volume is in preparation.

92   Macaulay, Ronald. LANGUAGE, SOCIAL CLASS, AND EDUCATION:
      A GLASGOW STUDY. Edinburgh: Edinburgh University Press, 1977.

93   Murison, David D. THE GUID SCOTS TONGUE. Edinburgh: Blackwood,
      1977.
      An excellent introduction by the editor of the SCOTTISH NA-
      TIONAL DICTIONARY.

94   McClure, J. Derrick, et al. THE SCOTS LANGUAGE: PLANNING
      FOR MODERN USAGE. Edinburgh: Ramsay Head Press, 1979.

95   Aitken, Adam Jack, and Tom McArthur, eds. LANGUAGES OF SCOT-
      LAND: A COMPREHENSIVE SURVEY. Edinburgh: Chambers, 1979.
      A collection of essays on various aspects of language in Scot-
      land--both historical and modern--that provide the essential
      background.

Place-Names

96   Watson, William J. THE HISTORY OF THE CELTIC PLACE-NAMES OF
      SCOTLAND. Edinburgh: Blackwood, 1926.

97   Johnston, James B. PLACE-NAMES OF SCOTLAND. 3rd ed. London:
      John Murray, 1934; rpt. Wakefield: S.R. Publishers, 1970.

98   Nicolaisen, William F.H. SCOTTISH PLACE-NAMES: THEIR STUDY
      AND SIGNIFICANCE. London: Batsford, 1976.
      An authoritative discussion.

Papers on Scottish linguistics are now being published regularly in one of the supplements issued each year with SCOTTISH LITERARY JOURNAL. The first LANGUAGE SUPPLEMENT (No. 6) appeared in 1978, the second (No. 9) in 1979, and the third (No. 12) in 1980.

F. DICTIONARIES

99 Jamieson, John. AN ETYMOLOGICAL DICTIONARY OF THE SCOTTISH LANGUAGE. Revised by J. Longmuir and D. Donaldson, with a supplement. 5 vols. Paisley: Gardner, 1879-87; rpt. New York: AMS, 1971.

Now superseded by THE SCOTTISH NATIONAL DICTIONARY (no. 102), but historically interesting.

100 Warrack, Alexander. CHAMBERS'S SCOTS DICTIONARY. Edinburgh: Chambers, 1911.

A convenient glossary, with no scholarly claims apart from the good descriptive introduction by William Grant. Frequently reprinted.

101 Jakobsen, Jakob. AN ETYMOLOGICAL DICTIONARY OF THE NORN LANGUAGE IN SHETLAND. 2 vols. London: Nutt, 1928-32.

102 THE SCOTTISH NATIONAL DICTIONARY. Ed. William Grant and David D. Murison. 10 vols. Edinburgh: Scottish National Dictionary Association, 1929-76.

The definitive work on Scots since about 1700. To mark the completion of the dictionary SCOTTISH REVIEW, No. 1 (1975), published three important articles: Adam Jack Aitken, "The Scottish National Dictionary: Comments on the Occasion of its Completion" (pp. 17-19); Robert William Burchfield, "Ayr., Ork., and A' That" (pp. 20-21); and Hugh MacDiarmid, "The Foundation Stone of the New Scotland" (pp. 21-25).

103 A DICTIONARY OF THE OLDER SCOTTISH TONGUE. Ed. Sir William A. Craigie and Adam Jack Aitken. Chicago: University of Chicago Press; London: OUP, 1931-- .

In progress, four volumes to date. Scots from the twelfth century to the end of the seventeenth. A monumental work of great scholarship.

104 Graham, William. THE SCOTS WORD BOOK. Edinburgh: Ramsay Head Press, 1977.

A popular handbook, with a two-way vocabulary of Scots and English.

G. COLLECTIVE BIOGRAPHY

105 Mackenzie, George. THE LIVES AND CHARACTERS OF THE MOST EMINENT WRITERS OF THE SCOTS NATION. 3 vols. Edinburgh, 1708-22; rpt. New York: Garland Press, 1971.

An interesting early work.

106 Chambers, Robert. A BIOGRAPHICAL DICTIONARY OF EMINENT SCOTS-MEN. Rev. Thomas Thomson. 3 vols. London, 1869-70; rpt. Hildesheim: Olms, 1971.

107 Scott, Hew, ed. FASTI ECCLESIAE SCOTICANAE: THE SUCCESSION OF MINISTERS IN THE CHURCH OF SCOTLAND FROM THE REFORMATION. New ed. 9 vols. Edinburgh: Oliver and Boyd, 1915-61.

108 MacDiarmid, Hugh. SCOTTISH ECCENTRICS. London: Routledge, 1936; rpt. New York: Johnson Reprint Corp., 1972.

A series of biographical essays from which one is led to believe that the eccentric is somehow typical in Scotland.

109 Watt, Donald E.R. A BIOGRAPHICAL DICTIONARY OF SCOTTISH GRADUATES TO A.D. 1410. Oxford: Clarendon Press, 1977.

Scots also figure in the more general biographical dictionaries:

110 THE DICTIONARY OF NATIONAL BIOGRAPHY. Ed. Sir Leslie Stephen and Sir Sidney Lee. 66 vols. 1885-1901; rpt. 22 vols. Oxford: Clarendon Press, 1921-22.

THE DICTIONARY OF NATIONAL BIOGRAPHY. [Seven supplements, covering the years 1901-70.] 7 vols. Oxford: Clarendon Press, 1912-81.

Continuing with decennial volumes.

THE DICTIONARY OF NATIONAL BIOGRAPHY. CORRECTIONS AND ADDITIONS, 1923-63. Boston: G.K. Hall, 1966.

The DNB is the standard source for information on notable British personalities no longer living.

111 THE CONCISE DICTIONARY OF NATIONAL BIOGRAPHY. 2 vols. Oxford: Clarendon Press, 1906-81.

THE CONCISE DNB contains summaries of every entry in the DNB.

112 WHO'S WHO. London: Black, 1849-- . Annual.

The standard source for information on living persons. At death

the latest entry for an individual is transferred to the next decennial volume in the companion series, WHO WAS WHO.

113 CHAMBERS'S BIOGRAPHICAL DICTIONARY. Edinburgh: Chambers, 1897;
new ed. 1961.

Frequently reprinted with additions and revisions.

114 EVERYMAN'S DICTIONARY OF LITERARY BIOGRAPHY: ENGLISH AND
AMERICAN. Ed. David C. Browning. 3rd ed. London: Dent, 1969;
London: Pan, 1972.

See also the Authors Series, published by the H.W. Wilson Co. of New York:

115 BRITISH AUTHORS BEFORE 1800. Ed. Stanley J. Kunitz and Howard
Haycraft. 1952.

116 BRITISH AUTHORS OF THE NINETEENTH CENTURY. Ed. Stanley J.
Kunitz and Howard Haycraft. 1936.

117 TWENTIETH CENTURY AUTHORS. Ed. Stanley J. Kunitz and Howard
Haycraft. 1942.

TWENTIETH CENTURY AUTHORS. First supplement. Ed. Stanley J.
Kunitz. 1955.

118 WORLD AUTHORS: 1950-1970. Ed. John Wakeman. 1975.

119 WORLD AUTHORS: 1970-1975. Ed. John Wakeman. 1980.

A general index to the Wilson Authors Series was published in
1976.

Three bibliographies are also useful:

120 BIOGRAPHY INDEX. New York: H.W. Wilson, 1946-- .

Published quarterly and cumulated annually and triennially. An
index to biographical material in a wide range of periodicals,
to current books of individual and collective biography in the
English language, and to incidental biographical information
elsewhere.

121 Matthews, William. BRITISH DIARIES: AN ANNOTATED BIBLIOGRAPHY
OF BRITISH DIARIES WRITTEN BETWEEN 1442 AND 1942. Berkeley and
Los Angeles: University of California Press, 1950.

122 _____. BRITISH AUTOBIOGRAPHIES: AN ANNOTATED BIBLIOGRAPHY OF BRITISH AUTOBIOGRAPHIES PUBLISHED OR WRITTEN BEFORE 1951. Berkeley and Los Angeles: University of California Press, 1955.

H. BACKGROUND STUDIES

General

123 Meikle, Henry W., ed. SCOTLAND: A DESCRIPTION OF SCOTLAND AND SCOTTISH LIFE. London: Nelson, 1947.

Authoritative essays on various aspects of Scottish life and culture.

124 Daiches, David, ed. A COMPANION TO SCOTTISH CULTURE. London: Edward Arnold, 1981.

A good general introduction.

History

125 Mathieson, William Law. POLITICS AND RELIGION: A STUDY IN SCOTTISH HISTORY FROM THE REFORMATION TO THE REVOLUTION [1550-1690]. 2 vols. Glasgow: Maclehose, 1902.

126 _____. SCOTLAND AND THE UNION: A HISTORY OF SCOTLAND, 1695-1747. Glasgow: Maclehose, 1905.

127 _____. THE AWAKENING OF SCOTLAND: A HISTORY, 1747-97. Glasgow: Maclehose, 1910.

128 _____. CHURCH AND REFORM IN SCOTLAND, 1797-1843. Glasgow: Maclehose, 1916.

Taken together, Mathieson's five volumes form a continuous history of Scotland from 1550 to 1843.

129 Brown, Peter Hume. HISTORY OF SCOTLAND. 3 vols. Cambridge: Cambridge University Press, 1911.

130 Notestein, Wallace. THE SCOT IN HISTORY: A STUDY OF THE INTERPLAY OF CHARACTER AND HISTORY. New Haven: Yale University Press, 1946; London: Cape, 1947.

131 Dickinson, William Croft. SCOTLAND FROM THE EARLIEST TIMES TO 1603. London: Nelson, 1961. 3rd ed. rev. Archibald A.M. Duncan. Oxford: Clarendon Press, 1977.

General Works

132 Pryde, George S. SCOTLAND FROM 1603 TO THE PRESENT DAY.
London: Nelson, 1962.

Together, these two volumes (131 and 132) constitute A NEW
HISTORY OF SCOTLAND.

133 McLaren, Moray. IF FREEDOM FAIL: BANNOCKBURN, FLODDEN,
THE UNION. London: Secker and Warburg, 1964.

A thematic essay.

134 THE EDINBURGH HISTORY OF SCOTLAND. 4 vols. Edinburgh: Oliver
and Boyd, 1965-75.

Duncan, Archibald A.M. SCOTLAND: THE MAKING OF THE
KINGDOM. 1975.

Nicholson, Ronald. SCOTLAND: THE LATER MIDDLE AGES.
1974.

Donaldson, Gordon. SCOTLAND: JAMES V TO JAMES VII.
1965.

Ferguson, William. SCOTLAND: 1689 TO THE PRESENT.
1968; rev. ed. 1979.

The standard modern history of Scotland.

135 Mitchison, Rosalind. A HISTORY OF SCOTLAND. London: Methuen,
1970.

A good one-volume history.

136 Donaldson, Gordon, and Robert S. Morpeth. A DICTIONARY OF SCOT-
TISH HISTORY. Edinburgh: John Donald, 1977.

137 Mackie, John Duncan. A HISTORY OF SCOTLAND. 2nd ed. rev.
Bruce Lenman and Geoffrey Parker. Harmondsworth: Penguin, 1978.

Church History

138 Burleigh, John H.S. A CHURCH HISTORY OF SCOTLAND. London:
OUP, 1960.

139 Drummond, Andrew L., and James Bulloch. THE SCOTTISH CHURCH,
1688-1843: THE AGE OF THE MODERATES. Edinburgh: St. Andrew
Press, 1973.

140 _____. THE CHURCH IN VICTORIAN SCOTLAND, 1843-1874. Edinburgh: St. Andrew Press, 1975.

16

141 _____. THE CHURCH IN LATE VICTORIAN SCOTLAND, 1874-1900. Edinburgh: St. Andrew Press, 1978.

Social History

142 THE STATISTICAL ACCOUNT OF SCOTLAND. Ed. Sir John Sinclair. 21 vols. Edinburgh, 1791-99.

Some volumes have appeared of a new reprint in which the in-dividual parish accounts, scattered throughout the volumes of the original edition, are being conveniently collected into county volumes. For Sinclair, see Rosalind Mitchison's AGRI-CULTURAL SIR JOHN: THE LIFE OF SIR JOHN SINCLAIR OF ULBSTER, 1754-1835 (London: Geoffrey Bles, 1962).

143 THE NEW STATISTICAL ACCOUNT OF SCOTLAND. 15 vols. Edinburgh, 1845.

144 Chambers, Robert. DOMESTIC ANNALS OF SCOTLAND. 3 vols. Edinburgh: Chambers, 1858-61.

From the Reformation to the Rebellion of 1745.

145 Johnston, Tom. HISTORY OF THE WORKING CLASSES IN SCOTLAND. Glasgow: Forward, 1920.

146 Fyfe, James G., ed. SCOTTISH DIARIES AND MEMOIRS, 1550-1746; 1746-1843. 2 vols. Stirling: Eneas Mackay, 1928, 1942.

147 Mackenzie, Agnes Mure. SCOTTISH PAGEANT. 4 vols. Edinburgh: Oliver and Boyd, 1946-50.

An anthology of contemporary writing by Scots or about Scotland (or both) from the first Roman invasion to the end of the eigh-teenth century.

148 THE THIRD STATISTICAL ACCOUNT OF SCOTLAND. Edinburgh: Oliver and Boyd [later, various publishers in different places], 1951-- .

In progress: volume 27 appeared in 1979. "By statistical is meant an inquiry into the state of a country for the purpose of ascertaining the quantum of happiness enjoyed by its inhabitants and the means of its future improvement." So Sir John Sinclair defined a word now used with rather a different meaning.

The three STATISTICAL ACCOUNTS (142, 143, and 148) provide a uniquely detailed survey of the social and economic life of Scotland, parish by parish, at three critical periods: on the eve of the Industrial Revolution, at the time of the Reform Bill of 1832, and at the end of the Second World War.

149 Smout, Thomas Christopher. A HISTORY OF THE SCOTTISH PEOPLE, 1560-1830. London: Collins, 1969.

150 Lenman, Bruce. AN ECONOMIC HISTORY OF MODERN SCOTLAND, 1660-1976. London: Batsford, 1977.

151 Harvie, Christopher. SCOTLAND AND NATIONALISM: SCOTTISH SO-CIETY AND POLITICS, 1707-1977. London: Allen and Unwin, 1977.

152 Mitchison, Rosalind. LIFE IN SCOTLAND. London: Batsford, 1978.

153 Young, James Douglas. THE ROUSING OF THE SCOTTISH WORKING CLASS. London: Croom Helm, 1979.

The Arts

154 Tonge, John. THE ARTS OF SCOTLAND. London: Kegan Paul, 1938.

155 Ramsay, Mary P. CALVIN AND ART CONSIDERED IN RELATION TO SCOTLAND. Edinburgh: Moray Press, 1938.

An essay which corrects some misapprehensions.

156 Farmer, Henry G. A HISTORY OF MUSIC IN SCOTLAND. London: Hinrichsen, 1947.

157 Cursiter, Stanley. SCOTTISH ART. London: Harrap, 1949.

A short account for the general reader.

Education

158 Neill, Alexander Sutherland. IS SCOTLAND EDUCATED? London: Routledge, 1936.

The author's contention is that Scotland is not educated, but merely learned.

159 Knox, Henry Macdonald. TWO HUNDRED AND FIFTY YEARS OF SCOT-TISH EDUCATION, 1696-1946. Edinburgh: Oliver and Boyd, 1953.

160 Davie, George Elder. THE DEMOCRATIC INTELLECT: SCOTLAND AND HER UNIVERSITIES IN THE NINETEENTH CENTURY. Edinburgh: Edin-burgh University Press, 1961; 2nd ed. 1964.

An important and essential study.

161   Scotland, James. THE HISTORY OF SCOTTISH EDUCATION. 2 vols.
      London: University of London Press, 1969.

162   Aitken, William R. A HISTORY OF THE PUBLIC LIBRARY MOVEMENT
      IN SCOTLAND TO 1955. Glasgow: Scottish Library Association, 1971.

I. SOCIETIES AND ORGANIZATIONS

163   The Scottish Text Society (c/o School of Scottish Studies, University of
      Edinburgh) was founded in 1882 "for the purpose of printing and editing
      texts illustrative of Scottish language and literature," and its program of
      publication still continues. The earlier period up to the seventeenth cen-
      tury has been more fully dealt with, but Ramsay and Fergusson are in-
      cluded. The society's editions are accepted as authoritative and indis-
      pensable.

164   The Saltire Society (13 Atholl Crescent, Edinburgh) was formed in 1936
      with the object of encouraging Scottish art, music, and literature. Its
      main contribution in the field of literature has been its series of Saltire
      Classics, begun in 1940: carefully edited selections from the main authors,
      attractively produced, and reasonably priced. The society also sponsored
      the SALTIRE REVIEW (1954-61) and its successor, NEW SALTIRE (1961-64);
      and it is currently publisher, with the Scottish Civic Trust, of the SCOT-
      TISH REVIEW (1975--).

165   The Scottish Arts Council (19 Charlotte Square, Edinburgh), the govern-
      ment's main agency for supporting the arts in Scotland, forms part of the
      Arts Council of Great Britain. From 1947 until 1967 it was the Scottish
      Committee of that body; in 1967 it was reconstituted under its present
      name, with virtual autonomy over the allocation of its funds. Its literature
      department was established in 1971. The council has a literature committee,
      and its professional staff includes a literature director. The council sup-
      ports writers in Scotland by granting bursaries, fellowships, and book
      awards, and by organizing the "Writers in Schools" scheme; it assists
      publishers by making grants towards the costs of publication and by sup-
      porting a number of Scotland's little magazines; it subsidizes the publication
      of books in Gaelic; and it seeks to stimulate a greater interest in con-
      temporary writing by supporting the visits to Scotland of novelists of inter-
      national distinction.

166   The Universities Committee on Scottish Literature (Department of Scottish
      Literature, University of Glasgow) first met in 1968, and has met regularly
      since, to discuss the teaching of Scottish literature and to encourage the
      publication of the necessary texts. The Association for Scottish Literary
      Studies grew out of the Universities Committee, but the committee continues
      to function as an organization representative of the departments involved
      in the teaching of Scottish literature in the Scottish universities.

167 The Association for Scottish Literary Studies (Department of English, University of Aberdeen, Old Aberdeen) was founded in 1970. Its aims are to promote the study, teaching, and writing of Scottish literature; to promote Scottish linguistic studies; to collect and disseminate information concerning these studies in Scotland and throughout the world; to stimulate and coordinate the publication and editing of works of Scottish literature; and to publish at suitable intervals edited texts, reprints, and such studies and periodicals as may from time to time be determined.

The association's first periodical, SCOTTISH LITERARY NEWS (1970-73), was succeeded in 1974 by SCOTTISH LITERARY JOURNAL, with two issues and three supplements a year. The association has arranged a number of conferences--local, national, and international--and published their proceedings. The general list of annual volumes already contains the following:

1971   James Hogg, THE THREE PERILS OF MAN.
1972-73 THE POEMS OF JOHN DAVIDSON. 2 vols.
1974   POEMS BY ALLAN RAMSAY AND ROBERT FERGUSSON.
1975   John Galt, THE MEMBER.
1976   POEMS OF DRUMMOND OF HAWTHORNDEN.
1977   Lockhart, PETER'S LETTERS TO HIS KINSFOLK.
1978   John Galt, SELECTED SHORT STORIES.
1979   Fletcher of Saltoun, SELECTED WRITINGS.
1980   SCOTT ON HIMSELF.

All are noted in their appropriate places in this guide.

168 The Scots Language Society (10 Wallace Street, Dunfermline, Fife) was founded in 1972, as the Lallans Society, to foster and promote the emergence of Lallans[1] as a language and to encourage a wider appreciation of Lallans literature. It holds branch meetings regularly in different parts of Scotland and national conferences annually, and publishes the periodical LALLANS twice a year.

1. For a comment on the word Lallans, see page xvii.

Section 2

MEDIEVAL-RENAISSANCE

This section deals with Scottish literature from the beginnings to 1660, including the early writers in prose and verse, the Middle Scots makars, and the poets and men of letters of the sixteenth and seventeenth centuries.

The general works relevant to the period are grouped under five headings:

A. Bibliographies
B. Literary History and Criticism
C. Anthologies
D. Background Studies
E. Printing and Publishing

Under each heading or subheading the works are arranged in chronological order by the year of publication.

A sixth heading, F. Individual Authors and Anonymous Works, lists the authors of the period in chronological order by their year of birth, giving for each author the standard editions of his work and the more important biographical and critical studies of the author and his work. Anonymous works are placed at appropriate points in the chronological sequence.

Medieval-Renaissance

A. BIBLIOGRAPHIES

See also pages 2-4.

169 Geddie, William. A BIBLIOGRAPHY OF MIDDLE SCOTS POETS. Edinburgh: STS, 1912.

Still a useful bibliography.

170 Heidtmann, Peter. "A Bibliography of Henryson, Dunbar and Douglas, 1912-1968." CHAUCER REVIEW, 5 (1970), 75-82.

171 Ridley, Florence H. "A Check List, 1956-1968, for Study of THE KING-IS QUAIR, the Poetry of Robert Henryson, Gawin Douglas, and William Dunbar." SSL, 8 (1970-71), 30-51.

Additions and comment by Robin Fulton and John C. Weston, SSL, 9 (1971-72), 169, 264.

172 _____. "Middle Scots Writers." In A MANUAL OF THE WRITINGS IN MIDDLE ENGLISH, 1050-1500. Ed. Albert E. Hartung. Vol. 4. Hamden, Conn.: Archon Books, 1973, pp. 961-1060, 1123-1284.

B. LITERARY HISTORY AND CRITICISM

See also pages 4-7.

173 Irving, David. THE HISTORY OF SCOTTISH POETRY. Ed. John Aitken Carlyle. Edinburgh: Edmonston and Douglas, 1861.

174 Ross, John M. SCOTTISH HISTORY AND LITERATURE TO THE PERIOD OF THE REFORMATION. Ed. James Brown. Glasgow: Maclehose, 1884.

175 Millar, John Hepburn. SCOTTISH PROSE OF THE SEVENTEENTH AND EIGHTEENTH CENTURIES. Glasgow: Maclehose, 1912.

176 Mill, Anna J. MEDIAEVAL PLAYS IN SCOTLAND. Edinburgh: Blackwood, 1927.

177 Mackenzie, Agnes Mure. AN HISTORICAL SURVEY OF SCOTTISH LITERATURE TO 1714. London: Maclehose, 1933.

178 Smith, Janet M. THE FRENCH BACKGROUND OF MIDDLE SCOTS LITERATURE. Edinburgh: Oliver and Boyd, 1934.

179 Brie, Friedrich. DIE NATIONALE LITERATUR SCHOTTLANDS VON DEN ANFÄNGEN BIS ZUR RENAISSANCE. Halle: Max Niemeyer, 1937.

180 Lewis, Clive Staples. ENGLISH LITERATURE IN THE SIXTEENTH CEN-TURY. Oxford History of English Literature, vol. 3. Oxford: Claren-don Press, 1954.

181 Kinsley, James, ed. SCOTTISH POETRY: A CRITICAL SURVEY. London: Cassell, 1955.

The relevant essays are James Kinsley, "The Mediaeval Makars," pages 1–32; Agnes Mure Mackenzie, "The Renaissance Poets: (1) Scots and English," pages 33–67; and James W.L. Adams, "The Renaissance Poets: (2) Latin," pages 68–98.

182 Shire, Helena M. SONG, DANCE AND POETRY OF THE COURT OF SCOTLAND UNDER KING JAMES VI. Cambridge: Cambridge University Press, 1969.

183 MacQueen, John. "The Case for Early Scottish Literature." In EDIN-BURGH STUDIES IN ENGLISH AND SCOTS. Ed. Adam Jack Aitken. London: Longman, 1971, pp. 234–47.

184 Jack, Ronald D.S. THE ITALIAN INFLUENCE ON SCOTTISH LITERA-TURE. Edinburgh: Edinburgh University Press, 1972.

185 Aitken, Adam Jack, et al., eds. BARDS AND MAKARS: SCOTTISH LANGUAGE AND LITERATURE, MEDIEVAL AND RENAISSANCE. Glas-gow: University of Glasgow Press, 1977.

186 MacQueen, John. "The Literature of Fifteenth-Century Scotland." In SCOTTISH SOCIETY IN THE FIFTEENTH CENTURY. Ed. Jennifer M. Brown. London: Edward Arnold, 1977, pp. 184–208.

C. ANTHOLOGIES

Manuscript Collections

For bibliographical notes see Smith (201), pages lxvi–lxxv.

187 PIECES FROM THE MAKCULLOCH AND THE GRAY MSS. [c. 1500] TO-GETHER WITH THE CHEPMAN AND MYLLAR PRINTS [1508]. Ed. George Stevenson. Edinburgh: STS, 1918.

188   THE ASLOAN MANUSCRIPT [c. 1515]. Ed. William A. Craigie. 2 vols.
      Edinburgh: STS, 1923–25.

189   THE BANNATYNE MANUSCRIPT [1568?]. Ed. William Tod Ritchie.
      4 vols. Edinburgh: STS, 1928–34.

      See also William Ramson, "On Bannatyne's Editing," in BARDS
      AND MAKARS, ed. Adam Jack Aitken et al. (Glasgow: Uni-
      versity of Glasgow Press, 1977), pages 172–83.

190   THE MAITLAND FOLIO MANUSCRIPT [c. 1580]. Ed. William A. Craigie.
      2 vols. Edinburgh: STS, 1919–27.

191   THE MAITLAND QUARTO MANUSCRIPT [1586]. Ed. William A. Craigie.
      Edinburgh: STS, 1920.

Printed Collections

See also pages 8–10.

192   Ramsay, Allan. THE EVER GREEN: BEING A COLLECTION OF SCOTS
      POEMS WROTE BY THE INGENIOUS BEFORE 1600. 2 vols. Edinburgh,
      1724; rpt. 2 vols. Glasgow: R. Forrester, 1876.

      Mainly from the Bannatyne Manuscript.

193   Pinkerton, John. ANCIENT SCOTISH POEMS NEVER BEFORE IN
      PRINT, BUT NOW PUBLISHED FROM THE MS. COLLECTIONS OF SIR
      RICHARD MAITLAND. 2 vols. London, 1786.

194   Laing, David, ed. SELECT REMAINS OF THE ANCIENT POPULAR AND
      ROMANCE POETRY OF SCOTLAND. Edinburgh, 1822; ed. J. Small.
      Edinburgh: Blackwood, 1885.

195   Cranstoun, James, ed. SATIRICAL POEMS OF THE TIME OF THE REFOR-
      MATION. 2 vols. Edinburgh: STS, 1891–93.

196   Eyre-Todd, George, ed. EARLY SCOTTISH POETRY. Glasgow: Hodge,
      1891.

197   _____. MEDIAEVAL SCOTTISH POETRY. Glasgow: Hodge, 1892.

198   _____. SCOTTISH POETRY OF THE SIXTEENTH CENTURY. Glasgow:
      Hodge, 1892.

199   _____. SCOTTISH POETRY OF THE SEVENTEENTH CENTURY. Glasgow: Hodge, 1895.

Four of the seven volumes in the Abbotsford Series of the Scottish Poets. Still useful.

200   Amours, François Joseph, ed. SCOTTISH ALLITERATIVE POEMS IN RIMING STANZAS. Edinburgh: STS, 1897.

201   Smith, George Gregory, ed. SPECIMENS OF MIDDLE SCOTS. Edinburgh: Blackwood, 1902.

202   Gray, Margaret M., ed. SCOTTISH POETRY FROM BARBOUR TO JAMES VI. London: Dent, 1935.

The spelling is modernized and simplified.

203   Girvan, Ritchie, ed. RATIS RAVING AND OTHER EARLY SCOTS POEMS ON MORALS. Edinburgh: STS, 1939.

204   Scott, Tom, ed. LATE MEDIEVAL SCOTS POETRY: A SELECTION FROM THE MAKARS AND THEIR HEIRS DOWN TO 1610. London: Heinemann, 1967.

205   Kinghorn, Alexander M., ed. THE MIDDLE SCOTS POETS. London: Edward Arnold, 1970.

206   MacQueen, John, ed. BALLATIS OF LUVE. Edinburgh: Edinburgh University Press, 1970.

207   Jack, Ronald D.S., ed. SCOTTISH PROSE, 1550-1700. London: Calder and Boyars, 1971.

208   MacQueen, John, and Winifred MacQueen, eds. A CHOICE OF SCOTTISH VERSE, 1470-1570. London: Faber, 1972.

209   Purcell, Sally, ed. MONARCHS AND THE MUSE: POEMS BY MONARCHS AND PRINCES OF ENGLAND, SCOTLAND AND WALES. Oxford: Carcanet Press, 1972.

Includes poems by James I, James IV, James V, Mary, Darnley, and James VI.

210   Jack, Ronald D.S., ed. A CHOICE OF SCOTTISH VERSE, 1560-1660. London: Hodder and Stoughton, 1978.

Provides a sequel to 208 above.

D. BACKGROUND STUDIES

See also pages 15-19.

211   Mathieson, William Law. POLITICS AND RELIGION: A STUDY IN
      SCOTTISH HISTORY FROM THE REFORMATION TO THE REVOLUTION
      [1550-1690]. 2 vols. Glasgow: Maclehose, 1902.
      Still useful for the political and religious background.

212   Grant, Isabel Frances. THE SOCIAL AND ECONOMIC DEVELOPMENT
      OF SCOTLAND BEFORE 1603. Edinburgh: Oliver and Boyd, 1930.

213   Mackenzie, Agnes Mure. SCOTTISH PAGEANT. [55 B.C.-A.D. 1513].
      Edinburgh: Oliver and Boyd, 1946.

214   _____. SCOTTISH PAGEANT, 1513-1625. Edinburgh: Oliver and
      Boyd, 1948.

215   _____. SCOTTISH PAGEANT, 1625-1707. Edinburgh: Oliver and
      Boyd, 1949.
      Three volumes of a four-part anthology of contemporary writing
      by Scots or about Scotland (or both).

216   THE EDINBURGH HISTORY OF SCOTLAND. 4 vols. Edinburgh: Oliver
      and Boyd, 1965-75.
      The first three volumes are relevant here:
      Duncan, Archibald A.M. SCOTLAND: THE MAKING OF THE
      KINGDOM. 1975.
      Nicholson, Ronald. SCOTLAND: THE LATER MIDDLE AGES.
      1974.
      Donaldson, Gordon. SCOTLAND: JAMES V TO JAMES VII.
      1965.

217   Bingham, Madeleine. SCOTLAND UNDER MARY STUART: AN AC-
      COUNT OF EVERYDAY LIFE. London: Allen and Unwin, 1971.

218   Barrow, Geoffrey W.S., ed. THE SCOTTISH TRADITION: ESSAYS IN
      HONOUR OF RONALD GEORGE CANT. Edinburgh: Scottish Academic
      Press, 1974.
      Includes an essay, "Some Early Scottish Books" (pp. 107-20),
      by William Beattie, formerly librarian of the National Library
      of Scotland.

219 Webster, Bruce. SCOTLAND FROM THE ELEVENTH CENTURY TO 1603. The Sources of History: Studies in the Uses of Historical Evidence. London: Hodder and Stoughton, 1975.

220 Dickinson, William Croft. SCOTLAND FROM THE EARLIEST TIMES TO 1603. 3rd ed. rev. Archibald A.M. Duncan. Oxford: Clarendon Press, 1977.

221 Brown, Jennifer M., ed. SCOTTISH SOCIETY IN THE FIFTEENTH CENTURY. London: Edward Arnold, 1977.

E. PRINTING AND PUBLISHING

222 Dickson, Robert, and John Philip Edmond. ANNALS OF SCOTTISH PRINTING FROM 1507 TO THE BEGINNING OF THE SEVENTEENTH CENTURY. Cambridge: Macmillan and Bowes, 1890.

The standard work.

223 Aldis, Harry G. A LIST OF BOOKS PRINTED IN SCOTLAND BEFORE 1700, WITH BRIEF NOTES ON THE PRINTERS AND STATIONERS. 1904; rpt., including entries for books published in 1700, and with additional notes by Robert Hay Carnie. Edinburgh: National Library of Scotland, 1970.

224 Duff, Edward Gordon. A CENTURY OF THE ENGLISH BOOK TRADE . . . 1457-1557. London: Bibliographical Society, 1905.

Includes Scotland.

225 McKerrow, Ronald B. A DICTIONARY OF THE PRINTERS AND BOOKSELLERS AT WORK IN ENGLAND, SCOTLAND AND IRELAND FROM 1557 TO 1640. London: Bibliographical Society, 1910.

226 Plomer, Henry R. A DICTIONARY OF THE BOOKSELLERS AND PRINTERS WHO WERE AT WORK IN ENGLAND, SCOTLAND AND IRELAND FROM 1641 TO 1667. London: Bibliographical Society, 1907.

F. INDIVIDUAL AUTHORS AND ANONYMOUS WORKS

This section deals with the authors of the period in chronological order by their year of birth. If the year of birth is doubtful or cannot be ascertained, the author is included in the chronological sequence in his probable place. Anonymous works are placed at appropriate points in the chronological sequence.

The bibliographies of individual authors follow a pattern. The author's works are listed first. For the earlier authors in this long period, the standard scholarly edition and any other modern collections and selections are listed in chronological order. For later authors, a chronological checklist of the author's separate works, giving the year of publication only, precedes the list of collected editions and selections. This primary bibliography is followed by a chronological list of the more important biographical and critical studies of the author and his work, the secondary bibliography, with the emphasis on books rather than articles. There is a final group for bibliographies of the author and reference works, if they exist.

John Barbour (1316?-95)

Barbour, archdeacon of Aberdeen from 1357 till his death, has been called the father of Scottish poetry and history. The BRUCE, partly written in 1375 and first printed in 1571, recounts the life and deeds of the national hero and his companions with remarkable historical accuracy and preserves many oral traditions.

227   BARBOUR'S BRUCE. Ed. Walter William Skeat. 4 vols. London: EETS, 1870–89; rpt. with corrections, 2 vols. Edinburgh: STS, 1894.

228   THE BRUCE. Ed. William Mackay Mackenzie. London: Black, 1909.

229   THE BRUCE: A SELECTION. Ed. Alexander M. Kinghorn. Saltire Classics. Edinburgh: Oliver and Boyd, 1960.

230   Scott, Tom. TALES OF KING ROBERT THE BRUCE: FREELY ADAPTED FROM THE BRUS OF JOHN BARBOUR. Oxford: Pergamon, 1969; rpt. Edinburgh: Reprographia, 1975.

BIOGRAPHY AND CRITICISM

231   Neilson, George. JOHN BARBOUR, POET AND TRANSLATOR. London: Kegan Paul, 1900.

232   Walker, Ian C. "Barbour, Blind Harry and Sir William Craigie." SSL, 1 (1963–64), 202–06.

233   Kinghorn, Alexander M. "Scottish Historiography in the 14th Century: A New Introduction to Barbour's BRUCE." SSL, 6 (1968–69), 131–45.

234   Kliman, B.W. "John Barbour and Rhetorical Tradition." ANNUALE MEDIAEVALE, 18 (1977), 106–35.

235   Barrow, Geoffrey W.S. "The Idea of Freedom in Late Medieval Scotland." INNES REVIEW, 30 (1979), 16–34.

BIBLIOGRAPHY

236   McKinlay, R. "Barbour's BRUCE." RECORDS OF THE GLASGOW BIB-
       LIOGRAPHICAL SOCIETY, 6 (1920), 20-38.

The Buik of Alexander

There is no extant manuscript of the Scottish Alexander Buik. This verse translation of parts of a French romance, sometimes attributed to Barbour, was first
printed in 1580. Dr. Ritchie's introduction discusses Barbour's claims to authorship.

237   THE BUIK OF ALEXANDER. Ed. by Robert Lindsay Graeme Ritchie. 4
       vols. Edinburgh: STS, 1921-29.

CRITICISM

238   Smith, Janet M. THE FRENCH BACKGROUND OF MIDDLE SCOTS
       LITERATURE. Edinburgh: Oliver and Boyd, 1934.

Legends of the Saints

The Scottish Legends of the Saints were written by an unknown hand, or by
unknown hands, about the year 1375. The only manuscript is in Cambridge
University Library.

239   LEGENDS OF THE SAINTS IN THE SCOTTISH DIALECT OF THE 14TH
       CENTURY. Ed. William M. Metcalfe. 3 vols. Edinburgh: STS,
       1888-96.

240   THE LEGENDS OF SS. NINIAN AND MACHOR. Ed. William M. Met-
       calfe. Paisley: Gardner, 1904.

Andrew of Wyntoun (1350?-1420?)

Wyntoun, a canon regular of St. Andrews, became prior of the monastery of
St. Serf on Loch Leven about 1395. His rhyming chronicle, "a compendium of
universal history, for Scottish use and with a Scottish foreground," is a valuable
specimen of early Scots.

241   THE ORIGINAL CHRONICLE OF ANDREW OF WYNTOUN. Ed. François
       Joseph Amours. 6 vols. Edinburgh: STS, 1903-14.

James I, King of Scotland (1394-1437)

James I, the ablest of the Stewart kings, was an accomplished poet.

242 THE KINGIS QUAIR, TOGETHER WITH A BALLAD OF GOOD COUNSEL. Ed. Walter William Skeat. Edinburgh: STS, 1884; rev. 1911.

243 THE KINGIS QUAIR. Ed. William Mackay Mackenzie. London: Faber, 1939.

244 THE KINGIS QUAIR. Ed. John Norton-Smith. Clarendon Medieval and Tudor Series. Oxford: Clarendon Press, 1971.

245 THE KINGIS QUAIR OF JAMES STEWART. Ed. Matthew P. McDiarmid. London: Heinemann, 1973.

BIOGRAPHY AND CRITICISM

246 Balfour-Melville, Evan W.M. JAMES I, KING OF SCOTS. London: Methuen, 1936.

247 Lewis, Clive Staples. THE ALLEGORY OF LOVE: A STUDY IN MEDIEVAL TRADITION. Oxford: Clarendon Press, 1936.

248 Craigie, William A. "The Language of THE KINGIS QUAIR." ESSAYS AND STUDIES, 25 (1939), 22-38.

249 MacQueen, John. "Tradition and the Interpretation of THE KINGIS QUAIR." RES, n.s. 12 (1961), 117-31.

250 Von Hendy, Andrew. "The Free Thrall: A Study of THE KINGIS QUAIR." SSL, 2 (1964-65), 141-51.

251 Brown, Ian. "The Mental Traveller: A Study of THE KINGIS QUAIR." SSL, 5 (1967-68), 246-52.

252 Scheps, Walter. "Chaucerian Synthesis: The Art of THE KINGIS QUAIR." SSL, 8 (1970-71), 143-65.

Gilbert of the Haye

Hay's manuscript is a translation from French and Latin of three works on the law of arms, knighthood, and chivalry. It is the earliest surviving literary Scots prose.

253 GILBERT OF THE HAYE'S PROSE MS. A.D. 1456. Ed. John Horne
Stevenson. 2 vols. Edinburgh: STS, 1901-14.

Robert Henryson (1425?-1506?)

Henryson, schoolmaster of Dunfermline, is remembered for his TESTAMENT OF
CRESSEID, a sequel to Chaucer's poem, his delightful fables, and the pastoral,
ROBENE AND MAKYNE.

254 POEMS. Ed. George Gregory Smith. 3 vols. Edinburgh: STS, 1906-14.

255 THE TESTAMENT OF CRESSEID. Ed. Bruce Dickins. Edinburgh: Porpoise Press, 1925; rev. London: Faber, 1943.

256 POEMS AND FABLES. Ed. Henry Harvey Wood. Edinburgh: Oliver
and Boyd, 1933; rev. 1958; rpt. Edinburgh: James Thin, Mercat Press,
1978.

257 SELECTIONS. Ed. David D. Murison. Saltire Classics. Edinburgh:
Oliver and Boyd, 1951.

258 THE TESTAMENT OF CRESSEID. Ed. Denton Fox. London: Nelson,
1968.

259 POEMS. Ed. Charles Elliott. Clarendon Medieval and Tudor Series.
2nd ed. Oxford: Clarendon Press, 1974.

BIOGRAPHY AND CRITICISM

260 Wood, Henry Harvey. "Robert Henryson." In EDINBURGH ESSAYS ON
SCOTS LITERATURE. Edinburgh: Oliver and Boyd, 1933, pp. 1-26.

261 Tillyard, Eustace M.W. "Robert Henryson: THE TESTAMENT OF CRES-
SEID, 1470?" In his FIVE POEMS, 1470-1870. London: Chatto and Windus, 1948, pp. 5-29.

262 Muir, Edwin. "Henryson." In his ESSAYS ON LITERATURE AND SOCI-
ETY. London: Hogarth Press, 1949; rev. 1965, pp. 10-21.

263 Stearns, Marshall W. ROBERT HENRYSON. New York: Columbia University Press, 1949.

264 Cruttwell, Patrick. "Two Scots Poets: Dunbar and Henryson." In THE
AGE OF CHAUCER. Ed. Boris Ford. Pelican Guide to English Literature,
vol. 1. Harmondsworth: Penguin, 1954, pp. 175-87.

265 Kinghorn, Alexander M. "The Minor Poems of Robert Henryson." SSL, 3 (1965–66), 30–40.

266 Macdonald, Donald. "Narrative Art in Henryson's FABLES." SSL, 3 (1965–66), 101–13.

267 Wood, Henry Harvey. "Robert Henryson." In his TWO SCOTS CHAUCERIANS: ROBERT HENRYSON, WILLIAM DUNBAR. London: Longmans, Green, for the British Council, 1967, pp. 9–23.

268 MacQueen, John. ROBERT HENRYSON: A STUDY OF THE MAJOR NARRATIVE POEMS. Oxford: Clarendon Press, 1967.

269 Jamieson, I.W.A. "Henryson's TAILL OF THE WOLF AND THE WEDDER." SSL, 6 (1968–69), 248–57.

270 Fox, Denton. "The 1663 Anderson Edition of Henryson's TESTAMENT OF CRESSEID." SSL, 8 (1970–71), 75–96.

     Includes a transcript of the text of that edition.

271 Jamieson, I.W.A. "The Minor Poems of Robert Henryson." SSL, 9 (1971–72), 125–41.

272 Aitken, Adam Jack, et al., eds. BARDS AND MAKARS: SCOTTISH LANGUAGE AND LITERATURE, MEDIEVAL AND RENAISSANCE. Glasgow: University of Glasgow Press, 1977.

     There are four essays on Henryson: Thomas W. Craik, "The Substance and Structure of THE TESTAMENT OF CRESSEID," pp. 22–26; Matthew P. McDiarmid, "Robert Henryson in his Poems," pp. 27–40; John McNamara, "Language as Action in Henryson's TESTAMENT OF CRESSEID," pp. 41–51; and Caroll Mills, "Romance Convention and Robert Henryson's ORPHEUS AND EURYDICE," pp. 52–60.

Harry the Minstrel (c. 1440?–92?)

To Harry the Minstrel, commonly known as Blind Harry, is attributed the long poem which collects and preserves the popular traditions concerning William Wallace, the earlier national hero of the War of Independence (Bruce is the other). Fragments survive of an edition printed about 1509. The WALLACE was extremely popular and numerous editions and versions appeared over three centuries. See, for example, the modernized version by William Hamilton of Gilbertfield, THE HISTORY OF THE LIFE AND ADVENTURES AND HEROIC ACTIONS OF THE RENOWNED SIR WILLIAM WALLACE (Edinburgh, 1722), which so impressed Robert Burns.

273 THE ACTIS AND DEIDIS OF THE ILLUSTERE AND VAILZEAND CAM-
PIOUN SCHIR WILLIAM WALLACE, KNICHT OF ELLERSLIE. Ed. James
Moir. Edinburgh: STS, 1889.

274 HARY'S WALLACE. Ed. Matthew P. McDiarmid. 2 vols. Edinburgh:
STS, 1968-69.

BIOGRAPHY AND CRITICISM

275 Schofield, William Henry. MYTHICAL BARDS AND THE LIFE OF WIL-
LIAM WALLACE. Cambridge: Harvard University Press, 1920.

276 Scheps, Walter. "William Wallace and His 'Buke': Some Instances of
Their Influence on Subsequent Literature." SSL, 6 (1968-69), 220-37.

BIBLIOGRAPHY

277 Miller, John F. "Blind Harry's WALLACE." RECORDS OF GLASGOW
BIBLIOGRAPHICAL SOCIETY, 3 (1914), 1-25; "Some Additions." 6
(1920), 14-19.

John of Ireland (1440-96?)

John of Ireland spent much of his life in France, but was rector of Yarrow
when he completed his book in 1490. It is the earliest extant example of
original literary prose in Scots.

278 THE MEROURE OF WYSSDOME, COMPOSED FOR THE USE OF JAMES
IV, KING OF SCOTS, A.D. 1490. Ed. Charles MacPherson and F.
Quinn. 2 vols. Edinburgh: STS, 1925-65.

William Dunbar (1460?-1513?)

Dunbar is the most versatile and individual of the Middle Scots poets, using a
variety of verse forms with great skill, and a vocabulary that ranges from the
aureate to the colloquial. It is not surprising that Hugh MacDiarmid, in
launching the modern Scottish literary renaissance in the 1920s, rallied his
followers with the cry, "Not Burns--Dunbar."

279 POEMS. Ed. John Small. 3 vols. Edinburgh: STS, 1884-93.

280 POEMS. Ed. William Mackay Mackenzie. London: Faber, 1932; rev.
1960.

281 POEMS. Ed. James Kinsley. Clarendon Medieval and Tudor Series.
Oxford: Clarendon Press, 1958.

This selection reprints appreciations of Dunbar by Clive Staples
Lewis, William Lindsay Renwick, Agnes Mure Mackenzie, and
others.

282 THE POEMS OF WILLIAM DUNBAR. Ed. James Kinsley. Oxford: Clarendon Press, 1979.

A magnificent new edition.

BIOGRAPHY AND CRITICISM

283 Taylor, Rachel Annand. DUNBAR: THE POET AND HIS PERIOD. London: Faber, 1931.

284 Mackenzie, William Mackay. "William Dunbar." In EDINBURGH ES-
SAYS ON SCOTS LITERATURE. Edinburgh: Oliver and Boyd, 1933,
pp. 27-55.

285 Baxter, John Walker. WILLIAM DUNBAR: A BIOGRAPHICAL STUDY.
Edinburgh: Oliver and Boyd, 1952.

286 Morgan, Edwin. "Dunbar and the Language of Poetry." ESSAYS IN
CRITICISM, 2 (1952), 138-58.

The essay is reprinted in Morgan's ESSAYS (Cheadle: Carcanet
Press, 1974), pp. 81-99.

287 Cruttwell, Patrick. "Two Scots Poets: Dunbar and Henryson." In THE
AGE OF CHAUCER. Ed. Boris Ford. Pelican Guide to English Literature, vol. 1. Harmondsworth: Penguin, 1954, pp. 175-87.

288 Scott, Tom. DUNBAR: A CRITICAL EXPOSITION OF THE POEMS.
Edinburgh: Oliver and Boyd, 1966.

Includes an extensive bibliographical review.

289 Wood, Henry Harvey. "William Dunbar." In his TWO SCOTS CHAUCER-
IANS: ROBERT HENRYSON, WILLIAM DUNBAR. London: Longmans,
Green, for the British Council, 1967, pp. 23-43.

290 Jack, Ronald D.S. "Dunbar and Lydgate." SSL, 8 (1970-71), 215-27.

291 Bawcutt, Priscilla. "Aspects of Dunbar's Imagery." In CHAUCER AND
MIDDLE ENGLISH STUDIES IN HONOUR OF R.H. ROBBINS. Ed. B.
Rowland. London: Allen and Unwin, 1974, pp. 190-200.

292 Aitken, Adam Jack, et al., eds. BARDS AND MAKARS: SCOTTISH
     LANGUAGE AND LITERATURE, MEDIEVAL AND RENAISSANCE. Glas-
     gow: University of Glasgow Press, 1977.
     There are three essays on Dunbar: W.F.H. Nicolaisen, "Line
     and Sentence in Dunbar's Poetry," pages 61-71; Jean-Jacques
     Blanchot, "William Dunbar and François Villon: The Literary
     PERSONAE," pages 72-87; and Ian Ross, "Dunbar's Vision of
     'The Four Last Things,'" pages 88-106.

293 Drexler, Robert D. "Dunbar's 'Lament for the Makaris' and the Dance
     of Death Tradition." SSL, 13 (1978), 144-58.

Gavin Douglas (1474?-1522)

Douglas, the first British translator of the AENEID, is at his best in the original
prologues he prefixed to each book: vivid descriptions of nature and the Scottish landscape in a strong and vigorous language which he was the first to call
Scots.

294 POETICAL WORKS OF GAVIN DOUGLAS, BISHOP OF DUNKELD. Ed.
     John Small. 4 vols. Edinburgh: W. Paterson, 1874.

295 VIRGIL'S AENEID TRANSLATED INTO SCOTTISH VERSE. Ed. David
     F.C. Coldwell. 4 vols. Edinburgh: STS, 1957-64.

296 GAVIN DOUGLAS: A SELECTION FROM HIS POETRY. Ed. Sydney
     Goodsir Smith. Saltire Classics. Edinburgh: Oliver and Boyd, 1959.

297 SELECTIONS FROM GAVIN DOUGLAS. Ed. David F.C. Coldwell.
     Clarendon Medieval and Tudor Series. Oxford: Clarendon Press, 1964.

298 SHORTER POEMS. Ed. Priscilla Bawcutt. Edinburgh: STS, 1967.

BIOGRAPHY AND CRITICISM

299 Watt, Lauchlan Maclean. DOUGLAS'S AENEID. Cambridge: Cambridge
     University Press, 1920.

300 Fulton, Robin. "Douglas and Virgil." SSL, 2 (1964-65), 125-28.

301 Bawcutt, Priscilla. GAVIN DOUGLAS: A CRITICAL STUDY. Edin-
     burgh: Edinburgh University Press, 1976.

302 Aitken, Adam Jack, et al., eds. BARDS AND MAKARS: SCOTTISH
LANGUAGE AND LITERATURE, MEDIEVAL AND RENAISSANCE. Glasgow: University of Glasgow Press, 1977.

> There are two essays on Douglas: Priscilla Bawcutt, "The 'Li-
> brary' of Gavin Douglas," pages 107-26; and Edwin Morgan,
> "Gavin Douglas and William Drummond as Translators," pages
> 194-200.

Murdoch Nisbet

Nisbet, an Ayrshire man who became a Protestant, completed his version of the
New Testament in Scots about 1520.

303 THE NEW TESTAMENT IN SCOTS, BEING PURVEY'S REVISION OF WY-
CLIFFE'S VERSION, TURNED INTO SCOTS. Ed. Thomas Graves Law.
3 vols. Edinburgh: STS, 1901-05.

Sir David Lindsay (1490?-1555)

Lindsay, a courtier, herald, and ambassador, joined the popular reforming party.
His poems are full of humor, good sense, and worldly wisdom; and he is an un-
relenting satirist of the nobles and clergy who batten on "John the Common-
weal," as Lindsay calls the common man of his day. He remained immensely
popular till at least the beginning of the nineteenth century, and his most
interesting work, the morality play, ANE SATIRE OF THE THRIE ESTAITIS,
first performed in 1540, was revived with great success at the Edinburgh Festival of 1948 in the adaptation by Robert Kemp, produced by Tyrone Guthrie.

304 THE WORKS OF SIR DAVID LINDSAY OF THE MOUNT. Ed. Douglas
Hamer. 4 vols. Edinburgh: STS, 1931-36.

305 POEMS. Ed. Maurice Lindsay. Saltire Classics. Edinburgh: Oliver
and Boyd, 1948.

306 THE SATIRE OF THE THREE ESTATES. Acting text by Robert Kemp.
Edinburgh: Scots Review, 1949.

307 ANE SATIRE OF THE THRIE ESTAITIS. Ed. James Kinsley. London:
Cassell, 1954.

308 THE HISTORY OF SQUYER MELDRUM. Ed. James Kinsley. London:
Nelson, 1959.

309 A SATIRE OF THE THREE ESTATES. Ed. Matthew P. McDiarmid. London: Heinemann, 1967.

A modernized acting version, from Robert Kemp's text (no. 306).

BIOGRAPHY AND CRITICISM

310 Murison, William. SIR DAVID LYNDSAY, POET AND SATIRIST OF THE OLD CHURCH IN SCOTLAND. Cambridge: Cambridge University Press, 1938.

311 MacQueen, John. "ANE SATYRE OF THE THRIE ESTAITIS." SSL, 3 (1965-66), 129-43.

312 Mill, Anna J. "The Original Version of Lindsay's SATYRE OF THE THRIE ESTAITIS." SSL, 6 (1968-69), 67-75.

313 Harwood, Vernon. "ANE SATYRE OF THE THRIE ESTAITIS Again." SSL, 7 (1969-70), 139-46.

314 Kantrowitz, Joanne Spencer. "Encore: Lindsay's THRIE ESTAITIS, Date and New Evidence." SSL, 10 (1972-73), 18-32.

315 _____. DRAMATIC ALLEGORY. Lincoln: University of Nebraska Press, 1974.

316 Graf, Claude. "Theatre and Politics: Lyndsay's SATYRE OF THE THRIE ESTAITIS." In BARDS AND MAKARS: SCOTTISH LANGUAGE AND LITERATURE, MEDIEVAL AND RENAISSANCE. Ed. Adam Jack Aitken et al. Glasgow: University of Glasgow Press, 1977, pp. 143-55.

John Bellenden (c. 1500-c. 1548)

John Bellenden or Ballantyne, who became archdeacon of Moray, is known for his translations from the Latin into easy and vigorous Scots. For his poetry, see SCOTTISH POETRY OF THE SIXTEENTH CENTURY, ed. George Eyre-Todd (Glasgow: Hodge, 1892).

317 LIVY'S HISTORY OF ROME: THE FIRST FIVE BOOKS. TRANSLATED INTO SCOTS. Ed. William A. Craigie. 2 vols. Edinburgh: STS, 1901.

318 THE CHRONICLES OF SCOTLAND, COMPILED BY HECTOR BOECE. TRANSLATED INTO SCOTS. Ed. Raymond W. Chambers et al. 2 vols. Edinburgh: STS, 1938-41.

There is a life of Bellenden by Elizabeth A. Sheppard in volume 2.

BIOGRAPHY AND CRITICISM

319   Chambers, Raymond W., and Walter Seton. "Bellenden's Translation of the History of Hector Boece." SHR, 17 (1920), 5-15; 19 (1922), 196-201.

The Complaynt of Scotlande

The author of this book is unknown. It discusses the contemporary state of Scotland, using the "domestic Scottis langage, maist intelligibil for the vulgare pepil," in a strange style which ranges from the aureate to the common; yet some have thought it to be the most thoroughly Scottish production of its age.

320   THE COMPLAYNT OF SCOTLANDE. Paris, 1549. Ed. James A.H. Murray. London: EETS, 1872.

322   THE COMPLAYNT OF SCOTLAND. Introd. A.M. Stewart. Edinburgh: STS, 1979.

Robert Lindsay of Pitscottie (1500?-1565?)

Nothing is known of the life of Lindsay of Pitscottie, who compiled the first history of Scotland to be written in Scots prose. For the last thirty years or so of his account, he was writing vividly as a contemporary.

323   THE HISTORIE AND CRONICLES OF SCOTLAND. Ed. Aeneas J.G. MacKay. 3 vols. Edinburgh: STS, 1899-1911.

The Gude and Godlie Ballatis

A unique collection of hymns, translations, and paraphrases, with other contemporary poems. The earliest known edition was published in 1567, but there may have been earlier editions. The authorship of the book is still obscure, but it is now generally accepted that the main responsibility rests with one or more of the Wedderburn brothers, John, James, and Robert. John Wedderburn took his degree at St. Andrews in 1528.

324   A COMPENDIOUS BOOK OF GODLY AND SPIRITUAL SONGS, COMMONLY KNOWN AS THE GUDE AND GODLIE BALLATIS. Ed. Alexander F. Mitchell. Edinburgh: STS, 1897.

The text of the 1567 edition.

325 THE GUDE AND GODLIE BALLATIS. Ed. Iain Ross. Saltire Classics. Edinburgh: Oliver and Boyd, 1940.

The text based mainly on the edition of 1578.

BIOGRAPHY AND CRITICISM

326 Mitchell, Alexander F. THE WEDDERBURNS AND THEIR WORK. Edinburgh: Blackwood, 1867.

George Buchanan (1506-82)

The great humanist and reformer, born near Killearn in Stirlingshire, taught in Paris for ten years, and after a brief return to Scotland, fled to the Continent again until 1561. During this second stay on the Continent, he was arrested and tried by the Lisbon Inquisition, but he put up a spirited defense and was released. Back in Scotland he was appointed tutor to Mary, Queen of Scots, and later to the young James VI. Buchanan had a European reputation as a Latin poet, and his history of Scotland is still valuable, despite its partisanship, for its account of contemporary affairs.

327 VERNACULAR WRITINGS. Ed. Peter Hume Brown. Edinburgh: STS, 1892.

328 THE TYRANNOUS REIGN OF MARY STEWART. Ed. W.A. Gatherer. Edinburgh: Edinburgh University Press, 1958.

A translation, with notes and commentary, of Buchanan's writings on Mary: the DETECTIO REGINAE MARIAE (1571), ANE ADMONITIOUN TO THE TREW LORDIS (1571), and the relevant books (17-19) of RERUM SCOTICARUM HISTORIA (1582).

329 JEPHTHAH [1554] AND THE BAPTIST [1578], TRANSLATIT FRAE LATIN IN SCOTS. By Robert Garioch Sutherland. Edinburgh: Oliver and Boyd, 1959.

330 THE ART AND SCIENCE OF GOVERNMENT AMONG THE SCOTS. By Duncan H. MacNeill. Glasgow: Maclellan, 1965.

A translation with commentary of DE JURE REGNI APUD SCOTOS (1579).

BIOGRAPHY AND CRITICISM

331 Brown, Peter Hume. GEORGE BUCHANAN: HUMANIST AND REFORMER. Edinburgh: David Douglas, 1890.

332 Millar, David Alexander, ed. GEORGE BUCHANAN: A MEMORIAL, 1506-1906. St. Andrews: Henderson, 1907.

333 Neilson, George, ed. GEORGE BUCHANAN: GLASGOW QUATER-CENTENARY STUDIES, 1906. Glasgow: Maclehose, 1907.

334 Aitken, James M. THE TRIAL OF GEORGE BUCHANAN BEFORE THE LISBON INQUISITION. Edinburgh: Oliver and Boyd, 1939.

The text of Buchanan's defenses, with a translation and commentary.

BIBLIOGRAPHY

335 Anderson, James Maitland. "The Writings of George Buchanan." In GEORGE BUCHANAN: A MEMORIAL, 1506-1906. Ed. David Alexander Millar. St. Andrews: Henderson, 1907, pp. 166-85.

336 Murray, David. "Catalogue of Printed Books, MSS., Charters, and Other Documents." In GEORGE BUCHANAN: GLASGOW QUATER-CENTENARY STUDIES, 1906. Ed. George Neilson. Glasgow: Maclehose, 1907, pp. 393-541.

John Knox (1513?-72)

Knox has been called the architect of the Scottish Reformation (Protestantism was established in Scotland in 1560), and his HISTORY is a unique record of contemporary affairs by an active participant, written in a Scots greatly influenced by English usage.

337 THE HISTORIE OF THE REFORMATIOUN OF RELIGIOUN WITHIN THE REALM OF SCOTLAND: A SELECTION. Ed. Ralph S. Walker. Saltire Classics. Edinburgh: Oliver and Boyd, 1940.

338 JOHN KNOX'S HISTORY OF THE REFORMATION IN SCOTLAND. Ed. William Croft Dickinson. 2 vols. Edinburgh: Nelson, 1949.

Complete, with modernized spelling.

339 THE FIRST BOOK OF DISCIPLINE. Introd. and commentary by James Kerr Cameron. Edinburgh: St. Andrew Press, 1972.

BIOGRAPHY AND CRITICISM

340 Brown, Peter Hume. JOHN KNOX: A BIOGRAPHY. 2 vols. London: Black, 1895.

341 Muir, Edwin. JOHN KNOX: PORTRAIT OF A CALVINIST. London: Cape, 1929.

342 Percy, Lord Eustace. JOHN KNOX. London: Hodder and Stoughton, 1937.

343 Ridley, Jasper. JOHN KNOX. Oxford: Clarendon Press, 1968.

344 Shaw, Duncan, ed. JOHN KNOX: A QUATERCENTENARY REAPPRAISAL. Edinburgh: St. Andrew Press, 1975.

See particularly two essays: Gordon Donaldson, "Knox the Man," pages 18-32; and David D. Murison, "Knox the Writer," pages 33-50.

Alexander Scott (1525?-84)

Scott's poems have been preserved in the Bannatyne Manuscript. Little is known of his life.

345 POEMS. Ed. James Cranstoun. Edinburgh: STS, 1896.

346 POEMS, EDITED FROM THE BANNATYNE MS. AND THE MAITLAND MS. Ed. Alexander K. Donald. London: EETS, 1902.

347 POEMS. Ed. Alexander Scott. Saltire Classics. Edinburgh: Oliver and Boyd, 1952.

A selection, for which the spelling has been simplified.

BIOGRAPHY AND CRITICISM

348 Maclean, Catherine Macdonald. ALEXANDER SCOTT, MONTGOMERIE AND DRUMMOND OF HAWTHORNDEN AS LYRIC POETS. Cambridge: Cambridge University Press, 1915.

349 MacQueen, John. "Alexander Scott and Scottish Court Poetry of the Middle Sixteenth Century." Warton Lecture. PROCEEDINGS OF THE BRITISH ACADEMY, 54 (1968), 93-116.

350 Shire, Helena M. SONG, DANCE AND POETRY OF THE COURT OF SCOTLAND UNDER KING JAMES VI. Cambridge: Cambridge University Press, 1969.

John Leslie, Bishop of Ross (1527-96)

Leslie studied at King's College, Aberdeen, and in Paris. His history of Scotland was translated from Latin into Scots in 1596.

351 LESLIE'S HISTORIE OF SCOTLAND. TRANSLATED INTO SCOTTISH FROM THE ORIGINAL LATIN BY FATHER JAMES DALRYMPLE. Ed. Elphege G. Cody. 2 vols. Edinburgh: STS, 1888-95.

Sir James Melville of Halhill (1535-1617)

The autobiography of Sir James Melville, courtier and privy councillor, is one of the original authorities for its period. It was first published in 1683.

352 THE MEMOIRES OF SIR JAMES MELVIL OF HAL-HILL. 1683. Ed. Thomas Thomson. Edinburgh: Bannatyne Club, 1827.

353 THE MEMOIRS OF SIR JAMES MELVILLE OF HALHILL. Ed. Gordon Donaldson. London: Folio Society, 1969.

John Stewart of Baldynneis (c. 1540-c. 1600)

Stewart was a minor poet with a felicitous turn of phrase and an inclination to experiment freely in his versification.

354 POEMS. Ed. Thomas Crockett. Edinburgh: STS, 1913.

BIOGRAPHY AND CRITICISM

355 McDiarmid, Matthew P. "Notes on the Poems of Stewart of Baldynneis." RES, 24 (1948), 12-18.

356 _____. "Stewart of Baldynneis." SHR, 29 (1950), 52-63.

Alexander Montgomerie (1556?-1610?)

Montgomerie is chiefly remembered for his allegorical poem, THE CHERRIE AND THE SLAE, and for the intricate stanza (which he may have invented) in which that poem is written. It was later used by Burns to great effect.

357 POEMS. Ed. James Cranstoun. Edinburgh: STS, 1887. Supplementary volume. Ed. George Stevenson. Edinburgh: STS, 1910.

358 THE CHERRIE AND THE SLAE. Ed. Henry Harvey Wood. London: Faber, 1937.

359 ALEXANDER MONTGOMERIE: A SELECTION FROM HIS SONGS AND POEMS. Ed. Helena M. Shire. Saltire Classics. Edinburgh: Oliver and Boyd, 1960.

BIOGRAPHY AND CRITICISM

360 Maclean, Catherine Macdonald. ALEXANDER SCOTT, MONTGOMERIE AND DRUMMOND OF HAWTHORNDEN AS LYRIC POETS. Cambridge: Cambridge University Press, 1915.

361 Shire, Helena M. "Alexander Montgomerie: The Oppositione of the Court to Conscience." SSL, 3 (1965-66), 144-50.

362 _____. SONG, DANCE AND POETRY OF THE COURT OF SCOTLAND UNDER KING JAMES VI. Cambridge: Cambridge University Press, 1969.

James Melville, Minister of Kilrenny (1556-1614)

James Melville, a nephew of the scholar and reformer, Andrew Melville, is best known for his diary, covering the period 1556 to 1601. It is written in a lively, idiomatic Scots, and reveals a particularly attractive personality.

363 THE AUTOBIOGRAPHY AND DIARY. Ed. Robert Pitcairn. Edinburgh: Wodrow Society, 1844.

364 THE HISTORIE OF THE LYFF OF JAMES MELVILL: A SELECTION. Ed. James G. Fyfe. Saltire Classics. Edinburgh: Oliver and Boyd, 1948.

Alexander Hume (1560?-1609)

Hume probably studied at St. Andrews, and then in France. He entered the ministry and held the charge at Logie, near Stirling.

365 POEMS. Ed. Alexander Lawson. Edinburgh: STS, 1902.

BIOGRAPHY AND CRITICISM

366 Fergusson, Robert Menzies. ALEXANDER HUME: AN EARLY POET-PASTOR OF LOGIE, AND HIS INTIMATES. Paisley: Gardner, 1899.

367 Lindsay, David W. "OF THE DAY ESTIVALL: A Textual Note." SSL, 4 (1966-67), 104-06.

William Fowler (1560-1612)

Fowler, well read in Latin, English, French, and Italian, held a post in the royal household, and was in charge of the masques at the baptism of Prince Henry in 1594.

368 WORKS. Ed. Henry W. Meikle, James Craigie, and John Purves. 3 vols. Edinburgh: STS, 1914-40.

> Volume 1, VERSE; volume 2, PROSE; volume 3, INTRODUCTION, NOTES, etc.

BIOGRAPHY AND CRITICISM

369 Purves, John. "William Fowler and Scoto-Italian Cultural Relations in the Sixteenth Century." In THE WORKS OF WILLIAM FOWLER. Ed. Henry W. Meikle et al. Edinburgh: STS, 1914-40, vol. 3, pp. lxxx-cl.

370 Jack, Ronald D.S. "William Fowler and Italian Literature." MLR, 65 (1970), 481-92.

James VI, King of Scotland (1566-1625)

King James early showed an intelligent interest in literature and the technique of writing, and is indeed rightly remembered as a critic and patron.

371 DAEMONOLOGIE. 1597. Ed. George B. Harrison. London: Lane, 1924.

372 BASILICON DORON. 1599. Ed. James Craigie. 2 vols. Edinburgh: STS, 1944-50.

> A treatise on kingship.

373 A COUNTERBLASTE TO TOBACCO. 1604. In A ROYAL RHETORICIAN. Ed. Robert S. Rait. London: Constable, 1900, pp. 29-59.

> Rait's volume also includes one of King James's critical essays, "Ane Schort Treatise" (1584).

374 POLITICAL WORKS. Ed. Charles Howard McIlwain. Cambridge: Harvard University Press, 1918.

375   POEMS. Ed. James Craigie. 2 vols. Edinburgh: STS, 1955-58.

BIOGRAPHY AND CRITICISM

376   Willson, David Harris. KING JAMES VI AND I. London: Cape, 1956.

377   McElwee, William. THE WISEST FOOL IN CHRISTENDOM. London: Faber, 1958.

378   Jack, Ronald D.S. "James VI and Renaissance Poetic Theory." ENGLISH, 16 (1966-67), 208-11.

379   Shire, Helena M. SONG, DANCE AND POETRY OF THE COURT OF SCOTLAND UNDER KING JAMES VI. Cambridge: Cambridge University Press, 1969.

Sir William Alexander, Earl of Stirling (1567?-1640)

Alexander, statesman and poet, followed James VI to England. Later he became Secretary of State for Scotland and was created an earl by Charles I. He wrote love lyrics and moral poems, an epic, and undramatic Senecan tragedies which were admired at the time.

380   AURORA. 1604.

Sonnets and other poems.

381   THE MONARCHICK TRAGEDIES. 1604; 1607.

Croesus; Darius; The Alexandraean Tragedy; Julius Caesar.

382   AN ELEGIE ON THE DEATH OF PRINCE HENRY. 1612.

383   DOOMES-DAY. 1614.

384   RECREATIONS WITH THE MUSES. 1637.

Alexander's collected and revised works.

385   POETICAL WORKS. Ed. Léon Emile Kastner and Henry B. Charlton. 2 vols. Edinburgh: STS, 1921-29.

With a bibliography and an essay on Senecan drama.

BIOGRAPHY AND CRITICISM

386   Fergusson, Robert Menzies. ALEXANDER HUME: AN EARLY POET—
PASTOR OF LOGIE, AND HIS INTIMATES. Paisley: Gardner, 1899.

387   McGrail, Thomas H. SIR WILLIAM ALEXANDER: A BIOGRAPHICAL
STUDY. Edinburgh: Oliver and Boyd, 1940.

388   Wiles, A.G.D. "Sir William Alexander's Continuation of the Revised
Version of Sir Philip Sidney's ARCADIA." SSL, 3 (1965–66), 221–29.

Sir Robert Ayton (1570-1638)

Ayton, who spent most of his life in various minor court offices, was one of the
first Scottish poets to write in English. He did so with grace and charm.

389   A CHOICE OF POEMS AND SONGS. Ed. Helena M. Shire. Cambridge: Ninth of May, 1961.

390   THE ENGLISH AND LATIN POEMS. Ed. Charles B. Gullans. Edinburgh: STS, 1963.

BIOGRAPHY AND CRITICISM

391   Shire, Helena M. SONG, DANCE AND POETRY OF THE COURT OF
SCOTLAND UNDER KING JAMES VI. Cambridge: Cambridge University Press, 1969.

392   Scott, Mary J.W. "Robert Ayton: Scottish Metaphysical." SLJ, 2
(July 1975), 5–16.

William Drummond of Hawthornden (1585-1649)

Drummond was an elegant poet, a bookman, and an inventor--he amassed a
considerable library and patented more than a dozen inventions. Ben Johnson
paid Drummond a memorable visit in the winter of 1618–19, walking the four
hundred miles from London to meet the Scottish poet in his home near Edinburgh
(see no. 394).

393   POETICAL WORKS. Ed. Léon Emile Kastner. 2 vols. Edinburgh: STS,
1913.

394   BEN JONSON'S CONVERSATIONS WITH WILLIAM DRUMMOND OF
HAWTHORNDEN. Ed. Richard F. Patterson. 1923; rpt. New York:
Haskell House, 1973.

395 POEMS AND PROSE. Ed. Robert H. MacDonald. Edinburgh: Scottish Academic Press, 1976.

BIOGRAPHY AND CRITICISM

396 Maclean, Catherine Macdonald. ALEXANDER SCOTT, MONTGOMERIE AND DRUMMOND OF HAWTHORNDEN AS LYRIC POETS. Cambridge: Cambridge University Press, 1915.

397 Fogle, French Rowe. A CRITICAL STUDY OF WILLIAM DRUMMOND. New York: King's Crown Press, 1952.

398 Jack, Ronald D.S. "Drummond of Hawthornden: The Major Scottish Sources." SSL, 6 (1968-69), 36-46.

399 MacDonald, Robert H. THE LIBRARY OF DRUMMOND OF HAWTHORNDEN. Edinburgh: Edinburgh University Press, 1971.

400 Rae, Thomas Ian. "The Political Attitudes of William Drummond of Hawthornden." In THE SCOTTISH TRADITION. Ed. Geoffrey W.S. Barrow. Edinburgh: Scottish Academic Press, 1974, pp. 132-46.

401 _____. "The Historical Writing of Drummond of Hawthornden." SHR, 54 (1975), 22-62.

402 Morgan, Edwin. "Gavin Douglas and William Drummond as Translators." In BARDS AND MAKARS: SCOTTISH LANGUAGE AND LITERATURE, MEDIEVAL AND RENAISSANCE. Ed. Adam Jack Aitken et al. Glasgow: University of Glasgow Press, 1977, pp. 194-200.

Sir John Scot of Scotstarvit (1585-1670)

Sir John Scot was a generous and intelligent supporter of literature and learning. The title of his chief work, as J.H. Millar points out, "especially in conjunction with the full territorial designation of its author, should keep it in everlasting remembrance."

403 THE STAGGERING STATE OF THE SCOTS STATESMEN FOR ONE HUNDRED YEARS. Ed. Charles Rogers. Edinburgh: Privately Printed, 1872.

With a memoir of the author.

BIOGRAPHY AND CRITICISM

404 Snoddy, Thomas G. SIR JOHN SCOT, LORD SCOTSTARVIT: HIS LIFE AND TIMES. Edinburgh: Constable, 1968.

405 Pringle, R.V. "An Early Humanity Class Library: The Gift of Sir John Scot and Friends to St. Leonard's College (1620)." BIBLIOTHECK, 7 (1974-75), 33-54.

Sir William Mure of Rowallan (1594-1657)

Mure of Rowallan was the major poet on the Covenanting side in the Scottish religious wars of the seventeenth century.

406 WORKS. Ed. William Tough. 2 vols. Edinburgh: STS, 1898.

407 "The Joy of Tears." Ed. C. Davis. In THE SCOTTISH TEXT SOCIETY MISCELLANY VOLUME. Edinburgh: STS, 1933, pp. 159-78.

BIOGRAPHY AND CRITICISM

408 Jack, Ronald D.S. "Scottish Sonneteer and Welsh Metaphysical: A Study of the Religious Poetry of Sir William Mure and Henry Vaughan." SSL, 3 (1965-66), 240-47.

409 Shire, Helena M. SONG, DANCE AND POETRY OF THE COURT OF SCOTLAND UNDER KING JAMES VI. Cambridge: Cambridge University Press, 1969.

Robert Sempill (1595?-1665)

Sempill earns a place in Scottish literary history for his poem, "The Life and Death of Habbie Simson, the Piper of Kilbarchan." Its metre and its mock-heroic tone became traditional for Scottish elegiac verse, being used to effect by Ramsay and Fergusson, and with superb genius by Burns. Robert Sempill's father, Sir James (1566-1625), and his son, Francis (1610-1682), also wrote poetry.

410 THE POEMS OF THE SEMPILLS OF BELTREES. Ed. James Paterson. Edinburgh: T.G. Stevenson, 1849.

BIOGRAPHY AND CRITICISM

411 Buthlay, Kenneth. "Habbie Simson." In BARDS AND MAKARS: SCOTTISH LANGUAGE AND LITERATURE, MEDIEVAL AND RENAISSANCE. Ed. Adam Jack Aitken et al. Glasgow: University of Glasgow Press, 1977, pp. 214-20.

Sir Thomas Urquhart (1611-60)

Urquhart is one of the great eccentrics. He was a polymath who revelled in his "volubility of utterance," spent a great part of his life in a hard struggle with the "impetuosity of the usurer," and died, it is said, of a fit of laughter on hearing of the Restoration of Charles II.

412 EPIGRAMS: DIVINE AND MORAL. 1641.

413 THE TRISSOTETRAS. 1645.

> A treatise on triangles.

414 PANTOCHRONOCHANON [THE TRUE PEDIGREE OF THE URQUHARTS]. 1652.

> The lineal descent of his family from Adam and Eve.

415 EKSKYBALAURON [THE JEWEL]. 1652.

416 LOGOPANDECTEISION [THE UNIVERSAL LANGUAGE]. 1653.

417 THE FIRST BOOK OF THE WORKS OF MR. FRANCIS RABELAIS . . . NOW FAITHFULLY TRANSLATED INTO ENGLISH. 1653.

> THE SECOND BOOK . . . 1653.

> THE THIRD BOOK . . . [Ed. Pierre Antoine Motteux.] 1693.

>> Motteux also revised Urquhart's first two books and completed the translation by publishing the fourth and fifth books in 1694. See Charles Whibley's edition, with a good introduction, in the Tudor Translations Series (3 vols., London: Nutt, 1900).

COLLECTIONS AND SELECTIONS

418 WORKS. Ed. Thomas Maitland. Edinburgh: Maitland Club, 1834.

419 SELECTIONS. Ed. John Purves. Saltire Classics. Edinburgh: Oliver and Boyd, 1942.

420 THE ADMIRABLE URQUHART: SELECTED WRITINGS. Ed. Richard Boston. London: Gordon Fraser, 1975.

BIOGRAPHY AND CRITICISM

421 Miller, Hugh. "Sir Thomas Urquhart." In his SCENES AND LEGENDS OF THE NORTH OF SCOTLAND. Edinburgh: Black, 1835, pp. 138-56.

422 Willcock, John. SIR THOMAS URQUHART OF CROMARTIE, KNIGHT. Edinburgh: Oliphant, Anderson and Ferrier, 1899.

423 MacDiarmid, Hugh. "Sir Thomas Urquhart, The Knight of Cromarty." In his SCOTTISH ECCENTRICS. London: Routledge, 1936, pp. 26-56.

424 Roe, Frederick Charles. SIR THOMAS URQUHART AND RABELAIS. Oxford: Clarendon Press, 1957.

James Graham, Marquis of Montrose (1612-50)

Montrose, a soldier and statesman, had the accomplished gentleman's talent for turning graceful verses.

425 POEMS. Ed. John Lowe Weir. London: John Murray, 1938.

BIOGRAPHY AND CRITICISM

426 Buchan, John. MONTROSE. London: Nelson, 1928; rpt. Edinburgh: James Thin, Mercat Press, 1979.

    Buchan's study of Montrose was also published in the World's Classics, with an introduction by Keith Feiling (London: OUP, 1957).

427 Wedgwood, C.V. "The Poems of Montrose." ESSAYS AND STUDIES, n.s. 13 (1960), 49-64.

428 Cowan, Edward J. MONTROSE: FOR COVENANT AND KING. London: Weidenfeld and Nicolson, 1977.

Section 3

1660-1800

This section deals with Scottish literature from 1660 to 1800, the period of the Enlightenment, the beginnings of the novel, and the eighteenth-century revival of Scots by Ramsay, Fergusson, and Burns.

The general works relevant to the period are grouped under six headings:

    A. Bibliographies
    B. Literary History and Criticism
    C. Anthologies
    D. Background Studies
    E. Printing and Publishing
    F. Periodicals

Under each heading or subheading the works are arranged in chronological order by the year of publication.

A seventh heading, G. Individual Authors, lists the authors of the period in chronological order by their year of birth, giving for each author a chronological checklist of his/her separate works, including standard editions and collections and selections, followed by a chronological list of the more important biographical and critical studies of the author and his/her work.

A. BIBLIOGRAPHIES

See also pages 2-4.

429   Dougan, Robert O. CATALOGUE OF AN EXHIBITION OF 18TH-CEN-
       TURY SCOTTISH BOOKS AT THE SIGNET LIBRARY, EDINBURGH. Cam-
       bridge: Cambridge University Press, 1951.

       A valuable record of a fine exhibition.

430   Tobin, Terence. "A List of Plays and Entertainments by Scottish Drama-
       tists, 1660-1800." STUDIES IN BIBLIOGRAPHY, 23 (1970), 103-17.

431   _____. "Plays Presented in Scotland, 1660-1700." RESTORATION AND
       EIGHTEENTH CENTURY THEATRE RESEARCH, 12 (1973), 51-53, 59.

432   _____. "A Check-List of Plays Printed in Scotland, 1700-1750." RES-
       TORATION AND EIGHTEENTH CENTURY THEATRE RESEARCH, 14 (1975),
       42-50.

B. LITERARY HISTORY AND CRITICISM

See also pages 4-7.

433   Graham, Henry Grey. SCOTTISH MEN OF LETTERS IN THE EIGHTEENTH
       CENTURY. London: Black, 1901.

434   Millar, John Hepburn. SCOTTISH PROSE OF THE SEVENTEENTH AND
       EIGHTEENTH CENTURIES. Glasgow: Maclehose, 1912.

435   Oliver, John W. "The Eighteenth Century Revival." In EDINBURGH
       ESSAYS ON SCOTS LITERATURE. Edinburgh: Oliver and Boyd, 1933,
       pp. 78-104.

436   Kinsley, James, ed. SCOTTISH POETRY: A CRITICAL SURVEY. Lon-
       don: Cassell, 1955.

       The relevant essays are A.M. Oliver, "The Scottish Augustans,"
       pages 119-49; David Daiches, "Eighteenth-Century Vernacular
       Poetry," pages 150-84; and Robert Dewar, "Burns and the Burns
       Tradition," pages 185-211.

437   Daiches, David. THE PARADOX OF SCOTTISH CULTURE: THE EIGH-
       TEENTH-CENTURY EXPERIENCE. London: OUP, 1964.

438 Crawford, Thomas. SOCIETY AND THE LYRIC: A STUDY OF THE
SONG CULTURE OF EIGHTEENTH-CENTURY SCOTLAND. Edinburgh:
Scottish Academic Press, 1979.

C. ANTHOLOGIES

See also pages 8-10.

439 [Watson, James.] A CHOICE COLLECTION OF COMIC AND SERIOUS
SCOTS POEMS. 3 parts. Edinburgh, 1706-11; 1 vol., Glasgow, 1869;
ed. Harriet Harvey Wood, 2 vols., Edinburgh: STS, 1977--.

> The first volume of the STS edition is a facsimile reprint of the
> Glasgow edition of 1869; the editor's notes are to follow in a
> second volume.

440 Ramsay, Allan. THE TEA-TABLE MISCELLANY. 4 vols. Edinburgh:
1723-37; 2 vols., Glasgow: R. Forrester, 1876.

441 [Herd, David.] ANCIENT AND MODERN SCOTTISH SONGS. 2 vols.
Edinburgh, 1776; Glasgow: Kerr and Richardson, 1869; rpt. Edinburgh:
Scottish Academic Press, 1973.

442 Johnson, James. THE SCOTS MUSICAL MUSEUM. 6 vols. Edinburgh,
1787-1803. Ed. William Stenhouse, David Laing, and Charles Kirkpatrick
Sharpe. 4 vols. Edinburgh: Blackwood, 1853; rpt., 2 vols., Hatboro,
Pa.: Folklore Associates, 1962.

> The collection with which Burns was greatly involved.

443 THE MERRY MUSES OF CALEDONIA: A COLLECTION OF FAVOURITE
SCOTS SONGS, ANCIENT AND MODERN. 1799. Ed. James Barke
and Sydney Goodsir Smith. Edinburgh: Privately Printed, 1959; London:
W.H. Allen, 1965.

> A collection of bawdy verse indiscriminately ascribed to Burns.
> See the bibliography by Gershon Legman in the facsimile of the
> 1799 edition (New Hyde Park, N.Y.: University Books, 1965).

444 Hogg, James. THE JACOBITE RELICS OF SCOTLAND. 2 vols. Edinburgh, 1819-21; Paisley: Gardner, 1874.

445 Eyre-Todd, George, ed. SCOTTISH POETRY OF THE EIGHTEENTH
CENTURY. 2 vols. Glasgow: Hodge, 1896.

446 Hecht, Hans, ed. SONGS FROM DAVID HERD'S MSS. Edinburgh: Hay,
1904.

447   Crawford, Thomas, ed. LOVE, LABOUR AND LIBERTY: THE EIGH-
TEENTH-CENTURY SCOTTISH LYRIC. Cheadle: Carcanet Press, 1976.

D. BACKGROUND STUDIES

See also pages 15-19.

448   Ramsay, John, of Ochtertyre. SCOTLAND AND SCOTSMEN IN THE
EIGHTEENTH CENTURY. Ed. Alexander Allardyce. 2 vols. Edinburgh:
Blackwood, 1888.

A valuable contemporary account.

449   Graham, Henry Grey. THE SOCIAL LIFE OF SCOTLAND IN THE EIGH-
TEENTH CENTURY. 1899; 5th ed., introd. Eric Linklater, London:
Black, 1969.

450   Lochhead, Marion. THE SCOTS HOUSEHOLD IN THE EIGHTEENTH
CENTURY: A CENTURY OF SCOTTISH DOMESTIC AND SOCIAL LIFE.
Edinburgh: Moray Press, 1948.

451   Mackenzie, Agnes Mure. SCOTTISH PAGEANT, 1707-1802. Edinburgh:
Oliver and Boyd, 1950.

An anthology of contemporary writing by Scots or about Scotland
(or both).

452   Plant, Marjorie. THE DOMESTIC LIFE OF SCOTLAND IN THE EIGH-
TEENTH CENTURY. Edinburgh: Edinburgh University Press, 1952.

453   Grave, Selwyn Alfred. THE SCOTTISH PHILOSOPHY OF COMMON
SENSE. Oxford: Clarendon Press, 1960.

454   Duncan, David. THOMAS RUDDIMAN: A STUDY IN SCOTTISH SCHOL-
ARSHIP OF THE EARLY EIGHTEENTH CENTURY. Edinburgh: Oliver and
Boyd, 1965.

455   Ferguson, William. SCOTLAND: 1689 TO THE PRESENT. Edinburgh
History of Scotland, vol. 4. Edinburgh: Oliver and Boyd, 1968; rev.
ed. 1979.

456   Smout, Thomas Christopher. A HISTORY OF THE SCOTTISH PEOPLE,
1560-1830. London: Collins, 1969.

457   Phillipson, Nicholas Tindal, and Rosalind Mitchison, eds. SCOTLAND IN
THE AGE OF IMPROVEMENT: ESSAYS IN SCOTTISH HISTORY IN THE
EIGHTEENTH CENTURY. Edinburgh: Edinburgh University Press, 1970.

458 Johnson, David. MUSIC AND SOCIETY IN LOWLAND SCOTLAND IN THE EIGHTEENTH CENTURY. London: OUP, 1972.

459 Ross, Ian S. LORD KAMES AND THE SCOTLAND OF HIS DAY. Oxford: Clarendon Press, 1972.

460 Rae, Thomas Ian, ed. THE UNION OF 1707: ITS IMPACT ON SCOTLAND. Glasgow: Blackie, 1974.

461 Todd, William Burton, ed. HUME AND THE ENLIGHTENMENT: ESSAYS PRESENTED TO ERNEST CAMPBELL MOSSNER. Edinburgh: Edinburgh University Press, 1974.

462 Hook, Andrew. SCOTLAND AND AMERICA: A STUDY OF CULTURAL RELATIONS, 1750-1835. Glasgow: Blackie, 1975.

463 Edwards, Owen Dudley, and George Shepperson, eds. SCOTLAND, EUROPE AND THE AMERICAN REVOLUTION. Edinburgh: EUSPB, 1976.

464 Chitnis, Anand C. THE SCOTTISH ENLIGHTENMENT: A SOCIAL HISTORY. London: Croom Helm, 1976.

Libraries and Education

465 Lough, John, and Muriel Lough. "Aberdeen Circulating Libraries in the Eighteenth Century." ABERDEEN UNIVERSITY REVIEW, 31 (1945), 17-24.

466 Kaufman, Paul. "The Rise of Community Libraries in Scotland." PAPERS OF THE BIBLIOGRAPHICAL SOCIETY OF AMERICA, 59 (1965), 233-94.

467 Law, Alexander. EDUCATION IN EDINBURGH IN THE EIGHTEENTH CENTURY. London: University of London Press, 1965.

468 MacDonald, William R. "Circulating Libraries in the North-East of Scotland in the Eighteenth Century." BIBLIOTHECK, 5 (1967-70), 119-37.

469 McElroy, Davis Dunbar. SCOTLAND'S AGE OF IMPROVEMENT: A SURVEY OF EIGHTEENTH-CENTURY CLUBS AND SOCIETIES. Pullman: Washington State University Press, 1969.

470 Carnie, Robert Hay. "Working Class Readers in Eighteenth-Century Scotland: The Evidence from Subscription Lists." SCOTTISH TRADITION, 7-8 (1978), 77-94.

E. PRINTING AND PUBLISHING

General

471 Aldis, Harry G. A LIST OF BOOKS PRINTED IN SCOTLAND BEFORE 1700, WITH BRIEF NOTES ON THE PRINTERS AND STATIONERS. 1904; rpt., including entries for books published in 1700, and with additional notes by Robert Hay Carnie. Edinburgh: National Library of Scotland, 1970.

472 Plomer, Henry R., et al. A DICTIONARY OF THE PRINTERS AND BOOKSELLERS WHO WERE AT WORK IN ENGLAND, SCOTLAND AND IRELAND, 1668-1725. London: Bibliographical Society, 1922.

473 _____. A DICTIONARY OF THE PRINTERS AND BOOKSELLERS WHO WERE AT WORK IN ENGLAND, SCOTLAND AND IRELAND, 1726-1775. London: Bibliographical Society, 1932.

The Scottish section is by George Herbert Bushnell.

474 Carnie, Robert Hay, and Ronald P. Doig. "Scottish Printers and Booksellers, 1668-1775." STUDIES IN BIBLIOGRAPHY, 12 (1959), 131-59; 14 (1961), 81-96; 15 (1962), 105-20.

Three supplements to Plomer, above.

475 Carnie, Robert Hay. "Scottish Printers and Booksellers, 1668-1775: A Study of Source-Material." BIBLIOTHECK, 4 (1963-66), 213-27.

476 Ross, Ian S., and Stephen Scobie. "Patriotic Publishing as a Response to the Union." In THE UNION OF 1707. Ed. Thomas Ian Rae. Glasgow: Blackie, 1974, pp. 94-119.

In Glasgow

477 Duncan, William James. NOTICES AND DOCUMENTS ILLUSTRATIVE OF THE LITERARY HISTORY OF GLASGOW. 1831; new ed. Glasgow: T.D. Morison, 1886.

478 MacLehose, James. THE GLASGOW UNIVERSITY PRESS, 1638-1931, WITH SOME NOTES ON SCOTTISH PRINTING IN THE LAST THREE HUNDRED YEARS. Glasgow: Glasgow University Press, 1931.

479 Gaskell, Philip. A BIBLIOGRAPHY OF THE FOULIS PRESS. London: Hart-Davis, 1964.

In Perth

480   Carnie, Robert Hay. PUBLISHING IN PERTH BEFORE 1807. Dundee: Abertay Historical Society, 1960.

F. PERIODICALS

481   THE SCOTS MAGAZINE. Edinburgh, 1739-1817. Monthly.

482   THE WEEKLY MAGAZINE, or EDINBURGH AMUSEMENT. 1768-84.
      Ed. Walter Ruddiman. Robert Fergusson was a contributor. See Ian C. Walker, "Scottish Verse in THE WEEKLY MAGAZINE," SSL, 5 (1967-68), 3-13.

483   THE MIRROR. Edinburgh, 1779-80. Weekly.
      Ed. Henry Mackenzie.

484   THE LOUNGER. Edinburgh, 1785-87. Weekly.
      Ed. Henry Mackenzie.

485   EDINBURGH MAGAZINE. 1785-1803. Monthly.
      Incorporated in THE SCOTS MAGAZINE from 1804.

Studies

486   Couper, William James. THE EDINBURGH PERIODICAL PRESS FROM THE EARLIEST TIMES TO 1800. 2 vols. Stirling: Eneas Mackay, 1908.

487   Craig, Mary E. THE SCOTTISH PERIODICAL PRESS, 1750-1789. Edinburgh: Oliver and Boyd, 1931.

488   MacDonald, William R. "Aberdeen Periodical Publishing, 1786-91." BIBLIOTHECK, 9 (1978-79), 1-12.

489   Knight, Charles A. "The Created World of the Edinburgh Periodicals." SLJ, 6 (December 1979), 20-36.

G. INDIVIDUAL AUTHORS

This section deals with the authors of the period in chronological order by their year of birth.

The bibliographies of individual authors follow a pattern. The author's works are listed first. A chronological checklist of the author's separate works, giving year of publication only, but adding after each title full details of any modern critical editions, precedes a list of the standard collections and selections of the author's work. This primary bibliography is followed by a chronological list of the more important biographical and critical studies of the author and his work, the secondary bibliography, with the emphasis on books rather than articles. There is a final group for bibliographies of the author and reference works, if they exist.

Sir George Mackenzie (1638-91)

The versatile lawyer, politician, and author, who in 1682 founded the Advocates' Library in Edinburgh, is commonly but unfairly known as "Bluidy Mackenzie," criminal prosecutor in the Covenanter Trials. His legal writings are not listed.

490 ARETINA: OR THE SERIOUS ROMANCE. 1660.

 A novel.

491 WORKS. Ed. Thomas Ruddiman. 2 vols. 1717-22.

492 MEMOIRS OF THE AFFAIRS OF SCOTLAND FROM THE RESTORATION OF KING CHARLES II. 1821.

BIOGRAPHY AND CRITICISM

493 Lang, Andrew. SIR GEORGE MACKENZIE, KING'S ADVOCATE: HIS LIFE AND TIMES. London: Longmans, Green, 1909.

494 Spiller, M.R.G. "The First Scots Novel: Sir George Mackenzie's ARETINA (1660)." SLJ, suppl. 11 (1979), 1-20.

BIBLIOGRAPHY

495 Ferguson, Frederic Sutherland. "A Bibliography of the Works of Sir George Mackenzie." TRANSACTIONS OF THE EDINBURGH BIBLIO-GRAPHICAL SOCIETY, 1 (1938), 1-60.

Archibald Pitcairne (1652-1713)

Pitcairne was a notable doctor and medical writer, a Jacobite, and the author of a vigorous satiric comedy, caricaturing the proceedings of the General Assembly of the Church of Scotland. His medical writings are not listed.

496   THE ASSEMBLY. 1722. Ed. Terence Tobin. Lafayette, Ind.:   Purdue University, 1972.

    A play.

BIOGRAPHY AND CRITICISM

497   Jolley, Leonard. "Archibald Pitcairne." EDINBURGH MEDICAL JOURNAL, 60 (1953), 39-51.

Andrew Fletcher of Saltoun (1655-1716)

Fletcher was a patriot in the Scottish Parliament of 1681 who advocated a federal relationship with England rather than the incorporating Union of 1707. Fletcher is the source for the opinion he attributes to a "very wise man": "If a man were permitted to make all the ballads, he need not care who should make the laws of a nation."

498   POLITICAL WORKS. 1732.

499   SELECTED POLITICAL WRITINGS AND SPEECHES. Ed. David Daiches. Edinburgh: Scottish Academic Press, 1979.

BIOGRAPHY AND CRITICISM

500   Mackenzie, William Cook. ANDREW FLETCHER OF SALTOUN: HIS LIFE AND TIMES. Edinburgh: Porpoise Press, 1935.

John Arbuthnot (1667-1735)

A physician and wit, the friend of Swift and Pope and most of the literary men of his day. His five anonymous pamphlets, THE HISTORY OF JOHN BULL (1712), mark the first appearance of that typical Englishman.

501   MISCELLANIES IN PROSE AND VERSE. 1727-32.

    The preface is signed by Swift and Pope.

502   LIFE AND WORKS. Ed. George A. Aitken. Oxford: Clarendon Press, 1892.

BIOGRAPHY AND CRITICISM

503   Beattie, Lester M. JOHN ARBUTHNOT, MATHEMATICIAN AND SATIRIST. Cambridge: Harvard University Press, 1935.

Allan Ramsay (1686-1758)

Ramsay is the poet and bookseller who opened in Edinburgh in 1725 the first circulating library in Britain. As a collector of popular poetry and an editor of the older Scots poets, he made Henryson, Dunbar, and others available to his contemporaries.

504 POEMS. 1720; 1721.

505 FABLES AND TALES. 1722.

506 THE GENTLE SHEPHERD: A SCOTS PASTORAL COMEDY. 1725.

507 POEMS. 1728.

508 THIRTY FABLES. 1730.

509 POEMS: EPISTLES, FABLES, SATIRES, ELEGIES & LYRICS, FROM THE EDITION PRINTED EDINBURGH, 1721-1728. Ed. Henry Harvey Wood. Saltire Classics. Edinburgh: Oliver and Boyd, 1940.

510 WORKS. Ed. Burns Martin, John W. Oliver, Alexander Law, and Alexander M. Kinghorn. 6 vols. Edinburgh: STS, 1951-74.

511 POEMS BY ALLAN RAMSAY AND ROBERT FERGUSSON. Ed. Alexander M. Kinghorn and Alexander Law. Edinburgh: Scottish Academic Press, 1974.

BIOGRAPHY AND CRITICISM

512 Gibson, Andrew. NEW LIGHT ON ALLAN RAMSAY. Edinburgh: W. Brown, 1927.

513 Martin, Burns. ALLAN RAMSAY: A STUDY OF HIS LIFE AND WORKS. Cambridge: Harvard University Press, 1931.

514 Craig, David. SCOTTISH LITERATURE AND THE SCOTTISH PEOPLE, 1680-1830. London: Chatto and Windus, 1961.

BIBLIOGRAPHY

515 Martin, Burns. "A Bibliography of the Writings of Allan Ramsay." RECORDS OF THE GLASGOW BIBLIOGRAPHICAL SOCIETY, 10 (1931), 1-114.

Alexander Ross (1699-1784)

Ross was a native of Aberdeenshire and for many years schoolmaster of Lochlee in Angus.

516 THE FORTUNATE SHEPHERDESS: A PASTORAL TALE IN THREE CANTOS, IN THE SCOTTISH DIALECT. 1768.

    Frequently known as HELENORE, OR THE FORTUNATE SHEP-HERDESS.

517 SCOTTISH WORKS. Ed. Margaret Wattie. Edinburgh: STS, 1938.

Robert Blair (1700-1746)

Blair, who was minister at Athelstaneford in East Lothian from 1731, is best known for his didactic blank-verse poem, THE GRAVE. With Edward Young's NIGHT THOUGHTS (1742-44), it belongs to the somber "graveyard" school of poetry.

518 THE GRAVE: A POEM. 1743.

    There is an edition of 1808 with illustrations by William Blake.

519 POETICAL WORKS OF BEATTIE, BLAIR AND FALCONER. Ed. George Gilfillan. Edinburgh: James Nichol, 1854.

BIOGRAPHY AND CRITICISM

520 Means, James A. "The Composition of THE GRAVE." SSL, 10 (1972-73), 3-9.

521 _____. "A Reading of THE GRAVE." SSL, 12 (1974-75), 270-81.

522 _____. "THE GRAVE in America: 1753-1860." SSL, 13 (1978), 57-62.

James Thomson (1700-1748)

Thomson was born in the Border country and his descriptions of nature in THE SEASONS reveal his origins. He had a genuine feeling for nature, his observation was keen and intelligent, and he had a considerable influence on both Burns and Wordsworth.

523 WINTER. 1726.

524 SUMMER. 1727.

525 SPRING. 1728.

526 BRITANNIA: A POEM. 1729.

527 THE SEASONS. 1730.
Includes the first edition of AUTUMN.

528 THE SEASONS. Ed. Otto Zippel. Berlin: Mayer and Müller, 1908.

529 THE TRAGEDY OF SOPHONISBA. 1730.
A play.

530 LIBERTY: A POEM. 1735-36.

531 ALFRED: A MASQUE. 1740.

532 THE CASTLE OF INDOLENCE: AN ALLEGORICAL POEM. 1748.

533 THE CASTLE OF INDOLENCE: AN ALLEGORICAL POEM. Ed. Alan D. McKillop. Lawrence: University of Kansas Press, 1961.

534 COMPLETE POETICAL WORKS. Ed. James Logie Robertson. London: OUP, 1908.

535 LETTERS AND DOCUMENTS. Ed. Alan D. McKillop. Lawrence: University of Kansas Press, 1958.

536 THE SEASONS AND THE CASTLE OF INDOLENCE. Ed. James Sambrook. Oxford: Clarendon Press, 1972.

BIOGRAPHY AND CRITICISM

537 McKillop, Alan D. THE BACKGROUND OF THOMSON'S SEASONS. Minneapolis: University of Minnesota Press, 1942.

538 Grant, Douglas. JAMES THOMSON: POET OF THE SEASONS. London: Cresset Press, 1951.

539 Cohen, Ralph. THE ART OF DISCRIMINATION: THOMSON'S THE SEASONS AND THE LANGUAGE OF CRITICISM. Berkeley and Los Angeles: University of California Press, 1964.

540 _____ . THE UNFOLDING OF THE SEASONS: A STUDY OF THOM-
SON'S POEM. Baltimore: Johns Hopkins Press, 1969; London: Routledge, 1970.

BIBLIOGRAPHY

541 Campbell, Hilbert H. JAMES THOMSON (1700-1748): AN ANNOTATED
BIBLIOGRAPHY OF SELECTED EDITIONS AND THE IMPORTANT CRITI-
CISM. New York: Garland, 1976.

William Hamilton of Bangour (1704-54)

Hamilton was a minor poet, but author of the fine ballad, "The Braes of Yarrow." The first collection of his poems was edited by Adam Smith.

542 POEMS ON SEVERAL OCCASIONS. Ed. Adam Smith. 1748.

543 POEMS AND SONGS. Ed. with notes and an account of the life of the
author by James Paterson. Edinburgh: T.G. Stevenson, 1850.

BIOGRAPHY AND CRITICISM

544 Bushnell, Nelson S. WILLIAM HAMILTON OF BANGOUR, POET AND
JACOBITE. Aberdeen: Aberdeen University Press, 1957.

With chronology and bibliography.

David Hume (1711-76)

Hume is one of the great figures of eighteenth-century Edinburgh: a philosopher and historian whose work had a considerable influence, both at home and
abroad. Hume awakened Kant from his "dogmatic slumbers" and stimulated the
Scottish "common sense" school of Thomas Reid (1710-96) and Dugald Stewart
(1753-1828).

545 A TREATISE OF HUMAN NATURE. 1739-40.

546 ESSAYS MORAL AND POLITICAL. 1741.

547 PHILOSOPHICAL ESSAYS CONCERNING HUMAN UNDERSTANDING.
1748.

548 ESSAYS AND TREATISES ON SEVERAL SUBJECTS. 1753-56.

549 ENQUIRIES CONCERNING HUMAN UNDERSTANDING. Ed. Lewis Amherst Selby-Bigge. 3rd ed. rev. Peter Harold Nidditch. Oxford: Clarendon Press, 1975.

550 THE HISTORY OF GREAT BRITAIN. [1603-49] 1754.

551 THE HISTORY OF GREAT BRITAIN. THE REIGNS OF JAMES I AND CHARLES I. Ed. Duncan Forbes. Pelican Classics. Harmondsworth: Penguin, 1970.

552 THE HISTORY OF GREAT BRITAIN. [1649-88] 1757.

553 FOUR DISSERTATIONS. 1757.

554 THE HISTORY OF ENGLAND UNDER THE HOUSE OF TUDOR. 1759.

555 THE HISTORY OF ENGLAND FROM THE INVASION OF JULIUS CAESAR TO THE ACCESSION OF HENRY VII. 1762.

556 THE HISTORY OF ENGLAND FROM THE INVASION OF JULIUS CAESAR TO THE REVOLUTION IN 1688. 1763; with the author's last corrections, 1778.

557 DIALOGUES CONCERNING NATURAL RELIGION. 1779.

558 DIALOGUES CONCERNING NATURAL RELIGION. Ed. Norman Kemp Smith. Oxford: Clarendon Press, 1935.

559 PHILOSOPHICAL WORKS. Ed. Thomas Hill Green and Thomas Hodge Grose. 4 vols. London: Longmans, Green, 1874-75.

560 THE NATURAL HISTORY OF RELIGION. Ed. A. Wayne Colver. DIALOGUES CONCERNING NATURAL RELIGION. Ed. John Valdimir Price. Oxford: Clarendon Press, 1976.

LETTERS

561 LETTERS. Ed. John Y.T. Greig. 2 vols. Oxford: Clarendon Press, 1932.

562 NEW LETTERS. Ed. Raymond Klibansky and Ernest Campbell Mossner. Oxford: Clarendon Press, 1954.

BIOGRAPHY AND CRITICISM

563   Mossner, Ernest Campbell. THE LIFE OF DAVID HUME. Edinburgh:
      Nelson, 1954; Oxford: Clarendon Press, 1970.

564   McGuiness, Arthur E. "Hume and Kames: The Burden of Friendship."
      SSL, 6 (1968-69), 3-19.

565   Todd, William Burton, ed. HUME AND THE ENLIGHTENMENT: ESSAYS
      PRESENTED TO ERNEST CAMPBELL MOSSNER. Edinburgh: Edinburgh
      University Press, 1974.

566   Sisson, Charles Hubert. DAVID HUME. Edinburgh: Ramsay Head Press,
      1976.

567   Livingston, Donald William, and James T. King, eds. HUME: A RE-
      EVALUATION. New York: Fordham University Press, 1976.

568   Stroud, Barry. HUME. London: Routledge and Kegan Paul, 1977.

569   Morice, G.P., ed. DAVID HUME: BICENTENARY PAPERS. Edinburgh:
      Edinburgh University Press, 1977.

BIBLIOGRAPHY

570   Jessop, Thomas Edmund. A BIBLIOGRAPHY OF HUME AND OF SCOT-
      TISH PHILOSOPHY FROM HUTCHESON TO BALFOUR. London: A.
      Brown, 1938.

571   Todd, William Burton. "David Hume: A Preliminary Bibliography." In
      HUME AND THE ENLIGHTENMENT: ESSAYS PRESENTED TO ERNEST
      CAMPBELL MOSSNER. Ed. William Burton Todd. Edinburgh: Edinburgh
      University Press, 1974.

572   Hall, Roland. FIFTY YEARS OF HUME SCHOLARSHIP: A BIBLIO-
      GRAPHICAL GUIDE. Edinburgh: Edinburgh University Press, 1978.

Tobias George Smollett (1721-71)

Smollett, born in Dunbartonshire, educated at Glasgow University, and thereafter apprenticed to a surgeon in Glasgow, went to London in 1739, to make
his fortune with a tragedy which no manager would produce. He sailed in 1740
as a naval surgeon and returned to Britain to write voluminously as a novelist
and miscellaneous writer. His picaresque novels have a vigor and exuberance

that too often run to coarseness and brutality. HUMPHRY CLINKER, his best book, is kindlier. His translations, which include GIL BLAS and DON QUIX-OTE, are not listed.

573   THE ADVENTURES OF RODERICK RANDOM. 1748.

574   THE ADVENTURES OF RODERICK RANDOM. Ed. Paul-Gabriel Boucé. Oxford English Novels. London: OUP, 1979.

575   THE ADVENTURES OF PEREGRINE PICKLE. 1751.

576   THE ADVENTURES OF PEREGRINE PICKLE. Ed. James L. Clifford. Oxford English Novels. London: OUP, 1964.

577   THE ADVENTURES OF FREDERICK, COUNT FATHOM. 1753.

578   THE ADVENTURES OF FREDERICK, COUNT FATHOM. Ed. Damian Grant. Oxford English Novels. London: OUP, 1971.

579   A COMPLETE HISTORY OF ENGLAND. 1757-65.

580   THE LIFE AND ADVENTURES OF SIR LAUNCELOT GREAVES. 1762.

581   THE LIFE AND ADVENTURES OF SIR LAUNCELOT GREAVES. Ed. David Evans. Oxford English Novels. London: OUP, 1973.

582   TRAVELS THROUGH FRANCE AND ITALY. 1766.

583   TRAVELS THROUGH FRANCE AND ITALY. Ed. Frank Felsenstein. Oxford: OUP, 1979.

584   THE HISTORY AND ADVENTURES OF AN ATOM. 1769.

585   THE EXPEDITION OF HUMPHRY CLINKER. 1771.

586   THE EXPEDITION OF HUMPHRY CLINKER. Ed. Lewis M. Knapp. Oxford English Novels. London: OUP, 1966.

587   THE EXPEDITION OF HUMPHRY CLINKER. Ed. Angus Ross. Harmondsworth: Penguin, 1967.

588   THE EXPEDITION OF HUMPHRY CLINKER. Ed. André Parreaux. Boston: Houghton Mifflin, 1968.

589   WORKS. Ed. George Saintsbury. 12 vols. London: Gibbings, 1895. The novels only.

590   LETTERS. Ed. Lewis M. Knapp. Oxford: Clarendon Press, 1970.

BIOGRAPHY AND CRITICISM

591   Scott, Sir Walter. "Tobias Smollett." In BALLANTYNE'S NOVELIST'S LIBRARY. 1821. Rpt. in Scott's LIVES OF THE NOVELISTS, Everyman's Library, London: Dent, 1910, pp. 71-119.

592   Read, Herbert. "Tobias Smollett." In his REASON AND ROMANTICISM. London: Faber and Gwyer, 1926, pp. 187-205.

593   Martz, Louis L. THE LATER CAREER OF TOBIAS SMOLLETT. New Haven: Yale University Press, 1942.

594   Kahrl, George M. TOBIAS SMOLLETT: TRAVELER-NOVELIST. Chicago: University of Chicago Press, 1945.

595   Boege, Fred W. SMOLLETT'S REPUTATION AS A NOVELIST. Princeton: Princeton University Press, 1947.

596   Pritchett, Victor Sawdon. "The Shocking Surgeon." In his THE LIVING NOVEL. London: Chatto and Windus, 1947, pp. 18-23.

597   Knapp, Lewis M. TOBIAS SMOLLETT: DOCTOR OF MEN AND MANNERS. Princeton: Princeton University Press, 1949; rpt. New York: Russell and Russell, 1963.

598   McKillop, Alan Dugald. "Smollett." In his THE EARLY MASTERS OF ENGLISH FICTION. Lawrence: University of Kansas Press, 1956, pp. 147-81.

599   Goldberg, Milton A. SMOLLETT AND THE SCOTTISH SCHOOL. Albuquerque: University of New Mexico Press, 1959.

600   Bruce, Donald. RADICAL DR. SMOLLETT. London: Gollancz, 1964.

601   Parreaux, André. SMOLLETT'S LONDON. Paris: A.G. Nizet, 1965.

602   Klukoff, Philip J. "Smollett and the CRITICAL REVIEW: Criticism of the Novel, 1756-1763." SSL, 4 (1966-67), 89-100.

603 Giddings, Robert. THE TRADITION OF SMOLLETT. London: Methuen, 1967.

604 Spector, R.D. TOBIAS GEORGE SMOLLETT. New York: Twayne, 1968.

605 Rousseau, George S., and Paul-Gabriel Boucé, eds. TOBIAS SMOLLETT: BICENTENNIAL ESSAYS PRESENTED TO LEWIS M. KNAPP. New York: OUP, 1971.

606 Boucé, Paul-Gabriel. LES ROMANS DE SMOLLETT: ÉTUDE CRITIQUE. Paris: Didier, 1971.

607 _____. THE NOVELS OF TOBIAS SMOLLETT. London: Longman, 1976.

       A translation of the preceding item.

608 Grant, Damian. TOBIAS SMOLLETT: A STUDY IN STYLE. Manchester: Manchester University Press, 1977.

609 Rice, Scott. "The Satiric Persona of Smollett's TRAVELS." SSL, 10 (1972-73), 33-47.

BIBLIOGRAPHY

610 Cordasco, Francesco. SMOLLETT CRITICISM, 1925-1945: A COMPILA-TION. Brooklyn: Long Island University Press, 1947.

611 _____. SMOLLETT CRITICISM, 1770-1924: A BIBLIOGRAPHY. Brooklyn: Long Island University Press, 1948.

612 Knapp, Lewis M. "Smollett." In THE ENGLISH NOVEL: SELECT BIB-LIOGRAPHICAL GUIDES. Ed. Anthony Edward Dyson. London: OUP, 1974, pp. 112-27.

613 Beasley, Jerry C. "Tobias George Smollett." In his ENGLISH FICTION, 1660-1800: A GUIDE TO INFORMATION SOURCES. American Litera-ture, English Literature, and World Literatures in English Information Guide Series, vol. 14. Detroit: Gale Research Co., 1978, pp. 223-36.

614 Cordasco, Francesco. TOBIAS GEORGE SMOLLETT: A BIBLIOGRAPHICAL GUIDE. New York: AMS Press, 1979.

Alexander Carlyle (1722-1805)

Carlyle, minister of Inveresk from 1748 till his death, was the friend of David Hume, Smollett, John Home, Adam Smith, and others. His reminiscences provide an invaluable contemporary account of the literary and intellectual life of Edinburgh.

615 AUTOBIOGRAPHY. Ed. John Hill Burton. 1860; new ed., Edinburgh: T.N. Foulis, 1910.

616 ANECDOTES AND CHARACTERS OF THE TIMES. Ed. James Kinsley. London: OUP, 1973.

> A scholarly edition of the AUTOBIOGRAPHY with its original title restored.

John Home (1722-1802)

Home was a minister and dramatist who resigned his charge when his successful first play, DOUGLAS, gave offense to the Edinburgh Presbytery. There is a story, often quoted but probably apocryphal, that this play provoked an enthusiastic admirer to cry out, "Whaur's your Wullie Shakespeare noo?"

617 DOUGLAS. 1757.

618 DOUGLAS. Ed. Hubert J. Tunney. Lawrence: University of Kansas Press, 1924.

619 DOUGLAS. Ed. Gerald D. Parker. Edinburgh: Oliver and Boyd, 1972.

620 AGIS. 1758.

621 THE SIEGE OF AQUILEIA. 1760.

622 THE FATAL DISCOVERY. 1769.

623 ALONZO. 1773.

624 ALFRED. 1778.

625 THE HISTORY OF THE REBELLION IN 1745. 1802.

626 WORKS. Ed. Henry Mackenzie. 3 vols. Edinburgh: Constable, 1822.

> Includes "An Account of the Life and Writings of John Home,
> Esq.," volume 1, pp. 1-182.

BIOGRAPHY AND CRITICISM

627 Gipson, Alice E. JOHN HOME: A STUDY OF HIS LIFE AND WORKS.
Caldwell, Idaho: Caxton Printers, 1917.

628 Malek, James S. "John Home's THE SIEGE OF AQUILEIA: A Re-Evalu-
ation." SSL, 10 (1972-73), 232-40.

629 Backscheider, Paula R. "John Home's DOUGLAS and the Theme of Un-
fulfilled Life." SSL, 14 (1979), 90-97.

BIBLIOGRAPHY

630 Lefèvre, Jean M. "John Home: A Check List of Editions." BIBLIO-
THECK, 3 (1960-62), 121-38, 222-28.

Adam Smith (1723-90)

Adam Smith belonged to the brilliant circle in Edinburgh which included David
Hume, John Home, Alexander Carlyle, and William Robertson, and later, in
London, he joined the literary club of Dr. Johnson, Garrick, and Reynolds.

631 THE THEORY OF MORAL SENTIMENTS. 1759.

632 THE THEORY OF MORAL SENTIMENTS. Ed. David Daiches Raphael
and Alec Lawrence Macfie. Glasgow Edition, vol. 1. Oxford: Clarendon Press, 1976.

633 AN INQUIRY INTO THE NATURE AND CAUSES OF THE WEALTH OF
NATIONS. 1776.

634 AN INQUIRY INTO THE NATURE AND CAUSES OF THE WEALTH OF
NATIONS. General editors: Roy Hutcheson Campbell and Andrew S.
Skinner. Textual editor: William Burton Todd. 2 vols. Glasgow Edi-
tion, vol. 2. Oxford: Clarendon Press, 1976.

635 ESSAYS ON PHILOSOPHICAL SUBJECTS. 1795.

> Includes an account of the life and writings of the author by
> Dugald Stewart. A new edition is to form volume 3 of the
> Glasgow edition.

636 LECTURES ON RHETORIC AND BELLES LETTRES. Reported by a student in 1762-63. Ed. John M. Lothian. London: Nelson, 1963.

A new edition is to form volume 4 of the Glasgow Edition.

637 LECTURES ON JURISPRUDENCE. Ed. Ronald Lindley Meek, David Daiches Raphael, and Peter Gonville Stein. Glasgow Edition, vol. 5. Oxford: Clarendon Press, 1978.

638 THE CORRESPONDENCE OF ADAM SMITH. Ed. Ernest Campbell Mossner and Ian Simpson Ross. Glasgow Edition, vol. 6. Oxford: Clarendon Press, 1977.

BIOGRAPHY AND CRITICISM

639 Fay, Charles Ryle. ADAM SMITH AND THE SCOTLAND OF HIS DAY. Cambridge: Cambridge University Press, 1956.

640 Skinner, Andrew S., and Thomas Wilson, eds. ESSAYS ON ADAM SMITH. Oxford: Clarendon Press, 1975.

641 Wilson, Thomas, and Andrew S. Skinner, eds. THE MARKET AND THE STATE: ESSAYS IN HONOUR OF ADAM SMITH. Oxford: Clarendon Press, 1976.

642 Skinner, Andrew S. ADAM SMITH: A SYSTEM OF SOCIAL SCIENCE. Oxford: Clarendon Press, 1978.

BIBLIOGRAPHY

643 Jessop, Thomas Edmund. A BIBLIOGRAPHY OF HUME AND OF SCOTTISH PHILOSOPHY FROM HUTCHESON TO BALFOUR. London: A. Brown, 1938.

John Moore (1729-1802)

Doctor, traveler, and novelist, and father of the General Sir John Moore who died at Corunna. Byron admitted that his intention in CHILDE HAROLD was to portray "a poetical Zeluco."

644 A VIEW OF SOCIETY AND MANNERS IN FRANCE, SWITZERLAND AND GERMANY. 1779.

645 A VIEW OF SOCIETY AND MANNERS IN ITALY. 1781.

646 ZELUCO: VARIOUS VIEWS OF HUMAN NATURE. 1786.
     A novel.

647 A JOURNAL DURING A RESIDENCE IN FRANCE. 1793.

648 EDWARD: VARIOUS VIEWS OF HUMAN NATURE. 1796.
     A novel.

649 MORDAUNT: BEING SKETCHES OF LIFE, CHARACTER AND MANNERS
     IN VARIOUS COUNTRIES. 1800.
     A novel.

650 MORDAUNT: BEING SKETCHES OF LIFE, CHARACTER AND MANNERS
     IN VARIOUS COUNTRIES. Ed. William Lindsay Renwick. Oxford En-
     glish Novels. London: OUP, 1965.

BIOGRAPHY AND CRITICISM

651 Oman, Carola. SIR JOHN MOORE. London: Hodder and Stoughton,
     1953.

William Falconer (1732-69)

Falconer went to sea as a boy and was shipwrecked off Greece in 1749. This
experience provided the subject of his best known poem, for which Burns had
a high regard. He later joined the navy, and his ship, the frigate AURORA,
was lost with all hands near Capetown.

652 THE SHIPWRECK: A POEM IN THREE CANTOS, BY A SAILOR. 1762;
     rev. 1764.

653 POETICAL WORKS OF BEATTIE, BLAIR AND FALCONER. Ed. George
     Gilfillan. Edinburgh: James Nichol, 1854.

BIOGRAPHY AND CRITICISM

654 Friedrich, Johann. WILLIAM FALCONER: THE SHIPWRECK. Vienna:
     W. Braumüller, 1901.

655 Joseph, Michael Kennedy. "William Falconer." STUDIES IN PHI-
     LOLOGY, 47 (1950), 72-101.

James Beattie (1735-1803)

After some years as a schoolmaster, Beattie became professor of moral philosophy in Aberdeen in 1760.

656 THE MINSTREL, OR THE PROGRESS OF GENIUS: A POEM. 1771-74.

657 POEMS ON SEVERAL OCCASIONS. 1776.

658 SCOTICISMS, ARRANGED IN ALPHABETICAL ORDER. 1779.

659 POETICAL WORKS OF BEATTIE, BLAIR AND FALCONER. Ed. George Gilfillan. Edinburgh: James Nichol, 1854.

660 LONDON DIARY 1773. Ed. Ralph S. Walker. Aberdeen: Aberdeen University Press, 1946.

661 DAY-BOOK 1773-1798. Ed. Ralph S. Walker. Aberdeen: Third Spalding Club, 1948.

BIOGRAPHY AND CRITICISM

662 Forbes, Margaret. BEATTIE AND HIS FRIENDS. London: Constable, 1904.

663 King, Everard H. JAMES BEATTIE. Boston: Twayne, 1977.

BIBLIOGRAPHY

664 Sinclair, William. "The Bibliography of James Beattie." RECORDS OF THE GLASGOW BIBLIOGRAPHICAL SOCIETY, 7 (1923), 27-35.

665 Kloth, Karen, and Bernhard Fabian. "James Beattie: Contributions Towards a Bibliography." BIBLIOTHECK, 5 (1967-70), 232-45.

James Macpherson (1736-96)

The "translator" of the Ossianic poems was born in Inverness-shire and had some knowledge of Gaelic poetry in the oral tradition of his district, but while he undoubtedly made use of these Gaelic fragments, the poems he published seem to have been at least to some extent his own creation. Despite an immediate and bitter controversy over their genuineness, they had a considerable influence, in Scotland, in England, and in Europe generally.

666 FRAGMENTS OF ANCIENT POETRY COLLECTED IN THE HIGHLANDS OF SCOTLAND, AND TRANSLATED FROM THE GALIC OR ERSE LANGUAGE. 1760.

667 FINGAL: AN ANCIENT EPIC POEM, WITH SEVERAL OTHER POEMS TRANSLATED FROM THE GALIC LANGUAGE. 1762.

668 TEMORA: AN ANCIENT EPIC POEM, WITH SEVERAL OTHER POEMS TRANSLATED FROM THE GALIC LANGUAGE. 1763.

669 THE WORKS OF OSSIAN, TRANSLATED BY JAMES MACPHERSON. 1765.

670 THE POEMS OF OSSIAN. Ed. Malcolm Laing. 2 vols. Edinburgh, 1805; rpt., introd. John MacQueen, Edinburgh: James Thin, Mercat Press, 1971.

BIOGRAPHY AND CRITICISM

671 Saunders, Thomas Bailey. THE LIFE AND LETTERS OF JAMES MACPHERSON. London: Swan Sonnenschein, 1894.

672 Smart, James Semple. JAMES MACPHERSON: AN EPISODE IN LITERATURE. London: Nutt, 1905.

673 Snyder, Edward Douglas. THE CELTIC REVIVAL IN ENGLISH LITERATURE. Cambridge: Harvard University Press, 1923.

674 Thomson, Derick S. THE GAELIC SOURCES OF MACPHERSON'S OSSIAN. Edinburgh: Oliver and Boyd, 1952.

675 _____. "Ossian Macpherson and the Gaelic World of the Eighteenth Century." ABERDEEN UNIVERSITY REVIEW, 40 (1963-64), 7-20.

676 SCOTTISH LITERARY NEWS, 3, No. 3 (November 1973), entire issue.

Ossian number with contributions by Matthew P. McDiarmid, Alasdair Stewart, Paul Dukes, and Andrew Hook.

James Boswell (1740-95)

The biographer of Dr. Johnson was born in Edinburgh and first met his famous subject on his second visit to London, in 1763. Together they journeyed to the Hebrides in 1773. After Johnson's death in 1784, Boswell worked assiduously on the biography that was published in 1791. The discovery in this century of

Boswell's journals and papers, their assembly at Yale, and their subsequent publication have corrected the traditional portrait of Boswell that Macaulay drew. Boswell is now recognized as a careful and meticulous artist, organizing his material to produce an accurate and completely lifelike portrait. He is indeed seen to be, as Bernard Shaw observed, "the dramatist who invented Dr. Johnson."

677   DORANDO: A SPANISH TALE. 1767.

678   AN ACCOUNT OF CORSICA, THE JOURNAL OF A TOUR TO THAT ISLAND AND MEMOIRS OF PASCAL PAOLI. 1768.

679   THE HYPOCHONDRIACK. 1777-83.

      Monthly essays contributed to the LONDON MAGAZINE.

680   THE HYPOCHONDRIACK. Ed. Margery Bailey. 2 vols. Stanford: Stanford University Press, 1928; rpt., with abridged annotation, as BOS-WELL'S COLUMN, London: Kimber, 1951.

681   THE JOURNAL OF A TOUR TO THE HEBRIDES WITH SAMUEL JOHNSON. 1785.

682   THE JOURNAL OF A TOUR TO THE HEBRIDES WITH SAMUEL JOHNSON. Ed. Robert William Chapman. Oxford: Clarendon Press, 1924.

      With Johnson's JOURNEY TO THE WESTERN ISLANDS OF SCOTLAND.

683   THE JOURNAL OF A TOUR TO THE HEBRIDES WITH SAMUEL JOHNSON. Ed. Frederick A. Pottle and Charles H. Bennett, from the original manu-script. London: Heinemann, 1936; rev. New York: McGraw Hill, 1961: London: Heinemann, 1963.

684   THE LIFE OF SAMUEL JOHNSON. 1791.

685   THE LIFE OF SAMUEL JOHNSON. Ed. George Birkbeck Hill; rev. Lawrence Fitzroy Powell. 6 vols. Oxford: Clarendon Press. Vols. 1-4, 1934; Vols. 5-6, 2nd ed., 1964.

686   LETTERS. Ed. Chauncey Brewster Tinker. 2 vols. Oxford: Clarendon Press, 1924.

687   THE PRIVATE PAPERS OF JAMES BOSWELL FROM MALAHIDE CASTLE. Ed. Geoffrey Scott (vols. 1-6) and Frederick A. Pottle (vols. 7-18). 18 vols. Mount Vernon: Privately Printed, 1928-34. INDEX. Comp. Frederick A. Pottle et al. London: OUP, 1937.

688   THE YALE EDITIONS OF THE PRIVATE PAPERS OF JAMES BOSWELL.

Two editions are in progress, a trade and a research edition.
The following have appeared in the trade edition, published in
New York by McGraw Hill and in London by Heinemann.

BOSWELL'S LONDON JOURNAL, 1762-1763. 1950.

BOSWELL IN HOLLAND, 1763-1764. 1952.

PORTRAITS [by Sir Joshua Reynolds]. 1952.

Includes new Boswell material.

BOSWELL ON THE GRAND TOUR: GERMANY AND SWITZER-
LAND, 1764. 1953.

BOSWELL ON THE GRAND TOUR: ITALY, CORSICA AND
FRANCE, 1765-1766. 1955.

BOSWELL IN SEARCH OF A WIFE, 1766-1769. 1957.

BOSWELL FOR THE DEFENCE, 1769-1774. 1960.

BOSWELL'S JOURNAL OF A TOUR TO THE HEBRIDES WITH
SAMUEL JOHNSON, 1773. 1961.

BOSWELL: THE OMINOUS YEARS, 1774-1776. 1963.

BOSWELL IN EXTREMES, 1776-1778. 1970.

BOSWELL, LAIRD OF AUCHINLECK, 1778-1782. 1977.

The following have appeared in the research edition:

THE CORRESPONDENCE OF JAMES BOSWELL AND JOHN
JOHNSTON OF GRANGE. 1966.

THE CORRESPONDENCE OF BOSWELL RELATING TO THE
MAKING OF THE LIFE OF JOHNSON. 1969.

BIOGRAPHY AND CRITICISM

689   Tinker, Chauncey Brewster. YOUNG BOSWELL. London: G.P. Putnam's
Sons, 1922.

690   Vulliamy, Colwyn Edward. JAMES BOSWELL. London: Geoffrey Bles,
1932.

691   Lewis, Dominic Bevan Wyndham. THE HOODED HAWK, OR THE CASE
OF MR. BOSWELL. London: Eyre and Spottiswoode, 1946; rpt. as
JAMES BOSWELL: A SHORT LIFE, London: Eyre and Spottiswoode,
1952.

692   JOHNSON, BOSWELL AND THEIR CIRCLE: ESSAYS PRESENTED TO
L.F. POWELL. Oxford: Clarendon Press, 1965.

693 Brooks, Alfred Russell. "The Scottish Education of James Boswell." SSL, 3 (1965–66), 151–57.

694 Pottle, Frederick A. JAMES BOSWELL: THE EARLIER YEARS, 1740–69. London: Heinemann, 1966; New York: McGraw Hill, 1966.

695 Brooks, Alfred Russell. JAMES BOSWELL. New York: Twayne, 1971.

696 Buchanan, David. THE TREASURE OF AUCHINLECK: THE STORY OF THE BOSWELL PAPERS. New York: McGraw Hill, 1974; London: Heinemann, 1975.

BIBLIOGRAPHY

697 Pottle, Frederick A. THE LITERARY CAREER OF JAMES BOSWELL: BEING THE BIBLIOGRAPHICAL MATERIALS FOR A LIFE OF BOSWELL. Oxford: Clarendon Press, 1929; rev. 1966.

698 Pottle, Frederick A., and Marion S. Pottle. THE PRIVATE PAPERS OF JAMES BOSWELL FROM MALAHIDE CASTLE: A CATALOGUE. London: OUP, 1931.

699 Abbott, Claude Colleer. A CATALOGUE OF PAPERS RELATING TO BOS-WELL, JOHNSON AND SIR WILLIAM FORBES FOUND AT FETTERCAIRN HOUSE. Oxford: Clarendon Press, 1936.

Henry Mackenzie (1745-1831)

For more than fifty years, Mackenzie was the leader of Edinburgh literary society. He was an early admirer of Burns, publishing his influential review of the Kilmarnock edition in No. 97 of the LOUNGER (9 December 1786). Scott dedicated WAVERLEY to Mackenzie, calling him "Our Scottish Addison."

700 THE MAN OF FEELING. 1771.

701 THE MAN OF FEELING. Ed. Brian Vickers. Oxford English Novels. London: OUP, 1967.

702 THE MAN OF THE WORLD. 1773.

703 JULIA DE ROUBIGNÉ, A TALE. 1777.

704 THE MIRROR. 1779-80.

110 numbers were issued.

705 THE LOUNGER. 1785-87.

One hundred one numbers were issued.

706 THE LIFE OF MR. JOHN HOME. 1822.

707 ANECDOTES AND EGOTISMS. Ed. Harold W. Thompson. London:
OUP, 1927.

708 LETTERS TO ELIZABETH ROSE OF KILRAVOCK: ON LITERATURE,
EVENTS AND PEOPLE. Ed. Horst Drescher. Münster: Aschendorff,
1967.

BIOGRAPHY AND CRITICISM

709 Scott, Sir Walter. "Henry Mackenzie." In BALLANTYNE'S NOVELIST'S
LIBRARY. 1823. Rpt. in Scott's LIVES OF THE NOVELISTS, Everyman's
Library, London: Dent, 1910, pp. 291-302.

710 Thompson, Harold W. A SCOTTISH MAN OF FEELING: SOME AC-
COUNT OF HENRY MACKENZIE AND OF THE GOLDEN AGE OF
BURNS AND SCOTT. London: OUP, 1931.

711 Jenkins, Ralph E. "The Art of the Theorist: Rhetorical Structure in
THE MAN OF FEELING." SSL, 9 (1971-72), 3-15.

712 Barker, Gerard A. HENRY MACKENZIE. New York: Twayne, 1975.

Michael Bruce (1746-67)

Michael Bruce, born at Kinnesswood, studied at Edinburgh University and became the schoolmaster at Forestmill in Clackmannanshire, where he died. His
friend, John Logan (1748-88), edited and published Bruce's poems in 1770, and
in 1781 published a volume of poems under his own name which contained,
according to Bruce's relatives, further poems by Bruce. The controversy is
not settled yet: there is a full but inconclusive discussion in Snoddy's book.

713 POEMS ON SEVERAL OCCASIONS. Ed. John Logan. 1770.

714 LIFE AND COMPLETE WORKS. Ed. James Mackenzie. Edinburgh:
J.B. Fairgrieve, 1914.

BIOGRAPHY AND CRITICISM

715 Snoddy, Thomas G. MICHAEL BRUCE, SHEPHERD-POET OF THE LO-
MOND BRAES, 1746-67. Edinburgh: Blackwood, 1947.

Robert Fergusson (1750-74)

Fergusson's poems are relatively few, but they enlarged and enriched the Scots poetic tradition. It is as the poet laureate of his native city, Edinburgh, "Auld Reekie," that he is chiefly remembered. In many directions, Fergusson inspired Burns: he set the form, style, and convention that Burns adopted in some of his best poems, and he encouraged the vigorous use of a rich vernacular. Fergusson died in the public asylum in Edinburgh, and fifteen years later Burns erected a stone over his unmarked grave. Many of Fergusson's poems were first published in Ruddiman's WEEKLY MAGAZINE, 1771-73.

716 POEMS. 1773.

717 POEMS ON VARIOUS SUBJECTS. 1779.

718 SCOTS POEMS. Ed. Bruce Dickins. Edinburgh: Porpoise Press, 1925.

719 SCOTS POEMS. Ed. Alexander Law. Saltire Classics. Edinburgh: Oliver and Boyd, 1947.

720 SCOTS POEMS. Ed. John Telfer. Edinburgh: Scottish Features, 1948.

721 POEMS. Ed. Matthew P. McDiarmid. 2 vols. Edinburgh: STS, 1954-56.

722 POEMS BY ALLAN RAMSAY AND ROBERT FERGUSSON. Ed. Alexander M. Kinghorn and Alexander Law. Edinburgh: Scottish Academic Press, 1974.

BIOGRAPHY AND CRITICISM

723 Smith, Sydney Goodsir, ed. ROBERT FERGUSSON, 1750-1774: ESSAYS BY VARIOUS HANDS TO COMMEMORATE THE BICENTENARY OF HIS BIRTH. Edinburgh: Nelson, 1952.

724 MacLaine, Allan H. ROBERT FERGUSSON. New York: Twayne, 1965.

725 Garioch, Robert, and Anne Smith. FERGUSSON: A BICENTENARY HANDSEL. Edinburgh: Reprographia, 1974.

BIBLIOGRAPHY

726 Fairley, John A. "Bibliography of Robert Fergusson." RECORDS OF THE GLASGOW BIBLIOGRAPHICAL SOCIETY, 3 (1915), 115-55.

Lady Anne Barnard (née Lindsay) (1750-1825)

Lady Barnard accompanied her husband to the Cape, in 1797, on his appointment as colonial secretary. Her letters give a vivid picture of colonial life at the time. The song on which her fame rests was written in 1772, although her authorship was not revealed until 1823.

727 AULD ROBIN GRAY: A BALLAD. Ed. John Lowe Weir. Brechin: D.H. Edwards, 1938.

Reprinted from the Bannatyne Club edition of 1825.

728 SOUTH AFRICA A CENTURY AGO: LETTERS WRITTEN FROM THE CAPE OF GOOD HOPE, 1797-1801. Ed. William Henry Wilkins. London: Smith, Elder, 1901.

729 THE LETTERS OF LADY ANNE BARNARD TO HENRY DUNDAS, FROM THE CAPE AND ELSEWHERE, 1793-1803; TOGETHER WITH HER JOURNAL OF A TOUR INTO THE INTERIOR, AND CERTAIN OTHER LETTERS. Ed. Anthony Meredith Lewin Robinson. Cape Town: Balkema, 1974.

Elizabeth Hamilton (1758-1816)

See page 97.

Robert Burns (1759-96)

When Burns went to Edinburgh in 1787, after the publication of the Kilmarnock edition of his poems in 1786, he was lionized as the "Heaven-taught ploughman," but there is no real foundation for the legend. Burns was in no sense unlettered: of his predecessors he had read "the excellent Ramsay, and the still more excellent Fergusson," and the story of Wallace (in Hamilton of Gilbertfield's version) had "poured a Scottish prejudice" in his veins. In his last years he contributed many songs to James Johnson's SCOTS MUSICAL MUSEUM (1787-1803) and to George Thomson's SELECT COLLECTION OF ORIGINAL SCOTISH AIRS (1793-1818).

Through the circumstances of his life and the nature of his work, Burns appeals to an extraordinarily wide range of admirers. The "Burns cult," with its heavy emphasis on his conviviality and the more conventionally sentimental of his poems, has tended to obscure the poet's true genius as the ironical observer of men and manners, the song collector who rescued and refurbished the Scottish folk tradition, and the incomparable poet of human love.

730 POEMS CHIEFLY IN THE SCOTTISH DIALECT. Kilmarnock, 1786.

One of the world's most famous first editions, frequently reissued in facsimile.

731 POEMS CHIEFLY IN THE SCOTTISH DIALECT. 1787; 1793; 1794.

732 ROBERT BURNS'S COMMONPLACE BOOK, 1783-1785. Ed. James Cameron Ewing and Davidson Cook. Glasgow: Gowans and Gray, 1938; rpt., with introd. by David Daiches. London: Centaur Press, 1965.

733 THE WORKS OF ROBERT BURNS, WITH AN ACCOUNT OF HIS LIFE AND A CRITICISM ON HIS WRITINGS. [Ed. James Currie.] 4 vols. London: Cadell and Davies, 1800.

   The first collected edition.

734 RELIQUES OF ROBERT BURNS. Ed. Robert Hartley Cromek. London: Cadell and Davies, 1808.

   An important early collection of letters, poems, and critical observations on Scottish songs.

735 WORKS. Ed. William Scott Douglas. 6 vols. Edinburgh: William Paterson, 1877-79.

   A monumental edition.

736 LIFE AND WORKS. Ed. Robert Chambers, rev. William Wallace. 4 vols. Edinburgh: Chambers, 1896.

   Burns's verse and prose in chronological order with the editors' connecting commentary and narrative.

737 POETRY. Ed. William Ernest Henley and Thomas F. Henderson. 4 vols. Edinburgh: Jack, 1896.

   Although superseded in many respects by Kinsley's edition (743), this centenary edition is still essential.

738 THE SONGS OF ROBERT BURNS, NOW FIRST PRINTED WITH THE MELODIES FOR WHICH THEY WERE WRITTEN. Ed. James C. Dick. London: OUP, 1903; rpt., with Burns's NOTES ON SCOTTISH SONG, ed. James C. Dick (London: OUP, 1908), Hatboro, Pa.: Folklore Associates, 1962.

   The text and annotation are excellent.

739 POEMS. Selected and ed. Laurence Brander. London: OUP, 1950.

740 POEMS. Selected and ed. Henry W. Meikle and William Beattie. Rev. ed. Harmondsworth: Penguin, 1953.

741 SELECTED POEMS. Ed. George Sutherland Fraser. London: Heinemann, 1960.

   There is a good introduction.

742 A CHOICE OF BURNS'S POEMS AND SONGS. Ed. Sydney Goodsir Smith. London: Faber, 1966.

743 POEMS AND SONGS. Ed. James Kinsley. 3 vols. Oxford: Clarendon Press, 1968.

> The standard modern edition. The text alone was published in one volume in the Oxford Standard Authors (London: OUP, 1969).

LETTERS

744 ROBERT BURNS AND MRS. DUNLOP: CORRESPONDENCE. Ed. William Wallace. 2 vols. London: Hodder and Stoughton, 1898.

> There is a fuller text in the American edition, New York: Dodd, Mead, 1898.

745 LETTERS. Ed. John DeLancey Ferguson. 2 vols. Oxford: Clarendon Press, 1931.

> This standard edition of Burns's letters will be superseded by the new edition in preparation by G. Ross Roy.

746 SELECTED LETTERS. Ed. John DeLancey Ferguson. London: OUP, 1953.

BIOGRAPHY AND CRITICISM

747 Lockhart, John Gibson. LIFE OF ROBERT BURNS. Edinburgh, 1828. Ed. William Scott Douglas, with an essay by Walter Raleigh. 2 vols. Liverpool: H. Young, 1914.

748 Angellier, Auguste. ROBERT BURNS: LA VIE, LES OEUVRES. 2 vols. Paris, 1893.

> Translated in part in the annual BURNS CHRONICLE, 1969-75.

749 Wilson, Sir James. THE DIALECT OF ROBERT BURNS. London: OUP, 1923.

750 _____. SCOTTISH POEMS OF ROBERT BURNS IN HIS NATIVE DIALECT. London: OUP, 1925.

751 Carswell, Catherine. THE LIFE OF ROBERT BURNS. London: Chatto and Windus, 1930; 1951.

752 Snyder, Franklyn Bliss. THE LIFE OF ROBERT BURNS. New York: Macmillan Co., 1932; rpt. Hamden, Conn.: Archon Books, 1968.

The best life, with a critical bibliography of the most important biographies, biographical studies, and editions.

753 _____. ROBERT BURNS: HIS PERSONALITY, HIS REPUTATION AND HIS ART. Toronto: University of Toronto Press, 1936.

754 Hecht, Hans. ROBERT BURNS: THE MAN AND HIS WORK. Trans. Jane Lymburn. Edinburgh: Hodge, 1936; 1950.

755 Ferguson, John DeLancey. PRIDE AND PASSION. New York: OUP, 1939.

756 Fitzhugh, Robert T., ed. ROBERT BURNS: HIS ASSOCIATES AND CON-TEMPORARIES, WITH THE JOURNAL OF THE BORDER TOUR. Chapel Hill: University of North Carolina Press, 1943.

757 Montgomerie, William, ed. ROBERT BURNS: SIX ESSAYS BY CON-TEMPORARY WRITERS. Glasgow: Maclellan, 1947.

The essayists are Edwin Muir, George Bruce, James Findlay Hendry, John Dick Scott, John Barclay Pick, and the editor.

758 Daiches, David. ROBERT BURNS. 1950; rev. London: Deutsch, 1966.

759 Lindsay, Maurice. ROBERT BURNS: THE MAN, HIS WORK, THE LE-GEND. 1954; rev. London: Robert Hale, 1979.

760 Strawhorn, John, ed. AYRSHIRE IN THE TIME OF ROBERT BURNS. Ayr: Ayrshire Archaeological and Natural History Society, 1959.

761 Crawford, Thomas. BURNS: A STUDY OF THE POEMS AND SONGS. Edinburgh: Oliver and Boyd, 1960; rpt. Edinburgh: James Thin, Mercat Press, 1978.

An excellent critical study.

762 Thornton, Robert D. JAMES CURRIE, THE ENTIRE STRANGER, AND ROBERT BURNS. Edinburgh: Oliver and Boyd, 1963.

A study of Burns's first editor and biographer (see 733).

763 Kinsley, James. "The Music of the Heart." RENAISSANCE AND MOD-ERN STUDIES, 8 (1964), 5-52.

764   Daiches, David. ROBERT BURNS AND HIS WORLD. London: Thames
       and Hudson, 1971.

765   Low, Donald A., ed. ROBERT BURNS: THE CRITICAL HERITAGE.
       London: Routledge and Kegan Paul, 1974.

       The first half century of Burns criticism.

766   Crawford, Thomas. "Burns since 1970." SLJ, suppl. 3 (1976), 4-14.

767   Ericson-Roos, Catarina. THE SONGS OF ROBERT BURNS: A STUDY
       OF THE UNITY OF POETRY AND MUSIC. Uppsala: Almqvist and
       Wiksell, 1977.

768   MacLaine, Allan H. "Radicalism and Conservatism in Burns's THE JOLLY
       BEGGARS." SSL, 13 (1978), 125-43.

BIBLIOGRAPHY AND REFERENCE WORKS

769   Gibson, James. THE BIBLIOGRAPHY OF ROBERT BURNS. Kilmarnock:
       McKie, 1881.

       Still useful, as it contains information not readily available
       elsewhere.

770   Reid, John Brown. A COMPLETE WORD AND PHRASE CONCORDANCE
       TO THE POEMS AND SONGS OF ROBERT BURNS. Glasgow: Kerr and
       Richardson, 1889; rpt. New York: Russell and Russell, 1967; rpt. New
       York: Burt Franklin, 1968.

771   CATALOGUE OF THE ROBERT BURNS COLLECTION IN THE MITCHELL
       LIBRARY, GLASGOW. Glasgow: Mitchell Library, 1959.

       The most comprehensive collection of printed material by and
       about Burns.

772   Egerer, Joel Warren. A BIBLIOGRAPHY OF ROBERT BURNS. Edinburgh:
       Oliver and Boyd, 1964.

773   Lindsay, Maurice. THE BURNS ENCYCLOPAEDIA. 3rd ed. rev. Lon-
       don: Robert Hale, 1980.

Alexander Wilson (1766-1813)

Wilson was born in Paisley and had published a number of poems before sailing
for America in 1794. There he developed a skill in drawing birds, and between

1808 and 1813 he brought out seven volumes of his AMERICAN ORNITHOLOGY.
He died in Philadelphia. Some of his Scots poetry was popularly attributed to
Burns.

774 POEMS. Paisley, 1790.

775 THE FORESTERS: A POEM DESCRIPTIVE OF A PEDESTRIAN JOURNEY
     TO THE FALLS OF NIAGARA IN THE AUTUMN OF 1803. 1804.

776 POEMS AND LITERARY PROSE. Ed. Alexander B. Grosart. 2 vols.
     Paisley: Gardner, 1876.

BIOGRAPHY AND CRITICISM

777 Ord, George. A SKETCH OF THE LIFE OF ALEXANDER WILSON,
     AUTHOR OF THE AMERICAN ORNITHOLOGY. Philadelphia: H. Hall,
     1828.

778 Hunter, Clark. "Alexander Wilson: Poet and Ornithologist." BURNS
     CHRONICLE, 3rd ser., 16 (1967), 42-50.

Section 4

1800-1900

This section deals with Scottish literature from 1800 to 1900, the century of Scott, Hogg, and Galt, of Carlyle and Stevenson, ending in the Kailyard of Thrums and Drumtochty.

The general works relevant to the period are grouped under six headings:

- A. Bibliographies
- B. Literary History and Criticism
- C. Anthologies
- D. Background Studies
- E. Printing, Publishing, and Bookselling
- F. Periodicals

Under each heading or subheading the works are arranged in chronological order by the year of publication.

A seventh heading, G. Individual Authors, lists the authors of the period in chronological order by their year of birth, giving for each author a chronological checklist of his/her separate works, including standard editions and collections and selections, followed by a chronological list of the more important biographical and critical studies of the author and his/her work.

A. BIBLIOGRAPHIES

See also pages 2-4.

779   Leclaire, Lucien. A GENERAL ANALYTICAL BIBLIOGRAPHY OF THE
      REGIONAL NOVELISTS OF THE BRITISH ISLES, 1800-1950. Paris:
      Société d'Édition "Les Belles Lettres," 1954; rev. 1969.

      Includes a number of Scottish novelists.

780   Aitken, William R., comp. SCOTTISH FICTION RESERVE: A LIST OF
      THE AUTHORS INCLUDED IN THE SCHEME. [Coatbridge]: Scottish
      Library Association, 1955.

      An alphabetical list of some 650 Scottish novelists, from Smol-
      lett onwards, showing the collecting libraries responsible for each
      author. A revised and greatly enlarged edition of the list, com-
      piled by Moira Stirling, is to be published in 1982 by the Na-
      tional Library of Scotland, Edinburgh.

781   Burgess, Moira. THE GLASGOW NOVEL, 1870-1970: A BIBLIOGRAPHY.
      Glasgow: Scottish Library Association, 1972.

782   Glen, Duncan. A BIBLIOGRAPHY OF SCOTTISH POETS FROM STEVEN-
      SON TO 1974. Preston: Akros, 1974.

Current research on all the major authors of the nineteenth century, including
a number of Scottish writers, is surveyed in the authoritative guides sponsored
by the Modern Language Association of America:

783   VICTORIAN FICTION: A GUIDE TO RESEARCH. Ed. Lionel Stevenson.
      Cambridge: Harvard University Press, 1964.

784   THE ENGLISH ROMANTIC POETS AND ESSAYISTS: A REVIEW OF RE-
      SEARCH AND CRITICISM. Ed. Carolyn Washburn Houtchens and Law-
      rence Huston Houtchens. Rev. ed. New York: New York University
      Press, 1966.

785   THE VICTORIAN POETS: A GUIDE TO RESEARCH. Ed. Frederick Ever-
      ett Faverty. Rev. ed. Cambridge: Harvard University Press, 1968.

786   THE ENGLISH ROMANTIC POETS: A REVIEW OF RESEARCH AND
      CRITICISM. 3rd rev. ed. Ed. Frank Jordan. New York: Modern Lan-
      guage Association, 1972.

787   VICTORIAN PROSE: A GUIDE TO RESEARCH. Ed. David J. DeLaura.
      New York: Modern Language Association, 1973.

788 VICTORIAN FICTION: A SECOND GUIDE TO RESEARCH. Ed. George
H. Ford. New York: Modern Language Association, 1978.

Current bibliographies recording the year's work in nineteenth-century literary
studies are now published annually in ENGLISH LANGUAGE NOTES (for the
Romantic movement) and in VICTORIAN STUDIES (for the Victorian period);
and there is an annual survey of critical writing on the nineteenth century in
the autumn number of STUDIES IN ENGLISH LITERATURE.

B. LITERARY HISTORY AND CRITICISM

See also pages 4-7.

789 Robertson, John M. "Belles Lettres in Scotland." In his CRITICISMS.
Vol. 2. London: Bonner, 1903.

790 Blake, George. BARRIE AND THE KAILYARD SCHOOL. London: Arthur Barker, 1951.

> The term "Kailyard" (cabbage patch) derives from the two lines
> of a Scots song--

>> There grows a bonnie brier bush in our kail-yard,
>> And white are the blossoms on't in our kail-yard.

> which Ian Maclaren chose as motto for his immensely popular
> collection of sketches of village life, published in 1894 as BE-
> SIDE THE BONNIE BRIER BUSH. It was first used by J.H.
> Millar and W.E. Henley in 1895 to describe the sentimentalized
> novels and stories of the Scottish countryside by Barrie, Mac-
> laren, Crockett, and others, which followed J.M. Barrie's
> AULD LICHT IDYLLS, published in 1888. Millar returned to
> the attack in 1903, in his LITERARY HISTORY OF SCOTLAND:

>> The circulating libraries became charged to over-
>> flowing with a crowd of ministers, precentors, and
>> beadles, whose dry and "pithy" wit had plainly been
>> recruited at the fountain-head of Dean Ramsay; while
>> the land was plangent with the sobs of grown men,
>> vainly endeavouring to stifle their emotion by an
>> elaborate affectation of "peching" and hoasting."

> The counterblast was to come with George Douglas Brown's THE
> HOUSE WITH THE GREEN SHUTTERS (1901) and John MacDou-
> gall Hay's GILLESPIE (1914). Lewis Grassic Gibbon, in SUN-
> SET SONG (1932) and its sequels, resolves the contradiction:
> his fictional village, Kinraddie, is described as "the Scots
> countryside itself, fathered between a kailyard and a bonny
> brier bush in the lee of a house with green shutters."

> For a more favorable recent assessment of the Kailyard school,
> see the essay by Eric Anderson, "The Kailyard Revisited," in

NINETEENTH-CENTURY SCOTTISH FICTION: CRITICAL ES-
SAYS, edited by Ian Campbell (Manchester: Carcanet New
Press, 1979), pages 130-47.

791 Kinsley, James, ed. SCOTTISH POETRY: A CRITICAL SURVEY. London: Cassell, 1955.

The relevant essays are John W. Oliver, "Scottish Poetry in
the Earlier Nineteenth Century," pages 212-35, and Douglas
Young, "Scottish Poetry in the Later Nineteenth Century,"
pages 236-55.

792 Craig, David. SCOTTISH LITERATURE AND THE SCOTTISH PEOPLE,
1680-1830. London: Chatto and Windus, 1961.

793 Gross, John. THE RISE AND FALL OF THE MAN OF LETTERS. London:
Weidenfeld and Nicolson, 1969.

A general study with some reference to Scottish writers.

794 Carter, Ian. "Kailyard: The Literature of Decline in Nineteenth-Century Scotland." SCOTTISH JOURNAL OF SOCIOLOGY, 1 (1976), 1-14.

795 Hart, Francis R. THE SCOTTISH NOVEL: A CRITICAL SURVEY. London: John Murray, 1978.

796 Campbell, Ian, ed. NINETEENTH-CENTURY SCOTTISH FICTION:
CRITICAL ESSAYS. Manchester: Carcanet New Press, 1979.

Nine essays by different writers on Scott, Galt, Hogg, Lockhart,
George MacDonald, Mrs. Oliphant, Stevenson, the Kailyarders,
and George Douglas Brown.

C. ANTHOLOGIES

See also pages 8-10.

797 WHISTLE-BINKIE, OR THE PIPER OF THE PARTY, BEING A COLLECTION
OF SONGS FOR THE SOCIAL CIRCLE. Glasgow: David Robertson, 1832.

The poetic equivalent of the Kailyard novel, this collection,
"wherein the vernacular muse appears at her very worst," was
frequently reprinted.

798 Young, Douglas, ed. SCOTTISH VERSE, 1851-1951. Edinburgh: Nelson,
1952.

Selected for the general reader.

799 Gifford, Douglas, ed. SCOTTISH SHORT STORIES, 1800-1900. London: Calder and Boyars, 1971.

800 Messenger, Nigel Philip, and John Richard Watson, eds. VICTORIAN POETRY: THE CITY OF DREADFUL NIGHT, AND OTHER POEMS. London: Dent, 1974.

This collection also includes Alexander Smith's poem, "Glasgow."

D. BACKGROUND STUDIES

See also pages 15-19.

801 Ramsay, Edward Bannerman. REMINISCENCES OF SCOTTISH LIFE AND CHARACTER. Edinburgh, 1857; 22nd ed. with the author's latest corrections and additions and a memoir of Dean Ramsay by Cosmo Innes. Edinburgh: Edmonston and Douglas, 1874.

802 Sage, Donald. MEMORABILIA DOMESTICA: PARISH LIFE IN THE NORTH OF SCOTLAND. 2nd ed. Wick, 1899; rpt., introd. Donald Withrington, Edinburgh: Albyn Press, 1976.

803 Crosland, Thomas W.H. THE UNSPEAKABLE SCOT. London: Grant Richards, 1902.

804 Carswell, Donald. BROTHER SCOTS. London: Constable, 1927.

A cultural picture of Scotland in the late nineteenth century through biographical studies of six intrinsically interesting Scotsmen.

805 Haldane, Elizabeth S. THE SCOTLAND OF OUR FATHERS. London: Maclehose, 1933.

806 Saunders, Laurance J. SCOTTISH DEMOCRACY, 1815-1840: THE SOCIAL AND INTELLECTUAL BACKGROUND. Edinburgh: Oliver and Boyd, 1950.

807 Davie, George Elder. THE DEMOCRATIC INTELLECT: SCOTLAND AND HER UNIVERSITIES IN THE NINETEENTH CENTURY. Edinburgh: Edinburgh University Press, 1961; 2nd ed. 1964.

An important and influential study.

808 Thompson, Alastair R. "The Use of Libraries by the Working Class in Scotland in the Early Nineteenth Century." SHR, 42 (1963), 21-29.

809   Young, Douglas. EDINBURGH IN THE AGE OF SIR WALTER SCOTT.
       Norman: University of Oklahoma Press, 1965.

810   Ferguson, William. SCOTLAND: 1689 TO THE PRESENT. Edinburgh
       History of Scotland, vol. 4. Edinburgh: Oliver and Boyd, 1968; rev.
       ed. 1979.

E. PRINTING, PUBLISHING, AND BOOKSELLING

General Studies

811   Myers, Robin. THE BRITISH BOOK TRADE FROM CAXTON TO THE
       PRESENT DAY: A BIBLIOGRAPHICAL GUIDE. London: Deutsch, 1973.

       A valuable survey.

812   Mumby, Frank A., and Ian Norrie. PUBLISHING AND BOOKSELLING.
       5th ed. London: Cape, 1974.

       Part 1: "From the Earliest Times to 1870," by Frank A. Mumby;
       Part 2: "1870-1970," by Ian Norrie. With an extensive "Bib-
       liography of Publishing and Bookselling" by William Peet and
       others. The current edition of Mumby's PUBLISHING AND
       BOOKSELLING: A HISTORY FROM THE EARLIEST TIMES TO
       THE PRESENT DAY (London: Cape, 1930), and the standard
       work, with many references to publishing in Scotland.

In Scotland

813   Macleod, Robert D. THE SCOTTISH PUBLISHING HOUSES. Glasgow:
       Holmes, 1953.

814   Carnie, Robert Hay. PUBLISHING IN PERTH BEFORE 1807. Dundee:
       Abertay Historical Society, 1960.

815   Gardner, Carreen S. PRINTING IN AYR AND KILMARNOCK: NEWS-
       PAPERS, PERIODICALS, BOOKS AND PAMPHLETS PRINTED FROM
       ABOUT 1780 UNTIL 1920. Ayr: Ayrshire Archaeological and Natural
       History Society, 1976.

Individual Firms (in alphabetical order)

ABERDEEN UNIVERSITY PRESS

816   Keith, Alexander. ABERDEEN UNIVERSITY PRESS, 1840-1963. Aber-
       deen: Aberdeen University Press, 1963.

BLACK

817　Nicolson, Alexander, ed.　MEMOIRS OF ADAM BLACK.　2nd ed.　London: Black, 1885.

818　ADAM AND CHARLES BLACK, 1807-1957: SOME CHAPTERS IN THE HISTORY OF A PUBLISHING HOUSE.　London: Black, 1957.

　　　Initialed J.D.N. [J.D. Newth].

BLACKIE

819　Blackie, Agnes A.C.　BLACKIE & SON, 1809-1959.　Glasgow: Blackie, 1959.

BLACKWOOD

820　Oliphant, Mrs. Margaret.　ANNALS OF A PUBLISHING HOUSE: WILLIAM BLACKWOOD AND HIS SONS, THEIR MAGAZINE AND FRIENDS. 2 vols.　Edinburgh: Blackwood, 1897.

　　　A third volume, JOHN BLACKWOOD, was added by his daughter, Mrs. Gerald Porter (Edinburgh: Blackwood, 1898).

821　Tredrey, Frank D.　THE HOUSE OF BLACKWOOD, 1804-1954.　Edinburgh: Blackwood, 1954.

822　National Library of Scotland. Edinburgh.　CATALOGUE OF MSS. ACQUIRED SINCE 1925.　Vol. 3, MSS. 4001-4940: BLACKWOOD PAPERS, 1805-1900.　Edinburgh: HMSO, 1969.

BROWN

823　BROWN'S BOOKSTALL.　[2 vols.] Aberdeen: Brown, 1892-99.

CADELL AND DAVIES

824　Besterman, Theodore, ed.　THE PUBLISHING FIRM OF CADELL AND DAVIES: SELECT CORRESPONDENCE AND ACCOUNTS, 1793-1836. London: OUP, 1938.

CHAMBERS

825　Chambers, William.　MEMOIR OF ROBERT CHAMBERS, WITH AUTOBIOGRAPHIC REMINISCENCES OF WILLIAM CHAMBERS.　Edinburgh, 1872; 13th ed. with suppl. chapter, Edinburgh: Chambers, 1884.

COLLINS

826 Keir, David. THE HOUSE OF COLLINS: THE STORY OF A SCOTTISH FAMILY OF PUBLISHERS FROM 1789 TO THE PRESENT DAY. London: Collins, 1952.

CONSTABLE

827 Constable, Thomas. ARCHIBALD CONSTABLE AND HIS LITERARY CORRESPONDENTS: A MEMORIAL BY HIS SON. 3 vols. Edinburgh: Edmonston and Douglas, 1873.

828 Quayle, Eric. THE RUIN OF SIR WALTER SCOTT. London: Hart-Davis, 1968.

GLASGOW UNIVERSITY PRESS

829 MacLehose, James. THE GLASGOW UNIVERSITY PRESS, 1638-1931, WITH SOME NOTES ON SCOTTISH PRINTING IN THE LAST THREE HUNDRED YEARS. Glasgow: Glasgow University Press, 1931.

LIVINGSTONE

830 FOOTPRINTS ON THE SANDS OF TIME, 1863-1963: THE STORY OF THE HOUSE OF LIVINGSTONE. Edinburgh: E. and S. Livingstone, 1963.

THE MILLERS

831 Couper, William James. THE MILLERS OF HADDINGTON, DUNBAR AND DUNFERMLINE: A RECORD OF SCOTTISH BOOKSELLING. London: T. Fisher Unwin, 1914.

NEILL

832 McLaren, Moray. THE HOUSE OF NEILL, 1749-1949. Edinburgh: Neill, 1949.

NELSON

833 Wilson, Sir Daniel. WILLIAM NELSON, 1816-87: A MEMOIR. Edinburgh: Nelson, 1889.

   Includes a sketch of Thomas Nelson (1780-1861), the founder of the firm.

PILLANS AND WILSON

834 A PRINTING HOUSE OF OLD AND NEW EDINBURGH, 1775-1925.
Edinburgh: Pillans and Wilson, 1925.

JOHN SMITH AND SON

835 A SHORT NOTE ON A LONG HISTORY, 1751-1925. Glasgow: John
Smith, 1925.

JAMES THIN

836 Thin, James. REMINISCENCES OF BOOKSELLERS AND BOOKSELLING
IN EDINBURGH IN THE TIME OF WILLIAM IV. Edinburgh: Oliver
and Boyd, 1905.

DAVID WYLLIE AND SONS

837 A CENTURY OF BOOKSELLING, 1814-1914. Aberdeen: Wyllie, 1914.

F. PERIODICALS

Many periodicals were founded and flourished in the nineteenth century, printing both trenchant criticism and much original imaginative writing. Scotland
had its share of these periodicals; some of the more important are listed.

For the location of runs of these periodicals the usual finding-lists should be
consulted: the BRITISH UNION CATALOGUE OF PERIODICALS (for the holdings of the major libraries in Britain) and the UNION LIST OF SERIALS (for
the United States and Canada). See Eugene P. Sheehy's GUIDE TO REFER-
ENCE BOOKS, and its supplements (Chicago: American Library Association,
1976--), for detailed descriptions of these guides.

Guides

838 WELLESLEY INDEX TO VICTORIAN PERIODICALS, 1824-1900. Vols. 1-
3. Toronto: University of Toronto Press, 1966-79.

> The INDEX identifies the authors of anonymous articles, citing
> evidence for each attribution. BLACKWOOD'S and the EDIN-
> BURGH REVIEW (with an initial section covering 1802-23) are
> included. The project is still in progress.

839 WATERLOO DIRECTORY OF VICTORIAN PERIODICALS, 1824-1900.
Phase 1. Waterloo, Ont.: University of Waterloo, 1976.

840   Vann, J. Don, and Rosemary T. Van Arsdel, eds. VICTORIAN PERI-
      ODICALS: A GUIDE TO RESEARCH. New York: Modern Language
      Association, 1978.

Individual Periodicals (in chronological order of first publication)

841   THE SCOTS MAGAZINE. Edinburgh, 1739-1817. Monthly.

      Continued as EDINBURGH MAGAZINE AND LITERARY MIS-
      CELLANY: A NEW SERIES OF THE SCOTS MAGAZINE.
      1817-26.

842   THE EDINBURGH REVIEW. 1802-1929. Quarterly

843   THE SPY. Edinburgh, 1810-11. Weekly.

      Edited and largely written by James Hogg.

844   BLACKWOOD'S. Edinburgh, 1817-1980. Monthly.

845   CHAMBERS'S JOURNAL. Edinburgh, 1832-1956. Originally weekly,
      monthly from 1932.

846   TAIT'S EDINBURGH MAGAZINE. 1832-61. Monthly.

847   THE NORTH BRITISH REVIEW. Edinburgh, 1844-71. Quarterly.

848   GOOD WORDS. Edinburgh, 1860-1906. Monthly.

849   THE SCOTTISH REVIEW. London [later Paisley; later Edinburgh], 1882-
      1900; n.s. 1914-20. Monthly.

850   SCOTTISH NOTES AND QUERIES. Aberdeen, 1887-1935. Monthly.

851   THE SCOTS OBSERVER. Edinburgh, 1888-90. Weekly.

      Continued in London as the NATIONAL OBSERVER. 1890-97.

852   BURNS CHRONICLE. Kilmarnock, 1892-- . Annual.

Studies

THE EDINBURGH REVIEW

853   Clive, John. SCOTCH REVIEWERS: A STUDY OF THE EDINBURGH
      REVIEW, 1802-1815. London: Faber, 1957.

854   . "The EDINBURGH REVIEW: The Life and Death of a Periodical."
In ESSAYS IN THE HISTORY OF PUBLISHING. Ed. Asa Briggs. London: Longman, 1974, pp. 113-40.

855 Taylor, J.A. "The 'Popular' Criticism of the EDINBURGH REVIEW."
JOURNAL OF POPULAR CULTURE, 9 (1975), 672-81.

BLACKWOOD'S

856 Strout, Alan Lang. "A Bibliography of Articles in BLACKWOOD'S MAG-
AZINE, 1817-1825." TEXAS TECHNICAL COLLEGE LITERARY BULLETIN,
5 (1959).

Newspapers

857 Stewart, William. THE GLASGOW HERALD: THE STORY OF A GREAT
NEWSPAPER FROM 1783 TO 1911. Glasgow: Privately Printed, 1911.

858 Cowan, Robert McNair Wilson. THE NEWSPAPER IN SCOTLAND: A
STUDY OF ITS FIRST EXPANSION, 1815-1860. Glasgow: Outram, 1946.

859 The Scotsman. THE GLORIOUS PRIVILEGE: THE HISTORY OF THE
SCOTSMAN. Edinburgh: Nelson, 1967.

G. INDIVIDUAL AUTHORS

This section deals with the authors of the period in chronological order by their
year of birth.

The bibliographies of individual authors follow a pattern. The author's works
are listed first. A chronological checklist of the author's separate works,
giving year of publication only, but adding after each title full details of any
modern critical editions, precedes a list of the standard collections and selections of the author's work. This primary bibliography is followed by a chronological list of the more important biographical and critical studies of the author
and his/her work, the secondary bibliography, with the emphasis on books rather
than articles. There is a final group for bibliographies of the author and reference works, if they exist.

Elizabeth Hamilton (1758-1816)

Elizabeth Hamilton was born in Belfast, of Scottish descent. When her father
died, she was adopted by an aunt who lived near Stirling. From 1804 she
lived in Edinburgh. THE COTTAGERS OF GLENBURNIE is a minor novel of

some interest as a faithful picture of a feckless Scots farming family called McClarty. The setting might well be Stirlingshire.

860   THE COTTAGERS OF GLENBURNIE. 1808; with memoir, 1851.

BIOGRAPHY AND CRITICISM

861   Benger, Elizabeth O. MEMOIRS OF MRS. ELIZABETH HAMILTON, WITH SELECTIONS FROM HER CORRESPONDENCE AND UNPUBLISHED WRITINGS. 2 vols. London: Longman, 1818.

Robert Burns (1759-96)

See page 80.

Joanna Baillie (1762-1851)

Joanna Baillie, poet and dramatist, was a close friend of Scott and the author of an ambitious series of plays which are impressive in style, but quite untheatrical: of her twenty-six plays only six or seven were staged. She ranks after Burns and Scott as one of the preservers and refurbishers of Scottish folk song.

862   FUGITIVE VERSES. 1790

863   A SERIES OF PLAYS IN WHICH IT IS ATTEMPTED TO DELINEATE THE STRONGER PASSIONS OF THE MIND. 1798-1812; rpt. introd. Donald H. Reiman. 3 vols. New York: Garland, 1977.

865   MISCELLANEOUS PLAYS. 1804.

866   THE FAMILY LEGEND: A TRAGEDY. 1810.

867   METRICAL LEGENDS. 1821.

868   POETICAL MISCELLANIES. 1822.

869   DRAMAS. 1836.

870   THE DRAMATIC AND POETIC WORKS OF JOANNA BAILLIE. London: Longman, 1851.

871 Carhart, Margaret S. THE LIFE AND WORK OF JOANNA BAILLIE. New Haven: Yale University Press, 1923; rpt. New York: Archon Books, 1970.

872 Carswell, Donald. "Joanna Baillie." In his SIR WALTER: A FOUR-PART STUDY IN BIOGRAPHY. London: John Murray, 1930, pp. 262-86.

Alexander Wilson (1766-1813)

See page 84.

Carolina Oliphant, Baroness Nairne (1766-1845)

Lady Nairne wrote nearly all her songs, over the initials B.B. (for Mrs. Bogan of Bogan), for THE SCOTTISH MINSTREL (1821-24). At her best she can stand comparison with Burns.

873 LIFE AND SONGS OF THE BARONESS NAIRNE. Ed. Charles Rogers. 2nd ed. enl. London: Griffin, 1869.

BIOGRAPHY AND CRITICISM

874 Oliphant, Thomas Lawrence Kington. THE JACOBITE LAIRDS OF GASK. London: Grampian Club, 1870.

875 Henderson, George. LADY NAIRNE AND HER SONGS. 1900; new ed. Paisley: Gardner, 1908.

James Hogg (1770-1835)

Hogg, the Ettrick Shepherd of the NOCTES AMBROSIANAE, was a friend of Scott, who encouraged his literary talent. At his best he is a considerable narrative poet, a clever imitator and parodist of his contemporaries, a lyric poet who can range from the hauntingly beautiful to the boisterously comic, and a prose writer of great power, particularly in his admirable use of the Scots vernacular. His present-day reputation dates from André Gide's "discovery" of the MEMOIRS AND CONFESSIONS OF A JUSTIFIED SINNER (see his introduction to the 1947 edition, below).

876 SCOTTISH PASTORALS, POEMS, SONGS. 1801.

877   THE MOUNTAIN BARD. 1807.

      Includes the (autobiographical) MEMOIR OF THE LIFE OF
      JAMES HOGG (see no. 901).

878   THE FOREST MINSTREL: A SELECTION OF SONGS. 1810.

879   THE QUEEN'S WAKE: A LEGENDARY POEM. 1813.

880   THE POETIC MIRROR, OR THE LIVING BARDS OF BRITAIN. 1816.

881   MADOR OF THE MOOR: A POEM. 1816.

882   DRAMATIC TALES. 1817.

883   THE BROWNIE OF BODSBECK, AND OTHER TALES. 1818.

884   THE BROWNIE OF BODSBECK. Ed. Douglas S. Mack. Edinburgh:
      Scottish Academic Press, 1976.

885   WINTER EVENING TALES. 1820.

886   THE THREE PERILS OF MAN, OR WAR, WOMEN, AND WITCHCRAFT:
      A BORDER ROMANCE. 1822.

887   THE THREE PERILS OF MAN, OR WAR, WOMEN, AND WITCHCRAFT:
      A BORDER ROMANCE. Ed. Douglas Gifford. Edinburgh: Scottish
      Academic Press, 1972.

888   THE THREE PERILS OF WOMAN, OR LOVE, LEASING, AND JEALOUSY:
      A SERIES OF DOMESTIC SCOTTISH TALES. 1823.

889   THE PRIVATE MEMOIRS AND CONFESSIONS OF A JUSTIFIED SINNER,
      WRITTEN BY HIMSELF. 1824.

890   THE PRIVATE MEMOIRS AND CONFESSIONS OF A JUSTIFIED SINNER,
      WRITTEN BY HIMSELF. Introd. André Gide. London: Cresset Press,
      1947.

891   THE PRIVATE MEMOIRS AND CONFESSIONS OF A JUSTIFIED SINNER,
      WRITTEN BY HIMSELF. Ed. John Carey. Oxford English Novels. Lon-
      don: OUP, 1969.

892 THE PRIVATE MEMOIRS AND CONFESSIONS OF A JUSTIFIED SINNER, WRITTEN BY HIMSELF. Introd. Douglas Gifford. London: Folio Society, 1978.

893 QUEEN HYNDE. 1825.

894 THE SHEPHERD'S CALENDAR. 1829.

895 SONGS. 1831.

896 THE DOMESTIC MANNERS AND PRIVATE LIFE OF SIR WALTER SCOTT. 1834.

See 901.

897 MEMOIR OF ROBERT BURNS. In THE WORKS OF ROBERT BURNS. Ed. James Hogg and William Motherwell, Vol. 5. 1836.

According to F.B. Snyder, "Perhaps the worst life of Burns written before the twentieth century."

898 A TOUR IN THE HIGHLANDS IN 1803. 1888.

COLLECTIONS AND SELECTIONS

899 SELECTED POEMS. Ed. John W. Oliver. Saltire Classics. Edinburgh: Oliver and Boyd, 1940.

900 SELECTED POEMS. Ed. Douglas S. Mack. Oxford: Clarendon Press, 1970.

901 MEMOIR OF THE AUTHOR'S LIFE and FAMILIAR ANECDOTES OF SIR WALTER SCOTT. Ed. Douglas S. Mack. Edinburgh: Scottish Academic Press, 1972.

BIOGRAPHY AND CRITICISM

902 Garden, Mrs. Mary Gray. MEMORIALS OF JAMES HOGG. Paisley: Gardner, 1885.

The author was Hogg's daughter.

903 Batho, Edith C. THE ETTRICK SHEPHERD. Cambridge: Cambridge University Press, 1927.

With a detailed bibliography.

904   Carswell, Donald. "The Ettrick Shepherd." In His SIR WALTER: A FOUR-
         PART STUDY IN BIOGRAPHY. London: John Murray, 1930, pp. 166-208.

905   Strout, Alan Lang. THE LIFE AND LETTERS OF JAMES HOGG. Vol.
         1, 1770-1825. Lubbock: Texas Technical College, 1946.

906   Craig, David. SCOTTISH LITERATURE AND THE SCOTTISH PEOPLE,
         1680-1830. London: Chatto and Windus, 1961.

907   Simpson, Louis. JAMES HOGG: A CRITICAL STUDY. Edinburgh:
         Oliver and Boyd, 1962.

908   Lee, L.L. "The Devil's Figure: James Hogg's JUSTIFIED SINNER."
         SSL, 3 (1965-66), 230-39.

909   SCOTTISH LITERARY NEWS, 3 (April 1973).

         This issue reprints papers on Hogg by Douglas S. Mack and
         Alexander Scott that were read at the Scott Bicentenary Con-
         ference in Edinburgh in 1971, and "A Note on Hogg's KIL-
         MENY," by John R. Mair.

910   Gifford, Douglas. JAMES HOGG. Edinburgh: Ramsay Head Press,
         1976.

         A new and wide-ranging assessment.

911   Mack, Douglas S. "'The Rage of Fanaticism in Former Days': James
         Hogg's CONFESSIONS OF A JUSTIFIED SINNER and the Controversy
         over OLD MORTALITY." In NINETEENTH-CENTURY SCOTTISH FICTION:
         CRITICAL ESSAYS. Ed. Ian Campbell. Manchester: Carcanet New
         Press, 1979, pp. 37-50.

912   Parr, Norah. JAMES HOGG AT HOME. Dollar: Douglas S. Mack,
         1980.

         Mrs. Parr, a great-granddaughter of the poet, bases her account
         of Hogg's domestic life in Yarrow on a series of letters and on
         family papers now in Stirling University Library.

Sir Walter Scott (1771-1832)

Scott bestrides the world of early nineteenth-century Scotland. His imagination
was early fired by the ballads, which he collected and arranged in his first major work, the MINSTRELSY OF THE SCOTTISH BORDER. His romantic narrative
poems were immensely popular, until Byron came to challenge their popularity.
Scott then turned to the novel. WAVERLEY, begun in 1805 and more than

once abandoned, was published in 1814 and went through four printings that year. The rest of the long series were eagerly awaited.

Scott has not lacked critics, but his virtues far exceed his faults. As a novelist he is preeminent in his portrayal of ordinary men and women, even when his heroes and heroines are conventional and unconvincing. The modern reader may be less impressed by IVANHOE and the English and foreign romances that followed it, but there is no abatement in his admiration of the Scottish novels. Scott may be said to have created the historical novel, and he had a profound influence both at home and abroad--on Fenimore Cooper, Pushkin, and the French novelists, among others.

Scott's huge output includes valuable editions of Dryden (1808) and Swift (1814), the BORDER ANTIQUITIES OF ENGLAND AND SCOTLAND (1814-17), and some first-rate criticism in his introductions for Ballantyne's Novelist's Library (1821-24), later collected as LIVES OF THE NOVELISTS.

913   MINSTRELSY OF THE SCOTTISH BORDER. 2 vols. Kelso, 1802. Vol.
       3. Edinburgh, 1803.

914   MINSTRELSY OF THE SCOTTISH BORDER. Ed. Thomas F. Henderson.
       4 vols. Edinburgh: Blackwood, 1902.

915   THE LAY OF THE LAST MINSTREL. 1805.

916   MARMION: A TALE OF FLODDEN FIELD. 1808.

917   THE LADY OF THE LAKE: A POEM. 1810.

918   THE VISION OF DON RODERICK: A POEM. 1811.

919   ROKEBY: A POEM. 1813.

920   THE BRIDAL OF TRIERMAIN, OR THE VALE OF ST. JOHN. 1813.

921   WAVERLEY, OR 'TIS SIXTY YEARS SINCE. 1814.

922   WAVERLEY, OR 'TIS SIXTY YEARS SINCE. Ed. Andrew Hook. Harmondsworth: Penguin, 1972.

923   GUY MANNERING, OR THE ASTROLOGER. 1815.

924   THE LORD OF THE ISLES: A POEM. 1815.

925 THE FIELD OF WATERLOO: A POEM. 1815.

926 THE ANTIQUARY. 1816.

927 TALES OF MY LANDLORD: THE BLACK DWARF; OLD MORTALITY. 1816.

928 OLD MORTALITY. Ed. Angus Calder. Harmondsworth: Penguin, 1975.

929 PAUL'S LETTERS TO HIS KINSFOLK. 1816.

930 HAROLD THE DAUNTLESS: A POEM. 1817.

931 ROB ROY. 1818.

932 TALES OF MY LANDLORD. 2nd series: THE HEART OF MIDLOTHIAN. 1818.

933 THE HEART OF MIDLOTHIAN. Ed. David Daiches. New York: Rinehart, 1948.

934 TALES OF MY LANDLORD. 3rd series: THE BRIDE OF LAMMERMOOR; A LEGEND OF MONTROSE. 1819.

935 IVANHOE: A ROMANCE. 1820.

936 THE MONASTERY: A ROMANCE. 1820.

937 THE ABBOT. 1820.

938 KENILWORTH: A ROMANCE. 1821.

939 THE PIRATE. 1822.

940 THE FORTUNES OF NIGEL. 1822.

941 HALIDON HILL: A DRAMATIC SKETCH. 1822.

942 PEVERIL OF THE PEAK. 1822.

943 QUENTIN DURWARD. 1823.

944 ST. RONAN'S WELL. 1824.

945 REDGAUNTLET: A TALE OF THE EIGHTEENTH CENTURY. 1824.

946 TALES OF THE CRUSADERS: THE BETROTHED; THE TALISMAN. 1825.

947 WOODSTOCK, OR THE CAVALIER. 1826.

948 CHRONICLES OF THE CANONGATE. 1st series: THE HIGHLAND WIDOW; THE TWO DROVERS; THE SURGEON'S DAUGHTER. 1827.

949 THE LIFE OF NAPOLEON BUONAPARTE. 1827.

950 TALES OF A GRANDFATHER. 1827-30.

951 CHRONICLES OF THE CANONGATE. 2nd series: ST. VALENTINE'S DAY, OR THE FAIR MAID OF PERTH. 1828.

952 ANNE OF GEIERSTEIN, OR THE MAIDEN OF THE MIST. 1829.

953 THE HISTORY OF SCOTLAND. 1829-30.

954 LETTERS ON DEMONOLOGY AND WITCHCRAFT. 1830.

955 THE DOOM OF DEVERGOIL: A MELODRAMA; AUCHINDRANE, OR THE AYRSHIRE TRAGEDY. 1830.

956 TALES OF MY LANDLORD. 4th series: COUNT ROBERT OF PARIS; CASTLE DANGEROUS. 1832.

COLLECTIONS AND SELECTIONS

957 THE WAVERLEY NOVELS. 48 vols. Edinburgh, 1830-34.

The author's last revision, with notes: his "magnum opus."

958 POETICAL WORKS. Ed. John Gibson Lockhart. 12 vols. Edinburgh, 1833-34.

959 MISCELLANEOUS PROSE WORKS. Ed. John Gibson Lockhart. 28 vols. Edinburgh, 1834-36.

960 THE WAVERLEY NOVELS. Dryburgh Edition. 25 vols. Edinburgh: Black, 1892-94.

961　THE WAVERLEY NOVELS.　Border Edition.　Ed. Andrew Lang.　48 vols.
　　　London: Nimmo, 1892-94.

962　POETICAL WORKS.　Ed. James Logie Robertson.　London: OUP, 1894.

963　POETICAL WORKS.　Dryburgh Edition.　Ed. Andrew Lang.　2 vols.
　　　London: Black, 1895.

964　THE WAVERLEY NOVELS.　Oxford Edition.　24 vols. London: OUP,
　　　1912-25.

965　SHORT STORIES.　Ed. Lord David Cecil.　London: OUP, 1934.

966　SIR WALTER SCOTT ON NOVELISTS AND FICTION.　Ed. Ioan Williams.
　　　London: Routledge and Kegan Paul, 1968.

　　　A collection of essays, reviews, and prefaces.

967　SELECTED POEMS.　Ed. Thomas Crawford.　Oxford: Clarendon Press,
　　　1972.

968　THE SUPERNATURAL SHORT STORIES.　Ed. Michael Hayes.　London:
　　　John Calder, 1977.

969　THE PREFACES TO THE WAVERLEY NOVELS.　Ed. Mark A. Weinstein.
　　　Lincoln: University of Nebraska Press, 1978.

LETTERS AND JOURNALS

970　THE LETTERS.　Ed. Sir Herbert Grierson et al.　12 vols.　London: Con-
　　　stable, 1932-37; rpt. New York: AMS, 1971.

971　THE LETTERS.　NOTES AND INDEX.　By James C. Corson.　Oxford:
　　　Clarendon Press, 1979.

972　THE JOURNAL.　Ed. John Guthrie Tait and William Mathie Parker.　3
　　　vols.　Edinburgh: Oliver and Boyd, 1939-46; 1 vol. ed., 1950.

973　THE JOURNAL.　Ed. William Eric Kinloch Anderson.　Oxford: Claren-
　　　don Press, 1972.

BIOGRAPHY AND CRITICISM

974　Hazlitt, William.　"Sir Walter Scott."　In his THE SPIRIT OF THE AGE.
　　　London, 1825; World's Classics, London: OUP, 1904, pp. 76-91.

975   Hogg, James. FAMILIAR ANECDOTES OF SIR WALTER SCOTT. 1834.
      Ed. Douglas S. Mack, with Hogg's MEMOIR OF THE AUTHOR'S LIFE.
      Edinburgh: Scottish Academic Press, 1972.

976   Lockhart, John Gibson. MEMOIRS OF THE LIFE OF SIR WALTER SCOTT,
      BART. 1837-38; ed. Alfred W. Pollard. 5 vols. London: Macmillan,
      1900.

977   _____. NARRATIVE OF THE LIFE OF SIR WALTER SCOTT, BART.
      1848.

      An abridgement of the foregoing, frequently reprinted.

978   Lang, Andrew. SIR WALTER SCOTT. London: Hodder and Stoughton,
      1906.

979   Crockett, William S. THE SCOTT ORIGINALS: AN ACCOUNT OF
      NOTABLES AND WORTHIES THE ORIGINALS OF CHARACTERS IN THE
      WAVERLEY NOVELS. Edinburgh: T.N. Foulis, 1912.

980   Carswell, Donald. SIR WALTER: A FOUR-PART STUDY IN BIOGRAPHY.
      London: John Murray, 1930; issued as SCOTT AND HIS CIRCLE, Gar-
      den City, N.Y.: Doubleday, Doran, 1930.

      Essays on Scott, Hogg, Lockhart, and Joanna Baillie.

981   Buchan, John. SIR WALTER SCOTT. London: Cassell, 1932.

      A readable biography with perceptive comments on the man and
      the novels.

982   Hillhouse, James T. THE WAVERLEY NOVELS AND THEIR CRITICS.
      Minneapolis: University of Minnesota Press, 1936.

983   Muir, Edwin. SCOTT AND SCOTLAND: THE PREDICAMENT OF THE
      SCOTTISH WRITER. London: Routledge, 1936.

      A stimulating essay.

984   Grierson, Sir Herbert. SIR WALTER SCOTT, BART.: A NEW LIFE, SUP-
      PLEMENTARY TO, AND CORRECTIVE OF, LOCKHART'S BIOGRAPHY.
      London: Constable, 1938.

      The author was principal editor of Scott's letters (see 970).

985   Pottle, Frederick A. "The Power of Memory in Boswell and Scott." In
      ESSAYS ON THE EIGHTEENTH CENTURY PRESENTED TO DAVID NICHOL
      SMITH. Oxford: Clarendon Press, 1945, pp. 168-89; rpt. in SCOTT'S
      MIND AND ART, ed. Alexander Norman Jeffares, Edinburgh: Oliver
      and Boyd, 1969, pp. 230-53.

986   Daiches, David. "Scott's Achievement as a Novelist." NINETEENTH
       CENTURY FICTION, 6 (1951-52); rpt. in LITERARY ESSAYS, Edinburgh:
       Oliver and Boyd, 1956, pp. 88-121; rpt. in WALTER SCOTT: MODERN
       JUDGEMENTS, ed. David Douglas Devlin, London: Macmillan, 1968,
       pp. 33-62; rpt. in SCOTT'S MIND AND ART, ed. Alexander Norman
       Jeffares, Edinburgh: Oliver and Boyd, 1969, pp. 21-52.

987   _____. "Scott's REDGAUNTLET." In FROM JANE AUSTEN TO JOSEPH
       CONRAD: ESSAYS COLLECTED IN MEMORY OF JAMES T. HILLHOUSE.
       Ed. Robert Charles Rathburn and Martin Steinmann. Minneapolis: Univer-
       sity of Minnesota Press, 1958, pp. 46-59; rpt. in WALTER SCOTT: MOD-
       ERN JUDGEMENTS, ed. David Douglas Devlin, London: Macmillan,
       1968, pp. 148-61.

988   Jack, Ian. SIR WALTER SCOTT. London: Longman, for the British
       Council, 1958.

       Reprinted with additions to the bibliography, 1964; 1971.

989   Davie, Donald. THE HEYDAY OF SIR WALTER SCOTT. London: Rout-
       ledge and Kegan Paul, 1961.

990   Lukács, Georg. THE HISTORICAL NOVEL. 1937; trans. Hannah and
       Stanley Mitchell. London: Merlin Press, 1962.

991   Welsh, Alexander. THE HERO OF THE WAVERLEY NOVELS. New
       Haven: Yale University Press, 1963.

992   Bushnell, Nelson S. "Walter Scott's Advent as Novelist of Manners."
       SSL, 1 (1963-64), 15-34.

993   _____. "Scott's Mature Achievement as Novelist of Manners." SSL,
       3 (1965-66), 3-29.

994   Parsons, Coleman O. WITCHCRAFT AND DEMONOLOGY IN SCOTT'S
       FICTION, WITH CHAPTERS ON THE SUPERNATURAL IN SCOTTISH
       LITERATURE. Edinburgh: Oliver and Boyd, 1964.

995   Crawford, Thomas. SCOTT. Edinburgh: Oliver and Boyd, 1965.

       An excellent introduction.

996   Hart, Francis R. SCOTT'S NOVELS: THE PLOTTING OF HISTORIC SUR-
       VIVAL. Charlottesville: University Press of Virginia, 1966.

997   Anderson, James. "Sir Walter Scott as Historical Novelist." SSL, 4
       (1966-67), 29-41, 63-78, 155-78; 5 (1967-68), 14-27, 83-97, 143-66.

998 Devlin, David Douglas, ed. WALTER SCOTT: MODERN JUDGEMENTS. London: Macmillan, 1968.

Includes a select bibliography.

999 Quayle, Eric. THE RUIN OF SIR WALTER SCOTT. London: Hart-Davis, 1968.

1000 Calder, Angus, and Jenni Calder. SCOTT. London: Evans Brothers, 1969.

1001 Cockshut, Anthony O.J. THE ACHIEVEMENT OF WALTER SCOTT. London: Collins, 1969.

1002 Clark, Arthur Melville. SIR WALTER SCOTT: THE FORMATIVE YEARS. Edinburgh: Blackwood, 1969.

1003 Gordon, Robert C. UNDER WHICH KING? A STUDY OF THE SCOTTISH WAVERLEY NOVELS. Edinburgh: Oliver and Boyd, 1969.

1004 Jeffares, Alexander Norman, ed. SCOTT'S MIND AND ART. Edinburgh: Oliver and Boyd, 1969.

A collection of ten essays, old and new.

1005 Morgan, Peter F. "Scott as Critic." SSL, 7 (1969-70), 90-101.

1006 Johnson, Edgar. SIR WALTER SCOTT: THE GREAT UNKNOWN. 2 vols. New York: Macmillan; London: Hamish Hamilton, 1970.

A comprehensive and accurate life. Indispensable.

1007 Hayden, John Olin, ed. SCOTT: THE CRITICAL HERITAGE. London: Routledge and Kegan Paul, 1970.

A selection of the best nineteenth-century writing on Scott.

1008 Daiches, David. SIR WALTER SCOTT AND HIS WORLD. London: Thames and Hudson, 1971.

1009 Devlin, David Douglas. THE AUTHOR OF WAVERLEY: A CRITICAL STUDY OF WALTER SCOTT. London: Macmillan, 1971.

1010 Fleishman, Avrom. THE ENGLISH HISTORICAL NOVEL: WALTER SCOTT TO VIRGINIA WOOLF. Baltimore: Johns Hopkins Press, 1971.

1011 Crawford, Thomas. "Scott as a Poet." ÉTUDES ANGLAISES, 24 (1971), 501-08.

One of the major papers at the Scott Bicentenary Conference in Edinburgh in 1971.

1012 Bell, Alan, ed. SCOTT BICENTENARY ESSAYS: SELECTED PAPERS READ AT THE SIR WALTER SCOTT BICENTENARY CONFERENCE [Edinburgh 1971]. Edinburgh: Scottish Academic Press, 1973.

See also 909, 1011, and 1015.

1013 Mayhead, Robin. WALTER SCOTT. Cambridge: Cambridge University Press, 1973.

1014 Hartveit, Lars. DREAM WITHIN A DREAM: A THEMATIC APPROACH TO SCOTT'S VISION OF FICTIONAL REALITY. Oslo: Universitetsforlaget, 1974.

1015 Chandler, Alice. "Chivalry and Romance: Scott's Medieval Novels." STUDIES IN ROMANTICISM, 14 (1975), 185-200.

A paper read at the Scott Bicentenary Conference in Edinburgh in 1971.

1016 Sultana, Donald E. THE SIEGE OF MALTA REDISCOVERED: AN ACCOUNT OF SIR WALTER SCOTT'S MEDITERRANEAN JOURNEY AND HIS LAST NOVEL. Edinburgh: Scottish Academic Press, 1976.

1017 Mitchell, Jerome. THE SIR WALTER SCOTT OPERAS: AN ANALYSIS OF OPERAS BASED ON THE WORKS OF SIR WALTER SCOTT. University: University of Alabama Press, 1977.

Examines the adaptations of Scott's poems and novels by British and European librettists.

1018 Alexander, John Huston. THE RECEPTION OF SCOTT'S POETRY BY HIS CORRESPONDENTS, 1796-1817. Salzburg: Salzburg Studies in English Literature, 1979.

1019 Brown, David. WALTER SCOTT AND THE HISTORICAL IMAGINATION. London: Routledge and Kegan Paul, 1979.

1020 Daiches, David. "Scott's WAVERLEY: The Presence of the Author." In NINETEENTH-CENTURY SCOTTISH FICTION: CRITICAL ESSAYS. Ed. Ian Campbell. Manchester: Carcanet New Press, 1979, pp. 6-17.

1021 Wilson, A.N. THE LAIRD OF ABBOTSFORD. Oxford: Clarendon Press, 1980.

1022 SCOTTISH LITERARY JOURNAL, 7 (May 1980), 7-201.

This special issue prints sixteen papers on Sir Walter Scott discussed at the Ruff Memorial Colloquium at the University of Florida Libraries, Gainesville, in 1979.

BIBLIOGRAPHY AND REFERENCE WORKS

1023 Husband, Margaret F. A DICTIONARY OF CHARACTERS IN THE WAVERLEY NOVELS. London: Routledge, 1910.

1024 Worthington, Greville. A BIBLIOGRAPHY OF THE WAVERLEY NOVELS. London: Constable, 1931.

1025 Ruff, William. "A Bibliography of the Poetical Works of Sir Walter Scott." TRANSACTIONS OF THE EDINBURGH BIBLIOGRAPHICAL SOCIETY, 1 (1938), 99-240, 277-82.

1026 Corson, James C. A BIBLIOGRAPHY OF SIR WALTER SCOTT: A CLASSIFIED AND ANNOTATED LIST OF BOOKS AND ARTICLES RELATING TO HIS LIFE AND WORKS, 1797-1940. Edinburgh: Oliver and Boyd, 1943; rpt. New York: Burt Franklin, 1969.

1027 Parsons, Coleman O. "Chapbook Versions of the Waverley Novels." SSL, 3 (1965-66), 189-220.

1028 Anderson, William Eric Kinloch. "Scott." In THE ENGLISH NOVEL: SELECT BIBLIOGRAPHICAL GUIDES. Ed. Anthony Edward Dyson. London: OUP, 1974, pp. 128-44.

1029 Bradley, Philip. AN INDEX TO THE WAVERLEY NOVELS. Metuchen, N.J.: Scarecrow Press, 1975.

1030 Ford, Richard. DRAMATISATIONS OF SCOTT'S NOVELS: A CATALOGUE. Oxford: Oxford Bibliographical Society, 1979.

Francis, Lord Jeffrey (1773-1850)

In 1802, along with Sydney Smith and others, Lord Jeffrey, an advocate and judge, founded the EDINBURGH REVIEW, of which he was editor. His numerous contributions--no fewer than two hundred articles on a wide range of subjects--are marked by a clean-cut, vivacious style and a self-confident, dogmatic, and even aggressive manner.

1031 CONTRIBUTIONS TO THE EDINBURGH REVIEW. 4 vols. 1844.

> For a full list of Jeffrey's contributions, see the WELLESLEY INDEX, Vol. 1 (1966), entry 838.

1032 JEFFREY'S LITERARY CRITICISM. Ed. David Nichol Smith. London: OUP, 1910.

> A judicious selection.

BIOGRAPHY AND CRITICISM

1033 Cockburn, Lord. THE LIFE OF LORD JEFFREY, WITH A SELECTION FROM HIS CORRESPONDENCE. 2 vols. Edinburgh: Black, 1852.

1034 Greig, James A. FRANCIS JEFFREY OF THE EDINBURGH REVIEW. Edinburgh: Oliver and Boyd, 1948.

1035 Clive, John. SCOTCH REVIEWERS: A STUDY OF THE EDINBURGH REVIEW, 1802-1815. London: Faber, 1957.

1036 Morgan, Peter F. "Principles and Perspective in Jeffrey's Criticism." SSL, 4 (1966-67), 179-93.

1037 Flynn, Philip. FRANCIS JEFFREY. Newark: University of Delaware Press, 1978.

Robert Tannahill (1774-1810)

Tannahill was a weaver in Paisley whose rather sentimental poems and songs proved popular when published in 1807, but when his publisher rejected a revised edition the poet burned his manuscripts and drowned himself.

1038 POEMS AND SONGS CHIEFLY IN THE SCOTS DIALECT. 1807.

1039 POEMS AND SONGS AND CORRESPONDENCE. Ed. David Semple. Paisley: Gardner, 1876.

BIOGRAPHY AND CRITICISM

1040 Hunter, Clark. "Robert Tannahill: A Bicentenary Study." BURNS CHRONICLE, 3rd series, 24 (1974), 18-22.

John Leyden (1775-1811)

Leyden, a Border shepherd's son, helped Scott with his MINSTRELSY before setting out for India, where he worked as a surgeon and naturalist, and later became a professor and a judge. He acquired an extensive knowledge of some thirty languages, publishing several important treatises and translations, not listed here. He died prematurely of fever while serving as an interpreter in Java.

1041 SCENES OF INFANCY: DESCRIPTIVE OF TEVIOTDALE. 1803.

1042 POETICAL WORKS. Ed. Thomas Brown. London: W.P. Nimmo, 1875.

1043 JOURNAL OF A TOUR IN THE HIGHLANDS AND WESTERN ISLANDS OF SCOTLAND IN 1800. Ed. J. Sinton. Edinburgh: Blackwood, 1903.
   Includes a bibliography of the life and writings of Leyden.

BIOGRAPHY AND CRITICISM

1044 Reith, John. LIFE OF DR. JOHN LEYDEN. Galashiels: Walker, [1908].

Thomas Campbell (1777-1844)

Campbell turned from the study of law to the reading and writing of poetry, where he won a quick popularity. His PLEASURES OF HOPE ran through four editions in Britain and America within a year. A stirring narrative poet, Campbell was also a prolific journalist, contributing articles to the EDINBURGH ENCYCLOPAEDIA and to the NEW MONTHLY MAGAZINE, which he edited from 1821 to 1830.

1045 THE PLEASURES OF HOPE, WITH OTHER POEMS. 1799.

1046 GERTRUDE OF WYOMING: A PENNSYLVANIAN TALE, AND OTHER POEMS. 1809.

1047 THEODRIC: A DOMESTIC TALE, AND OTHER POEMS. 1824.

1048 THE LIFE OF MRS. SIDDONS. 1834.

1049 LETTERS FROM THE SOUTH. 1837.
   Issued as THE JOURNAL OF A RESIDENCE IN ALGIERS. 1842.

1050 THE PILGRIM OF GLENCOE, AND OTHER POEMS. 1842.

1051 COMPLETE POETICAL WORKS. Ed. James Logie Robertson. Oxford: OUP, 1907.

BIOGRAPHY AND CRITICISM

1052 Beattie, William. THE LIFE AND LETTERS OF THOMAS CAMPBELL. 3 vols. London: Moxon, 1849.

1053 Redding, Cyrus. LITERARY REMINISCENCES AND MEMOIRS OF THOMAS CAMPBELL. 2 vols. London: Skeet, 1860.

1054 Hadden, James Cuthbert. THOMAS CAMPBELL. Edinburgh: Oliphant, Anderson and Ferrier, 1899.

1055 Miller, Mary R. THOMAS CAMPBELL. Boston: Twayne, 1978.

Mary Brunton (1778-1818)

Mrs. Brunton, wife of the professor of Hebrew in the University of Edinburgh, gained some success with the two novels she published, but the posthumous EMMELINE is considered her best.

1056 SELF CONTROL. 1811.

1057 DISCIPLINE. 1814.

1058 EMMELINE, WITH SOME OTHER PIECES, TO WHICH IS PREFIXED A MEMOIR OF HER LIFE, INCLUDING SOME EXTRACTS FROM HER CORRESPONDENCE. 1819.

   The memoir is by the author's husband, Alexander Brunton.

John Galt (1779-1839)

Galt, born in Irvine and brought up in Greenock, traveled in the Levant, where he met Byron. For BLACKWOOD'S MAGAZINE, in 1820, he wrote the first of the novels he called "theoretical histories," following it in quick succession with others of the same kind, in which he is unrivaled. In 1826 he went to Canada, where he pioneered the town of Guelph, but he later returned to London and to literature. In his best work he is a careful observer, rich in humor and warm in sympathy, with an excellent ear for his native Scots.

1059 THE BATTLE OF LARGS: A GOTHIC POEM. 1804.

1060 LETTERS FROM THE LEVANT. 1813.

1061 THE MAJOLO: A TALE. 1816.

1062 THE LIFE AND STUDIES OF BENJAMIN WEST. 1816-20.

1063 THE CRUSADE: A POEM. 1816.

1064 THE EARTHQUAKE: A TALE. 1820.

1065 THE WANDERING JEW. 1820.

1066 THE AYRSHIRE LEGATEES, OR THE PRINGLE FAMILY. 1821.

1067 ANNALS OF THE PARISH, OR THE CHRONICLE OF DALMAILING. 1821.

1068 ANNALS OF THE PARISH, OR THE CHRONICLE OF DALMAILING. Ed. James Kinsley. Oxford English Novels. London: OUP, 1967.

1069 SIR ANDREW WYLIE OF THAT ILK. 1822.

1070 THE PROVOST. 1822.

1071 THE PROVOST. Ed. Ian A. Gordon. Oxford English Novels. London: OUP, 1973.

1072 THE STEAMBOAT. 1822.

1073 THE ENTAIL, OR THE LAIRDS OF GRIPPY. 1823.

1074 THE ENTAIL, OR THE LAIRDS OF GRIPPY. Ed. Ian A. Gordon. Oxford English Novels. London: OUP, 1970.

1075 RINGAN GILHAIZE, OR THE COVENANTERS. 1823.

1076 GLENFELL, OR MACDONALDS AND CAMPBELLS. 1823.

1077 THE SPAEWIFE: A TALE OF THE SCOTTISH CHRONICLES. 1823.

1078 ROTHELAN: A ROMANCE OF THE ENGLISH HISTORIES. 1824.

1079 THE OMEN. 1825.

1080 THE LAST OF THE LAIRDS, OR THE LIFE AND OPINIONS OF MALACHI MAILINGS ESQ. OF AULDBIGGINGS. 1826.

1081 THE LAST OF THE LAIRDS, OR THE LIFE AND OPINIONS OF MALACHI MAILINGS ESQ. OF AULDBIGGINGS. Ed. Ian A. Gordon. Edinburgh: Scottish Academic Press, 1976.

1082 LAWRIE TODD, OR THE SETTLERS IN THE WOODS. 1830.

1083 SOUTHENNAN. 1830.

1084 THE LIFE OF LORD BYRON. 1830.

1085 THE LIVES OF THE PLAYERS. 1831.

1086 BOGLE CORBET, OR THE EMIGRANTS. 1831.

1087 BOGLE CORBET, OR THE EMIGRANTS. Ed. Elizabeth Waterston. Toronto: McClelland and Stewart, 1977.

1088 THE MEMBER: AN AUTOBIOGRAPHY. 1832.
  A novel.

1089 THE MEMBER: AN AUTOBIOGRAPHY. Ed. Ian A. Gordon: Edinburgh: Scottish Academic Press, 1975.

1090 THE RADICAL: AN AUTOBIOGRAPHY. 1832.
  A novel.

1091 STANLEY BUXTON, OR THE SCHOOLFELLOWS. 1832.

1092 POEMS. 1833.

1093 EBEN ERSKINE, OR THE TRAVELLER. 1833.

1094 THE STOLEN CHILD: A TALE OF THE TOWN. 1833.

1095 STORIES OF THE STUDY. 1833.

1096 THE AUTOBIOGRAPHY OF JOHN GALT. 1833.

1097 THE LITERARY LIFE AND MISCELLANIES. 1834.

1098 THE HOWDIE AND OTHER TALES. Ed. William Roughead. Edinburgh: T.N. Foulis, 1923.

1099 A RICH MAN AND OTHER STORIES. Ed. William Roughead. Edinburgh: T.N. Foulis, 1925.

1100 WORKS. Ed. David S. Meldrum and William Roughead. 10 vols. Edinburgh: John Grant, 1936.

Collects, in fact, only seven of Galt's novels.

1101 POEMS: A SELECTION. Ed. George Henry Needler. Toronto: Burns and MacEachern, 1954.

1102 SELECTED SHORT STORIES. Ed. Ian A. Gordon. Edinburgh: Scottish Academic Press, 1978.

BIOGRAPHY AND CRITICISM

1103 Kitchin, George. "John Galt." In EDINBURGH ESSAYS ON SCOTS LITERATURE. Edinburgh: Oliver and Boyd, 1933, pp. 105-24.

1104 Aberdein, Jennie W. JOHN GALT. London: OUP, 1936.

1105 Lyell, Frank H. A STUDY OF THE NOVELS OF JOHN GALT. Princeton: Princeton University Press, 1942.

1106 Frykman, Erik. JOHN GALT'S SCOTTISH STORIES. Uppsala: Lundequistska, 1959.

An illuminating study.

1107 Parker, William Mathie. "John Galt." In his SUSAN FERRIER AND JOHN GALT. London: Longmans, Green, for the British Council, 1965, pp. 24-43.

1108 Costain, Keith M. "The Prince and the Provost." SSL, 6 (1968-69), 20-35.

1109 Gordon, Ian A. JOHN GALT: THE LIFE OF A WRITER. Edinburgh: Oliver and Boyd, 1972.

The standard modern study, with a good bibliography.

1110 MacQueen, John. "John Galt and the Analysis of Social History." In SCOTT BICENTENARY ESSAYS. Ed. Alan Bell. Edinburgh: Scottish Academic Press, 1973, pp. 332-42.

1111 Gordon, Ian A. "Three New Chapters by Galt: THE PUBLISHER."
SLJ, 3 (July 1976), 23-30.

1112 Costain, Keith M. "Theoretical History and the Novel: The Scottish
Fiction of John Galt." ELH, 43 (1976), 342-65.

1113 Timothy, Hamilton B. THE GALTS: A CANADIAN ODYSSEY. JOHN
GALT, 1779-1839. Toronto: McClelland and Stewart, 1977.

1114 Aldrich, Ruth I. JOHN GALT. Boston: Twayne, 1978.

1115 Gibault, Henri. JOHN GALT, ROMANCIER ÉCOSSAIS. Grenoble:
Université des Langues et Lettres de Grenoble, 1979.

1116 Buchan, David. "Galt's ANNALS: Treatise and Fable." In NINETEENTH-
CENTURY SCOTTISH FICTION: CRITICAL ESSAYS. Ed. Ian Campbell.
Manchester: Carcanet New Press, 1979, pp. 18-36.

1117 Whatley, Christopher A., ed. JOHN GALT 1779-1979. Edinburgh:
Ramsay Head Press, 1979.

  A collection of ten essays on Galt to mark the bicentenary of
  his birth.

BIBLIOGRAPHY

1118 Lumsden, Harry. "The Bibliography of John Galt." RECORDS OF THE
GLASGOW BIBLIOGRAPHICAL SOCIETY, 9 (1931), 1-41.

1119 Booth, Bradford A. "A Bibliography of John Galt." BULLETIN OF BIB-
LIOGRAPHY, 16 (1936-39), 7-9.

Henry, Lord Cockburn (1779-1854)

Lord Cockburn was a companion of Francis Jeffrey, whose life he wrote, and a
contributor (but mainly on legal topics) to the EDINBURGH REVIEW. He is
remembered for his posthumous volumes of reminiscences, part autobiography and
part a shrewdly observed account of contemporary Edinburgh and its personalities
from his youth to his old age.

1120 THE LIFE OF LORD JEFFREY. 2 vols. Edinburgh: Black, 1852.

1121 MEMORIALS OF HIS TIME. Edinburgh: Black, 1856; rpt. Edinburgh:
James Thin, Mercat Press, 1971; ed. Karl Miller, Chicago: University
of Chicago Press, 1974.

1122 JOURNAL, 1831-1854. 2 vols. Edinburgh: Edmonston and Douglas, 1874.

1123 CIRCUIT JOURNEYS. Edinburgh: David Douglas, 1888; rpt. Edinburgh: James Thin, Mercat Press, 1975.

BIOGRAPHY AND CRITICISM

1124 Miller, Karl. COCKBURN'S MILLENIUM. London: Duckworth, 1975.

1125 Bell, Alan. "Lord Cockburn as a Letter-Writer." SLJ, 6 (May 1979), 43-57.

1126 _____, ed. LORD COCKBURN: A BICENTENARY COMMEMORATION, 1779-1979. Edinburgh: Scottish Academic Press, 1979.

   A collection of eight essays.

Charles Kirkpatrick Sharpe (1781-1851)

According to J.H. Millar, in a footnote in his LITERARY HISTORY OF SCOT-LAND, Sharpe was "a singular character, with an unusual appetite for all manner of scandal past and present, and also with a really sound knowledge of the antiquarian side of some periods in Scottish history." He is chiefly remembered by his correspondence.

1127 A HISTORICAL ACCOUNT OF THE BELIEF IN WITCHCRAFT IN SCOT-LAND. 1884; rpt. Wakefield: S.R. Publishers, 1972.

1128 LETTERS FROM AND TO CHARLES KIRKPATRICK SHARPE. Ed. Alexander Allardyce. 2 vols. Edinburgh: Blackwood, 1888.

BIOGRAPHY AND CRITICISM

1129 Caird, James B. "Charles Kirkpatrick Sharpe." LIBRARY REVIEW, 23 (1971-72), 75-80.

Susan Ferrier (1782-1854)

When Susan Ferrier's novels were first published, anonymously, they were for a time attributed by some to Scott, whose friendship she enjoyed. They present a closely observed picture of Scottish society.

1130 MARRIAGE: A NOVEL. 1818.

1131 MARRIAGE: A NOVEL. Ed. Herbert Foltinek. Oxford English Novels.
London: OUP, 1971.

1132 THE INHERITANCE. 1824.

1133 DESTINY, OR THE CHIEF'S DAUGHTER. 1831.

1134 WORKS. Ed. Lady Margaret Sackville. 4 vols. London: Nash and
Grayson, 1928.

> The first three volumes contain the three novels; volume 4 is
> Doyle's MEMOIR AND CORRESPONDENCE OF SUSAN FERRIER,
> first published in 1898 (see 1135).

BIOGRAPHY AND CRITICISM

1135 Doyle, John A. MEMOIR AND CORRESPONDENCE OF SUSAN FERRIER.
London: John Murray, 1898.

1136 Grant, Aline. SUSAN FERRIER OF EDINBURGH: A BIOGRAPHY. Den-
ver: A. Swallow, 1957.

1137 Parker, William Mathie. "Susan Ferrier." In his SUSAN FERRIER AND
JOHN GALT. London: Longmans, Green, for the British Council, 1965,
pp. 8-23.

> Includes a select bibliography.

1138 Bushnell, Nelson S. "Susan Ferrier's MARRIAGE as Novel of Manners."
SSL, 5 (1967-68), 216-28.

1139 Craik, Wendy. "Susan Ferrier." In SCOTT BICENTENARY ESSAYS.
Ed. Alan Bell. Edinburgh: Scottish Academic Press, 1973, pp. 322-31.

Allan Cunningham (1784-1842)

Cunningham was born in Dumfriesshire and at an early age took an interest in
poetry, contributing to R.H. Cromek's spurious REMAINS OF NITHSDALE AND
GALLOWAY SONG (1810). He moved to London, where he wrote regularly
for the LONDON MAGAZINE (1820-25), edited a collection of songs (1825)
and the works of Burns (1834), and published his pioneer work on British artists.
Some of his songs are popular still.

1140 TRADITIONAL TALES OF THE ENGLISH AND SCOTTISH PEASANTRY.
1822.

1141 THE SONGS OF SCOTLAND, ANCIENT AND MODERN. 1825.

1142 LIVES OF THE MOST EMINENT BRITISH PAINTERS, SCULPTORS, AND ARCHITECTS. 1829-33.

1143 THE LIFE OF SIR DAVID WILKIE. 1843.

1144 POEMS AND SONGS. Ed. Peter Cunningham. 1847.

BIOGRAPHY AND CRITICISM

1145 Hogg, David. THE LIFE OF ALLAN CUNNINGHAM, WITH SELECTIONS FROM HIS WORKS AND CORRESPONDENCE. Dumfries: Anderson, 1875.

"Christopher North"
John Wilson (1785-1854)

John Wilson was born in Paisley, the eldest son of a rich manufacturer. In his twenties he settled in the Lake District, and became acquainted with Wordsworth and his circle, but returned to Edinburgh, where he joined Lockhart on the founding of BLACKWOOD'S MAGAZINE. In 1820 he was appointed professor of moral philosophy in Edinburgh University, but continued his connection with "Maga," contributing some forty of the seventy NOCTES AMBROSIANAE (1822-35), imaginary conversation pieces in which issues of the day were vigorously argued by "Christopher North," "The Ettrick Shepherd" (Hogg), and "Timothy Tickler," a character loosely based on Wilson's uncle.

1146 THE ISLE OF PALMS, AND OTHER POEMS. 1812.

1147 THE CITY OF THE PLAGUE, AND OTHER POEMS. 1816.

1148 LIGHTS AND SHADOWS OF SCOTTISH LIFE. 1822.
     Tales and sketches.

1149 THE TRIALS OF MARGARET LYNDSAY. 1823.

1150 THE FORESTERS. 1825.

1151 POEMS: A NEW EDITION. 1825.

1152 THE RECREATIONS OF CHRISTOPHER NORTH. 1842.

1153 THE NOCTES AMBROSIANAE. 1843.

> Mainly by Wilson, but with contributions from Hogg, Lockhart, William Maginn, and others. First published in BLACKWOOD'S MAGAZINE, 1822-35. See the WELLESLEY INDEX (838).

1154 THE NOCTES AMBROSIANAE. Ed. Robert Shelton Mackenzie. 5 vols. New York: Redfield, 1854; rev. ed., New York: Widdleton, 1866; rev. ed., New York: Hagemann, 1894.

1155 WORKS. Ed. James F. Ferrier. 12 vols. Edinburgh: Blackwood, 1855-58.

BIOGRAPHY AND CRITICISM

1156 Gordon, Mary. CHRISTOPHER NORTH: A MEMOIR OF JOHN WILSON. 2 vols. Edinburgh: Edmonston and Douglas, 1862.

> Mrs. Gordon was Wilson's daughter.

1157 Douglas, Sir George. THE BLACKWOOD GROUP. Edinburgh: Oliphant, Anderson and Ferrier, 1897.

1158 Swann, Elsie. CHRISTOPHER NORTH (JOHN WILSON). Edinburgh: Oliver and Boyd, 1934.

> Includes a detailed bibliography.

George Gordon Byron, 6th Baron Byron (1788-1824)

Byron was born in London, but spent his formative years in Aberdeen, and there is a discernible Scottish element in his life and work. His early poems were savagely reviewed by Brougham in the EDINBURGH REVIEW; Byron's reply was the powerful satire, ENGLISH BARDS AND SCOTCH REVIEWERS. He made a Grand Tour for two years or so, returning to publish CHILDE HAROLD'S PILGRIMAGE, which immediately challenged Scott's position as a popular writer of verse romances. This was followed by a series of oriental tales in verse, with "Byronic" heroes who were popularly identified with the poet himself. After separating from his wife, Byron settled in Italy, where much of his best work was written. He actively supported the liberal revolutionaries, and in 1823 he left for Greece to join the insurgents there. He died of marsh fever at Missolonghi.

His influence was immense and far-reaching, leaving its mark on Hugo, Leopardi, Heine, Pushkin and Lermontov, among others.

1159 HOURS OF IDLENESS: A SERIES OF POEMS, ORIGINAL AND TRANSLATED. 1807.

1160 ENGLISH BARDS AND SCOTCH REVIEWERS: A SATIRE. [1809].

1161 CHILDE HAROLD'S PILGRIMAGE. Cantos 1-2. 1812.
    Canto 3. 1816. Canto 4. 1818.

1162 CHILDE HAROLD'S PILGRIMAGE. Ed. Alexander Hamilton Thompson. Cambridge: Cambridge University Press, 1913.

1163 THE GIAOUR: A FRAGMENT OF A TURKISH TALE. 1813.

1164 THE BRIDE OF ABYDOS: A TURKISH TALE. 1813.

1165 THE CORSAIR: A TALE. 1814.

1166 LARA: A TALE. 1814.

1167 HEBREW MELODIES, ANCIENT AND MODERN. 1815.

1168 THE SIEGE OF CORINTH: A POEM; PARISINA: A POEM. 1816.

1169 THE PRISONER OF CHILLON, AND OTHER POEMS. 1816.

1170 MANFRED: A DRAMATIC POEM. 1817.

1171 BEPPO: A VENETIAN STORY. 1818.

1172 MAZEPPA: A POEM. 1819.

1173 DON JUAN. Cantos 1-16. 1819-24.

1174 DON JUAN. Ed. Truman Guy Steffan and Willis W. Pratt. 4 vols. Austin: University of Texas Press, 1957.
    A variorum edition.

1175 DON JUAN. Ed. Leslie A. Marchand. Boston: Houghton Mifflin, 1958.

1176 DON JUAN. Ed. Truman Guy Steffan and Willis W. Pratt. Harmondsworth: Penguin, 1973.

1177 MARINO FALIERO, DOGE OF VENICE: AN HISTORICAL TRAGEDY IN FIVE ACTS. 1821.

1178 THE PROPHECY OF DANTE: A POEM. 1821.

1179 SARDANAPALUS: A TRAGEDY; THE TWO FOSCARI: A TRAGEDY; CAIN: A MYSTERY. 1821.

1180 CAIN. Ed. Truman Guy Steffan. Austin: University of Texas Press, 1968.

Twelve essays and a text with variants and annotations.

1181 THE VISION OF JUDGMENT. 1822.

1182 THE AGE OF BRONZE. 1823.

1183 THE ISLAND, OR CHRISTIAN AND HIS COMRADES. 1823.

1184 WERNER: A TRAGEDY. 1823.

1185 THE DEFORMED TRANSFORMED: A DRAMA. 1824.

COLLECTIONS AND SELECTIONS

1186 WORKS. New rev. and enl. ed. 13 vols. London: John Murray, 1898-1904.

POETRY. Ed Ernest Hartley Coleridge. 7 vols. 1898-1904.
LETTERS AND JOURNALS. Ed. Rowland E. Prothero. 6 vols. 1898-1901.

This is still the standard edition for the poetry, but a new edition of the complete poems and plays, edited by Jerome J. McGann, is in preparation. An authoritative edition of the LETTERS AND JOURNALS by Leslie A. Marchand is nearing completion (see 1189).

1187 BYRON: SELECTIONS FROM POETRY, LETTERS AND JOURNAL. Ed. Peter Quennell. London: Nonesuch Press, 1949.

1188 SELECTED POETRY AND PROSE: Ed. Wystan Hugh Auden. New York: New American Library, 1966.

1189 BYRON'S LETTERS AND JOURNALS. Ed. Leslie A. Marchand. London: John Murray, 1973-- .

The definitive edition. Nine volumes have appeared so far:

Vol. 1. "IN MY HOT YOUTH": 1798-1810. 1973.
Vol. 2. "FAMOUS IN MY TIME": 1810-1812. 1973.

Vol. 3.   "ALAS! THE LOVE OF WOMEN!": 1813-1814. 1974.
Vol. 4.   "WEDLOCK'S THE DEVIL": 1814-1815. 1975.
Vol. 5.   "SO LATE INTO THE NIGHT": 1816-1817. 1976.
Vol. 6.   "THE FLESH IS FRAIL": 1818-1819. 1976.
Vol. 7.   "BETWEEN TWO WORLDS": 1820. 1977.
Vol. 8.   "BORN FOR OPPOSITION": 1821. 1978.
Vol. 9.   "IN THE WIND'S EYE": 1821-1822. 1979.

1190 CHILDE HAROLD'S PILGRIMAGE, AND OTHER ROMANTIC POEMS.
Ed. John D. Jump. London: Dent, 1975.

BIOGRAPHY AND CRITICISM

1191 Medwin, Thomas. CONVERSATIONS OF LORD BYRON AT PISA. 1824.
Ed. Ernest J. Lovell. Princeton: Princeton University Press, 1966.

1192 Blessington, Lady. CONVERSATIONS OF LORD BYRON. 1834. Ed.
Ernest J. Lovell. Princeton: Princeton University Press, 1969.

1193 Trelawny, Edward J. RECOLLECTIONS OF THE LAST DAYS OF SHELLEY
AND BYRON. 1858. Ed. Jack Eric Morpurgo. London: Folio Society,
1952.

1194 Mayne, Ethel Colburn. BYRON. 2 vols. London: Methuen, 1912;
rev. ed. (1 vol.), 1924.

1195 Chew, Samuel C. BYRON IN ENGLAND: HIS FAME AND AFTERFAME.
London: John Murray, 1924; rpt. New York: Russell and Russell, 1965.

A bibliographical study.

1196 Nicolson, Harold. BYRON: THE LAST JOURNEY. London: Constable,
1924; new ed. with a suppl. chapter, 1940.

1197 Calvert, William J. BYRON: ROMANTIC PARADOX. Chapel Hill:
University of North Carolina Press, 1935.

1198 Quennell, Peter. BYRON: THE YEARS OF FAME. London: Faber,
1935; new ed., London: Collins, 1967.

1199 Eliot, Thomas Stearns. "Byron." In FROM ANNE TO VICTORIA. Ed.
Bonamy Dobrée. London: Cassell, 1937, pp. 601-19.

1200 Quennell, Peter. BYRON IN ITALY. London: Collins, 1941.

1201 Boyd, Elizabeth F. BYRON'S DON JUAN: A CRITICAL STUDY. New Brunswick, N.J.: Rutgers University Press, 1945.

1202 Trueblood, Paul G. THE FLOWERING OF BYRON'S GENIUS: STUDIES IN BYRON'S DON JUAN. Stanford: Stanford University Press, 1945.

1203 Origo, Iris. THE LAST ATTACHMENT: BYRON AND TERESA GUICCIO-LI. London: Cape and John Murray, 1949.

1204 Lovell, Ernest J. BYRON: THE RECORD OF A QUEST. STUDIES IN A POET'S CONCEPT AND TREATMENT OF NATURE. Austin: University of Texas Press, 1949.

1205 _____. HIS VERY SELF AND VOICE: COLLECTED CONVERSATIONS OF LORD BYRON. New York: Macmillan, 1954.

The major first-hand accounts expertly edited.

1206 Escarpit, Robert. LORD BYRON: UN TEMPÉRAMENT LITTÉRAIRE. 2 vols. Paris: Cercle du Livre, 1955-57.

1207 Marchand, Leslie A. BYRON: A BIOGRAPHY. 3 vols. London: John Murray, 1957.

The standard full-scale work.

1208 Moore, Doris Langley. THE LATE LORD BYRON. London: John Murray, 1961.

1209 Rutherford, Andrew. BYRON: A CRITICAL STUDY. Edinburgh: Oliver and Boyd, 1961.

1210 Elwin, Malcolm. LORD BYRON'S WIFE. London: Macdonald, 1962.

1211 Marshall, William H. THE STRUCTURE OF BYRON'S MAJOR POEMS. Philadelphia: University of Pennsylvania Press, 1962.

1212 Thorslev, Peter L. THE BYRONIC HERO: TYPES AND PROTOTYPES. Minneapolis: University of Minnesota Press, 1962.

1213 Joseph, Michael Kennedy. BYRON THE POET. London: Gollancz, 1964.

1214 Marchand, Leslie A. BYRON'S POETRY: A CRITICAL INTRODUCTION. Boston: Houghton Mifflin, 1965; London: John Murray, 1966.

1215 Gleckner, Robert Francis. BYRON AND THE RUINS OF PARADISE. Baltimore: Johns Hopkins Press, 1967.

1216 Buxton, John. BYRON AND SHELLEY: THE HISTORY OF A FRIEND-SHIP. London: Macmillan, 1968.

1217 McGann, Jerome J. FIERY DUST: BYRON'S POETIC DEVELOPMENT. Chicago: University of Chicago Press, 1968.

1218 Marchand, Leslie A. BYRON: A PORTRAIT. London: John Murray, 1970.

1219 Rutherford, Andrew, ed. BYRON: THE CRITICAL HERITAGE. London: Routledge and Kegan Paul, 1970.

1220 Jump, John D. BYRON. London: Routledge and Kegan Paul, 1972.

1221 Moore, Doris Langley. LORD BYRON: ACCOUNTS RENDERED. London: John Murray, 1974.

1222 McGann, Jerome J. DON JUAN IN CONTEXT. London: John Murray, 1976.

1223 Speer, Roderick S. "Byron and the Scottish Literary Tradition." SSL, 14 (1979), 196-206.

BIBLIOGRAPHY AND REFERENCE WORKS

1224 Coleridge, Ernest Hartley. "A Bibliography of the Successive Editions and Translations of Lord Byron's Poetical Works." In THE POETICAL WORKS OF LORD BYRON. Vol. 7. London: John Murray, 1904, pp. 89-348.

1225 Hagelman, Charles W., and Robert J. Barnes. A CONCORDANCE TO BYRON'S DON JUAN. Ithaca: Cornell University Press, 1967.

1226 Jump, John D. "Byron." In ENGLISH POETRY: SELECT BIBLIOGRAPHI-CAL GUIDES. Ed. Anthony Edward Dyson. London: OUP, 1971, pp. 211-23.

1227 Young, Ione Dodson. A CONCORDANCE TO THE POETRY OF BYRON. 4 vols. Austin, Tex.: Best Printing Co., 1975.

1228 Santucho, Oscar J. GEORGE GORDON, LORD BYRON: A COMPRE-HENSIVE BIBLIOGRAPHY OF SECONDARY MATERIALS IN ENGLISH, 1807-1974. Metuchen, N.J.: Scarecrow Press, 1977.

1229 Reiman, Donald H., ed. ENGLISH ROMANTIC POETRY, 1800-1835: A GUIDE TO INFORMATION SOURCES. American Literature, English Literature, and World Literatures in English Information Guide Series, vol. 27. Detroit: Gale Research Co., 1979, pp. 121-42.

Michael Scott (1789-1835)

At the age of seventeen, Scott sought his fortune in Jamaica. His experiences supplied the material for TOM CRINGLE'S LOG, which first appeared serially in BLACKWOOD'S MAGAZINE, 1829-33.

1230 TOM CRINGLE'S LOG. 1833.

1231 TOM CRINGLE'S LOG. Ed. Richard Armstrong. London: Dent, 1969.

1232 THE CRUISE OF THE MIDGE. 1836.

BIOGRAPHY AND CRITICISM

1233 Douglas, Sir George. THE BLACKWOOD GROUP. Edinburgh: Oliphant, Anderson and Ferrier, 1897.

John Gibson Lockhart (1794-1854)

Lockhart could be a savage critic—he was responsible for the notorious review of Keats's ENDYMION in BLACKWOOD'S MAGAZINE—yet he wrote in PETER'S LETTERS TO HIS KINSFOLK a witty and urbane account of the society of his time. He is chiefly remembered for his biography of his father-in-law, Sir Walter Scott. It has sterling qualities: natural affection and warm sympathy, a sense of drama, and a gallery of convincingly lifelike pen-portraits.

1234 PETER'S LETTERS TO HIS KINSFOLK. 1819.

1235 PETER'S LETTERS TO HIS KINSFOLK. Ed. William Ruddick. Edinburgh: Scottish Academic Press, 1977.

1236 VALERIUS: A ROMAN STORY. 1821.

1237 SOME PASSAGES IN THE LIFE OF MR. ADAM BLAIR, MINISTER OF THE GOSPEL AT CROSS MEIKLE: A NOVEL. 1822.

1238 SOME PASSAGES IN THE LIFE OF MR. ADAM BLAIR, MINISTER OF THE GOSPEL AT CROSS MEIKLE: A NOVEL. Ed. David Craig. Edinburgh: Edinburgh University Press, 1963.

1239 REGINALD DALTON: A STORY OF ENGLISH UNIVERSITY LIFE. 1823.

1240 THE HISTORY OF MATTHEW WALD: A NOVEL. 1824.

1241 LIFE OF ROBERT BURNS. 1828.

1242 LIFE OF ROBERT BURNS. Ed. William Scott Douglas, with an essay by Walter Raleigh. 2 vols. Liverpool: H. Young, 1914.

1243 THE HISTORY OF NAPOLEON BUONAPARTE. 1829.

1244 MEMOIRS OF THE LIFE OF SIR WALTER SCOTT, BART. 1837-38.

1245 MEMOIRS OF THE LIFE OF SIR WALTER SCOTT, BART. Ed. Alfred W. Pollard. 5 vols. London: Macmillan, 1900.

1246 NARRATIVE OF THE LIFE OF SIR WALTER SCOTT, BART. 1848.

   An abridgement of 1244.

1247 LOCKHART'S LITERARY CRITICISM. Ed. Margaret Clive Hildyard. London: OUP, 1931.

   Includes a list of Lockhart's contributions to BLACKWOOD'S MAGAZINE (1817-46) and the QUARTERLY REVIEW, which he edited, 1826-53.

BIOGRAPHY AND CRITICISM

1248 Lang, Andrew. THE LIFE AND LETTERS OF JOHN GIBSON LOCKHART. 2 vols. London: J.C. Nimmo, 1897.

1249 Carswell, Donald. "John Gibson Lockhart." In his SIR WALTER: A FOUR-PART STUDY IN BIOGRAPHY. London: John Murray, 1930, pp. 209-61.

1250 Macbeth, Gilbert. JOHN GIBSON LOCKHART: A CRITICAL STUDY. Urbana, Ill.: University of Illinois, 1935.

1251 Lochhead, Marion. JOHN GIBSON LOCKHART. London: John Murray, 1954.

1252 Hart, Francis R. LOCKHART AS ROMANTIC BIOGRAPHER. Edinburgh: Edinburgh University Press, 1971.

1253 Richardson, Thomas C. "Character and Craft in Lockhart's ADAM BLAIR."
In NINETEENTH-CENTURY SCOTTISH FICTION: CRITICAL ESSAYS.
Ed. Ian Campbell. Manchester: Carcanet New Press, 1979, pp. 51-67.

Thomas Carlyle (1795-1881)

Carlyle, the outstanding Scottish writer of the generation succeeding Scott, was
born in Dumfriesshire and his formative years were spent in Scotland--he was
nearly forty when he moved to London. Known to the intellectual world as
"the Sage of Chelsea," he remained characteristically Scottish, from his education and background. His highly individual style is a strange amalgam of
Scots pulpit rhetoric, the diction of the King James' Bible, and German syn-
tax. The modern reader recognizes the interest and power of his historical
writings and his political and social thought without necessarily accepting his
message as the revelations of the prophet he was once claimed to be.

Carlyle's life and work are inevitably intertwined with those of the accomplished
Jane Welsh (1801-66), from their first meeting in 1821, to their marriage in
1826, and her death forty years later.

1254 WILHELM MEISTER'S APPRENTICESHIP: A NOVEL FROM THE GERMAN
OF GOETHE. 1824.

1255 THE LIFE OF SCHILLER. 1825.

1256 GERMAN ROMANCE: SPECIMENS OF ITS CHIEF AUTHORS. 1827.

1257 SARTOR RESARTUS. 1836.

First published in FRASER'S MAGAZINE, 1833-34.

1258 SARTOR RESARTUS. Ed. Charles Frederick Harrold. Garden City, N.Y.:
Doubleday, Doran, 1937.

1259 THE FRENCH REVOLUTION: A HISTORY. 1837.

1260 THE FRENCH REVOLUTION: A HISTORY. Ed. Charles R.L. Fletcher.
3 vols. London: Methuen, 1902.

1261 CRITICAL AND MISCELLANEOUS ESSAYS. 1838.

Contains most of his contributions to periodicals to 1838.

1262 CHARTISM. 1840.

1263 ON HEROES, HERO-WORSHIP, AND THE HEROIC IN HISTORY. 1841.

1264 PAST AND PRESENT. 1843.

1265 PAST AND PRESENT. Ed. Richard D. Altick. Boston: Houghton Mifflin, 1965.

1266 OLIVER CROMWELL'S LETTERS AND SPEECHES. 1845.

1267 LATTER-DAY PAMPHLETS. 1850.

1268 LIFE OF JOHN STERLING. 1851.

1269 THE HISTORY OF FRIEDRICH II OF PRUSSIA, CALLED FREDERICK THE GREAT. 1858-65.

1270 THE HISTORY OF FRIEDRICH II OF PRUSSIA, CALLED FREDERICK THE GREAT. Abridged and ed. John Clive. Chicago: University of Chicago Press, 1969.

1271 ON THE CHOICE OF BOOKS. 1866.

1272 REMINISCENCES. Ed. James Anthony Froude. 1881; ed. Charles Eliot Norton, 1887.

1273 REMINISCENCES. Ed. Ian Campbell. London: Dent, 1972.

1274 LAST WORDS. 1892.

Includes WOTTON REINFRED, an unfinished semi-autobiographical novel, written c. 1827, and the EXCURSION (FUTILE ENOUGH) TO PARIS, AUTUMN 1851.

COLLECTIONS AND SELECTIONS

1275 COLLECTED WORKS. Centenary Edition. Ed. Henry D. Traill. 30 vols. London: Chapman and Hall, 1896-99.

The standard edition.

1276 SELECTED WORKS, REMINISCENCES AND LETTERS. Ed. Julian Symons. London: Hart-Davis, 1955.

An attractive introduction to Carlyle's work.

1277 A CARLYLE READER. Ed. George B. Tennyson. New York: Modern Library, 1969.

1278 SELECTED WRITINGS. Ed. Alan Shelston. Harmondsworth: Penguin, 1971.

LETTERS

1279 LETTERS AND MEMORIALS OF JANE WELSH CARLYLE. Ed. James Anthony Froude. 3 vols. London: Longmans, Green, 1883.

1280 THE CORRESPONDENCE OF EMERSON AND CARLYLE. 1883; ed. Joseph Slater. New York: Columbia University Press, 1964.

1281 EARLY LETTERS OF CARLYLE, 1814–26; 1826–36. Ed. Charles Eliot Norton. 4 vols. London: Macmillan, 1886–88.

1282 CORRESPONDENCE BETWEEN GOETHE AND CARLYLE. Ed. Charles Eliot Norton. London: Macmillan, 1887.

1283 EARLY LETTERS OF JANE WELSH CARLYLE. Ed. David G. Ritchie. London: Sonnenschein, 1889.

1284 NEW LETTERS AND MEMORIALS OF JANE WELSH CARLYLE. Ed. Alexander Carlyle. 2 vols. London: John Lane, 1903.

1285 NEW LETTERS OF THOMAS CARLYLE. Ed. Alexander Carlyle. 2 vols. London: John Lane, 1904.

1286 THE LOVE LETTERS OF THOMAS CARLYLE AND JANE WELSH CARLYLE. Ed. Alexander Carlyle. 2 vols. London: John Lane, 1909.

1287 LETTERS OF CARLYLE TO JOHN STUART MILL, JOHN STERLING AND ROBERT BROWNING. Ed. Alexander Carlyle. London: T. Fisher Unwin, 1923.

1288 JANE WELSH CARLYLE: A NEW SELECTION OF HER LETTERS. Ed. Trudy Bliss. London: Gollancz, 1950.

1289 THOMAS CARLYLE: LETTERS TO HIS WIFE. Ed. Trudy Bliss. London: Gollancz, 1953.

1290 THE LETTERS OF THOMAS CARLYLE TO HIS BROTHER ALEXANDER, WITH RELATED FAMILY LETTERS. Ed. Edwin W. Marrs. Cambridge: Harvard University Press, 1968.

1291 THE COLLECTED LETTERS OF THOMAS AND JANE WELSH CARLYLE.
Duke-Edinburgh Edition. Ed. Charles Richard Sanders and Kenneth J.
Fielding. Durham, N.C.: Duke University Press, 1970-- .

> This monumental edition will eventually supersede all previous
> partial collections.

BIOGRAPHY AND CRITICISM

1292 Froude, James Anthony. THOMAS CARLYLE. 4 vols. London: Longmans, Green, 1882-84.

1293 _____. FROUDE'S LIFE OF CARLYLE. Abridged and ed. John Clubbe.
London: John Murray, 1979.

1294 _____. MY RELATIONS WITH CARLYLE. London: Longmans, Green,
1903.

> See also Waldo Hilary Dunn's FROUDE AND CARLYLE (London:
> Longmans, Green, 1930) and his biography, JAMES ANTHONY
> FROUDE (2 vols. Oxford: Clarendon Press, 1963).

1295 Wilson, David Alec. CARLYLE. 6 vols. London: Kegan Paul, 1923-34.

> The last volume completed by David Wilson MacArthur.

1296 Storrs, Margaret. THE RELATION OF CARLYLE TO KANT AND FICHTE.
Bryn Mawr, Pa.: Bryn Mawr College, 1929.

1297 Neff, Emery. CARLYLE. London: Allen and Unwin, 1932.

1298 Harrold, Charles Frederick. CARLYLE AND GERMAN THOUGHT, 1819-
1834. New Haven: Yale University Press, 1934.

1299 Shine, Hill. CARLYLE'S FUSION OF POETRY, HISTORY AND RELI-
GION BY 1834. Chapel Hill: University of North Carolina Press, 1937.

1300 Young, Louise M. THOMAS CARLYLE AND THE ART OF HISTORY.
Philadelphia: University of Pennsylvania Press, 1939.

1301 Calder, Grace J. THE WRITING OF PAST AND PRESENT: A STUDY
OF CARLYLE'S MANUSCRIPTS. New Haven: Yale University Press,
1949.

1302 Halliday, James L. MR. CARLYLE: MY PATIENT. London: Heinemann,
1949.

> A psychosomatic biography.

1303 Symons, Julian. THOMAS CARLYLE: THE LIFE AND IDEAS OF A PROPHET. London: Gollancz, 1952.

1304 Hanson, Lawrence, and Elisabeth Hanson. NECESSARY EVIL: THE LIFE OF JANE WELSH CARLYLE. London: Constable, 1952.

1305 Holloway, John. THE VICTORIAN SAGE: STUDIES IN ARGUMENT. London: Macmillan, 1953.

1306 Shine, Hill. CARLYLE'S EARLY READING TO 1834. Lexington: University of Kentucky, 1953.

1307 Holme, Thea. THE CARLYLES AT HOME. London: OUP, 1965.

1308 Tennyson, George B. SARTOR CALLED RESARTUS: GENESIS, STRUCTURE AND STYLE. Princeton: Princeton University Press, 1965.

1309 VaValley, Albert J. CARLYLE AND THE IDEA OF THE MODERN. New Haven: Yale University Press, 1968.

1310 Seigel, Jules Paul, ed. CARLYLE: THE CRITICAL HERITAGE. London: Routledge and Kegan Paul, 1971.

   A selection of contemporary criticism.

1311 Goldberg, Michael. CARLYLE AND DICKENS. Athens: University of Georgia Press, 1972.

1312 Campbell, Ian. THOMAS CARLYLE. London: Hamish Hamilton, 1974.

   A good introduction with an annotated bibliography.

1313 Tarr, Rodger L. "Thomas Carlyle's Libraries at Chelsea and Ecclefechan." STUDIES IN BIBLIOGRAPHY, 27 (1974), 249-65.

1314 Clubbe, John, ed. CARLYLE AND HIS CONTEMPORARIES: ESSAYS IN HONOR OF CHARLES RICHARD SANDERS. Durham, N.C.: Duke University Press, 1976.

1315 Fielding, Kenneth J., and Rodger L. Tarr, eds. CARLYLE PAST AND PRESENT: A COLLECTION OF NEW ESSAYS. London: Vision Press, 1976.

1316 Sanders, Charles Richard. CARLYLE'S FRIENDSHIPS AND OTHER STUDIES. Durham, N.C.: Duke University Press, 1977.

1317 Campbell, Ian. THOMAS CARLYLE. Harlow: Longman, for the British Council, 1978.

An essay, with a select bibliography.

BIBLIOGRAPHY

1318 Dyer, Isaac W. A BIBLIOGRAPHY OF CARLYLE'S WRITINGS AND ANA. Portland, Maine: Southworth Press, 1928.

1319 Tarr, Rodger L. THOMAS CARLYLE: A BIBLIOGRAPHY OF ENGLISH LANGUAGE CRITICISM, 1824-1974. Charlottesville: University Press of Virginia, 1976.

1320 CARLYLE NEWSLETTER. Edinburgh: University of Edinburgh, Department of English Literature, 1979-- . Annual.

Number 1 includes a Carlyle bibliography: 1977-78 (pp. 28-35).

David Macbeth Moir (1798-1851)

Moir was a doctor in Musselburgh who contributed prose and verse regularly and voluminously to BLACKWOOD'S MAGAZINE, and also wrote a number of medical works not listed here. His sketches of life in a small town broaden and sentimentalize the perceptive realism of Galt.

1321 THE BOMBARDMENT OF ALGIERS, AND OTHER POEMS. 1816.

1322 THE LEGEND OF GENEVIEVE, WITH OTHER TALES AND POEMS. 1824.

1323 THE LIFE OF MANSIE WAUCH, TAILOR IN DALKEITH, WRITTEN BY HIMSELF. 1828.

First published in BLACKWOOD'S MAGAZINE, 1824-28.

1324 THE LIFE OF MANSIE WAUCH, TAILOR IN DALKEITH, WRITTEN BY HIMSELF. Ed. Thomas F. Henderson. London: Methuen, 1902.

1325 MEMOIR OF JOHN GALT. 1841.

1326 DOMESTIC VERSES. 1843.

1327 POETICAL WORKS. Ed. with a memoir by Thomas Aird. 2 vols. 1852.

BIOGRAPHY AND CRITICISM

1328 Douglas, Sir George. THE BLACKWOOD GROUP. Edinburgh: Oliphant, Anderson and Ferrier, 1897.

Jane Welsh Carlyle (1801-66)

See THOMAS CARLYLE (1795-1881), page 130.

Hugh Miller (1802-56)

Miller, born in Cromarty, worked at first as a stonemason, devoting his winter months to reading, writing, and natural history. After a few years as a bank clerk, he came to Edinburgh in 1839 to edit the Free Church paper, THE WITNESS, in which he printed the popular geological articles, later published in book form.

1329 POEMS WRITTEN IN THE LEISURE HOURS OF A JOURNEYMAN MASON. 1829.

1330 SCENES AND LEGENDS OF THE NORTH OF SCOTLAND. 1835.

1331 THE OLD RED SANDSTONE, OR NEW WALKS IN AN OLD FIELD. 1841.

Reprinted from THE WITNESS.

1332 FIRST IMPRESSIONS OF ENGLAND AND ITS PEOPLE. 1847.

1333 FOOTPRINTS OF THE CREATOR. 1849.

A reply to Robert Chambers's VESTIGES OF CREATION (see 1350).

1334 MY SCHOOLS AND SCHOOLMASTERS, OR THE STORY OF MY EDUCATION. 1854.

1335 MY SCHOOLS AND SCHOOLMASTERS, OR THE STORY OF MY EDUCATION. Ed. William Mackay Mackenzie. Edinburgh: George A. Morton, 1905.

A notable autobiography.

1336 THE TESTIMONY OF THE ROCKS. 1857.

1337 THE CRUISE OF THE BETSY. Ed. William Samuel Symonds. 1858.

1338 ESSAYS. Ed. Peter Bayne. 1862.

1339 TALES AND SKETCHES. Ed. Lydia F.F. Miller. 1863.

1340 SELECTIONS. Ed. William Mackay Mackenzie. Paisley: Gardner, 1908.

BIOGRAPHY AND CRITICISM

1341 Bayne, Peter. THE LIFE AND LETTERS OF HUGH MILLER. 2 vols. London: Strahan, 1871.

1342 Mackenzie, William Mackay. HUGH MILLER: A CRITICAL STUDY. London: Hodder and Stoughton, 1905.

Robert Chambers (1802-71)

Robert Chambers began business as a bookseller in Edinburgh in 1818, and later joined his older brother, William, in launching CHAMBERS'S JOURNAL, to which he contributed essays "familiar and humorous," and in founding the publishing firm of W. and R. Chambers. Robert wrote voluminously for the rapidly growing public of new readers. In his VESTIGES OF THE NATURAL HISTORY OF CREATION, he anticipated the theories of Darwin by arguing the case for evolution.

1343 TRADITIONS OF EDINBURGH. 1824.

1344 TRADITIONS OF EDINBURGH. Illus. James Riddel. Introd. C.E.S. Chambers. Edinburgh: Chambers, 1912; 1967.

1345 THE POPULAR RHYMES OF SCOTLAND. 1826; rev. 1870; rpt. Detroit: Singing Tree Press, Gale Research Co., 1969.

1346 HISTORY OF THE REBELLION IN SCOTLAND IN 1745-46. 1827.

1347 THE PICTURE OF SCOTLAND. 1827.

1348 LIFE OF SIR WALTER SCOTT. 1832.

1349 A BIOGRAPHICAL DICTIONARY OF EMINENT SCOTSMEN. 1832-35.

1350 VESTIGES OF THE NATURAL HISTORY OF CREATION. 1844.

1351 CYCLOPAEDIA OF ENGLISH LITERATURE. 1844.

1352 LIFE AND WORKS OF ROBERT BURNS. 1851.

1353 DOMESTIC ANNALS OF SCOTLAND. 1858-61.

1354 THE BOOK OF DAYS: A MISCELLANY OF POPULAR ANTIQUITIES. 1862-64.

BIOGRAPHY AND CRITICISM

1355 Chambers, William. MEMOIR OF ROBERT CHAMBERS, WITH AUTO-BIOGRAPHIC REMINISCENCES OF WILLIAM CHAMBERS. Edinburgh, 1872; 13th ed. with suppl. chapter, Edinburgh: Chambers, 1884.

1356 Cruse, Amy. THE VICTORIANS AND THEIR BOOKS. London: Allen and Unwin, 1935.

1357 Lehmann, John. ANCESTORS AND FRIENDS. London: Eyre and Spottiswoode, 1962.

John Mackay Wilson (1804-35)

Wilson edited and was also a contributor to the long-running series, TALES OF THE BORDERS, originally issued in weekly numbers and continued after Wilson's death by Alexander Leighton (1800-1874). The best of the stories are still reprinted in anthologies.

1358 TALES OF THE BORDERS. 6 vols. Edinburgh, 1835-40; new ed. rev. Alexander Leighton. 20 vols. Edinburgh: W.P. Nimmo, 1857-59.

There have been many subsequent editions and selections.

Alicia Ann Spottiswoode, Lady John Scott (1810-1900)

A poet and song writer, remembered for a version of "Annie Laurie."

1359 SONGS AND VERSES. Edinburgh: David Douglas, 1904.

BIOGRAPHY AND CRITICISM

1360 Warrender, Margaret. "Preface." In SONGS AND VERSES, by Lady
John Scott. Edinburgh: David Douglas, 1904, pp. ix-lxiv.

Samuel Smiles (1812-1904)

Smiles was a doctor who turned journalist and biographer, writing the lives of
a number of successful self-taught engineers, business men, and industrialists.
His SELF-HELP was immensely popular.

1361 SELF-HELP, WITH ILLUSTRATIONS OF CHARACTER AND CONDUCT.
1859.

1362 SELF-HELP, WITH ILLUSTRATIONS OF CHARACTER AND CONDUCT.
New ed., introd. Asa Briggs. London: John Murray, 1958.

1363 LIVES OF THE ENGINEERS. 1861.

1364 CHARACTER. 1871.

1365 DUTY. 1880.

1366 AUTOBIOGRAPHY. Ed. Thomas Mackay. 1905.

BIOGRAPHY AND CRITICISM

1367 Smiles, Aileen. SAMUEL SMILES AND HIS SURROUNDINGS. London:
Robert Hale, 1956.

1368 Cockshut, Anthony O.J. "Smiles as Biographer." In his TRUTH TO LIFE.
London: Collins, 1974, pp. 105-24.

William Edmondstoune Aytoun (1813-65)

Aytoun, an advocate, was appointed professor of rhetoric at Edinburgh University in 1845. He was a frequent and versatile contributor to BLACKWOOD'S
MAGAZINE.

1369 POLAND, HOMER, AND OTHER POEMS. 1832.

1370 THE LIFE AND TIMES OF RICHARD THE FIRST, KING OF ENGLAND.
1840.

1371 THE BOOK OF BALLADS [by "Bon Gaultier"]. 1845.

>In collaboration with Theodore Martin, who was to be Aytoun's biographer.

1372 LAYS OF THE SCOTTISH CAVALIERS. 1849.

1373 FIRMILIAN: A SPASMODIC TRAGEDY. 1854.

1374 BOTHWELL: A POEM IN SIX PARTS. 1856.

1375 THE GLENMUTCHKIN RAILWAY. 1858.

1376 POEMS AND BALLADS OF GOETHE. 1859.

>Translated with Theodore Martin.

1377 NORMAN SINCLAIR: A NOVEL. 1861.

For Aytoun's contributions to BLACKWOOD'S MAGAZINE, see the WELLESLEY INDEX (838).

1378 STORIES AND VERSE. Ed. William Lindsay Renwick. Edinburgh: Edinburgh University Press, 1964.

BIOGRAPHY AND CRITICISM

1379 Martin, Theodore. MEMOIR OF W.E. AYTOUN. Edinburgh: Blackwood, 1867.

1380 Frykman, Erik. WILLIAM EDMONDSTOUNE AYTOUN: PIONEER PROFESSOR OF ENGLISH AT EDINBURGH. Gothenburg, 1963.

1381 Weinstein, Mark A. WILLIAM EDMONDSTOUNE AYTOUN AND THE SPASMODIC CONTROVERSY. New Haven: Yale University Press, 1968.

James Grant (1822-87)

After some years of military service, Grant produced a long series of novels, many with an army background, and a number of historical works. The NCBEL lists sixty-eight titles from 1838 to 1888. Only a selection is given here.

1382 THE ROMANCE OF WAR. 1846-47.

1383 ADVENTURES OF AN AIDE-DE-CAMP. 1848.

1384 THE SCOTTISH CAVALIER: AN HISTORICAL ROMANCE. 1850.

1385 BOTHWELL, OR THE DAYS OF MARY, QUEEN OF SCOTS. 1854.

1386 PHILIP ROLLO, OR THE SCOTTISH MUSKETEERS. 1854.

1387 THE YELLOW FRIGATE, OR THE THREE SISTERS. 1855.

> The novel by which Grant is remembered, at least locally, if he is remembered at all.

1388 HARRY OGILVIE, OR THE BLACK DRAGOONS. 1856.

1389 THE HIGHLANDERS OF GLEN ORA. 1857.

1390 HOLLYWOOD HALL: A TALE OF 1715. 1859.

1391 MARY OF LORRAINE: AN HISTORICAL ROMANCE. 1860.

1392 THE CAPTAIN OF THE GUARD. 1862.

1393 SECOND TO NONE: A MILITARY ROMANCE. 1864.

1394 OLD AND NEW EDINBURGH. 1880-83.

> A history of his native town.

BIOGRAPHY AND CRITICISM

1395 Ellis, Stewart M. "James Grant." In his MAINLY VICTORIAN. London: Hutchinson, [1925], pp. 108-12.

1396 Horsburgh, A. "James Grant: Edinburgh's Novelist of War." JOURNAL OF THE SOCIETY FOR ARMY HISTORICAL RESEARCH, 53 (Spring 1975), 48-53.

George MacDonald (1824-1905)

George MacDonald was a Congregational minister who turned to literature. His earlier novels, realistically set in his native Aberdeenshire, were greatly admired, but later he became better known for his charming and original children's books and allegorical fantasies, which influenced C.S. Lewis, among others. More recently, there has been a revival of interest in his Scottish novels.

1397 WITHIN AND WITHOUT: A POEM. 1855.

1398 POEMS. 1857.

1399 PHANTASTES: A FAERIE ROMANCE FOR MEN AND WOMEN. 1858.

1400 DAVID ELGINBROD. 1863.

1401 ALEC FORBES OF HOWGLEN. 1865.

1402 ANNALS OF A QUIET NEIGHBOURHOOD. 1867.

1403 ROBERT FALCONER. 1868.

1404 AT THE BACK OF THE NORTH WIND. 1871.

1405 RANALD BANNERMAN'S BOYHOOD. 1871.

1406 THE PRINCESS AND THE GOBLIN. 1872.

1407 GUTTA PERCHA WILLIE: THE WORKING GENIUS. 1873.

1408 MALCOLM. 1875.

1409 THE MARQUIS OF LOSSIE. 1877.

1410 SIR GIBBIE. 1879.

1411 THE DIARY OF AN OLD SOUL. 1880.

1412 CASTLE WARLOCK: A HOMELY ROMANCE. 1882.

1413 DONALD GRANT. 1883.

1414 THE PRINCESS AND CURDIE. 1883.

1415 WHAT'S MINE'S MINE. 1886.

1416 THE ELECT LADY. 1888.

1417 HEATHER AND SNOW. 1893.

1418 POETICAL WORKS. 1893.

1419 LILITH: A ROMANCE. 1895.

1420 GEORGE MacDONALD: AN ANTHOLOGY. Ed. Clive Staples Lewis. London: Geoffrey Bles, 1946.

1421 THE VISIONARY NOVELS. Ed. Anne Fremantle. Introd. Wystan Hugh Auden. New York: Noonday Press, 1954.

   Contains PHANTASTES and LILITH.

1422 PHANTASTES AND LILITH. Introd. Clive Staples Lewis. London: Gollancz, 1962.

BIOGRAPHY AND CRITICISM

1423 MacDonald, Greville. GEORGE MacDONALD AND HIS WIFE. London: Allen and Unwin, 1924.

1424 Wolff, Robert Lee. THE GOLDEN KEY: A STUDY OF THE FICTION OF GEORGE MacDONALD. New Haven: Yale University Press, 1961.

1425 Reis, Richard H. GEORGE MacDONALD. New York: Twayne, 1972.

1426 Manlove, Colin. MODERN FANTASY: FIVE STUDIES. Cambridge: Cambridge University Press, 1975.

   Considers MacDonald, along with Charles Kingsley, C.S. Lewis, J.R.R. Tolkien, and Mervyn Peake.

1427 Lochhead, Marion. THE RENAISSANCE OF WONDER IN CHILDREN'S LITERATURE. Edinburgh: Canongate, 1977.

1428 Manlove, Colin. "George MacDonald's Early Scottish Novels." In NINETEENTH-CENTURY SCOTTISH FICTION: CRITICAL ESSAYS. Ed. Ian Campbell. Manchester: Carcanet New Press, 1979, pp. 68-88.

BIBLIOGRAPHY

1429 Bulloch, John Malcolm. A CENTENNIAL BIBLIOGRAPHY OF GEORGE MacDONALD. Aberdeen: Aberdeen University Press, 1925.

R[obert] M[ichael] Ballantyne (1825-94)

As a young man R.M. Ballantyne worked in Canada for the Hudson's Bay Company. He published a rough diary of these years and drew on the same experience for the first of his long series of boys' adventure stories. Altogether, he wrote more than a hundred books: only a selection of the better known is listed here.

1430 HUDSON'S BAY, OR EVERYDAY LIFE IN THE WILDS OF NORTH AMERICA. Edinburgh: Blackwood, 1848.

1431 SNOWFLAKES AND SUNBEAMS, OR THE YOUNG FUR TRADERS. 1856.

1432 UNGAVA: A TALE OF ESQUIMAUX-LAND. 1858.

1433 MARTIN RATTLER, OR A BOY'S ADVENTURES IN THE FORESTS OF BRAZIL. 1858.

1434 THE CORAL ISLAND. 1858.

1435 THE WORLD OF ICE. 1860.

1436 THE DOG CRUSOE AND HIS MASTER. 1861.

1437 THE GORILLA HUNTERS. 1861.

1438 THE LIFEBOAT. 1864.

1439 THE LIGHTHOUSE. 1865.

1440 ERLING THE BOLD: A TALE OF THE NORSE SEA-KINGS. 1869.

1441 THE IRON HORSE, OR LIFE ON THE LINE. 1871.

1442 PERSONAL REMINISCENCES IN BOOK-MAKING. London: Nisbet, 1893.

BIOGRAPHY AND CRITICISM

1443 Osborne, Edgar. "Ballantyne the Pioneer." JUNIOR BOOKSHELF, 8 (1944), 6-11.

1444 Quayle, Eric. BALLANTYNE THE BRAVE: A VICTORIAN WRITER AND HIS FAMILY. London: Hart-Davis, 1967.

BIBLIOGRAPHY

1445 Quayle, Eric. R.M. BALLANTYNE: A BIBLIOGRAPHY OF FIRST EDI-
TIONS. London: Dawsons, 1968.

William Alexander (1826-94)

Alexander was a farm boy and ploughman. After an accident in which he lost
a leg, he turned to journalism and eventually became editor of the ABERDEEN
FREE PRESS. He writes in a rich Buchan Scots.

1446 JOHNNY GIBB OF GUSHETNEUK IN THE PARISH OF PYKETILLIM,
WITH GLIMPSES OF THE PARISH POLITICS ABOUT A.D. 1843. 1871;
illus. George Reid, Edinburgh: David Douglas, 1880.

1447 SKETCHES OF LIFE AMONG MY AIN FOLK. Edinburgh: David Douglas, 1875.

1448 NOTES AND SKETCHES ILLUSTRATIVE OF NORTHERN RURAL LIFE IN
THE EIGHTEENTH CENTURY. Edinburgh: David Douglas, 1877.

1449 TWENTY-FIVE YEARS: A PERSONAL RETROSPECT. Aberdeen, 1878.

BIOGRAPHY AND CRITICISM

1450 Carter, Ian. "'To Roose the Countra fae the Caul' Morality o' a Deid
Moderation': William Alexander and JOHNNY GIBB OF GUSHETNEUK."
NORTHERN SCOTLAND, 2 (1976-77), 145-62.

Margaret Oliphant (1828-97)

Over a period of fifty years, Mrs. Oliphant published nearly a hundred novels
and historical and biographical studies and wrote more than two hundred articles
and stories for BLACKWOOD'S MAGAZINE. She has been described as "a
George Eliot with talent instead of genius," but that judgment scarcely does
her justice. She is rather sadly neglected.

1451 PASSAGES IN THE LIFE OF MRS. MARGARET MAITLAND OF SUNNY-
SIDE. 1849.

1452 CALEB FIELD: A TALE OF THE PURITANS. 1851.

1453 MERKLAND: A STORY OF SCOTTISH LIFE. 1851.

1454 MEMOIRS AND RESOLUTIONS OF ADAM GRAEME OF MOSSGRAY. 1852.

1455 KATIE STEWART: A TRUE STORY. 1853.

1456 HARRY MUIR: A STORY OF SCOTTISH LIFE. 1853.

1457 MAGDALEN HEPBURN: A STORY OF THE SCOTTISH REFORMATION. 1854.

1458 THE QUIET HEART: A STORY. 1854.

1459 LILLIESLEAF, BEING A CONCLUDING SERIES OF PASSAGES IN THE LIFE OF MRS. MARGARET MAITLAND. 1855.

1460 THE LAIRD OF NORLAW: A SCOTTISH STORY. 1858.

1461 SALEM CHAPEL. 1863.
   Chronicles of Carlingford.

1462 THE RECTOR AND THE DOCTOR'S FAMILY. 1863.
   Chronicles of Carlingford.

1463 THE PERPETUAL CURATE. 1864.
   Chronicles of Carlingford.

1464 MISS MARJORIBANKS. 1866.
   Chronicles of Carlingford.

1465 MISS MARJORIBANKS. Introd. Queenie D. Leavis. London: Chatto and Windus (Zodiac Press), 1969.

1466 THE BROWNLOWS. 1868.

1467 THE MINISTER'S WIFE. 1869.

1468 THE STORY OF VALENTINE AND HIS BROTHER. 1875.

1469 PHOEBE JUNIOR: A LAST CHRONICLE OF CARLINGFORD. 1876.

1470 THE PRIMROSE PATH: A CHAPTER IN THE ANNALS OF THE KINGDOM OF FIFE. 1878.

1471 A BELEAGUERED CITY. 1880.

1472 SHERIDAN. 1883.

A volume in the English Men of Letters series.

1473 THE LADIES LINDORES. 1883.

1474 EFFIE OGILVIE. 1886.

1475 KIRSTEEN: A STORY OF A SCOTTISH FAMILY SEVENTY YEARS AGO. 1890.

1476 AUTOBIOGRAPHY AND LETTERS. 1899; rpt. introd. Queenie D. Leavis. Leicester: Leicester University Press, 1974.

BIOGRAPHY AND CRITICISM

1477 Colby, Vineta, and Robert Colby. THE EQUIVOCAL VIRTUE: MRS. OLIPHANT AND THE VICTORIAN LITERARY MARKET PLACE. Hamden, Conn.: Archon Books, 1966.

1478 Cunningham, Valentine. "Mrs. Oliphant and the Tradition." In her EVERY-WHERE SPOKEN AGAINST: DISSENT IN THE VICTORIAN NOVEL. Oxford: Clarendon Press, 1975, pp. 231-48.

1479 Colby, Robert, and Vineta Colby. "Mrs. Oliphant's Scotland: The Romance of Reality." In NINETEENTH-CENTURY SCOTTISH FICTION: CRITICAL ESSAYS. Ed. Ian Campbell. Manchester: Carcanet New Press, 1979, pp. 89-104.

Alexander Smith (1830-67)

Smith, who became secretary of Edinburgh University in 1854, was a poet, essayist, and journalist. As a poet, he belonged to the group satirized by Aytoun as the "spasmodic" school.

1480 POEMS. 1853.

1481 CITY POEMS. 1857.

1482 EDWIN OF DEIRA. 1861.

1483 DREAMTHORP: A BOOK OF ESSAYS. 1863; ed. Hugh Walker. World's Classics. London: OUP, 1914.

1484 A SUMMER IN SKYE. 1865; ed. Lauchlan Maclean Watt. London: Routledge, 1907; ed. William Forbes Gray. Edinburgh: Nimmo, Hay, 1912.

1485 ALFRED HAGART'S HOUSEHOLD. 1866.

A novel.

1486 MISS OONA McQUARRIE. 1866.

A novel.

1487 LAST LEAVES: SKETCHES AND CRITICISMS. Ed. with memoir by Patrick P. Alexander. Edinburgh: W.P. Nimmo, 1868.

1488 POETICAL WORKS. Ed. William Sinclair. Edinburgh: W.P. Nimmo, 1909.

BIOGRAPHY AND CRITICISM

1489 Brisbane, Thomas. THE EARLY YEARS OF ALEXANDER SMITH, POET AND ESSAYIST. London: Hodder and Stoughton, 1869.

1490 Scott, Mary Jane W. "Alexander Smith: Poet of Victorian Scotland." SSL, 14 (1979), 98-111.

William McGonagall (1830-1902)

McGonagall has been called "the only truly memorable bad poet." He was sublimely unconscious of the bathos of his pedestrian and prosaic vocabulary. The one poetic necessity in his versification was that his lines should rhyme, eventually and however ludicrously, and there is indeed a curious fascination in the absolute flatness of his verse, which is still, as David Daiches points out, "savoured by connoisseurs of doggerel." He published his first book of verse in 1877, and the selection he entitled POETIC GEMS was first issued in two parts in 1890.

1491 WM. McGONAGALL: A LIBRARY OMNIBUS. Dundee: Winter; London: Duckworth, 1969.

A collected reissue of POETIC GEMS, MORE POETIC GEMS, and LAST POETIC GEMS.

BIOGRAPHY AND CRITICISM

1492 MacDiarmid, Hugh. "The Great McGonagall." In his SCOTTISH ECCENTRICS. London: Routledge, 1936, pp. 57-75.

1493 Smith, James L. "William McGonagall and the Poet Laureate." SSL, 7 (1969-70), 21-28.

1494 Henderson, Hamish. "McGonagall and the Irish Question." NEW EDINBURGH REVIEW, no. 14 (August-September 1971), pp. 38-44.

1495 Phillips, David. NO POETS' CORNER IN THE ABBEY: THE DRAMATIC STORY OF WILLIAM McGONAGALL. Dundee: Winter; London: Duckworth, 1971.

James Thomson ("B.V.") (1834-92)

James Thomson, born in Port Glasgow, was orphaned as a child in London. He became a teacher and later an army schoolmaster, but was discharged in 1862 for a trivial breach of discipline. He contributed poetry and essays to Charles Bradlaugh's NATIONAL REFORMER. His long poem, "The City of Dreadful Night," first published there in installments in 1874, expresses a profound pessimism. He lived his last years, alone and melancholy, in London, where he died in hospital, a victim of despair, alcohol and drugs.

His pseudonym, Bysshe Vanolis (B.V.), consists of Shelley's middle name and an anagram of Novalis, the pseudonym of Friedrich von Hardenberg, the German Romantic poet who died in 1801 in his twenty-ninth year.

1496 THE CITY OF DREADFUL NIGHT, AND OTHER POEMS. 1880.

1497 VANE'S STORY, AND OTHER POEMS. 1881.

1498 ESSAYS AND FANTASIES. 1881.

1499 A VOICE FROM THE NILE, AND OTHER POEMS. 1884.

1500 SHELLEY: A POEM, WITH OTHER WRITINGS RELATING TO SHELLEY. 1884.

1501 POETICAL WORKS. Ed. Bertram Dobell. 1895.

1502 BIOGRAPHICAL AND CRITICAL STUDIES. Ed. Bertram Dobell. 1896.

1503 POEMS AND SOME LETTERS. Ed. Anne Ridler. London: Centaur Press; Carbondale: Southern Illinois University Press, 1963.

1504 THE SPEEDY EXTINCTION OF EVIL AND MISERY: SELECTED PROSE OF JAMES THOMSON. Ed. William David Schaefer. Berkeley and Los Angeles: University of California Press, 1967.

BIOGRAPHY AND CRITICISM

1505 Salt, Henry S. THE LIFE OF JAMES THOMSON (B.V.). 1889; rev.
ed. London: Watts, 1914.

1506 Dobell, Bertram. THE LAUREATE OF PESSIMISM. London: Privately
Printed, 1910.

1507 Walker, Imogene B. JAMES THOMSON (B.V.): A CRITICAL STUDY.
Ithaca: Cornell University Press, 1950.

Includes a bibliography.

1508 Schaefer, William David. JAMES THOMSON: BEYOND "THE CITY."
Berkeley and Los Angeles: University of California Press, 1965.

1509 Campbell, Ian. "'And I Burn Too': Thomson's CITY OF DREADFUL
NIGHT." VICTORIAN POETRY, 16 (1978), 123-33.

Robert Williams Buchanan (1841-1901)

Robert Buchanan, the son of a Scottish socialist, was born in Staffordshire, but
brought up and educated in Glasgow. In 1860 he set out, with his friend David
Gray, for London, where he had some success with his poetry and one of his plays,
ALONE IN LONDON (performed 1885; unpublished), but his novels (there are
more than twenty of them) are largely forgotten. He is perhaps best known for
the essay he published in the CONTEMPORARY REVIEW, October 1871, "The
Fleshly School of Poetry," attacking Rossetti and the Pre-Raphaelites (see 1517).

1510 UNDERTONES. 1863.

1511 IDYLLS AND LEGENDS OF INVERBURN. 1865.

1512 LONDON POEMS. 1866.

1513 NORTH COAST AND OTHER POEMS. 1868.

1514 DAVID GRAY, AND OTHER ESSAYS, CHIEFLY ON POETRY. 1868.

1515 THE DRAMA OF KINGS. 1871.

Three plays: BUONAPARTE, NAPOLEON FALLEN, and THE
TEUTON AGAINST PARIS. It has been suggested that these
plays, which may have been derived from Victor Hugo's LA
LÉGENDE DES SIÈCLES (1859), are the immediate source of
Thomas Hardy's DYNASTS (1903-08). (See Hoxie N. Fairchild,

"The Immediate Source of THE DYNASTS," PMLA, 67 [1952], 43–64; and John A. Cassidy, "The Original Source of Hardy's DYNASTS," PMLA, 69 [1954], 1085–1100).

1516 THE LAND OF LORNE. 1871.

1517 THE FLESHLY SCHOOL OF POETRY AND OTHER PHENOMENA OF THE DAY. 1872.

1518 THE SHADOW OF THE SWORD. 1876.

A novel.

1519 GOD AND THE MAN. 1881.

A novel.

1520 BALLADS OF LIFE, LOVE AND HUMOUR. 1882.

1521 THE OUTCAST: A RHYME FOR THE TIME. 1891.

1522 THE WANDERING JEW: A CHRISTMAS CAROL. 1893.

1523 COMPLETE POETICAL WORKS. 1901.

BIOGRAPHY AND CRITICISM

1524 Jay, Harriet. ROBERT BUCHANAN: SOME ACCOUNT OF HIS LIFE, HIS LIFE'S WORK, AND HIS LITERARY FRIENDSHIPS. London: T. Fisher Unwin, 1903.

A biography "suffused with adulation."

1525 Cassidy, John A. ROBERT W. BUCHANAN. New York: Twayne, 1974.

William Black (1841-98)

William Black, born in Glasgow, studied art, but became a journalist and a popular and prolific writer of romantic novels.

1526 IN SILK ATTIRE. 1869.

1527 KILMENY. 1870.

1528 A DAUGHTER OF HETH. 1871.

1529 THE STRANGE ADVENTURES OF A PHAETON. 1872.

1530 A PRINCESS OF THULE. 1874.

1531 THE MAID OF KILLEENA, AND OTHER STORIES. 1874.

1532 MACLEOD OF DARE. 1878.

1533 OLIVER GOLDSMITH. 1878.
     A volume in the English Men of Letters series.

1534 WHITE WINGS: A YACHTING ROMANCE. 1880.

1535 WHITE HEATHER. 1885.

1536 THE WISE WOMEN OF INVERNESS, AND OTHER MISCELLANIES. 1885.

1537 IN FAR LOCHABER. 1888.

1538 DONALD ROSS OF HEIMRA. 1891.

1539 WILD EELIN: HER ESCAPADES, ADVENTURES AND BITTER SORROWS. 1898.

1540 NOVELS. New and rev. ed. 28 vols. London: Sampson Low, 1892-98.

BIOGRAPHY AND CRITICISM

1541 Reid, Thomas Wemyss. WILLIAM BLACK, NOVELIST: A BIOGRAPHY. London: Cassell, 1902.

Andrew Lang (1844-1912)

Andrew Lang, Stevenson's "dear Andrew, with the brindled hair," was born in Selkirk and educated in Edinburgh, St. Andrews, Glasgow, and Oxford. He soon won distinction as a man of letters of great versatility: historian, scholar and translator, poet, novelist, and student of philosophy and folklore. He is perhaps most often remembered now for the series of twelve rainbow-colored fairy books he edited, beginning with THE BLUE FAIRY BOOK in 1889.

1542 BALLADS AND LYRICS OF OLD FRANCE. 1872.

1543 THE ODYSSEY OF HOMER, DONE INTO ENGLISH PROSE. With S.H. Butcher. 1879.

1544 THEOCRITUS, BION, AND MOSCHUS, RENDERED INTO ENGLISH PROSE. 1880.

1545 BALLADES IN BLUE CHINA. 1880; 1881.

1546 THE LIBRARY. 1881.

1547 HELEN OF TROY. 1882.

1548 THE ILIAD OF HOMER, DONE INTO ENGLISH PROSE. With Walter Leaf and Ernest Myers. 1883.

1549 CUSTOM AND MYTH. 1884.

1550 RHYMES À LA MODE. 1884.

1551 LETTERS TO DEAD AUTHORS. 1886.

1552 BOOKS AND BOOKMEN. 1886.

1553 MYTH, RITUAL AND RELIGION. 1887.

1554 GRASS OF PARNASSUS: RHYMES OLD AND NEW. 1888.

1555 THE GOLD OF FAIRNILEE. 1888.

For young people.

1556 THE BLUE FAIRY BOOK. 1889.

The first of the series of twelve FAIRY BOOKS of different colors, 1889-1910. See 1574.

1557 THE WORLD'S DESIRE. 1890.

A novel; with Sir Henry Rider Haggard.

1558 ST. ANDREWS. 1893; ed. George Herbert Bushnell. St. Andrews: Henderson, 1951.

1559 A MONK OF FIFE. 1896.

A novel.

1560 PICKLE⸴THE SPY, OR THE INCOGNITO OF PRINCE CHARLES. 1897.

1561 THE COMPANIONS OF PICKLE. 1898.

1562 PARSON KELLY. 1899.
   A novel; with Alfred E.W. Mason.

1563 THE HOMERIC HYMNS: A NEW PROSE TRANSLATION. 1899.

1564 PRINCE CHARLES EDWARD. 1900.

1565 A HISTORY OF SCOTLAND. 4 vols. 1900-1907.

1566 MAGIC AND RELIGION. 1901.

1567 THE BOOK OF ROMANCE. 1902.
   For young people.

1568 JAMES VI AND THE GOWRIE MYSTERY. 1902.

1569 HISTORICAL MYSTERIES. 1904.

1570 ADVENTURES AMONG BOOKS. 1905.

1571 TALES OF TROY AND GREECE. 1907.
   For young people.

1572 THE MAID OF FRANCE: THE LIFE AND DEATH OF JEANNE D'ARC.
   1908.

1573 HIGHWAYS AND BYWAYS IN THE BORDER. 1913.
   With Jean Lang.

SELECTIONS

1574 FIFTY FAVOURITE FAIRY TALES, CHOSEN FROM THE COLOUR FAIRY
   BOOKS OF ANDREW LANG. Ed. Kathleen M. Lines. London: Nonesuch Library, 1963; Bodley Head, 1973.

BIOGRAPHY AND CRITICISM

1575 Elwin, Malcolm. OLD GODS FALLING. London: Collins, 1939.

> See in particular chapter 6, "Andrew Lang and Other Critics," pages 182-202.

1576 Green, Roger Lancelyn. ANDREW LANG: A CRITICAL BIOGRAPHY. Leicester: Edmund Ward, 1946.

> Includes a short-title bibliography of Lang's writings.

1577 Webster, Adam Blyth, ed. CONCERNING ANDREW LANG: BEING THE LANG LECTURES, 1927-37. Oxford: Clarendon Press, 1949.

1578 Green, Roger Lancelyn. ANDREW LANG. London: Bodley Head, 1962.

1579 Langstaff, Eleanor DeS. ANDREW LANG. Boston: Twayne, 1978.

J[ames] Logie Robertson (1846-1922)
"Hugh Haliburton"

Robertson was born in Milnathort in Kinross-shire and was for many years an English teacher in Edinburgh. Under his own name he edited collected editions of many English and Scottish poets, but for much of his original writing he adopted the persona of "Hugh Haliburton," who is represented as a shepherd of the Ochil Hills.

1580 HORACE IN HOMESPUN: A SERIES OF SCOTTISH PASTORALS. 1886.

1581 "FOR PUIR AULD SCOTLAND'S SAKE." 1887.

> Essays.

1582 IN SCOTTISH FIELDS. 1890.

> Essays.

1583 OCHIL IDYLLS AND OTHER POEMS. 1891.

1584 FURTH IN FIELD. 1895.

> Essays.

1585 HORACE IN HOMESPUN, AND OTHER SCOTS POEMS. Memorial volume. Edinburgh: Blackwood, 1925.

> Includes a six-page memoir by his wife, Janet Logie Robertson.

Robert Louis Stevenson (1850-94)

Stevenson's long fight against ill-health and his wanderings in search of a congenial climate are well known. He is an amazingly versatile novelist, essayist, and poet, with a graceful prose style, and in WEIR OF HERMISTON he left unfinished a masterpiece of tremendous power and character.

1586 AN INLAND VOYAGE. 1878.

1587 EDINBURGH: PICTURESQUE NOTES. 1879.

1588 TRAVELS WITH A DONKEY IN THE CEVENNES. 1879.

1589 VIRGINIBUS PUERISQUE AND OTHER PAPERS. 1881.

1590 FAMILIAR STUDIES OF MEN AND BOOKS. 1882.

1591 THE NEW ARABIAN NIGHTS. 1882.

1592 THE SILVERADO SQUATTERS: SKETCHES FROM A CALIFORNIAN MOUNTAIN. 1883.

1593 TREASURE ISLAND. 1883.
    First serialized, as THE SEA-COOK, in YOUNG FOLKS, 1881-82.

1594 A CHILD'S GARDEN OF VERSES. 1885.

1595 PRINCE OTTO: A ROMANCE. 1885.

1596 THE STRANGE CASE OF DR. JEKYLL AND MR. HYDE. 1886.

1597 KIDNAPPED. 1886.

1598 THE MERRY MEN, AND OTHER TALES AND FABLES. 1887.
    Collected from the CORNHILL and other magazines.

1599 UNDERWOODS. 1887.
    Poems in English and Scots.

1600 MEMORIES AND PORTRAITS. 1887.
    Mainly reprinted from periodicals.

1601 THE BLACK ARROW: A TALE OF THE TWO ROSES. 1888.

1602 THE MASTER OF BALLANTRAE: A WINTER'S TALE. 1889.

1603 THE WRONG BOX. 1889.
  With Lloyd Osbourne.

1604 ACROSS THE PLAINS, WITH OTHER MEMORIES AND ESSAYS. 1892.

1605 THREE PLAYS: DEACON BRODIE, BEAU AUSTIN, ADMIRAL GUINEA. 1892.
  With William Ernest Henley.

1606 THE WRECKER. 1892.
  With Lloyd Osbourne.

1607 ISLAND NIGHTS' ENTERTAINMENTS. 1893.

1608 CATRIONA: A SEQUEL TO KIDNAPPED. 1893.

1609 THE EBB-TIDE: A TRIO AND A QUARTETTE. 1894.
  With Lloyd Osbourne.

1610 SONGS OF TRAVEL, AND OTHER VERSES. 1895.

1611 WEIR OF HERMISTON: AN UNFINISHED ROMANCE. 1896.

1612 ST. IVES: BEING THE ADVENTURES OF A FRENCH PRISONER IN ENG-
  LAND. 1897.
  Unfinished, but completed by A.T. Quiller Couch.

COLLECTIONS AND SELECTIONS

1613 WORKS. Edinburgh Edition. Ed. Sidney Colvin. 28 vols. London:
  Chatto and Windus, 1894-98.

1614 WORKS. Vailima Edition. Ed. Lloyd Osbourne and Fanny Van de Grift
  Stevenson. 26 vols. London: Heinemann, 1922-23.

1615 WORKS. Tusitala Edition. 35 vols. London: Heinemann, 1923-24.
  The introductory essays by Lloyd Osbourne, Stevenson's stepson
  (and collaborator), are interesting and illuminating.

1616 FROM SCOTLAND TO SILVERADO. Ed. James D. Hart. Cambridge: Harvard University Press, 1966.

> Complete texts of THE AMATEUR EMIGRANT (1895) and THE SILVERADO SQUATTERS (1883), with some material previously unpublished.

1617 COLLECTED POEMS. Ed. Janet Adam Smith. 2nd ed. London: Hart-Davis, 1971.

1618 THE STRANGE CASE OF DR. JEKYLL AND MR. HYDE, AND OTHER STORIES. Ed. Jenni Calder. Harmondsworth: Penguin, 1979.

1619 WEIR OF HERMISTON, AND OTHER STORIES. Ed. Paul Binding. Harmondsworth: Penguin, 1979.

LETTERS

A definitive edition of Stevenson's letters is in preparation.

1620 THE LETTERS OF ROBERT LOUIS STEVENSON TO HIS FAMILY AND FRIENDS. Ed. Sidney Colvin. 4 vols. London: Methuen, 1911.

1621 HENRY JAMES AND ROBERT LOUIS STEVENSON: A RECORD OF FRIENDSHIP AND CRITICISM. Ed. Janet Adam Smith. London: Hart-Davis, 1948.

1622 R.L.S.: STEVENSON'S LETTERS TO CHARLES BAXTER. Ed. John DeLancey Ferguson and Marshall Waingrow. New Haven: Yale University Press, 1956; rpt. Port Washington: Kennikat Press, 1973.

BIOGRAPHY AND CRITICISM

1623 Balfour, Graham. THE LIFE OF ROBERT LOUIS STEVENSON. 2 vols. London: Methuen, 1901.

> The authorized biography, by Stevenson's cousin.

1624 Steuart, John A. ROBERT LOUIS STEVENSON, MAN AND WRITER: A CRITICAL BIOGRAPHY. 2 vols. London: Sampson Low, Marston, 1924.

1625 Daiches, David. ROBERT LOUIS STEVENSON. Glasgow: Maclellan; Norfolk: New Directions, 1947.

1626 Elwin, Malcolm. THE STRANGE CASE OF ROBERT LOUIS STEVENSON. London: Macdonald, 1950.

1627 Furnas, Joseph Chamberlain. VOYAGE TO WINDWARD: THE LIFE OF ROBERT LOUIS STEVENSON. New York: Sloane, 1951; London: Faber, 1952.

The standard modern biography.

1628 Caldwell, Elsie N. LAST WITNESS FOR ROBERT LOUIS STEVENSON. Norman: University of Oklahoma Press, 1960.

1629 Kiely, Robert. ROBERT LOUIS STEVENSON AND THE FICTION OF ADVENTURE. Cambridge: Harvard University Press, 1964.

1630 Eigner, Edwin M. ROBERT LOUIS STEVENSON AND ROMANTIC TRADITION. Princeton: Princeton University Press, 1966.

1631 Kilroy, James F. "Narrative Technique in THE MASTER OF BALLANTRAE." SSL, 5 (1967-68), 98-106.

1632 MacKay, Margaret. THE VIOLENT FRIEND: THE STORY OF MRS. ROBERT LOUIS STEVENSON, 1840-1914. New York: Doubleday, 1968; abridged ed., London: Dent, 1969.

1633 Eliott, N. "Robert Louis Stevenson and Scottish Literature." ENGLISH LITERATURE IN TRANSITION, 12 (1969), 79-85.

1634 Daiches, David. ROBERT LOUIS STEVENSON AND HIS WORLD. London: Thames and Hudson, 1973.

1635 Morgan, Edwin. "The Poetry of Robert Louis Stevenson." SLJ, 1 (1974), 29-44; rpt. in his ESSAYS, Cheadle: Carcanet New Press, 1974, pp. 135-49.

1636 Saposnik, Irving S. ROBERT LOUIS STEVENSON. New York: Twayne, 1974.

1637 Fowler, Alistair. "Parables of Adventure: The Debatable Novels of Robert Louis Stevenson." In NINETEENTH-CENTURY SCOTTISH FICTION: CRITICAL ESSAYS. Ed. Ian Campbell. Manchester: Carcanet New Press, 1979, pp. 105-29.

1638 Calder, Jenni. R.L.S.: A LIFE STUDY. London: Hamish Hamilton, 1980.

BIBLIOGRAPHY

1639 Prideaux, William Francis. A BIBLIOGRAPHY OF THE WORKS OF ROBERT LOUIS STEVENSON. New and rev. ed. London: Frank Hollings, 1917.

1640 McKay, George L. A STEVENSON LIBRARY. CATALOGUE OF A COL-
LECTION OF WRITINGS BY AND ABOUT ROBERT LOUIS STEVENSON
FORMED BY EDWIN J. BEINECKE. 6 vols. New Haven: Yale Uni-
versity Library, 1951-64.

1641 Swearingen, Roger G. "The Prose Writings of Robert Louis Stevenson:
An Index and Finding-List, 1850-81." SSL, 11 (1973-74), 178-96,
237-49.

"Ian Maclaren"
John Watson (1850-1907)

Brought up in Perth and Stirling and educated at Edinburgh University, John
Watson became a Free Church minister in Perthshire and Glasgow, before moving to a charge in Liverpool. The couthy sketches of Scottish village life
which he contributed to the BRITISH WEEKLY, a church paper founded and
edited by the Aberdonian, Robertson Nicoll, were immensely popular and
reached an even wider public when they were collected and published as BE-
SIDE THE BONNIE BRIER BUSH. (Hence the term "Kailyard" attached to
stories of this kind: see the note at 790.)

1642 BESIDE THE BONNIE BRIER BUSH. 1894; rpt. Edinburgh: Albyn Press,
1977.

1643 A DOCTOR OF THE OLD SCHOOL. 1895; rpt. Edinburgh: Albyn Press,
1977.

1644 THE DAYS OF AULD LANG SYNE. 1895; rpt. Edinburgh: Albyn Press,
1977.

1645 KATE CARNEGIE AND THOSE MINISTERS. 1896.

1646 AFTERWARDS, AND OTHER STORIES. 1898.

1647 YOUNG BARBARIANS. 1901.
    A partly autobiographical novel of school days in Perth.

1648 GRAHAM OF CLAVERHOUSE. 1908.

BIOGRAPHY AND CRITICISM

1649 Nicoll, Sir William Robertson. "IAN MACLAREN": A LIFE OF THE
REV. JOHN WATSON. London: Hodder and Stoughton, 1908.

1650 Blake, George. BARRIE AND THE KAILYARD SCHOOL. London: Arthur Barker, 1951.

1651 Anderson, [William] Eric [Kinloch]. "The Kailyard Revisited." In NINETEENTH-CENTURY SCOTTISH FICTION: CRITICAL ESSAYS. Ed. Ian Campbell. Manchester: Carcanet New Press, 1979, pp. 130-47.

R[obert] B[ontine] Cunninghame Graham (1852-1936)

See page 193.

Sir James George Frazer (1854-1941)

The noted anthropologist was born in Glasgow. THE GOLDEN BOUGH is a monumental study of man's early beliefs, religion, and culture; and a work of literature in its own right.

1652 THE GOLDEN BOUGH: A STUDY IN COMPARATIVE RELIGION. 1890; 1900; 3rd ed., rev. and enl. 12 vols. London: Macmillan, 1911-15.

Vols. 1-2. THE MAGIC ART AND THE EVOLUTION OF KINGS. 1911.
Vol. 3. TABOO AND THE PERILS OF THE SOUL. 1911.
Vol. 4. THE DYING GOD. 1911.
Vols. 5-6. ADONIS, ATTIS, OSIRIS. 1914.
Vols. 7-8. SPIRITS OF THE CORN AND THE WILD. 1912.
Vol. 9. THE SCAPEGOAT. 1913.
Vols.10-11.BALDER THE BEAUTIFUL. 1913.
Vol. 12. BIBLIOGRAPHY AND GENERAL INDEX. 1915.

1653 TOTEMISM AND EXOGAMY. 4 vols. 1910.

1654 THE BELIEF IN IMMORTALITY AND THE WORSHIP OF THE DEAD. 3 vols. 1913-24.

1655 FOLKLORE IN THE OLD TESTAMENT: STUDIES IN COMPARATIVE RELIGION, LEGEND AND LAW. 3 vols. 1918-19.

1656 THE MAGICAL ORIGIN OF KINGS. 1920.

1657 THE GOLDEN BOUGH. Abridged ed. 1922.

1658 FOLKLORE IN THE OLD TESTAMENT. Abridged ed. 1923.

1659 THE WORSHIP OF NATURE. 1926.

1660 THE GORGON'S HEAD, AND OTHER LITERARY PIECES. 1927.

1661 MAN, GOD AND IMMORTALITY: THOUGHTS ON HUMAN PROGRESS. 1927.

1662 MYTHS OF THE ORIGIN OF FIRE. 1930.

1663 GARNERED SHEAVES: ESSAYS, ADDRESSES AND REVIEWS. 1931.

1664 THE FEAR OF THE DEAD IN PRIMITIVE RELIGION. 3 vols. 1933-36.

1665 AFTERMATH: A SUPPLEMENT TO THE GOLDEN BOUGH. London: Macmillan, 1936.

BIOGRAPHY AND CRITICISM

1666 Hyman, Stanley E. THE TANGLED BANK: DARWIN, MARX, FRAZER AND FREUD AS IMAGINATIVE WRITERS. New York: Atheneum, 1962.

1667 Downie, Robert Angus. JAMES GEORGE FRAZER: THE PORTRAIT OF A SCHOLAR. London: Watts, 1940.

1668 _____. FRAZER AND THE GOLDEN BOUGH. London: Gollancz, 1970.

BIBLIOGRAPHY

1669 Besterman, Theodore. A BIBLIOGRAPHY OF SIR JAMES GEORGE FRAZER. London: Macmillan, 1934.

"Fiona Macleod"
William Sharp (1855-1905)

Sharp was born in Paisley, and spent his boyhood in the Western Isles. He settled in London in 1879, and under his own name edited several anthologies and wrote a number of books and articles, including poems, novels, boys' stories, and literary criticism, but he published his most distinctive work under the pseudonym of "Fiona Macleod," a supposed cousin, whose real identity he refused to reveal. "Her" Celtic tales and poems form part of the Celtic revival begun with W.B. Yeats's stories of THE CELTIC TWILIGHT (1893). Only the work of "Fiona Macleod" is listed here.

1670 PHARAIS: A ROMANCE OF THE ISLES. 1894.

1671 THE MOUNTAIN LOVERS. 1895.

1672 THE SIN EATER, AND OTHER TALES. 1895.

1673 THE WASHER OF THE FORD, AND OTHER LEGENDARY MORALITIES. 1896.

1674 GREEN FIRE: A ROMANCE. 1896.

1675 FROM THE HILLS OF DREAM: MOUNTAIN SONGS AND ISLAND RUNES. 1896; 1907.

1676 THE LAUGHTER OF PETERKIN. 1896.

1677 THE DOMINION OF DREAMS. 1899.

1678 THE HOUSE OF USNA: A DRAMA. 1903.

1679 THE WINGED DESTINY: STUDIES IN THE SPIRITUAL HISTORY OF THE GAEL. 1904.

1680 WHERE THE FOREST MURMURS: NATURE ESSAYS. 1906.

1681 THE IMMORTAL HOUR: A DRAMA. 1908.

1682 THE WRITINGS OF FIONA MACLEOD. 7 vols. London: Heinemann, 1909-10.

BIOGRAPHY AND CRITICISM

1683 Sharp, Elizabeth A. WILLIAM SHARP (FIONA MACLEOD): A MEMOIR. 2 vols. London: Heinemann, 1912.

1684 Alaya, Flavia. WILLIAM SHARP--"FIONA MACLEOD"--1855-1905. Cambridge: Harvard University Press, 1970.

1685 Halloran, William F. "William Sharp as Bard and Craftsman." VICTORIAN POETRY, 10 (1972), 57-78.

William Archer (1856-1924)

The translator and champion of Ibsen was born in Perth. He went to London in 1878, where he was active as a critic and dramatist. The first of Archer's translations from Ibsen, PILLARS OF SOCIETY, was published in 1888; the first to be performed was A DOLL'S HOUSE in 1889. The work of translation, revision, and editing occupied much of his time for nearly sixteen years.

1686 ENGLISH DRAMATISTS OF TODAY. 1882.

1687 HENRY IRVING, ACTOR AND MANAGER: A CRITICAL STUDY. 1883.

1688 ABOUT THE THEATRE: ESSAYS AND STUDIES. 1886.

1689 MASKS OR FACES? A STUDY IN THE PSYCHOLOGY OF ACTING. 1888.

1690 THE THEATRICAL "WORLD," 1893-97. 5 vols. 1894-98.

1691 POETS OF THE YOUNGER GENERATION. 1902.

1692 PLAYMAKING: A MANUAL OF CRAFTMANSHIP. 1912.

1693 THE GREEN GODDESS: A PLAY IN FOUR ACTS. 1921.

1694 THE OLD DRAMA AND THE NEW: AN ESSAY IN REVALUATION. 1923.

1695 WILLIAM ARCHER AS RATIONALIST: A COLLECTION OF HIS HETERODOX WRITINGS. Ed. J.M. Robertson. London: Watts, 1925.

1696 THREE PLAYS. London: Constable, 1927.

> There is a personal note by Bernard Shaw. The plays are MARTHA WASHINGTON, BEATRIZ-JUANA, and LIDIA.

BIOGRAPHY AND CRITICISM

1697 Parker, William Mathie. "Our Dramatic Mentor: William Archer." In his MODERN SCOTTISH WRITERS. Edinburgh: Hodge, 1917, pp. 163-94.

1698 Shaw, Bernard. "Archer." In his PEN PORTRAITS AND REVIEWS. London: Constable, 1931; 1932, pp. 1-30.

1699 Archer, Charles. WILLIAM ARCHER: LIFE, WORKS AND FRIENDSHIPS. London: Allen and Unwin, 1931.

1700 Schmid, Hans. THE DRAMATIC CRITICISM OF WILLIAM ARCHER. Bern: Francke, 1964.

James Pittendrigh Macgillivray (1856-1938)

See page 196.

John Davidson (1857-1909)

After teaching in a number of Scottish schools, Davidson went to London in 1890, where he published a moderately successful novel and made some reputation as a poet of city life. His later work is powerful but somber. He drowned himself near Penzance.

1701 BRUCE. 1886.

A verse play.

1702 SMITH: A TRAGEDY. 1888.

1703 PLAYS. 1889.

The plays are AN UNHISTORICAL PASTORAL, A ROMANTIC FARCE, and SCARAMOUCHE IN NAXOS.

1704 PERFERVID: THE CAREER OF NINIAN JAMIESON. 1890.

A novel.

1705 IN A MUSIC HALL. 1891.

Poems.

1706 FLEET STREET ECLOGUES. 1893; 1896.

1707 BALLADS AND SONGS. 1894.

1708 BAPTIST LAKE: A NOVEL. 1894.

1709 NEW BALLADS. 1897.

1710 THE LAST BALLAD, AND OTHER POEMS. 1899.

1711 SELF'S THE MAN: A TRAGI-COMEDY. 1901.

1712 THE TESTAMENT OF A VIVISECTOR. 1901.

1713 THE TESTAMENT OF A MAN FORBID. 1901.

1714 THE TESTAMENT OF AN EMPIRE-BUILDER. 1902.

1715 THE TESTAMENT OF A PRIME MINISTER. 1904.

1716 A QUEEN'S ROMANCE. 1904.
    A translation of Hugo's RUY BLAS.

1717 THE THEATROCRAT: A TRAGIC PLAY OF CHURCH AND STATE. 1905.

1718 GOD AND MAMMON. 1907.

1719 THE TESTAMENT OF JOHN DAVIDSON. 1908.

COLLECTIONS AND SELECTIONS

1720 POEMS AND BALLADS. Ed. Robert D. Macleod. London: Unicorn
    Press, 1959.

1721 JOHN DAVIDSON: A SELECTION OF HIS POEMS. Ed. Maurice Lind-
    say. Preface by Thomas Stearns Eliot. With an essay by Hugh Mac-
    Diarmid. London: Hutchinson, 1961.

1722 THE POEMS OF JOHN DAVIDSON. Ed. Andrew Turnbull. 2 vols.
    Edinburgh: Scottish Academic Press, 1973.

BIOGRAPHY AND CRITICISM

1723 Parker, William Mathie. "A Princely Decadent: John Davidson." In his
    MODERN SCOTTISH WRITERS. Edinburgh: Hodge, 1917, pp. 223-41.

1724 Macleod, Robert D. JOHN DAVIDSON: A STUDY IN PERSONALITY.
    Glasgow: Holmes, 1957.

1725 Townsend, James B. JOHN DAVIDSON: POET OF ARMAGEDDON.
    New Haven: Yale University Press, 1961.

1726 Peterson, Carroll V. JOHN DAVIDSON. New York: Twayne, 1972.

BIBLIOGRAPHY

1726a Stonehill, Charles A., and Helen W. Stonehill. "John Davidson." In their BIBLIOGRAPHIES OF MODERN AUTHORS. 2nd ser. London: John Castle, 1925, pp. 3-38.

Sir Arthur Conan Doyle (1859-1930)

Conan Doyle was born of Irish parentage in Edinburgh, where he studied medicine, working under Dr. Joseph Bell, who was in part the prototype of Sherlock Holmes. The famous detective first appeared in 1887, but became widely known only with the publication of his ADVENTURES in the STRAND Magazine, beginning in July 1891. Conan Doyle wrote many other novels and stories, including a number of scientific adventures in the manner of H.G. Wells. In his later years he became deeply interested in spiritualism.

1727 A STUDY IN SCARLET. 1888.

1728 MICAH CLARKE. 1889.

1729 THE SIGN OF FOUR. 1890.

1730 THE CAPTAIN OF THE POLESTAR, AND OTHER TALES. 1890.

1731 THE WHITE COMPANY. 1891.

1732 THE ADVENTURES OF SHERLOCK HOLMES. 1892.

1733 THE REFUGEES. 1893.

1734 THE MEMOIRS OF SHERLOCK HOLMES. 1894.

1735 ROUND THE RED LAMP: BEING FACTS AND FANCIES OF MEDICAL LIFE. 1894.

1736 THE STARK-MUNRO LETTERS. 1895.

1737 THE EXPLOITS OF BRIGADIER GERARD. 1896.

1738 RODNEY STONE. 1896.

1739 UNCLE BERNAC: A MEMORY OF THE EMPIRE. 1897.

1740 THE TRAGEDY OF THE KOROSKO. 1898.

1741 THE HOUND OF THE BASKERVILLES. 1902.

1742 ADVENTURES OF GERARD. 1903.

1743 THE RETURN OF SHERLOCK HOLMES. 1905.

1744 SIR NIGEL. 1906.

1745 ROUND THE FIRE STORIES. 1908.

1746 THE LOST WORLD. 1912.

1747 THE POISON BELT. 1913.

1748 THE VALLEY OF FEAR. 1915.

1749 HIS LAST BOW. 1917.

1750 MEMORIES AND ADVENTURES. 1924.
    Autobiography.

1751 THE HISTORY OF SPIRITUALISM. 1926.

1752 THE CASE-BOOK OF SHERLOCK HOLMES. 1927.

1753 THE MARACOT DEEP, AND OTHER STORIES. 1929.

COLLECTIONS AND SELECTIONS

Various "omnibus" volumes of Conan Doyle's novels and stories have been published from time to time, and frequently reprinted.

1754 THE POEMS OF ARTHUR CONAN DOYLE. Collected Edition. London: John Murray, 1922.

1755 SHERLOCK HOLMES: SELECTED STORIES. Introd. Sydney Castle Roberts. London: OUP, 1951.

1756 THE ANNOTATED SHERLOCK HOLMES. Ed. William Stuart Baring-Gould. 2 vols. London: John Murray, 1968.

BIOGRAPHY AND CRITICISM

1757 Pearson, Hesketh. CONAN DOYLE: HIS LIFE AND ART. London: Methuen, 1943.

1758 Doyle, Adrian Conan. THE TRUE CONAN DOYLE. London: John Murray, 1945.

1759 Carr, John Dickson. THE LIFE OF SIR ARTHUR CONAN DOYLE. London: John Murray, 1949.

1760 Nordon, Pierre. CONAN DOYLE: A BIOGRAPHY. New York: Rinehart and Winston, 1967.

There is a considerable literature relating to Conan Doyle's famous detective, from which a selection follows. See also Margaret Patterson's AUTHOR NEWS-LETTERS AND JOURNALS: A GUIDE TO INFORMATION SOURCES; volume 19 in the American Literature, English Literature, and World Literatures in English Information Guide Series (Detroit: Gale Research Co., 1979), which lists no fewer than fifty-two journals devoted to Conan Doyle and Sherlock Holmes. Only Shakespeare, with sixty-eight journals, exceeds this number.

1761 Brend, Gavin. MY DEAR HOLMES: A STUDY IN SHERLOCK. London: Allen and Unwin, 1951.

1762 Roberts, Sydney Castle. HOLMES AND WATSON: A MISCELLANY. London: OUP, 1953.

1763 Starrett, Vincent. THE PRIVATE LIFE OF SHERLOCK HOLMES. Rev. and enl. ed. Chicago: University of Chicago Press, 1960.

1764 Baring-Gould, William Stuart. SHERLOCK HOLMES: A BIOGRAPHY. London: Hart-Davis, 1962.

1765 Hardwick, Michael, and Mollie Hardwick. THE SHERLOCK HOLMES COMPANION. London: John Murray, 1962.

1766 Dakin, David Martin. A SHERLOCK HOLMES COMMENTARY. Newton Abbott: David and Charles, 1972.

BIBLIOGRAPHY

1767 Locke, Harold. A BIBLIOGRAPHICAL CATALOGUE OF THE WRITINGS OF SIR ARTHUR CONAN DOYLE. Tunbridge Wells: Webster, 1928.

Kenneth Grahame (1859-1932)

Kenneth Grahame, bank clerk and secretary, showed in his early work a subtle understanding of the child mind, though the books are not juvenile reading. THE WIND IN THE WILLOWS, originally devised to entertain his son, has become a perennially popular children's classic.

1768 PAGAN PAPERS. 1894; 1898.

1769 THE GOLDEN AGE. 1895; 5th ed. illus. E.H. Shepard, 1928; rpt. London: Bodley Head, 1979.

1770 DREAM DAYS. 1898; 4th ed. illus. E.H. Shepard, 1930; rpt. London: Bodley Head, 1979.

1771 THE WIND IN THE WILLOWS. 1908; illus. E.H. Shepard. London: Methuen, 1931.

1772 THE CAMBRIDGE BOOK OF POETRY FOR CHILDREN. Cambridge: Cambridge University Press, 1916.

1773 Chalmers, Patrick R. THE LIFE, LETTERS AND UNPUBLISHED WORK OF KENNETH GRAHAME. London: Methuen, 1933.

BIOGRAPHY AND CRITICISM

1774 Parker, William Mathie. "The Children's Advocate: Kenneth Grahame." In his MODERN SCOTTISH WRITERS. Edinburgh: Hodge, 1917, pp. 125-38.

1775 Grahame, Elspeth. FIRST WHISPERS OF THE WIND IN THE WILLOWS. London: Methuen, 1944.

1776 Green, Peter. KENNETH GRAHAME: A STUDY OF HIS LIFE, WORK AND TIMES. London: John Murray, 1959.

1777 Graham, Eleanor. KENNETH GRAHAME. London: Bodley Head, 1963.

1778 Ray, L.K. "Kenneth Grahame and the Literature of Childhood." ENGLISH LITERATURE IN TRANSITION, 20 (1977), 3-12.

Annie S. Swan (1859-1943)

Annie S. Swan published her first novel in 1878 and went on to publish over two hundred altogether, along with a prodigious number of magazine articles.

She wrote in the Kailyard mode (see note at 790), and had no literary pretensions; with disarming modesty and great good sense she regarded herself simply as a competent writer of simple, sentimental stories for the commercial market, aimed mainly at the woman at home. (THE WOMAN AT HOME was launched by the astute Robertson Nicoll in 1893 to meet that particular market, and he recruited Annie Swan as a contributor from the start.)

The nature and the extent of her immense popularity, particularly in Scotland, is a literary phenomenon that deserves investigation. Only a selection of her novels can be listed here, including her earlier and her more specifically Scottish work.

1779 ALDERSYDE: A BORDER STORY OF SEVENTY YEARS AGO. 1883.

1780 CARLOWRIE, OR AMONG LOTHIAN FOLK. 1884.

1781 THE GATES OF EDEN. 1886.

1782 SHEILA. 1889.

1783 MAITLAND OF LAURIESTON. 1891.

1784 THE GUINEA STAMP: A TALE OF MODERN GLASGOW. 1892.

1785 HOMESPUN: A STUDY OF SIMPLE FOLK. 1893.

1786 A VICTORY WON. 1895.

1787 MEMORIES OF MARGARET GRAINGER, SCHOOLMISTRESS: A SCOTTISH TALE. 1896.

1788 THE CURSE OF COWDEN. 1897.

1789 THE BRIDGE BUILDERS. 1913.

1790 A VEXED INHERITANCE. 1924.

1791 THE LAST OF THE LAIDLAWS: A ROMANCE OF THE BORDER. 1933.

1792 MY LIFE. London: Nicholson and Watson, 1934.
Autobiography.

1793 LETTERS. Ed. Mildred Robertson Nicoll. London: Hodder and Stoughton, 1945.

BIOGRAPHY AND CRITICISM

1794 Blake, George. BARRIE AND THE KAILYARD SCHOOL. London: Arthur Barker, 1951.

1795 Gardiner, Edmond F. "Annie S. Swan: Forerunner of Modern Popular Fiction." LIBRARY REVIEW, 24 (1973-74), 251-54.

Samuel Rutherford Crockett (1860-1914)

Crockett, who was born in Galloway, became a Free Church minister in 1886, but left the ministry for authorship. His first two novels place him firmly in the sentimental Kailyard school (see note at 790), but THE RAIDERS is an exciting Stevensonian adventure story of smuggling in Galloway.

1796 THE STICKIT MINISTER AND SOME COMMON MEN. 1893.

1797 THE LILAC SUNBONNET. 1894.

1798 THE RAIDERS. 1894.

1799 BOG-MYRTLE AND PEAT: TALES, CHIEFLY OF GALLOWAY. 1895.

1800 THE MEN OF THE MOSS HAGS. 1895.

1801 THE GREY MAN. 1896.

1802 CLEG KELLY, ARAB OF THE CITY. 1896.

1803 LOCHINVAR. 1897.

1804 THE STANDARD BEARER. 1898.

1805 THE RED AXE. 1898.

1806 THE BLACK DOUGLAS. 1899.

1807 KIT KENNEDY. 1899.

1808 THE SILVER SKULL. 1901.

1809 THE DARK O' THE MOON. 1902.

1810 RAIDERLAND: ALL ABOUT GREY GALLOWAY. 1904.

1811 THE CHERRY RIBAND. 1905.

1812 MAID MARGARET OF GALLOWAY. 1905.

1813 THE WHITE PLUMES OF NAVARRE. 1909.

1814 THE MOSS TROOPERS. 1912.

BIOGRAPHY AND CRITICISM

1815 Harper, Malcolm M. CROCKETT AND GREY GALLOWAY: THE NOVEL-
IST AND HIS WORKS. London: Hodder and Stoughton, 1907.

1816 Blake, George. BARRIE AND THE KAILYARD SCHOOL. London: Arthur
Barker, 1951.

1817 Anderson, [William] Eric [Kinloch]. "The Kailyard Revisited." In
NINETEENTH-CENTURY SCOTTISH FICTION: CRITICAL ESSAYS. Ed.
Ian Campbell. Manchester: Carcanet New Press, 1979, pp. 130-47.

Sir James Matthew Barrie (1860-1937)

Barrie was born in Kirriemuir, his fictional Thrums, and educated at Dumfries
Academy and Edinburgh University. He settled in London in 1885, where he
wrote a number of sketches of life in his native village some fifty years before,
and a successful novel which marked the emergence of what has been called
the Kailyard school (see explanatory note at 790). From about 1900 he wrote
almost entirely for the theatre. His plays are listed below by their year of
performance [in brackets]: the year of publication is also given. Barrie showed
himself a complete master of dialogue and stagecraft, but his peculiar blend of
sentiment and whimsy has not worn well. PETER PAN, however, first presented
in 1904, although not published until 1928, remains perennial. Like its hero,
it does not grow old.

1818 BETTER DEAD. 1887.

A novel.

1819 AULD LICHT IDYLLS. 1888.

1820 A WINDOW IN THRUMS. 1889.

1821 THE LITTLE MINISTER. 1891.

> A novel. It was dramatized by the author and first performed in 1897. The play was published in 1942, in the definitive edition of Barrie's plays.

1822 MARGARET OGILVY. 1896.

> A memoir of his mother.

1823 SENTIMENTAL TOMMY: THE STORY OF HIS BOYHOOD. 1896.

> A novel.

1824 TOMMY AND GRIZEL. 1900.

> A novel.

1825 THE LITTLE WHITE BIRD. 1902.

1826 QUALITY STREET. [1902]. 1913.

1827 THE ADMIRABLE CRICHTON. [1902]. 1914.

1828 PETER PAN. [1904]. 1928.

1829 ALICE SIT-BY-THE-FIRE. [1905]. 1919.

1830 PETER PAN IN KENSINGTON GARDENS. 1906.

1831 WHAT EVERY WOMAN KNOWS. [1908]. 1918.

1832 PETER AND WENDY. 1911.

1833 A KISS FOR CINDERELLA. [1916]. 1920.

1834 DEAR BRUTUS. [1917]. 1922.

1835 MARY ROSE. [1920]. 1924.

1836 FAREWELL, MISS JULIE LOGAN. 1932.

1837 THE BOY DAVID. [1936]. 1938.

1838 THE GREENWOOD HAT. 1937.

> Autobiographical

COLLECTIONS AND SELECTIONS

1839 PLAYS. Ed. Albert Edward Wilson. London: Hodder and Stoughton, 1942.

    The definitive edition.

1840 LETTERS. Ed. Viola Meynell. London: Peter Davies, 1942.

1841 PLAYS AND STORIES. Ed. Roger Lancelyn Green. London: Dent, 1962.

BIOGRAPHY AND CRITICISM

1842 Parker, William Mathie. "A Northern Puck: Sir James Barrie, Bart." In his MODERN SCOTTISH WRITERS. Edinburgh: Hodge, 1917, pp. 75-83.

1843 Grieve, Christopher Murray ["Hugh MacDiarmid"]. "Sir J.M. Barrie." In his CONTEMPORARY SCOTTISH STUDIES. 1926; rpt. Edinburgh: Scottish Educational Journal, 1976, pp. 3-4.

1844 Hammerton, John Alexander. BARRIE: THE STORY OF A GENIUS. London: Sampson Low, Marston, 1929.

1845 Darlington, William A. J.M. BARRIE. London: Blackie, 1938.

1846 Mackail, Denis. THE STORY OF J.M.B.: A BIOGRAPHY. London: Peter Davies, 1941; rpt. Freeport, N.Y.: Books for Libraries, 1972.

    The authorized biography.

1847 Blake, George. BARRIE AND THE KAILYARD SCHOOL. London: Arthur Barker, 1951.

1848 Asquith, Cynthia. PORTRAIT OF BARRIE. London: James Barrie, 1954.

1849 Green, Roger Lancelyn. FIFTY YEARS OF PETER PAN. London: Peter Davies, 1954.

1850 _____. J.M. BARRIE. London: Bodley Head, 1960.

1851 McGraw, William R. "Barrie and the Critics." SSL, 1 (1963-64), 111-30.

1852 Dunbar, Janet. J.M. BARRIE: THE MAN BEHIND THE IMAGE. London: Collins, 1970.

1853 Wright, Allen. J.M. BARRIE: GLAMOUR OF TWILIGHT. Edinburgh: Ramsay Head Press, 1976.

1854 Anderson, [William] Eric [Kinloch]. "The Kailyard Revisited." In NINE-TEENTH-CENTURY SCOTTISH FICTION: CRITICAL ESSAYS. Ed. Ian Campbell. Manchester: Carcanet New Press, 1979, pp. 130-47.

1855 Birkin, Andrew. J.M. BARRIE AND THE LOST BOYS. London: Constable, 1979.

BIBLIOGRAPHY

1856 Garland, Herbert. A BIBLIOGRAPHY OF THE WRITINGS OF SIR JAMES M. BARRIE. London: Bookman's Journal, 1928.

1857 Cutler, Bradley D. SIR JAMES M. BARRIE: A BIBLIOGRAPHY WITH FULL COLLATIONS OF THE AMERICAN UNAUTHORIZED EDITIONS. New York: Greenberg, 1931.

1858 Shields, Katharine G. "Sir James Matthew Barrie, Bart.: A Bibliography." BULLETIN OF BIBLIOGRAPHY, 16 (1936-39), 44-46, 68-69, 97, 119, 140-41, 162.

Section 5

1900-1980

This section deals with Scottish literature from 1900 to 1980, the period of the modern Renaissance initiated and inspired by Hugh MacDiarmid. It is the age of MacDiarmid, Muir and Gunn, of James Bridie and William Soutar, of Lewis Grassic Gibbon and Sydney Goodsir Smith, and their successors to the present day.

The general works relevant to the period are grouped under five headings:

    A.   Bibliographies and Reference Works
    B.   Literary History and Criticism
    C.   Anthologies
    D.   Background Studies
    E.   Periodicals

Under each heading or subheading the works are arranged in chronological order by the year of publication.

A sixth heading, F. Individual Authors, lists the authors of the period in chronological order by their year of birth, giving for each author a chronological checklist of his/her separate works, and of any collections and selections, followed by a chronological list of the more important biographical and critical studies of the author and his/her work.

A. BIBLIOGRAPHIES AND REFERENCE WORKS

See also pages 2-4.

General

Most of the general bibliographies and reference works giving bibliographical, biographical, and critical information on authors of the twentieth century include a number of Scottish writers.

1859 Muir, Edwin. THE PRESENT AGE, FROM 1914. London: Cresset Press, 1939.

> Volume 5 of the INTRODUCTIONS TO ENGLISH LITERATURE, ed. Bonamy Dobrée. It was later replaced by the volume by David Daiches (see no. 1862).

1860 TWENTIETH CENTURY AUTHORS. Ed. Stanley J. Kunitz and Howard Haycraft. New York: H.W. Wilson, 1942.

TWENTIETH CENTURY AUTHORS. First supplement. Ed. Stanley J. Kunitz. New York: H.W. Wilson, 1955.

1861 Leclaire, Lucien. A GENERAL ANALYTICAL BIBLIOGRAPHY OF THE REGIONAL NOVELISTS OF THE BRITISH ISLES, 1800-1950. Paris: Société d'Édition "Les Belles Lettres," 1954; rev. 1969.

1862 Daiches, David. THE PRESENT AGE: AFTER 1920. London: Cresset Press, 1958; 1969.

> Volume 5 of the INTRODUCTIONS TO ENGLISH LITERATURE, ed. Bonamy Dobrée. It replaced the volume by Edwin Muir (see no. 1859).

1863 CONTEMPORARY AUTHORS. Detroit: Gale Research Co., 1962-- .

> This current and continuing series is a basic source for reliable and informative biobibliographies of contemporary writers. An alphabetical index of the authors included in the series is cumulated in alternate volumes.

CONTEMPORARY AUTHORS. Permanent series. Detroit: Gale Research Co., 1975-78.

> A parallel series to which the biobibliographies from the current series are transferred when the authors die, or seem to have completed their work.

CONTEMPORARY AUTHORS. New Revision series. Detroit: Gale Research Co., 1981-- .

> Each volume provides updated biobibliographical sketches on

active authors covered in regular CA volumes.

1864 Temple, Ruth Z., and Martin Tucker, eds. TWENTIETH–CENTURY BRITISH LITERATURE: A REFERENCE GUIDE AND BIBLIOGRAPHY. New York: Ungar, 1968.

1865 CONTEMPORARY POETS. Ed. Rosalie Murphy, 1970; 2nd ed. Ed. James Vinson. London: St. James Press, 1975.

1866 CONTEMPORARY NOVELISTS. Ed. James Vinson. London: St. James Press, 1972.

1867 CONTEMPORARY DRAMATISTS. Ed. James Vinson. London: St. James Press, 1973; 2nd ed. 1977.

1868 CONTEMPORARY LITERARY CRITICISM. Detroit: Gale Research Co., 1973-- .

A continuing series which provides a judicious selection of critical comment on contemporary writers. Volume 22 (1982) includes a cumulative index to volumes 1-22.

1869 ENCYCLOPEDIA OF WORLD LITERATURE IN THE 20TH CENTURY. Ed. Frederick Ungar and Lina Mainiero. 4 vols. New York: Ungar, 1975.

1870 WORLD AUTHORS: 1950-1970. Ed. John Wakeman. New York: H.W. Wilson, 1975.

WORLD AUTHORS: 1970-1975. Ed. John Wakeman. New York: H.W. Wilson, 1980.

1871 Seymour–Smith, Martin, ed. WHO'S WHO IN TWENTIETH–CENTURY LITERATURE. London: Weidenfeld and Nicolson, 1976.

1872 Mellown, Elgin W. A DESCRIPTIVE CATALOGUE OF THE BIBLIOG-RAPHIES OF TWENTIETH–CENTURY BRITISH POETS, NOVELISTS AND DRAMATISTS. 2nd ed. Troy, N.Y.: Whitston, 1978.

1873 TWENTIETH–CENTURY LITERARY CRITICISM. Detroit: Gale Research Co., 1978-- .

A parallel series to CONTEMPORARY LITERARY CRITICISM (see no. 1868) providing a similar selection of critical comment on twentieth–century authors who died before 1960. Volume 7 (1982) includes a cumulative index to volumes 1-7.

Current research on the major writers of the period has been summarized since 1955 in the periodical TWENTIETH CENTURY LITERATURE and since 1971 in the annual review numbers of the JOURNAL OF MODERN LITERATURE.

Scottish Literature

1874 Macleod, Robert D. MODERN SCOTTISH LITERATURE: A POPULAR
GUIDE-BOOK CATALOGUE. Glasgow: Holmes, 1933.

1875 Dougan, Robert O. CATALOGUE OF AN EXHIBITION OF 20TH-CEN-
TURY SCOTTISH BOOKS AT THE MITCHELL LIBRARY, GLASGOW.
Glasgow: Scottish Committee, Festival of Britain, 1951.

1876 Aitken, William R., comp. SCOTTISH FICTION RESERVE: A LIST OF
THE AUTHORS INCLUDED IN THE SCHEME. [Coatbridge]: Scottish
Library Association, 1955.

> An alphabetical list of some 650 Scottish novelists, from Smol-
> lett onwards, showing the collecting libraries responsible for
> each author. A revised and greatly enlarged edition of the
> list, compiled by Moira Stirling, is to be published in 1982 by
> the National Library of Scotland, Edinburgh.

1877 Glen, Duncan. "Bibliography." In his HUGH MacDIARMID (CHRISTOPHER
MURRAY GRIEVE) AND THE SCOTTISH RENAISSANCE. Edinburgh:
Chambers, 1964, pp. 245-80.

1878 Kidd, James. "Current Scottish Prose and Verse." 1969-- .

> Annual lists, which attempt to record "current original imagi-
> native writing which can claim, however broadly, to be Scot-
> tish," published for the years from 1969 to 1972 in SCOTTISH
> LITERARY NEWS (1970-73) and from 1973 in that periodical's
> successor, SCOTTISH LITERARY JOURNAL, or its supplements.

1879 Burgess, Moira. THE GLASGOW NOVEL, 1870-1970: A BIBLIOGRAPHY.
Glasgow: Scottish Library Association, 1972.

1880 Glen, Duncan. A BIBLIOGRAPHY OF SCOTTISH POETS FROM STEVEN-
SON TO 1974. Preston: Akros, 1974.

1881 _____. FORWARD FROM HUGH MacDIARMID. FIFTEEN YEARS OF
DUNCAN GLEN/AKROS PUBLICATIONS, 1962-1977. Preston: Akros,
1977.

> A bibliography of Glen's own enterprise.

1882 Fraser, Kenneth C. A BIBLIOGRAPHY OF THE SCOTTISH NATIONAL
MOVEMENT (1844-1973). Dollar: Douglas S. Mack, 1976.

1883 "A Checklist of Modern Scottish Literary MSS. in the National Library of
Scotland." BIBLIOTHECK, 9 (1978-79), 81-152.

B. LITERARY HISTORY AND CRITICISM

See also pages 4-7.

1884 Grieve, Christopher Murray. [Hugh MacDiarmid]. CONTEMPORARY
SCOTTISH STUDIES: FIRST SERIES. London: Leonard Parsons, 1926.

Articles reprinted from the SCOTTISH EDUCATIONAL JOUR-
NAL, June 1925-July 1926, with an introductory chapter, conclusion, and bibliography.

CONTEMPORARY SCOTTISH STUDIES. Edinburgh: Scottish Educational
Journal, 1976.

A new edition reprinting the complete series of articles, June
1925-February 1927, with the "furious and fascinating" correspondence they evoked. The introductory chapter, conclusion,
and bibliography of the 1926 edition are not reprinted.

1885 EDINBURGH ESSAYS ON SCOTS LITERATURE. Edinburgh: Oliver and
Boyd, 1933.

The relevant essays are Ian A. Gordon, "Modern Scots Poetry,"
pages 125-48, and Angus Macdonald, "Modern Scots Novelists,"
pages 149-73.

1886 MacDiarmid, Hugh. AT THE SIGN OF THE THISTLE: A COLLECTION
OF ESSAYS. London: Stanley Nott, 1934.

1887 Reid, James M. MODERN SCOTTISH LITERATURE. Edinburgh: Oliver
and Boyd, 1945.

1888 Young, Douglas. "PLASTIC SCOTS" AND THE SCOTTISH LITERARY TRA-
DITION: AN AUTHORITATIVE INTRODUCTION TO A CONTROVERSY.
Glasgow: Maclellan, 1947.

A spirited defense of the modern revival of Braid Scots or
Lallans.

1889 Lindsay, Maurice. THE SCOTTISH RENAISSANCE. Edinburgh: Serif
Books, 1948.

1890 Kitchin, George. "The Modern Makars." In SCOTTISH POETRY: A
CRITICAL SURVEY. Ed. James Kinsley. London: Cassell, 1955, pp.
256-79.

1891 Blake, George. ANNALS OF SCOTLAND, 1895-1955: AN ESSAY ON
THE TWENTIETH-CENTURY SCOTTISH NOVEL. London: British Broadcasting Corp., 1956.

1892 Glen, Duncan. HUGH MacDIARMID (CHRISTOPHER MURRAY GRIEVE) AND THE SCOTTISH RENAISSANCE. Edinburgh: Chambers, 1964.

1893 Smith, Sydney Goodsir. "Trahison des Clercs, or The Anti-Scottish Lobby in Scottish Letters." SSL, 2 (1964-65), 71-86.

1894 Broom, John L. "Some Neglected Scottish Novelists." CATALYST, 2, No. 4 (Autumn 1969), 24-26.

1895 Scott, Alexander. THE MacDIARMID MAKARS, 1923-72: AN ESSAY. Preston: Akros, 1972.

1896 Crawford, Thomas, ed. SCOTTISH WRITING TODAY. Aberdeen: ASLS, 1972.

     Three papers: George Bruce, "Scottish Poetry Today," pages 2-14; James B. Caird, "The Scottish Novel Yesterday and Today," pages 15-25; Christopher Small, "Scottish Drama Today," pages 26-36.

1897 Mitchell, Jack. "The Struggle for the Working-Class Novel in Scotland, 1900-1939." ZEITSCHRIFT FUR ANGLISTIK UND AMERIKANISTIK, 24 (1973), 384-413.

1898 Fulton, Robin. CONTEMPORARY SCOTTISH POETRY: INDIVIDUALS AND CONTEXTS. Loanhead: Macdonald, 1974.

1899 Morgan, Edwin. ESSAYS. Cheadle: Carcanet Press, 1974.

1900 Thornton, Robert D. "Scottish Literature." In ENCYCLOPEDIA OF WORLD LITERATURE IN THE 20TH CENTURY. Ed. Frederick Ungar and Lina Mainiero. 4 vols. New York: Ungar, 1975. Vol. 3, pp. 251-54.

     An admirable summary.

1901 "Scottish Poetry, 1920-1975." AKROS, No. 28 (August 1975), entire issue.

     A series of essays by Albert D. Mackie, James King Annand, Maurice Lindsay, Alexander Scott, and David Black.

1902 Hutchison, David. THE MODERN SCOTTISH THEATRE. Glasgow: Molendinar Press, 1977.

1903 Mackie, Alastair. "Change and Continuity in Modern Scottish Poetry." AKROS, No. 33 (April 1977), 13-40.

1904 Wilson, Norman, ed. SCOTTISH WRITING AND WRITERS. Edinburgh: Ramsay Head Press, 1977.

But see also the review by Isobel Murray in SLJ, suppl. 5 (1977), 63-65.

1905 Hart, Francis R. THE SCOTTISH NOVEL: A CRITICAL SURVEY. London: John Murray, 1978.

1906 Lindsay, Maurice, ed. AS I REMEMBER: TEN SCOTTISH AUTHORS RECALL HOW WRITING BEGAN FOR THEM. London: Robert Hale, 1979.

Surveys

1907 Scott, Alexander. "Scottish Poetry in 1968." SSL, 6 (1968-69), 199-219.

Similar surveys appeared regularly in SSL thereafter for 1969, 1970, 1971, 1972, 1973, and 1974-76.

1908 Gifford, Douglas. "Modern Scottish Fiction." SSL, 13 (1978), 250-73.

1909 _____. "Scottish Fiction, 1975-1977." SSL, 14 (1979), 207-37.

It is intended that these surveys should appear regularly.

C. ANTHOLOGIES

See also pages 8-10.

General

1910 White, James H., ed. TOWARDS A NEW SCOTLAND, BEING A SELECTION FROM THE MODERN SCOT. London: Maclehose, 1935.

1911 Linklater, Eric, ed. THE THISTLE AND THE PEN: AN ANTHOLOGY OF MODERN SCOTTISH WRITERS. Edinburgh: Nelson, 1950.

Poetry

1912 Grieve, Christopher Murray [Hugh MacDiarmid], ed. NORTHERN NUMBERS, BEING REPRESENTATIVE SELECTIONS FROM CERTAIN LIVING SCOTTISH POETS. Edinburgh: T.N. Foulis, 1920; 2nd ser. Edinburgh: T.N. Foulis, 1921; 3rd ser. Montrose: Grieve, 1922.

1913 Hamilton, William H., ed. HOLYROOD: A GARLAND OF MODERN SCOTS POEMS. London: Dent, 1929.

1914 Grieve, Christopher Murray [Hugh MacDiarmid], ed. LIVING SCOTTISH POETS. London: Ernest Benn, 1931.

1915 POETRY SCOTLAND. Ed. Maurice Lindsay. Nos. 1-3, Glasgow: Maclellan, 1943-46; no. 4, Edinburgh: Serif Books, 1949.

1916 Lindsay, Maurice, ed. MODERN SCOTTISH POETRY: AN ANTHOLOGY OF THE SCOTTISH RENAISSANCE, 1920-1945. London: Faber, 1946.

    For later editions, see 1920 and 1927.

1917 NEW SCOTS POETRY: A SELECTION OF SHORT POEMS FROM THE FESTIVAL OF BRITAIN SCOTS POETRY COMPETITION. Edinburgh: Serif Books, 1952.

1918 Young, Douglas, ed. SCOTTISH VERSE, 1851-1951. Edinburgh: Nelson, 1952.

    Selected for the general reader.

1919 MacCaig, Norman, ed. HONOUR'D SHADE: AN ANTHOLOGY OF NEW SCOTTISH POETRY TO MARK THE BICENTENARY OF THE BIRTH OF ROBERT BURNS. Edinburgh: Chambers, 1959.

1920 Lindsay, Maurice, ed. MODERN SCOTTISH POETRY: AN ANTHOLOGY OF THE SCOTTISH RENAISSANCE. 2nd ed. London: Faber, 1966.

    For other editions, see 1916 and 1927.

1921 SCOTTISH POETRY. Nos. 1-9. 1966-76.

    A series of nine collections published over ten years with various editors and publishers.

1922 Bruce, George, ed. THE SCOTTISH LITERARY REVIVAL: AN ANTHOLOGY OF TWENTIETH CENTURY POETRY. London: Collier-Macmillan; New York: Macmillan, 1968.

    A representative anthology with a good introduction.

1923 Glen, Duncan, ed. THE AKROS ANTHOLOGY OF SCOTTISH POETRY, 1965-70. Preston: Akros, 1970.

1924 MacCaig, Norman, and Alexander Scott, eds. CONTEMPORARY SCOTTISH VERSE, 1959-1969. London: Calder and Boyars, 1970.

1925 King, Charles, ed. TWELVE MODERN SCOTTISH POETS. London: University of London Press, 1971; Hodder and Stoughton, 1980.

Generous selections from the twelve poets included.

1926 Bold, Alan, ed. CAMBRIDGE BOOK OF ENGLISH VERSE, 1939-1975. Cambridge: Cambridge University Press, 1976.

Includes Edwin Muir and Hugh MacDiarmid.

1927 Lindsay, Maurice, ed. MODERN SCOTTISH POETRY: AN ANTHOLOGY OF THE SCOTTISH RENAISSANCE, 1925-1975. Manchester: Carcanet Press, 1976.

For earlier editions, see 1916 and 1920.

1928 Scott, Alexander, ed. MODERN SCOTS VERSE, 1922-1977. Preston: Akros, 1978.

Plays

1929 Reid, John Macnair, ed. SCOTTISH ONE-ACT PLAYS. Edinburgh: Porpoise Press, 1935.

1930 Bannister, Winifred, ed. NORTH LIGHT: TEN NEW ONE-ACT PLAYS FROM THE NORTH. Glasgow: Maclellan, 1947.

1931 Millar, Robert, and John T. Low, eds. FIVE SCOTTISH ONE-ACT PLAYS. London: Heinemann, 1972.

Short Stories

1932 Lindsay, Maurice, and Fred Urquhart, eds. NO SCOTTISH TWILIGHT: NEW SCOTTISH SHORT STORIES. Glasgow: Maclellan, 1947.

1933 SCOTTISH SHORT STORIES. London: Collins, 1973-- .

Annual volumes sponsored by the Scottish Arts Council. Nine have appeared from 1973 to 1981.

1934 Millar, Robert, and John T. Low, eds. TEN MODERN SCOTTISH STORIES. London: Heinemann, 1973.

1935 _____. FURTHER MODERN SCOTTISH STORIES. London: Heinemann, 1976.

1936 Urquhart, Fred, and Giles Gordon, eds. MODERN SCOTTISH SHORT STORIES. London: Hamish Hamilton, 1978.

1937 Millar, Robert, and John T. Low, eds. A THIRD BOOK OF MODERN
SCOTTISH STORIES. London: Heinemann, 1979.

D. BACKGROUND STUDIES

See also pages 15-19.

1938 Gibbon, Lewis Grassic, and Hugh MacDiarmid. SCOTTISH SCENE, OR
THE INTELLIGENT MAN'S GUIDE TO ALBYN. London: Jarrolds, 1934.

A remarkable survey of contemporary Scotland from two different points of view.

1939 Cammell, Charles Richard. HEART OF SCOTLAND: A MEMOIR. London: Robert Hale, 1956.

Reminiscences and gossip of Edinburgh literary life in the 1930s.

1940 Wolfe, James Nathaniel, ed. GOVERNMENT AND NATIONALISM IN
SCOTLAND: AN ENQUIRY BY MEMBERS OF THE UNIVERSITY OF
EDINBURGH. Edinburgh: Edinburgh University Press, 1969.

1941 Hanham, Harold John. SCOTTISH NATIONALISM. London: Faber,
1969.

1942 Miller, Karl, ed. MEMOIRS OF A MODERN SCOTLAND. London:
Faber, 1970.

1943 Glen, Duncan, ed. WHITHER SCOTLAND? A PREJUDICED LOOK AT
THE FUTURE OF A NATION. London: Gollancz, 1971.

1944 Brown, Gordon, ed. THE RED PAPER ON SCOTLAND. Edinburgh:
EUSPB, 1975.

This series of essays on Scotland today includes one by David
Craig, "The Radical Literary Tradition," pages 289-303.

1945 Webb, Keith. THE GROWTH OF NATIONALISM IN SCOTLAND. Glasgow: Molendinar Press, 1977; Harmondsworth: Penguin, 1978.

1946 Brand, Jack. THE NATIONAL MOVEMENT IN SCOTLAND. London:
Routledge and Kegan Paul, 1978.

1947 Lindsay, Maurice. FRANCIS GEORGE SCOTT AND THE SCOTTISH RE-
NAISSANCE. Edinburgh: Paul Harris, 1980.

The composer Francis George Scott was a close friend of both
Edwin Muir and Hugh MacDiarmid.

E. PERIODICALS

Many periodicals have been published in Scotland in the present century. A selective list follows, in chronological order of first publication, starting with a few survivors from the nineteenth century. Many were short lived, few enjoyed a large circulation, but even of these a number have been of outstanding importance and influence.

For publication details of current periodicals, see the appropriate sections of directories such as ULRICH's and the other bibliographies of new serials. To locate runs of these periodicals, consult the BRITISH UNION CATALOGUE OF PERIODICALS for the holdings of the major libraries in Britain, and the UNION LIST OF SERIALS for the United States and Canada.

Relevant articles in the periodicals listed, and in many other more general periodicals, have been indexed since 1969 in the ANNUAL BIBLIOGRAPHY OF SCOTTISH LITERATURE, published as a supplement to THE BIBLIOTHECK. The indexing of material on Scottish literature in periodicals prior to 1969 is unpredictable and haphazard, but occasional references may be found in the SUBJECT INDEX TO PERIODICALS and its successor, BRITISH HUMANITIES INDEX, in the H.W. Wilson Company's HUMANITIES INDEX and its predecessors, and in the READERS' GUIDE TO PERIODICAL LITERATURE. See Eugene P. Sheehy's GUIDE TO REFERENCE BOOKS and its supplements (Chicago: American Library Association, 1976--) for detailed descriptions of these guides and indexes.

1948 THE EDINBURGH REVIEW. 1802-1929. Quarterly.

1949 BLACKWOOD'S. Edinburgh, 1817-1980. Monthly.

1950 CHAMBERS'S JOURNAL. Edinburgh, 1832-1956. Originally weekly, monthly from 1932.

1951 SCOTTISH NOTES AND QUERIES. Aberdeen, 1887-1935. Monthly.

1952 BURNS CHRONICLE. Kilmarnock, 1892-- . Annual.

1953 SCOTTISH ART AND LETTERS. Glasgow, 1901-04. Quarterly.

1954 CELTIC REVIEW. Edinburgh, 1904-16. Quarterly.

1955 ABERDEEN UNIVERSITY REVIEW. Aberdeen: Aberdeen University Alumnus Association, 1913-- . Two issues a year.

1956 THE SCOTTISH CHAPBOOK. Montrose: C.M. Grieve, 1922-23. Monthly. Ed. C.M. Grieve [Hugh MacDiarmid]. The first periodical of the Scottish Renaissance.

1957 THE SCOTTISH NATION. Montrose: C.M. Grieve, 1923. Weekly.
Ed. C.M. Grieve [Hugh MacDiarmid].

1958 THE NORTHERN REVIEW. Edinburgh, 1924. Monthly. (4 issues only).
Ed. C.M. Grieve [Hugh MacDiarmid].

1959 THE SCOTS MAGAZINE. New ser. Dundee: D.C. Thomson, 1924-- .
Monthly.

1960 THE SCOTS REVIEW. Glasgow, 1925. Monthly. (4 issues only).

1961 UNIVERSITY OF EDINBURGH JOURNAL. Edinburgh: University of
Edinburgh Graduates' Association, 1925-- . Two issues a year.

1962 SCOTS OBSERVER. Glasgow, 1926-33. Weekly.

1963 SCOTS INDEPENDENT. Stirling, 1926-- . Monthly (weekly from 1954-
71).

1964 PICTISH REVIEW. Aberdeen, 1927-28. Monthly. (8 issues only).

1965 LIBRARY REVIEW. Dunfermline [later Glasgow]: W. and R. Holmes,
1927-- . Quarterly.

1966 THE MODERN SCOT. Dundee [later St. Andrews], 1930-36. Quarterly.
Indexed in Barry C. Bloomfield, AN AUTHOR INDEX TO SE-
LECTED BRITISH "LITTLE MAGAZINES," 1930-1939. London:
Mansell, 1976. See also TOWARDS A NEW SCOTLAND,
BEING A SELECTION FROM THE MODERN SCOT. Ed. James
H. White. London: Maclehose, 1935.

1967 THE FREE MAN. Edinburgh, 1932-34. Weekly.
Continued as NEW SCOTLAND, 1935-36 (Glasgow, weekly);
and again as THE FREE MAN (Glasgow, weekly) until 1947.

1968 SCOTTISH BOOKMAN. Dunfermline, 1935-36. Monthly. (6 issues only).

1969 SCOTTISH STANDARD. Glasgow, 1935-36. Monthly.

1970 OUTLOOK. Edinburgh, 1936-37. Monthly. (10 issues only).
Amalgamating the MODERN SCOT and SCOTTISH STANDARD.

1971 ALBANNACH. Dingwall, 1938. (1 issue only).

1972 THE VOICE OF SCOTLAND. Dunfermline, 1938-39; Glasgow, 1945-49; Edinburgh, 1955-58. Quarterly (irregular).

> Ed. Hugh MacDiarmid. The numbers for 1938-39 are indexed in Barry C. Bloomfield, AN AUTHOR INDEX TO SELECTED BRITISH "LITTLE MAGAZINES," 1930-1939. London: Mansell, 1976.

1973 NEW ALLIANCE. Edinburgh, 1939-46. Irregular.

> Continued as NEW ALLIANCE AND SCOTS REVIEW. 1946-51.

1974 MILLION. Glasgow, 1943-45. Irregular.

1975 POETRY SCOTLAND. Nos. 1-3, Glasgow: Maclellan, 1943-46. No.4, Edinburgh: Serif Books, 1949. Irregular.

1976 SCOTTISH ART AND LETTERS. Glasgow: Maclellan, 1944-50. Irregular. (5 issues only).

1977 NEW SCOT. Glasgow: Scottish Reconstruction Committee, 1945-49. Monthly.

1978 NEW SHETLANDER. Lerwick: Shetland Council of Social Service, 1947-- . Originally monthly, now quarterly.

> See also NEW SHETLANDER WRITING: AN ANTHOLOGY FROM THE FIRST HUNDRED NUMBERS. Lerwick: Shetland Times, 1973.

1979 SCOTTISH PERIODICAL. Edinburgh, 1947-48. Irregular (2 issues only).

1980 NEW ATHENIAN BROADSHEET. Edinburgh, 1947-51. Irregular (16 issues only).

1981 NATIONAL WEEKLY. Glasgow: Caledonian Press, 1948-53.

> Hugh MacDiarmid was a regular contributor.

1982 SCOTTISH JOURNAL. Glasgow: Maclellan, 1952-54. Monthly. (12 issues only).

> MacDiarmid was a major contributor.

1983 LINES REVIEW. Edinburgh [later Loanhead]: Macdonald, 1952-- . Quarterly.

1984 SALTIRE REVIEW. Edinburgh: Saltire Society, 1954-61. Three issues a year.

    Continued as NEW SALTIRE. Edinburgh: Saltire Society, 1961-64. Quarterly.

1985 THE BIBLIOTHECK. Edinburgh: Library Association (University, College, and Research Section: Scottish Group), 1956-- . Three issues a year, with an annual supplement.

1986 SCOTTISH STUDIES. Edinburgh: University of Edinburgh, School of Scottish Studies, 1957-- . Originally two issues a year, now annual.

1987 STUDIES IN SCOTTISH LITERATURE. Columbia: University of South Carolina Press, 1963-- . Vols. 1-12, quarterly; vol. 13-- , annual.

1988 AKROS. Preston [later Nottingham]: Akros Publications, 1965-- . Three issues a year.

1989 SCOTTISH POETRY. 1966-76. Nine issues published over ten years by various publishers in Edinburgh, Glasgow, and Manchester.

1990 CATALYST. 1967-74. Published by the 1320 Club from various addresses in Scotland. Quarterly.

1991 SCOTTISH INTERNATIONAL. Edinburgh, 1968-74. Originally quarterly, later monthly.

1992 NEW EDINBURGH REVIEW. Edinburgh: EUSPB, 1969-- . Originally monthly, now quarterly.

1993 CHAPMAN. Hamilton [later Edinburgh], 1970-- . Irregular.

1994 SCOTIA. Thurso, Caithness, 1970-72. Monthly.

    Continued as SCOTIA REVIEW. Thurso, Caithness [later Wick], 1972-78. Three issues a year.

1995 SCOTTISH LITERARY NEWS. Aberdeen: ASLS, 1970-73. Quarterly.

    Continued as SCOTTISH LITERARY JOURNAL. Aberdeen: ASLS, 1974-- . Two issues a year, with two or three supplements.

1996 KNOWE. Preston: Akros Publications, 1971. Monthly. (3 issues only).

1997 TOCHER. Edinburgh: University of Edinburgh, School of Scottish Studies, 1971-- . Quarterly.

1998 NORTHERN SCOTLAND. Aberdeen: University of Aberdeen, Centre for Scottish Studies, 1972-- . Annual.

1999 LALLANS. Dunfermline: Scots Language Society, 1973-- . Two issues a year.

2000 LEOPARD. Aberdeen, 1973-- . Monthly.

2001 Q. Edinburgh, 1975-76. Fortnightly.

2002 CALGACUS. Breakish, Isle of Skye, 1975-- . Bimonthly.

2003 SCOTTISH REVIEW. Glasgow: Scottish Civic Trust and Saltire Society, 1975-- . Quarterly.

2004 BRUNTON'S MISCELLANY. Edinburgh, 1977-- . Quarterly.

2005 BOOKS IN SCOTLAND. Edinburgh: Ramsay Head Press, 1978-- . Quarterly.

2006 CENCRASTUS. Edinburgh, 1979-- . Quarterly.

2007 LITERARY REVIEW. Edinburgh, 1979-- . Fortnightly.

Bibliography

2008 Fraser, Kenneth C. "Scottish Nationalist Periodicals, 1880-1973: A Chronological Checklist." BIBLIOTHECK, 7 (1974-75), 21-25.

F. INDIVIDUAL AUTHORS

This section deals with the authors of the period in chronological order by their year of birth. When it has not been possible to ascertain the year of birth, or when the author has explicitly requested that this information should not be revealed, the author is included in the chronological sequence at an appropriate place.

The bibliographies of individual authors follow a pattern. The author's separate works (or with some prolific authors a selection of the more interesting of their separate works) are listed first, in chronological order, with subheadings, where necessary, for any collections and selections or letters. This primary bibliography is followed by a chronological list of the more important biographical and critical studies of the author and the work, the secondary bibliography, with the emphasis on books rather than articles. With many of the authors, particularly when there is little to record in the way of biography and criticism, references are given to the entries for these authors in the following publications, using the abbreviations indicated:

CA   CONTEMPORARY AUTHORS. Detroit: Gale Research Co., 1962-- .

CAP   CONTEMPORARY AUTHORS. Permanent series. Detroit: Gale Research Co., 1975-- .

CD   CONTEMPORARY DRAMATISTS. Ed. James Vinson. 2nd ed. London: St. James Press, 1977.

CN   CONTEMPORARY NOVELISTS. Ed. James Vinson. London: St. James Press, 1972.

CP   CONTEMPORARY POETS. Ed. James Vinson. 2nd ed. London: St. James Press, 1975.

CSS   CONTEMPORARY SCOTTISH STUDIES. By Hugh MacDiarmid. 1926; new ed. Edinburgh: Scottish Educational Journal, 1976.

D   Daiches, David. THE PRESENT AGE: AFTER 1920. London: Cresset Press, 1958.

H   Hart, Francis R. THE SCOTTISH NOVEL: A CRITICAL SURVEY. London: John Murray, 1978.

P   PENGUIN COMPANION TO LITERATURE: BRITAIN AND THE COMMONWEALTH. Ed. David Daiches. London: Allen Lane, Penguin Press, 1971.

T   Temple, Ruth Z., and Martin Tucker, eds. TWENTIETH-CENTURY BRITISH LITERATURE: A REFERENCE GUIDE AND BIBLIOGRAPHY. New York: Ungar, 1968.

TCA   TWENTIETH CENTURY AUTHORS. Ed. Stanley J. Kunitz and Howard Haycraft. New York: H.W. Wilson, 1942.

TCA-1 TWENTIETH CENTURY AUTHORS. First supplement. Ed. Stanley J. Kunitz. New York: H.W. Wilson, 1955.

W   WHO'S WHO IN TWENTIETH-CENTURY LITERATURE. Ed. Martin Seymour-Smith. London: Weidenfeld and Nicolson, 1976.

WA-50 WORLD AUTHORS: 1950-1970. Ed. John Wakeman. New York: H.W. Wilson, 1975.

WA-70 WORLD AUTHORS: 1970-1975. Ed. John Wakeman. New York: H.W. Wilson, 1980.

Page references are cited for CSS and H. The required information is readily located in the other works, which are arranged alphabetically.

A final group in each individual author bibliography lists bibliographies of the author and reference works, if they exist.

R[obert] B[ontine] Cunninghame Graham (1852-1936)

Traveler, short-story writer, and historian of South America.

2009 NOTES ON THE DISTRICT OF MENTEITH. London: Black, 1895.

2010 FATHER ARCHANGEL OF SCOTLAND, AND OTHER ESSAYS. London: Black, 1896.

With Gabriela Cunninghame Graham.

2011 MOGREB-EL-ACKSA: A JOURNEY IN MOROCCO. London: Heinemann, 1898.

2012 THE IPANÉ. London: Fisher Unwin, 1899.

Tales and sketches.

2013 THIRTEEN STORIES. London: Heinemann, 1900.

2014 A VANISHED ARCADIA, BEING SOME ACCOUNT OF THE JESUITS IN PARAGUAY, 1607 TO 1767. London: Heinemann, 1901.

2015 SUCCESS. London: Duckworth, 1902.

Tales and sketches.

2016 HERNANDO DE SOTO, TOGETHER WITH AN ACCOUNT OF ONE OF HIS CAPTAINS, GONCALO SILVESTRE. London: Heinemann, 1903.

2017 PROGRESS, AND OTHER SKETCHES. London: Duckworth, 1906.

2018 HIS PEOPLE. London: Duckworth, 1906.

Tales and sketches.

2019 FAITH. London: Duckworth, 1909.

Tales and sketches.

2020 HOPE. London: Duckworth, 1910.

Tales and sketches.

2021 CHARITY. London: Duckworth, 1912.

Tales and sketches.

2022 A HATCHMENT. London: Duckworth, 1913.

Tales and sketches.

2023 SCOTTISH STORIES. London: Duckworth, 1914.

2024 BERNAL DIAZ DEL CASTILLO, BEING SOME ACCOUNT OF HIM TAKEN FROM HIS TRUE HISTORY OF THE CONQUEST OF NEW SPAIN. London: Eveleigh Nash, 1915.

2025 BROUGHT FORWARD. London: Duckworth, 1916.

Tales and sketches.

2026 A BRAZILIAN MYSTIC, BEING THE LIFE AND MIRACLES OF ANTONIO CONSELHEIRO. London: Heinemann, 1920.

2027 CARTAGENA AND THE BANKS OF THE SINÚ. London: Heinemann, 1920.

2028 THE CONQUEST OF NEW GRANADA, BEING THE LIFE OF GONZALO JIMENEZ DE QUESADA. London: Heinemann, 1922.

2029 THE CONQUEST OF THE RIVER PLATE. London: Heinemann, 1924.

2030 DOUGHTY DEEDS: AN ACCOUNT OF THE LIFE OF ROBERT GRAHAM OF GARTMORE, POET AND POLITICIAN, 1735-1797. London: Heinemann, 1925.

2031 PEDRO DE VALDIVIA, CONQUEROR OF CHILE. London: Heinemann, 1926.

2032 REDEEMED, AND OTHER SKETCHES. London: Heinemann, 1927.

2033 JOSÉ ANTONIO PÁEZ. London: Heinemann, 1929.

2034 THE HORSES OF THE CONQUEST. London: Heinemann, 1930.

2035 WRIT IN SAND. London: Heinemann, 1932.

Tales and sketches.

2036 PORTRAIT OF A DICTATOR: FRANCISCO SOLANO LOPEZ, PARAGUAY, 1865-1870. London: Heinemann, 1933.

2037 MIRAGES. London: Heinemann, 1936.

Essays and sketches.

COLLECTIONS AND SELECTIONS

2038 THIRTY TALES AND SKETCHES. Ed. Edward Garnett. London: Duckworth, 1929.

2039 RODEO: A COLLECTION OF THE TALES AND SKETCHES. Ed. Aimé Felix Tschiffely. London: Heinemann, 1936.

2040 THE ESSENTIAL R.B. CUNNINGHAME GRAHAM. Ed. Paul Bloomfield. London: Cape, 1952.

2041 THE SOUTH-AMERICAN SKETCHES OF R.B. CUNNINGHAME GRAHAM. Ed. John Walker. Norman: University of Oklahoma Press, 1978.

2042 BEATTOCK FOR MOFFAT AND THE BEST OF R.B. CUNNINGHAME GRAHAM. Ed. Alanna Knight. Edinburgh: Paul Harris, 1979.

BIOGRAPHY AND CRITICISM

CSS, pages 10-12; D; P; T; TCA; TCA-1.

2043 West, Herbert Faulkner. A MODERN CONQUISTADOR: ROBERT BONTINE CUNNINGHAME GRAHAM, HIS LIFE AND WORKS. London: Cranley and Day, 1932.

2044 Tschiffely, Aimé Felix. DON ROBERTO, BEING AN ACCOUNT OF THE LIFE AND WORKS OF R.B. CUNNINGHAME GRAHAM, 1852-1936. London: Heinemann, 1937.

2045 Niles, Blair, ed. JOURNEYS IN TIME. New York: Coward-McCann, 1946.

2046 MacDiarmid, Hugh. CUNNINGHAME GRAHAM: A CENTENARY STUDY. Glasgow: Caledonian Press, 1952.

2047 Davies, Laurence. "R.B. Cunninghame Graham: The Kailyard and After." SSL, 11 (1973-74), 156-77.

2048 Meyers, Jeffrey. "The Genius of Fashion: R.B. Cunninghame Graham." LONDON MAGAZINE, 15 (October-November 1975), 54-73.

2049 Watts, Cedric, and Laurence Davies. CUNNINGHAME GRAHAM: A
CRITICAL BIOGRAPHY. Cambridge: Cambridge University Press, 1979.

BIBLIOGRAPHY

2050 Chaundy, Leslie. A BIBLIOGRAPHY OF THE FIRST EDITIONS OF THE
WORKS OF ROBERT BONTINE CUNNINGHAME GRAHAM. London:
Dulau, 1924.

2051 West, Herbert Faulkner. THE HERBERT FAULKNER WEST COLLECTION
OF R.B. CUNNINGHAME GRAHAM. Hanover, N.H.: Privately Printed,
1938.

2052 Watts, Cedric. "R.B. Cunninghame Graham (1852-1936): A List of his
Contributions to Periodicals." BIBLIOTHECK, 4 (1963-66), 186-99.

2053 Walker, John. "A Chronological Bibliography of Works on R.B. Cunninghame Graham (1852-1936)." BIBLIOTHECK, 9 (1978-79), 47-64.

2054 _____. "R.B. Cunninghame Graham: An Annotated Bibliography of
Writings about Him." ELT, 22 (1979), 77-156.

Sir James George Frazer (1854-1941)

See page 161.

"Fiona Macleod"
William Sharp (1855-1905)

See page 162.

William Archer (1856-1924)

See page 164.

James Pittendrigh Macgillivray (1856-1938)

The King's Sculptor for Scotland was also a poet, recognized by Hugh Mac-
Diarmid as one of the forerunners of the Scottish literary renaissance.

2055 PRO PATRIA. Edinburgh: Privately Printed, 1915.

Poems.

2056 BOG-MYRTLE AND PEAT REEK: VERSE MAINLY IN THE NORTH AND SOUTH COUNTRY DIALECTS OF SCOTLAND. Edinburgh: Privately Printed, 1922.

BIOGRAPHY AND CRITICISM

CSS, pages 13-16.

2057 Cammell, Charles Richard. HEART OF SCOTLAND. London: Robert Hale, 1956.

  Particularly chapter 4, pages 91-120.

John Davidson (1857-1909)

See page 165.

Sir Arthur Conan Doyle (1859-1930)

See page 167.

Kenneth Grahame (1859-1932)

See page 170.

Annie S. Swan (1859-1943)

See page 170.

Samuel Rutherford Crockett (1860-1914)

See page 172.

Sir James Matthew Barrie (1860-1937)

See page 173.

Violet Jacob (1863-1946)

Although Violet Jacob began as a novelist, she is best known for her poems, mainly "Songs of Angus," written in a racy and fluent Scots.

2058 THE SHEEP STEALERS. London: Heinemann, 1902.
   A novel.

2059 THE GOLDEN HEART, AND OTHER FAIRY STORIES. London: Heine-mann, 1904.

2060 THE INTERLOPER. London: Heinemann, 1904.
   A novel.

2061 VERSES. London: Heinemann, 1905.

2062 THE HISTORY OF AYTHAN WARING. London: Heinemann, 1908.
   A novel.

2063 IRRESOLUTE CATHERINE. London: John Murray, 1908.
   A novel.

2064 STORIES TOLD BY THE MILLER. London: John Murray, 1909.

2065 THE FORTUNE HUNTERS, AND OTHER STORIES. London: John Murray, 1910.

2066 FLEMINGTON. London: John Murray, 1911.
   A novel.

2067 SONGS OF ANGUS. London: John Murray, 1915.

2068 MORE SONGS OF ANGUS AND OTHERS. London: Country Life, 1918.

2069 BONNIE JOANN, AND OTHER POEMS. London: John Murray, 1921.

2070 TALES OF MY OWN COUNTRY. London: John Murray, 1922.

2071 TWO NEW POEMS. Edinburgh: Porpoise Press, 1924.

2072 THE NORTHERN LIGHTS, AND OTHER POEMS. London: John Murray, 1927.

2073 THE LAIRDS OF DUN. London: John Murray, 1931.
   Family history.

2074 "Anderson." "The Yellow Dog." SLJ, 9 (May 1979), 58–68.

Two recently discovered short stories.

COLLECTIONS

2075 THE SCOTTISH POEMS OF VIOLET JACOB. Edinburgh: Oliver and Boyd, 1944.

BIOGRAPHY AND CRITICISM

CSS, pages 8–10; P.

Neil Munro (1864-1930)
"Hugh Foulis"

Poet, journalist and writer of romantic novels and stories. As Hugh Foulis, he wrote a number of highly amusing tales.

2076 THE LOST PIBROCH, AND OTHER SHEILING STORIES. Edinburgh: Blackwood, 1896.

2077 JOHN SPLENDID: THE TALE OF A POOR GENTLEMAN AND THE LITTLE WARS OF LORN. Edinburgh: Blackwood, 1898.

2078 GILIAN THE DREAMER. London: Isbister, 1899.

2079 THE SHOES OF FORTUNE. London: Isbister, 1901.

2080 DOOM CASTLE: A ROMANCE. Edinburgh: Blackwood, 1901.

2081 CHILDREN OF TEMPEST: A TALE OF THE OUTER ISLES. Edinburgh: Blackwood, 1903.

2082 ERCHIE, MY DROLL FRIEND. [by H.F.] Edinburgh: Blackwood, 1904.

2083 THE VITAL SPARK AND HER QUEER CREW. [by H.F.] Edinburgh: Blackwood, 1906.

Tales of Para Handy, skipper of the Clyde puffer s.s. VITAL SPARK.

2084 THE CLYDE, RIVER AND FIRTH. London: Black, 1907.

2085 THE DAFT DAYS. Edinburgh: Blackwood, 1907; issued as BUD: A NOVEL, New York: Harper, 1907.

2086 FANCY FARM. Edinburgh: Blackwood, 1910.

2087 IN HIGHLAND HARBOURS WITH PARA HANDY, s.s. VITAL SPARK. [by H.F.] Edinburgh: Blackwood, 1911.

2088 AYRSHIRE IDYLLS. London: Black, 1912.

2089 THE NEW ROAD. Edinburgh: Blackwood, 1914.

2090 JIMMY SWAN, THE JOY TRAVELLER. [by H.F.] Edinburgh: Blackwood, 1917.

2091 JAUNTY JOCK AND OTHER STORIES. Edinburgh: Blackwood, 1918.

2092 HURRICANE JACK OF THE VITAL SPARK. [by H.F.] Edinburgh: Blackwood, 1923.

COLLECTIONS AND SELECTIONS

2093 THE POETRY OF NEIL MUNRO. Introd. John Buchan. Edinburgh: Blackwood, 1931.

2094 THE BRAVE DAYS: A CHRONICLE FROM THE NORTH. Ed. George Blake. Edinburgh: Porpoise Press, 1931.

2095 THE LOOKER-ON. Ed. George Blake. Edinburgh: Porpoise Press, 1933. Essays.

2096 PARA HANDY TALES. Edinburgh: Blackwood, 1958.

BIOGRAPHY AND CRITICISM

CSS, pages 5-6; H, pages 164-69; P; TCA.

Charles Murray (1864-1941)

An Aberdeenshire man who wrote the poems of an exile in the dialect of his native district, while living in South Africa.

2097 HAMEWITH. Aberdeen: Wyllie, 1900; London: Constable, 1909.

2098 A SOUGH O' WAR. London: Constable, 1917.

2099 IN THE COUNTRY PLACES. London: Constable, 1920.

2100 THE LAST POEMS. Aberdeen: Aberdeen University Press, 1969.
    With an appreciation of Charles Murray by Dr. Nan Shepherd.

COLLECTIONS AND SELECTIONS

2101 HAMEWITH AND OTHER POEMS. London: Constable, 1927.

2102 HAMEWITH: THE COMPLETE POEMS OF CHARLES MURRAY. Aberdeen: Aberdeen University Press, 1979.

BIOGRAPHY AND CRITICISM

CSS, pages 6-8; P.

Marion Angus (1866-1946)

A sensitive and wistful poet whose use of Scots is natural and poignant.

2103 THE LILT, AND OTHER VERSES. Aberdeen: Wyllie, 1922.

2104 THE TINKER'S ROAD, AND OTHER VERSES. Glasgow: Gowans and Gray, 1924.

2105 SUN AND CANDLELIGHT. Edinburgh: Porpoise Press, 1927.

2106 THE SINGIN' LASS. Edinburgh: Porpoise Press, 1929.

2107 THE TURN OF THE DAY. Edinburgh: Porpoise Press, 1931.

2108 LOST COUNTRY, AND OTHER VERSES. Glasgow: Gowans and Gray, 1937.

SELECTIONS

2109 SELECTED POEMS. Ed. Maurice Lindsay. Edinburgh: Serif Books, 1950.

BIOGRAPHY AND CRITICISM

CSS, pages 61–63; P.

2110 Lindsay, Maurice, "Introduction," and Helen B. Cruickshank, "A Personal Note." In SELECTED POEMS OF MARION ANGUS. Edinburgh: Serif Books, 1950, pp. ix–xxi.

Norman Douglas (1868-1952)

Novelist, essayist, and the author of several travel books, stylishly written and attractively urbane.

2111 SIREN LAND. London: Dent, 1911.

Travels in southern Italy.

2112 FOUNTAINS IN THE SAND. London: Secker, 1912.

Travels in Tunisia.

2113 OLD CALABRIA. London: Secker, 1915.

2114 SOUTH WIND. London: Secker, 1917.

A novel.

2115 THEY WENT. London: Chapman and Hall, 1920.

A novel.

2116 ALONE. London: Chapman and Hall, 1921.

Travel in Italy.

2117 TOGETHER. London: Chapman and Hall, 1923.

Travel in Austria.

2118 EXPERIMENTS. London: Chapman and Hall, 1925.

2119 BIRDS AND BEASTS OF THE GREEK ANTHOLOGY. London: Chapman and Hall, 1928.

2120 IN THE BEGINNING. London: Chatto and Windus, 1928.

A romance.

2121 HOW ABOUT EUROPE? London: Chatto and Windus, 1930; issued as GOOD-BYE TO WESTERN CULTURE, New York: Harper, 1930.

2122 PANEROS: SOME WORDS ON APHRODISIACS AND THE LIKE. London: Chatto and Windus, 1931.

2123 LOOKING BACK: AN AUTOBIOGRAPHICAL EXCURSION. 2 vols. London: Chatto and Windus, 1933.

2124 LATE HARVEST. London: Lindsay Drummond, 1946; 1947.

Bibliographical comment on his work, essays, and reviews.

SELECTIONS

2125 AN ALMANAC. London: Chatto and Windus, with Secker and Warburg, 1945.

Selected by the author.

2126 NORMAN DOUGLAS: A SELECTION FROM HIS WORKS. Introd. David Morrice Low. London: Chatto and Windus, with Secker and Warburg, 1955.

BIOGRAPHY AND CRITICISM

2127 Tomlinson, Henry Major. NORMAN DOUGLAS. London: Chatto and Windus, 1931; enl. and rev., London: Hutchinson, 1952.

2128 Fitzgibbon, Constantine. NORMAN DOUGLAS: A PICTORIAL RECORD. London: Richards Press, 1953.

2129 Aldington, Richard. PINORMAN: PERSONAL RECOLLECTIONS OF NORMAN DOUGLAS AND PINO ORIOLI. London: Heinemann, 1954.

2130 Cunard, Nancy. GRAND MAN: MEMORIES OF NORMAN DOUGLAS. London: Secker and Warburg, 1954.

2131 Lindeman, Ralph. NORMAN DOUGLAS. New York: Twayne, 1965.

2132 Fitzgibbon, Constantine. "Norman Douglas: Memoir of an Unwritten Biography." ENCOUNTER, 43 (September 1974), 23-37.

2133 Holloway, Mark. NORMAN DOUGLAS: A BIOGRAPHY. London: Secker and Warburg, 1976.

BIBLIOGRAPHY

2134 Woolf, Cecil. A BIBLIOGRAPHY OF NORMAN DOUGLAS. London:
Hart-Davis, 1954.

George Douglas Brown (1869-1902)
"Kennedy King"

His great novel, a grim picture of life in a small Scottish town, shattered the
Kailyarders' cozy picture. For a note on the Kailyard school, see 790.

2135 LOVE AND A SWORD. [by K.K.] London: Macqueen, 1899.

2136 THE HOUSE WITH THE GREEN SHUTTERS. London: Macqueen, 1901;
memorial edition, London: Melrose, 1923.

> Includes a biographical sketch and an appreciation of the man
> and his book by Andrew Melrose. There are also editions of
> this important novel with good introductions by George Blake
> (New York: Modern Library, 1927), J.B. Priestley (London:
> Cape, 1929), and W. Somerset Maugham (London: OUP, 1938).

2137 THE HOUSE WITH THE GREEN SHUTTERS. Ed. John T. Low. Edinburgh:
Holmes McDougall, 1975.

BIOGRAPHY AND CRITICISM

2138 Crosland, Thomas W.H. THE UNSPEAKABLE SCOT. London: Grant
Richards, 1902.

2139 Lennox, Cuthbert. GEORGE DOUGLAS BROWN: A BIOGRAPHICAL
MEMOIR. London: Hodder and Stoughton, 1903.

> Includes REMINISCENCES by Andrew Melrose.

2140 Parker, William Mathie. "A Herald of Revolt: George Douglas Brown."
In his MODERN SCOTTISH WRITERS. Edinburgh: Hodge, 1917, pp. 245-55.

2141 Muir, Edwin. "George Douglas." In his LATITUDES. London: Melrose,
1924, pp. 31-46.

2142 Scott, John Dick. "R.L. Stevenson and G.D. Brown." HORIZON, 13
(1946), 298-310.

2143 Blake, George. BARRIE AND THE KAILYARD SCHOOL. London: Arthur
Barker, 1951.

2144 Veitch, James. GEORGE DOUGLAS BROWN. London: Jenkins, 1952.

2145 McClure, J. Derrick. "Dialect in THE HOUSE WITH THE GREEN SHUT-TERS." SSL, 9 (1971-72), 148-63.

2146 Campbell, Ian. "George Douglas Brown's Kailyard Novel." SSL, 12 (1974-75), 62-73.

2147 _____. "George Douglas Brown: A Study in Objectivity." In NINE-TEENTH-CENTURY SCOTTISH FICTION: CRITICAL ESSAYS. Ed. Ian Campbell. Manchester: Carcanet New Press, 1979, pp. 148-63.

2148 Manson, John. "Young Gourlay." SLJ, 7 (December 1980), 44-54.

"John Brandane"
John MacIntyre (1869-1947)

A doctor who wrote several presentable plays and three novels. His plays are listed below by their year of first performance [in brackets]; details of their publication in book form are given under the year of publication.

2149 MY LADY OF AROS. London: Pitman, 1910.

A novel.

2150 GLENFORSA: A PLAY IN ONE ACT. With A.W. Yuill. [1921] Glasgow: Gowans and Gray, 1921.

2151 THE CHANGE-HOUSE: A PLAY IN ONE ACT. [1921] Glasgow: Gowans and Gray, 1921.

2152 THE SPANISH GALLEON: A PLAY IN ONE ACT. With A.W. Yuill. [1922]

2153 THE CAPTAIN MORE. London: Cape, 1923.

A novel.

2154 THE GLEN IS MINE. [1923]

2155 THE TREASURE SHIP. [1924]

2156 THE LIFTING. [1925]

2157 THE GLEN IS MINE AND THE LIFTING: TWO PLAYS OF THE HEB-RIDES. London: Constable, 1925.

2158 THE INN OF ADVENTURE. [1925]

2159 RORY AFORESAID. [1925]

2160 HEATHER GENTRY. [1927]

2161 THE TREASURE SHIP, RORY AFORESAID, THE HAPPY WAR: THREE PLAYS.
London: Constable, 1928.

2162 THE SPANISH GALLEON: A PLAY IN ONE ACT. With A.W. Yuill.
Glasgow: Gowans and Gray, 1932.

2163 STRAW-FEET. London: Constable, 1932.

A novel.

2164 THE INN OF ADVENTURE, HEATHER GENTRY: TWO COMEDIES. London: Constable, 1933.

2165 MAN OF UZ. London: Muller, 1938.

BIOGRAPHY AND CRITICISM

CSS, pages 74-76.

2166 Bannister, Winifred. JAMES BRIDIE AND HIS THEATRE. London: Rockliff, 1955.

Lewis Spence (1874-1955)

A poet who chose to write in a highly stylized literary Scots, more widely
known for his substantial works on mythology and anthropology, of which only
a selection of the more important is listed here.

2167 THE MYTHOLOGY OF ANCIENT MEXICO AND PERU. London: Constable, 1908.

2168 A DICTIONARY OF MYTHOLOGY. London: Cassell, 1910.

2169 LE ROI D'YS AND OTHER POEMS. London: Elkin Mathews, 1910.

2170 THE CIVILISATION OF ANCIENT MEXICO. Cambridge: Cambridge
University Press, 1912.

2171 THE MYTHS OF MEXICO AND PERU. London: Harrap, 1913.

2172 SONGS, SATANIC AND CELESTIAL. London: Elkin Mathews, 1913.

2173 AN ENCYCLOPAEDIA OF OCCULTISM. London: Routledge, 1920.

2174 AN INTRODUCTION TO MYTHOLOGY. London: Harrap, 1921.

2175 THE GODS OF MEXICO. London: T. Fisher Unwin, 1922.

2176 THE PHOENIX AND OTHER POEMS. Edinburgh: Porpoise Press, 1923.

2177 THE PROBLEM OF ATLANTIS. London: Rider, 1924.

2178 PLUMES OF TIME. London: Allen and Unwin, 1926.
Poems.

2179 WEIRDS AND VANITIES. Edinburgh: Porpoise Press, 1927.
Poems.

2180 THE ARCHER IN THE ARRAS, AND OTHER TALES OF MYSTERY. Edinburgh: Grant and Murray, 1932.

2181 THE MAGIC ARTS IN CELTIC BRITAIN. London: Rider, 1946.

2182 SECOND SIGHT: ITS HISTORY AND ORIGINS. London: Rider, 1951.

COLLECTIONS AND SELECTIONS

2183 COLLECTED POEMS. Edinburgh: Serif Books, 1953.

BIOGRAPHY AND CRITICISM

CSS, pages 61-63; P; TCA-1.

John Buchan, 1st Baron Tweedsmuir (1875-1940)

Biographer, historian, statesman, and writer of adventure stories.

2184 SCHOLAR GIPSIES. London: John Lane, 1896.
Essays.

2185 JOHN BURNET OF BARNS: A ROMANCE. London: John Lane, 1898; rpt. Edinburgh: Canongate, 1978.

2186 GREY WEATHER: MOORLAND TALES OF MY OWN PEOPLE. London: John Lane, 1899.

2187 A LOST LADY OF OLD YEARS: A ROMANCE. London: John Lane, 1899.

2188 THE HALF—HEARTED. London: Isbister, 1900.

2189 THE WATCHER BY THE THRESHOLD, AND OTHER TALES. Edinburgh: Blackwood, 1902.

2190 A LODGE IN THE WILDERNESS. Edinburgh: Blackwood, 1906.

2191 SOME EIGHTEENTH-CENTURY BYWAYS AND OTHER ESSAYS. Edinburgh: Blackwood, 1908.

2192 PRESTER JOHN. London: Nelson, 1910; issued as THE GREAT DIAMOND PIPE, New York: Dodd, Mead, 1910.

2193 SIR WALTER RALEIGH. London: Nelson, 1911.

2194 THE MOON ENDURETH: TALES AND FANCIES. Edinburgh: Blackwood, 1912.

2195 SALUTE TO ADVENTURERS. London: Nelson, 1915.

2196 THE THIRTY-NINE STEPS. Edinburgh: Blackwood, 1915.

2197 NELSON'S HISTORY OF THE GREAT WAR. 24 vols. London: Nelson, 1915-19; issued as A HISTORY OF THE GREAT WAR, London: Nelson, 1921-22.

2198 THE POWER-HOUSE. Edinburgh: Blackwood, 1916.

2199 GREENMANTLE. London: Hodder and Stoughton, 1916.

2200 POEMS, SCOTS AND ENGLISH. Edinburgh: Jack, 1917.

2201 MR. STANDFAST. London: Hodder and Stoughton, 1919.

2202 THE PATH OF THE KING. London: Hodder and Stoughton, 1921.

2203 A BOOK OF ESCAPES AND HURRIED JOURNEYS. London: Nelson, 1922.

2204 HUNTINGTOWER. London: Hodder and Stoughton, 1922; rpt. Edinburgh: EUSPB, 1978.

2205 THE LAST SECRETS. London: Nelson, 1923.

2206 MIDWINTER. London: Hodder and Stoughton, 1923.

2207 THE THREE HOSTAGES. London: Hodder and Stoughton, 1924.

2208 JOHN MACNAB. London: Hodder and Stoughton, 1925.

2209 THE DANCING FLOOR. London: Hodder and Stoughton, 1926.

2210 HOMILIES AND RECREATIONS. London: Nelson, 1926.

2211 WITCH WOOD. London: Hodder and Stoughton, 1927.

2212 MONTROSE. London: Nelson, 1928; rpt. Edinburgh: James Thin, Mercat Press, 1979.

    This study of Montrose was also published in the World's Classics, introd. Keith Feiling (London: OUP, 1957).

2213 THE RUNAGATES CLUB. London: Hodder and Stoughton, 1928.

2214 THE COURTS OF THE MORNING. London: Hodder and Stoughton, 1929.

2215 THE KIRK IN SCOTLAND, 1560-1929. With George Adam Smith. London: Hodder and Stoughton, 1930.

2216 CASTLE GAY. London: Hodder and Stoughton, 1930.

2217 THE BLANKET OF THE DARK. London: Hodder and Stoughton, 1931.

2218 SIR WALTER SCOTT. London: Cassell, 1932.

2219 THE GAP IN THE CURTAIN. London: Hodder and Stoughton, 1932.

2220 JULIUS CAESAR. London: Peter Davies, 1932.

2221 THE MAGIC WALKING STICK. London: Hodder and Stoughton, 1932.

2222 THE MASSACRE OF GLENCOE. London: Peter Davies, 1933.

2223 A PRINCE OF THE CAPTIVITY. London: Hodder and Stoughton, 1933.

2224 THE FREE FISHERS. London: Hodder and Stoughton, 1934.

2225 GORDON AT KHARTOUM. London: Peter Davies, 1934.

2226 OLIVER CROMWELL. London: Hodder and Stoughton, 1934.

2227 THE KING'S GRACE, 1910-35. London: Hodder and Stoughton, 1935; issued as THE PEOPLE'S KING, GEORGE V: A NARRATIVE OF TWENTY-FIVE YEARS, Boston: Houghton Mifflin, 1935.

2228 THE HOUSE OF THE FOUR WINDS. London: Hodder and Stoughton, 1935.

2229 THE ISLAND OF SHEEP. London: Hodder and Stoughton, 1936; issued as THE MAN FROM THE NORLANDS, Boston: Houghton Mifflin, 1936.

2230 AUGUSTUS. London: Hodder and Stoughton, 1937.

2231 MEMORY HOLD-THE-DOOR. London: Hodder and Stoughton, 1940; issued as PILGRIM'S WAY: AN ESSAY IN RECOLLECTION, Boston: Houghton Mifflin, 1940.

2232 COMMENTS AND CHARACTERS. Ed. William Forbes Gray. London: Nelson, 1940.

A selection of Buchan's contributions to the SCOTTISH REVIEW.

2233 SICK HEART RIVER. London: Hodder and Stoughton, 1941; issued as MOUNTAIN MEADOW, Boston: Houghton Mifflin, 1941.

2234 THE LONG TRAVERSE. London: Hodder and Stoughton, 1941; issued as LAKE OF GOLD, Boston: Houghton Mifflin, 1941.

COLLECTIONS AND SELECTIONS

Various "omnibus" volumes of John Buchan's novels have been published from time to time, and frequently reprinted.

2235 MEN AND DEEDS. London: Peter Davies, 1935.

> Includes JULIUS CAESAR, THE MASSACRE OF GLENCOE, and GORDON AT KHARTOUM, with other essays and papers.

2236 THE CLEARING HOUSE: A SURVEY OF ONE MAN'S MIND. London: Hodder and Stoughton, 1946.

> A selection arranged by Susan Buchan, Lady Tweedsmuir.

2237 BEST SHORT STORIES. Ed. David Daniell. London: Michael Joseph, 1980.

BIOGRAPHY AND CRITICISM

CSS, pages 1-3; D; P; T; TCA; TCA-1.

2238 Buchan, Susan, et al. JOHN BUCHAN, BY HIS WIFE AND FRIENDS. London: Hodder and Stoughton, 1947.

2239 Turner, Arthur C. MR. BUCHAN, WRITER. London: S.C.M. Press, 1949.

2240 Usborne, Richard. CLUBLAND HEROES: A NOSTALGIC STUDY OF SOME RECURRENT CHARACTERS IN THE ROMANTIC FICTION OF DORNFORD YATES, BUCHAN AND SAPPER. London: Constable, 1953.

2241 Smith, Janet Adam. JOHN BUCHAN. London: Hart-Davis, 1965.

2242 Sandison, Alan. THE WHEEL OF EMPIRE: A STUDY OF THE IMPERIAL IDEA IN SOME LATE NINETEENTH AND EARLY TWENTIETH-CENTURY FICTION. London: Macmillan, 1967.

2243 Daniell, David. THE INTERPRETER'S HOUSE: A CRITICAL ASSESSMENT OF JOHN BUCHAN. London: Nelson, 1975.

2244 Smith, Janet Adam. JOHN BUCHAN AND HIS WORLD. London: Thames and Hudson, 1979.

BIBLIOGRAPHY

2245 Hanna, Archibald. JOHN BUCHAN, 1875-1940: A BIBLIOGRAPHY.
Hamden, Conn.: Shoe String Press, 1953.

George Reston Malloch (1875-1953)

A dramatist, poet, and critic now undeservedly neglected. Five of his plays,
first performed between 1909 and 1928, have not been published, and are not
listed here (see Allardyce Nicoll's ENGLISH DRAMA, 1900-1930 [Cambridge:
Cambridge University Press, 1973], pp. 265, 811, 1052). The year of first
performance of the separately published plays is given in brackets.

2246 ARABELLA: A PLAY IN THREE ACTS. [1912] London: Stephen Swift,
1912.

2247 LYRICS AND OTHER POEMS. London: Elkin Mathews, 1913.

2248 POEMS AND LYRICS. London: Heinemann, 1916.

2249 POEMS. London: Heinemann, 1920.

2250 THE HOUSE OF THE QUEEN. [1926] Montrose: Scottish Poetry Bookshop, 1923.

   A play in one act.

2251 THOMAS THE RHYMER. [1924] Montrose: Scottish Poetry Bookshop,
1924.

   A play in one act.

2252 SOUTARNESS WATER: A PLAY IN THREE ACTS. [1926] Glasgow:
Gowans and Gray, 1927.

2253 THE GRENADIER: A PLAY IN ONE ACT. Stirling: Eneas Mackay,
1930.

2254 HUMAN VOICES: NEW POEMS. Stirling: Eneas Mackay, 1930.

2255 THE MOMENT'S MONUMENTS: SEVENTY SONNETS. Stirling: Eneas
Mackay, 1932.

2256 DOWN IN THE FOREST: A PLAY. [1935]

2257 PROLOGUE TO FLODDEN. Stirling: Eneas Mackay, 1936.

    A play in one act.

BIOGRAPHY AND CRITICISM

CSS, pages 35-37, 78-80.

Rachel Annand Taylor (1876-1960)

A poet, and student of the Italian Renaissance.

2258 POEMS. London: John Lane, 1904.

2259 ROSE AND VINE. London: Elkin Mathews, 1909.

2260 THE HOURS OF FIAMETTA: A SONNET SEQUENCE. London: Elkin Mathews, 1910.

2261 THE END OF FIAMETTA. London: Grant Richards, 1923.

2262 ASPECTS OF THE ITALIAN RENAISSANCE. London: Grant Richards, 1923; rev. and enl. as INVITATION TO RENAISSANCE ITALY, New York: Harper, 1930.

2263 LEONARDO THE FLORENTINE: A STUDY IN PERSONALITY. London: Richards Press, 1927; New York: Harper, 1928.

    The American edition has a note on the author's work by Gilbert Murray.

2264 DUNBAR: THE POET AND HIS PERIOD. Poets on the Poets. London: Faber, 1931.

BIOGRAPHY AND CRITICISM

CSS, pages 102-3; TCA; TCA-1.

"O. Douglas"
Anna Buchan (1877-1948)

A writer of plain, homely novels, with a shrewd if somewhat sentimental eye for character.

2265 OLIVIA IN INDIA. London: Hodder and Stoughton, 1913.
Reissued by the same publisher in 1918 as OLIVIA.

2266 THE SETONS. London: Hodder and Stoughton, 1917.

2267 PENNY PLAIN. London: Hodder and Stoughton, 1920.

2268 ANN AND HER MOTHER. London: Hodder and Stoughton, 1922.

2269 PINK SUGAR. London: Hodder and Stoughton, 1924.

2270 THE PROPER PLACE. London: Hodder and Stoughton, 1926.

2271 ELIZA FOR COMMON. London: Hodder and Stoughton, 1928.

2272 THE DAY OF SMALL THINGS. London: Hodder and Stoughton, 1930.

2273 PRIORSFORD. London: Hodder and Stoughton, 1932.

2274 TAKEN BY THE HAND. London: Hodder and Stoughton, 1935.

2275 JANE'S PARLOUR. London: Hodder and Stoughton, 1937.

2276 THE HOUSE THAT IS OUR OWN. London: Hodder and Stoughton, 1940.

2277 UNFORGETTABLE, UNFORGOTTEN. London: Hodder and Stoughton, 1945.
Autobiography.

BIOGRAPHY AND CRITICISM

2278 FAREWELL TO PRIORSFORD: A BOOK BY AND ABOUT ANNA BUCHAN (O. DOUGLAS). London: Hodder and Stoughton, 1950.
Includes five short stories, a sketch, and eight chapters from an unfinished novel.

Frederick Niven (1878-1944)

A novelist who is at his best in describing Glasgow life of the period 1890-1914. After the war he made his home in British Columbia: hence his inclusion in McCourt's survey (2316).

2279 THE LOST CABIN MINE. London: John Lane, 1908.

2280 THE ISLAND PROVIDENCE. London: John Lane, 1910.

2281 A WILDERNESS OF MONKEYS. London: Martin Secker, 1911.

2282 ABOVE YOUR HEADS. London: Martin Secker, 1911.
     Short stories.

2283 DEAD MEN'S BELLS: A ROMANCE. London: Martin Secker, 1912.

2284 THE PORCELAIN LADY. London: Martin Secker, 1913.

2285 ELLEN ADAIR. London: Eveleigh Nash, 1913.

2286 HANDS UP! London: Martin Secker, 1913.

2287 THE JUSTICE OF THE PEACE. London: Eveleigh Nash, 1914.

2288 THE S.S. GLORY. London: Heinemann, 1915.

2289 CINDERELLA OF SKOOKUM CREEK. London: Eveleigh Nash, 1916.

2290 TWO GENERATIONS. London: Eveleigh Nash, 1916.

2291 MAPLE-LEAF SONGS. London: Sidgwick and Jackson, 1917.

2292 SAGE-BRUSH STORIES. London: Eveleigh Nash, 1917.

2293 PENNY SCOT'S TREASURE. London: Collins, 1918.

2294 THE LADY OF THE CROSSING: A NOVEL OF THE NEW WEST. London: Hodder and Stoughton, 1919.

2295 A TALE THAT IS TOLD. London: Collins, 1920.

2296 TREASURE TRAIL. New York: Dodd, Mead, 1923.

2297 THE WOLFER. New York: Dodd, Mead, 1923.

2298 A LOVER OF THE LAND, AND OTHER POEMS. New York: Boni and Liveright, 1925.

2299 QUEER FELLOWS. London: John Lane, 1927; issued as WILD HONEY, New York: Dodd, Mead, 1927.

2300 THE STORY OF ALEXANDER SELKIRK. London: Wells Gardner, Darton, 1927.

2301 CANADA WEST. London: Dent, 1930.

2302 THE THREE MARYS. London: Collins, 1930.

2303 THE PAISLEY SHAWL. London: Collins, 1931.

2304 THE RICH WIFE. London: Collins, 1932.

2305 MRS. BARRY. London: Collins, 1933.

2306 TRIUMPH. London: Collins, 1934.

2307 THE FLYING YEARS. London: Collins, 1935.

2308 OLD SOLDIER: A NOVEL. London: Collins, 1936.

2309 THE STAFF AT SIMSON'S: A NOVEL. London: Collins, 1937.

2310 COLOURED SPECTACLES. London: Collins, 1938.
Autobiography.

2311 THE STORY OF THEIR DAYS. London: Collins, 1939.

2312 MINE INHERITANCE. London: Collins, 1940.

2313 BROTHERS IN ARMS. London: Collins, 1942.

2314 UNDER WHICH KING? London: Collins, 1943.

2315 THE TRANSPLANTED. London: Collins, 1944.

BIOGRAPHY AND CRITICISM

CSS, pages 20-23; TCA; TCA-1.

2316 McCourt, Edward A. THE CANADIAN WEST IN FICTION. Toronto: Ryerson, 1949; rev. and enl. ed., 1970.

2317 Dunlop, John. "The Spirit of Niven." SCOTTISH FIELD, 102 (November 1954), 45.

2318 Reid, Alexander. "A Scottish Chekhov?" SCOTLAND'S MAGAZINE, 58 (March 1962), 45-46.

David Lindsay (1878-1945)

A novelist of powerful originality, strangely neglected in his day but now winning belated recognition.

2319 A VOYAGE TO ARCTURUS. London: Methuen, 1920; London: Gollancz, 1946.

2320 THE HAUNTED WOMAN. London: Methuen, 1922; London: Gollancz, 1947.

2321 SPHINX. London: John Long, 1923.

2322 ADVENTURES OF MONSIEUR DE MAILLY. London: Melrose, 1926; issued as A BLADE FOR SALE, New York: McBride, 1927.

2323 DEVIL'S TOR. London: Putnam, 1932.

2324 THE VIOLET APPLE and THE WITCH. Ed. John Barclay Pick. Chicago: Swallow Press, 1976.

2325 THE VIOLET APPLE. Introd. John Barclay Pick. London: Sidgwick and Jackson, 1978.

BIOGRAPHY AND CRITICISM

2326 Pick, John Barclay, et al. THE STRANGE GENIUS OF DAVID LINDSAY: AN APPRECIATION. London: Baker, 1970.

   The collaborators in this volume are Colin Wilson and E.H. Visiak.

2327 McClure, J. Derrick. "'Purely as Entertainment'? ADVENTURES OF M. DE MAILLY as a Representative Work of David Lindsay." SSL, 11 (1973-74), 226-36.

2328 ____. "Language and Logic in A VOYAGE TO ARCTURUS." SLJ, 1 (July 1974), 20-38.

2329 Wolfe, Gary K. "David Lindsay and George MacDonald." SSL, 12 (1974-75), 131-45.

2330 Herdman, John. "The Previously Unpublished Novels of David Lindsay." SLJ, suppl. 3 (1976), 14-25.

A review of the two novels first published posthumously by the Swallow Press (see 2324).

2331 Hume, Kathryn. "Visionary Allegory in David Lindsay's A VOYAGE TO ARCTURUS." JOURNAL OF ENGLISH AND GERMANIC PHILOLOGY, 77 (1978), 72-91.

Catherine Carswell (1879-1946)

A perceptive biographer and novelist.

2332 OPEN THE DOOR! London: Melrose, 1920; Chatto and Windus, 1931.

A novel.

2333 THE CAMOMILE: AN INVENTION. London: Chatto and Windus, 1922.

2334 THE LIFE OF ROBERT BURNS. London: Chatto and Windus, 1930; 1951.

2335 THE SAVAGE PILGRIMAGE: A NARRATIVE OF D.H. LAWRENCE. London: Chatto and Windus, 1932.

Withdrawn under threat of legal action.

THE SAVAGE PILGRIMAGE: A NARRATIVE OF D.H. LAWRENCE. Rev. ed. London: Secker and Warburg, 1932.

2336 ROBERT BURNS. London: Duckworth, 1933.

2337 THE FAYS OF THE ABBEY THEATRE: AN AUTOBIOGRAPHICAL RECORD. With William G. Fay. London: Rich and Cowan, 1935.

2338 THE SCOTS WEEK-END AND CALEDONIAN VADEMECUM. With Donald Carswell. London: Routledge, 1936.

2339 THE TRANQUIL HEART: PORTRAIT OF GIOVANNI BOCCACIO. London: Lawrence and Wishart, 1937.

2340 LYING AWAKE: AN UNFINISHED AUTOBIOGRAPHY, AND OTHER POSTHUMOUS PAPERS. Ed. John Carswell. London: Secker and Warburg, 1950.

BIOGRAPHY AND CRITICISM

D; P; TCA; TCA-1.

2341 Murry, John Middleton. REMINISCENCES OF D.H. LAWRENCE. London: Cape, 1933.

2342 Carswell, John. LIVES AND LETTERS, 1906-1957. London: Faber, 1978.

Reminiscences by Mrs. Carswell's son.

John MacDougall Hay (1881-1919)

A minister who wrote, in his first book, one of the outstanding Scottish novels of this century.

2343 GILLESPIE. London: Constable, 1914; introd. Robert Kemp, London: Duckworth, 1963; introd. Bob Tait and Isobel Murray, Edinburgh: Canongate, 1979.

2344 BARNACLES. London: Constable, 1916.

2345 THEIR DEAD SONS. London: Erskine Macdonald, 1918.

Poems.

BIOGRAPHY AND CRITICISM

H, pages 137-39.

2346 Hart, Francis R. "Reviewing Hay's GILLESPIE: Modern Scottish Fiction and the Critic's Plight." SSL, 2 (1964-65), 19-31.

2347 Scott, Tom. "A Note on J. MacDougall Hay." SCOTIA REVIEW, 7 (1974), 35-39.

2348 Spring, Ian. "Determinism in John MacDougall Hay's GILLESPIE." SLJ, 6 (December 1979), 55-68.

Sir Alexander Gray (1882-1968)

A professor of political economy and a poet who excelled at translation into Scots.

2349 SONGS AND BALLADS, CHIEFLY FROM HEINE. London: Grant Richards, 1920.

2350 ANY MAN'S LIFE: A BOOK OF POEMS. Oxford: Blackwell, 1924.

2351 POEMS. Edinburgh: Porpoise Press, 1925.

2352 GOSSIP: A BOOK OF NEW POEMS. Edinburgh: Porpoise Press, 1928.

2353 SONGS FROM HEINE. Edinburgh: Porpoise Press, 1928.

2354 ARROWS: A BOOK OF GERMAN BALLADS AND FOLK-SONGS ATTEMPTED IN SCOTS. Edinburgh: Grant and Murray, 1932.

2355 THE SOCIALIST TRADITION: MOSES TO LENIN. London: Longmans, Green, 1946.

2356 SIR HALEWYN: EXAMPLES IN EUROPEAN BALLADRY AND FOLKSONG. Edinburgh: Oliver and Boyd, 1949.

2357 FOUR-AND-FORTY: A SELECTION OF DANISH BALLADS PRESENTED IN SCOTS. Edinburgh: Edinburgh University Press, 1954.

2358 HISTORICAL BALLADS OF DENMARK. Edinburgh: Edinburgh University Press, 1958.

SELECTIONS

2359 SELECTED POEMS. Ed. Maurice Lindsay. Glasgow: Maclellan, 1948.

BIOGRAPHY AND CRITICISM

CA-7/8.

2360 Scott, Alexander. "Sir Alexander Gray, 1882-1968." SSL, 8 (1970-71), 123-26.

Sir Compton Mackenzie (1883-1972)

A prolific and versatile writer of novels, entertainments, and reminiscences. His seventeen books for children are not listed here.

2361 POEMS. Oxford: Blackwell, 1907.

2362 THE PASSIONATE ELOPEMENT. London: John Lane, 1911.

2363 CARNIVAL. London: Martin Secker, 1912.

2364 SINISTER STREET. 2 vols. London: Martin Secker, 1913-14; New York: Appleton, 1913-14.

In the American edition, volume 1 has a separate title, YOUTH'S ENCOUNTER.

2365 GUY AND PAULINE. London: Martin Secker, 1915; issued as PLASHER'S MEAD, New York: Harper, 1915.

2366 THE EARLY LIFE AND ADVENTURES OF SYLVIA SCARLETT. London: Martin Secker, 1918.

2367 POOR RELATIONS. London: Martin Secker, 1919.

2368 SYLVIA AND MICHAEL: THE LATER ADVENTURES OF SYLVIA SCAR- LETT. London: Martin Secker, 1919.

2369 THE VANITY GIRL. London: Cassell, 1920.

2370 RICH RELATIVES. London: Martin Secker, 1921.

2371 THE ALTAR STEPS. London: Cassell, 1922.

2372 GRAMOPHONE NIGHTS. With Archibald Marshall. London: Heine- mann, 1923.

2373 THE PARSON'S PROGRESS. London: Cassell, 1923.

A sequel to THE ALTAR STEPS.

2374 THE SEVEN AGES OF WOMAN. London: Martin Secker, 1923.

2375 THE HEAVENLY LADDER. London: Cassell, 1924.

A sequel to THE PARSON'S PROGRESS.

2376 THE OLD MEN OF THE SEA. London: Cassell, 1924; issued as PARA-
DISE FOR SALE, London: Macdonald, 1963.

2377 CORAL: A SEQUEL TO CARNIVAL. London: Cassell, 1925.

2378 FAIRY GOLD. London: Cassell, 1926.

2379 ROGUES AND VAGABONDS. London: Cassell, 1927.

2380 VESTAL FIRE. London: Cassell, 1927.

2381 EXTRAORDINARY WOMEN: THEME AND VARIATIONS. London: Martin
Secker, 1928.

2382 EXTREMES MEET. London: Cassell, 1928.

2383 GALLIPOLI MEMORIES. London: Cassell, 1929.
Volume 1 of his war memoirs.

2384 THE THREE COURIERS. London: Cassell, 1929.

2385 APRIL FOOLS: A FARCE OF MANNERS. London: Cassell, 1930.

2386 BUTTERCUPS AND DAISIES. London: Cassell, 1931; issued as FOR
SALE, Garden City, N.Y.: Doubleday, Doran, 1931.

2387 FIRST ATHENIAN MEMORIES. London: Cassell, 1931.
Volume 2 of his war memoirs.

2388 OUR STREET. London: Cassell, 1931.

2389 GREEK MEMORIES. London: Cassell, 1932.
Volume 3 of his war memoirs.

2390 PRINCE CHARLIE. London: Peter Davies, 1932.

2391 UNCONSIDERED TRIFLES. London: Martin Secker, 1932.
A collection of articles.

2392 LITERATURE IN MY TIME. London: Rich and Cowan, 1933.

2393 THE LOST CAUSE: A JACOBITE PLAY. Edinburgh: Oliver and Boyd, 1933.

2394 REAPED AND BOUND. London: Martin Secker, 1933.
Essays.

2395 WATER ON THE BRAIN. London: Cassell, 1933.

2396 THE DARKENING GREEN. London: Cassell, 1934.

2397 MARATHON AND SALAMIS. London: Peter Davies, 1934.

2398 PRINCE CHARLIE AND HIS LADIES. London: Cassell, 1934.

2399 CATHOLICISM AND SCOTLAND. London: Routledge, 1936.

2400 FIGURE OF EIGHT. London: Cassell, 1936.

2401 PERICLES. London: Hodder and Stoughton, 1937.

2402 THE EAST WIND OF LOVE. London: Rich and Cowan, 1937.

2403 THE SOUTH WIND OF LOVE. London: Rich and Cowan, 1937.

2404 THE WINDSOR TAPESTRY. London: Rich and Cowan, 1938.
A study of the life, heritage, and abdication of Edward VIII, Duke of Windsor.

2405 A MUSICAL CHAIR. London: Chatto and Windus, 1939.
Articles reprinted from THE GRAMOPHONE, which Mackenzie founded in 1923, and edited for many years.

2406 AEGEAN MEMORIES. London: Chatto and Windus, 1940.
Volume 4 of his war memoirs.

2407 THE WEST WIND OF LOVE. London: Chatto and Windus, 1940.

2408 WEST TO NORTH. London: Chatto and Windus, 1940.

2409 THE MONARCH OF THE GLEN. London: Chatto and Windus, 1941.

2410 THE RED TAPE WORM. London: Chatto and Windus, 1941.

2411 CALVARY. With Faith Compton Mackenzie. London: John Lane, 1942.

2412 KEEP THE HOME GUARD TURNING. London: Chatto and Windus, 1943.

2413 MR. ROOSEVELT. London: Harrap, 1943.

2414 WIND OF FREEDOM: THE HISTORY OF THE INVASION OF GREECE BY THE AXIS POWERS, 1940–41. London: Chatto and Windus, 1943.

2415 THE NORTH WIND OF LOVE: BOOK ONE. London: Chatto and Windus, 1944.

2416 THE NORTH WIND OF LOVE: BOOK TWO. London: Chatto and Windus, 1945; issued as AGAIN TO THE NORTH, New York: Dodd, Mead, 1946.

2417 DR. BENES. London: Harrap, 1946.

2418 THE VITAL FLAME. London: Muller, 1947.
Written for the British Gas Council.

2419 WHISKY GALORE. London: Chatto and Windus, 1947; issued as TIGHT LITTLE ISLAND, Boston: Houghton Mifflin, 1950.

2420 ALL OVER THE PLACE: FIFTY THOUSAND MILES BY SEA, AIR, ROAD, AND RAIL. London: Chatto and Windus, 1949.

2421 HUNTING THE FAIRIES. London: Chatto and Windus, 1949.

2422 EASTERN EPIC. London: Chatto and Windus, 1951.
The story of the Indian Army in World War II.

2423 THE HOUSE OF COALPORT, 1750–1950. London: Collins, 1951.

2424 I TOOK A JOURNEY: A TOUR OF NATIONAL TRUST PROPERTIES. London: Naldrett Press, for the National Trust, 1951.

2425 THE RIVAL MONSTER. London: Chatto and Windus, 1952.

2426 THE QUEEN'S HOUSE: A HISTORY OF BUCKINGHAM PALACE. London: Hutchinson, 1953.

2427 THE SAVOY OF LONDON. London: Harrap, 1953.
The story of the Savoy Hotel.

2428 BEN NEVIS GOES EAST. London: Chatto and Windus, 1954.

2429 ECHOES. London: Chatto and Windus, 1954.
Broadcast talks.

2430 REALMS OF SILVER: ONE HUNDRED YEARS OF BANKING IN THE EAST. London: Routledge and Kegan Paul, 1954.
The story of the Chartered Bank of India, Australia and China.

2431 MY RECORD OF MUSIC. London: Hutchinson, 1955.

2432 THIN ICE. London: Chatto and Windus, 1956.

2433 ROCKETS GALORE. London: Chatto and Windus, 1957.

2434 SUBLIME TOBACCO. London: Chatto and Windus, 1957.

2435 THE LUNATIC REPUBLIC. London: Chatto and Windus, 1959.

2436 CAT'S COMPANY. London: Paul Elek, 1960.

2437 GREECE IN MY LIFE. London: Chatto and Windus, 1961.

2438 MEZZOTINT. London: Chatto and Windus, 1961.

2439 MY LIFE AND TIMES. 10 vols. London: Chatto and Windus, 1963-71.

2440 THE STOLEN SOPRANO. London: Chatto and Windus, 1965.

2441 PAPER LIVES. London: Chatto and Windus, 1966.

2442 ROBERT LOUIS STEVENSON. London: Morgan-Grampian, 1968.

BIOGRAPHY AND CRITICISM

CN (Stewart F. Sanderson); D; P; T; TCA; TCA-1; W.

2443 Robertson, Leo. COMPTON MACKENZIE: AN APPRAISAL OF HIS LITERARY WORK. London: Richards Press, 1955.

2444 Sanderson, Stewart F. "The Four Winds of Love." ARIEL, 2, No. 3 (1971), 7-15.

2445 Dooley, D.J. COMPTON MACKENZIE. New York: Twayne, 1974.

2446 Guégen, P., and A. Louis-David. "Compton Mackenzie (1883-1972)." ÉTUDES ANGLAISES, 27 (1974), 302-16.

2447 Campbell, John Lorne. "Our Barra Years." SCOTS MAGAZINE, n.s. 103 (1975), 494-503, 613-23.

Andrew Young (1885-1971)

His poetry reflects the acute observation of nature that marks his writings on flowers.

2448 SONGS OF NIGHT. London: Alexander Moring, [1910].

2449 BOAZ AND RUTH, AND OTHER POEMS. London: Wilson, 1920.

2450 THE DEATH OF ELI, AND OTHER POEMS. London: Wilson, 1921.

2451 THIRTY-ONE POEMS. London: Wilson, 1922.

2452 THE ADVERSARY. London: Wilson, 1923.
Two verse plays.

2453 THE BIRD-CAGE. London: Bumpus, 1926.
Poems.

2454 THE CUCKOO CLOCK. London: Bumpus, 1928.
Poems.

2455 THE NEW SHEPHERD. London: Bumpus, 1931.
Poems.

2456 WINTER HARVEST. London: Nonesuch Press, 1933.
Poems.

2457 THE WHITE BLACKBIRD. London: Cape, 1935.

Poems.

2458 NICODEMUS: A MYSTERY. London: Cape, 1937.

A verse play.

2459 SPEAK TO THE EARTH. London: Cape, 1939.

Poems.

2460 A PROSPECT OF FLOWERS: A BOOK ABOUT WILD FLOWERS. London: Cape, 1945.

2461 THE GREEN MAN. London: Cape, 1947.

Poems.

2462 A RETROSPECT OF FLOWERS. London: Cape, 1950.

2463 INTO HADES. London: Hart-Davis, 1952.

A poem, revised and reprinted in no. 2465.

2464 A PROSPECT OF BRITAIN. London: Hutchinson, 1956.

2465 OUT OF THE WORLD AND BACK: INTO HADES and A TRAVELLER IN TIME. TWO POEMS. London: Hart-Davis, 1958.

2466 THE POET AND THE LANDSCAPE. London: Hart-Davis, 1962.

2467 THE NEW POLY-OLBION: TOPOGRAPHICAL EXCURSIONS WITH AN INTRODUCTORY ACCOUNT OF THE POET'S EARLY DAYS. London: Hart-Davis, 1967.

COLLECTIONS AND SELECTIONS

2468 COLLECTED POEMS. London: Cape, 1936.

2469 COLLECTED POEMS. London: Cape, 1950.

2470 QUIET AS MOSS: THIRTY-SIX POEMS. Ed. Leonard Clark. London: Hart-Davis, 1959.

2471 COLLECTED POEMS. London: Hart-Davis, 1960.

2472 BURNING AS LIGHT: THIRTY-SEVEN POEMS. Ed. Leonard Clark.
London: Hart-Davis, 1967.

2473 COMPLETE POEMS. Ed. Leonard Clark. London: Secker and Warburg,
1974.

BIOGRAPHY AND CRITICISM

CA-7/8; CP (Maurice Lindsay); D; P; W; WA-50.

2474 Clark, Leonard, ed. ANDREW YOUNG, PROSPECT OF A POET: ES-
SAYS AND TRIBUTES BY FOURTEEN WRITERS. London: Hart-Davis,
1957.

> The contributors include John Betjeman, Richard Church, and
> Norman Nicholson.

Helen B[urness] Cruickshank (1886-1975)

She takes her place with her predecessors from the same part of Scotland, Violet Jacob and Marion Angus. As secretary of the Scottish PEN for many years,
she was active in literary affairs in the country (see her OCTOBIOGRAPHY,
2479).

2475 UP THE NORAN WATER, AND OTHER SCOTS POEMS. London: Methuen,
1934.

2476 SEA BUCKTHORN. Dunfermline: Macpherson, 1954.

2477 THE PONNAGE POOL. Edinburgh: Macdonald, 1968.

2478 COLLECTED POEMS. Edinburgh: Reprographia, 1971.

2479 OCTOBIOGRAPHY. Montrose: Standard Press, 1976.

> Reminiscences.

2480 MORE COLLECTED POEMS. Edinburgh: Gordon Wright, 1978.

BIOGRAPHY AND CRITICISM

CP (George Bruce); P.

2481 Wright, Gordon. "Helen B. Cruickshank's Fifty Years of Verse Writing."
CATALYST, 2 (Summer 1969), 34-35.

Edwin Muir (1887-1959)

Scotland's most distinguished poet of the century writing in English was also a sensitive critic and, with his wife, the translator of many important contemporary German writers.

2482 WE MODERNS: ENIGMAS AND GUESSES. By "Edward Moore." London: Allen and Unwin, 1918.

2483 LATITUDES. London: Melrose, 1924.

Essays.

2484 FIRST POEMS. London: Hogarth Press, 1925.

2485 CHORUS OF THE NEWLY DEAD. London: Hogarth Press, 1926.

2486 TRANSITION: ESSAYS ON CONTEMPORARY LITERATURE. London: Hogarth Press, 1926.

2487 THE MARIONETTE. London: Hogarth Press, 1927.

A novel.

2488 THE STRUCTURE OF THE NOVEL. London: Hogarth Press, 1928.

2489 JOHN KNOX: PORTRAIT OF A CALVINIST. London: Cape, 1929.

2490 THE THREE BROTHERS. London: Heinemann, 1931.

A novel.

2491 POOR TOM. London: Dent, 1932.

A novel.

2492 VARIATIONS ON A TIME THEME. London: Dent, 1934.

Poems.

2493 SCOTTISH JOURNEY. London: Heinemann with Gollancz, 1935; rpt. introd. Thomas Christopher Smout, Edinburgh: Mainstream, 1979.

2494 SCOTT AND SCOTLAND: THE PREDICAMENT OF THE SCOTTISH WRITER. London: Routledge, 1936.

2495 JOURNEYS AND PLACES. London: Dent, 1937.

Poems.

2496 THE PRESENT AGE, FROM 1914. London: Cresset Press, 1939.

2497 THE STORY AND THE FABLE: AN AUTOBIOGRAPHY. London: Harrap, 1940.

See also 2502.

2498 THE NARROW PLACE. London: Faber, 1943.

Poems.

2499 THE VOYAGE, AND OTHER POEMS. London: Faber, 1946.

2500 ESSAYS ON LITERATURE AND SOCIETY. London: Hogarth Press, 1949; rev. and enl. ed. 1965.

2501 THE LABYRINTH. London: Faber, 1949.

Poems.

2502 AN AUTOBIOGRAPHY. London: Hogarth Press, 1954.

A revision of 2497.

2503 ONE FOOT IN EDEN. London: Faber, 1956.

Poems.

2504 THE ESTATE OF POETRY. London: Hogarth Press, 1962.

COLLECTIONS AND SELECTIONS

2505 COLLECTED POEMS, 1921-1951. London: Faber, 1952.

2506 COLLECTED POEMS, 1921-1958. London: Faber, 1960.

2507 COLLECTED POEMS. London: Faber, 1963.

A second edition of 2506, with minor corrections and an additional poem.

2508 SELECTED POEMS. Introd. Thomas Stearns Eliot. London: Faber, 1965.

2509 [SELECTION] In PENGUIN MODERN POETS, 23. Harmondsworth: Penguin, 1973, pp. 63-102.

LETTERS

2510 SELECTED LETTERS. Ed. Peter H. Butter. London: Hogarth Press, 1974.

BIOGRAPHY AND CRITICISM

CSS, pages 29-32; D; P; T; TCA; TCA-1; W.

2511 Bruce, George. "Edwin Muir: Poet." SALTIRE REVIEW, 6 (1959), 12-16.

2512 Butter, Peter H. EDWIN MUIR. Edinburgh: Oliver and Boyd, 1962.

2513 Morgan, Edwin. "Edwin Muir." REVIEW, 5 (February 1963), 3-10; rpt. in his ESSAYS, Cheadle: Carcanet Press, 1974, pp. 186-93.

2514 Butter, Peter H. EDWIN MUIR: MAN AND POET. Edinburgh: Oliver and Boyd, 1966.

2515 Muir, Willa. BELONGING: A MEMOIR. London: Hogarth Press, 1968.

2516 Huberman, Elizabeth. THE POETRY OF EDWIN MUIR: THE FIELD OF GOOD AND ILL. New York: OUP, 1971.

2517 Brown, George Mackay. EDWIN MUIR: A BRIEF MEMOIR. West Linton: Castlelaw Press, 1975.

2518 Scott, Tom. "Orkney's Greatest Poet, Edwin Muir." SCOTIA REVIEW, 18 (1977-78), 29-37.

2519 Wiseman, Christopher. BEYOND THE LABYRINTH: A STUDY OF ED-WIN MUIR'S POETRY. Victoria, B.C.: Sono Nis Press, 1978.

2520 Mellown, Elgin W. EDWIN MUIR. Boston: Twayne, 1979.

BIBLIOGRAPHY

2521 Mellown, Elgin W. BIBLIOGRAPHY OF THE WRITINGS OF EDWIN MUIR. University: University of Alabama Press, 1964; rev. ed., London: Nicholas Vane, 1966; 1970.

2522 Hoy, Peter, and Elgin W. Mellown. A CHECKLIST OF WRITINGS ABOUT EDWIN MUIR. Troy, N.Y.: Whitston, 1971.

"James Bridie"
Osborne Henry Mavor (1888-1951)

A fertile dramatist whose plays are rich in character, wit, and humor. His plays are listed below by their year of first performance [in brackets] in the chronological sequence of his published work.

2523 SOME TALK OF ALEXANDER. London: Methuen, 1925.

War-time experiences in the Far East.

2524 THE SUNLIGHT SONATA. [1928]

In 2527.

2525 THE SWITCHBACK. [1929]

In 2527.

2526 WHAT IT IS TO BE YOUNG. [1929]

In 2538.

2527 THE SWITCHBACK; THE PARDONER'S TALE; THE SUNLIGHT SONATA: A COMEDY, A MORALITY, A FARCE-MORALITY. London: Constable, 1930; 2nd ed., with a revised version of THE SWITCHBACK [1931], 1932.

2528 THE ANATOMIST. [1930]

In 2531.

2529 THE GIRL WHO DID NOT WANT TO GO TO KUALA LUMPUR. [1930]

In 2538.

2530 TOBIAS AND THE ANGEL. [1930]

In 2531.

2531 THE ANATOMIST AND OTHER PLAYS. London: Constable, 1931.

The other plays are TOBIAS AND THE ANGEL and THE AMAZED EVANGELIST.

2532 THE DANCING BEAR. [1931]

In 2538.

2533 THE AMAZED EVANGELIST. [1932]
   In 2531.

2534 JONAH AND THE WHALE. [1932] London: Constable, 1932.

2535 A SLEEPING CLERGYMAN. [1933] London: Constable, 1933.

2536 MARRIAGE IS NO JOKE. [1934] London: Constable, 1934.

2537 COLONEL WOTHERSPOON. [1934]
   In 2538.

2538 COLONEL WOTHERSPOON AND OTHER PLAYS. London: Constable, 1934.
   The other plays are WHAT IT IS TO BE YOUNG, THE DANC-
   ING BEAR, and THE GIRL WHO DID NOT WANT TO GO TO
   KUALA LUMPUR.

2539 MR. BRIDIE'S ALPHABET FOR LITTLE GLASGOW HIGHBROWS. London:
   Constable, 1934.
   Satirical essays reprinted from the GLASGOW HERALD.

2540 MARY READ. With Claud Gurney. [1934] London: Constable, 1935.

2541 THE BLACK EYE. [1935] London: Constable, 1935.

2542 STORM IN A TEA-CUP. [1936] London: Constable, 1936.
   An Anglo-Scottish version of STURM IM WASSERGLAS by Bruno
   Frank.

2543 SUSANNAH AND THE ELDERS. [1937]
   In 2552.

2544 THE KING OF NOWHERE. [1938]
   In 2547.

2545 BABES IN THE WOOD. [1938]
   In 2547.

2546 THE LAST TRUMP. [1938]
   In 2547.

2547 THE KING OF NOWHERE AND OTHER PLAYS. London: Constable, 1938.

The other plays are BABES IN THE WOOD and THE LAST TRUMP.

2548 THE KITCHEN COMEDY. [1938]

In 2552.

2549 THE GOLDEN LEGEND OF SHULTS. [1939]

In 2552.

2550 WHAT SAY THEY? [1939] London: Constable, 1939.

Also in 2552.

2551 ONE WAY OF LIVING. London: Constable, 1939.

Autobiography.

2552 SUSANNAH AND THE ELDERS AND OTHER PLAYS. London: Constable, 1940.

The other plays are WHAT SAY THEY?, THE GOLDEN LEGEND OF SHULTS, and THE KITCHEN COMEDY.

2553 THE SIGN OF THE PROPHET JONAH. [1942]

In 2560. A version for broadcasting of JONAH AND THE WHALE.

2554 JONAH 3: A NEW VERSION OF JONAH AND THE WHALE. [1942]

In 2560.

2555 HOLY ISLE. [1942]

In 2560.

2556 THE DRAGON AND THE DOVE. [1942]

In 2560.

2557 A CHANGE FOR THE WORSE. [1943]

In 2561.

2558 MR. BOLFRY. [1943]

In 2560.

2559 MR. BOLFRY. Ed. John T. Low. London: Constable, 1978.

2560 PLAYS FOR PLAIN PEOPLE. London: Constable, 1944.

The plays are LANCELOT, HOLY ISLE, MR. BOLFRY, JONAH 3, THE SIGN OF THE PROPHET JONAH, and THE DRAGON AND THE DOVE.

2561 TEDIOUS AND BRIEF. London: Constable, 1944.

A mixture of short plays, occasional verses, anecdotes, essays, and stories, connected by a running commentary.

2562 IT DEPENDS WHAT YOU MEAN. [1944]

In 2568.

2563 THE FORRIGAN REEL. [1944]

A revised (but less successful) version [1945] in 2568.

2564 LANCELOT. [1945]

In 2560.

2565 DR. ANGELUS. [1947]

In 2568.

2566 JOHN KNOX. [1947]

In 2568.

2567 "Gog and Magog." [1948]

Unpublished. Manuscript in the British Drama League Library, London.

2568 JOHN KNOX AND OTHER PLAYS. London: Constable, 1949.

The other plays are DR. ANGELUS, IT DEPENDS WHAT YOU MEAN, and THE FORRIGAN REEL [1945].

2569 DAPHNE LAUREOLA. [1949] London: Constable, 1949.

2570 A SMALL STIR: LETTERS ON THE ENGLISH. With Moray McLaren. London: Hollis and Carter, 1949.

2571 MR. GILLIE. [1950] London: Constable, 1950.

2572 THE QUEEN'S COMEDY. [1950] London: Constable, 1950.

2573 THE BAIKIE CHARIVARI. [1952] London: Constable, 1953.

2574 MEETING AT NIGHT. With Archibald Batty. [1954] London: Constable, 1956.

COLLECTIONS

2575 A SLEEPING CLERGYMAN AND OTHER PLAYS. London: Constable, 1934.

> The other plays are TOBIAS AND THE ANGEL, JONAH AND THE WHALE, THE ANATOMIST, and THE AMAZED EVANGELIST.

2576 MORAL PLAYS. London: Constable, 1936.

> Includes MARRIAGE IS NO JOKE (with an alternative version of Act II, Scene I), MARY READ, and THE BLACK EYE, with a preface, "The Anatomy of Failure."

BIOGRAPHY AND CRITICISM

D; P; T; W; WA-50.

2577 Williamson, Audrey. THEATRE OF TWO DECADES. London: Rockliff, 1951.

2578 Bannister, Winifred. JAMES BRIDIE AND HIS THEATRE: A STUDY OF JAMES BRIDIE'S PERSONALITY, HIS STAGE PLAYS AND HIS WORK FOR THE FOUNDATION OF A SCOTTISH NATIONAL THEATRE. London: Rockliff, 1955.

2579 Greene, Anne. "Bridie's Concept of the Master Experimenter." SSL, 2 (1964-65), 96-110.

2580 Luyben, Helen L. JAMES BRIDIE: CLOWN AND PHILOSOPHER. Philadelphia: Pennsylvania University Press, 1965.

2581 Morgan, Edwin. "James Bridie." SCOTTISH INTERNATIONAL (November 1971), 22-26; rpt. in his ESSAYS, Cheadle: Carcanet Press, 1974. pp. 232-41.

Willa Muir (1890-1970)

With Edwin Muir, her husband, Willa Muir translated many works by contemporary German authors, including Sholem Asch, Hermann Broch, Lion Feuchtwanger, Gerhart Hauptmann, and Franz Kafka. They are listed in Elgin W. Mellown's BIBLIOGRAPHY OF THE WRITINGS OF EDWIN MUIR (see 2521).

2582 IMAGINED CORNERS. London: Martin Secker, 1931.

A novel.

2583 FIVE SONGS FROM THE AUVERGNAT, DONE INTO MODERN SCOTS. Warlingham: Samson Press, 1931.

2584 MRS. RITCHIE. London: Martin Secker, 1933.

A novel.

2585 MRS. GRUNDY IN SCOTLAND. London: Routledge, 1936.

2586 LIVING WITH BALLADS. London: Hogarth Press, 1965.

2587 BELONGING: A MEMOIR. London: Hogarth Press, 1968.

Neil M[iller] Gunn (1891-1973)

One of the two most important Scottish novelists of the twentieth century (the other is Lewis Grassic Gibbon). Neil Gunn writes of the Highland crofting and fishing community, in the past and today, and of the development of the individual within that community and environment.

2588 THE GREY COAST. London: Cape, 1926; rpt. London: Souvenir Press, 1976.

The author carefully revised his first novel for a second edition, Edinburgh: Porpoise Press, 1931.

2589 HIDDEN DOORS. Edinburgh: Porpoise Press, 1929.

Short stories.

2590 MORNING TIDE. Edinburgh: Porpoise Press, 1931; rpt. London: Souvenir Press, 1975.

2591 BACK HOME. Glasgow: Wilson, 1932.

A play in one act.

2592 THE LOST GLEN. Edinburgh: Porpoise Press, 1932.

2593 SUN CIRCLE. Edinburgh: Porpoise Press, 1933.

2594 BUTCHER'S BROOM. Edinburgh: Porpoise Press, 1934; rpt. London: Souvenir Press, 1977; issued as HIGHLAND NIGHT, New York: Harcourt, Brace, 1935.

2595 WHISKY AND SCOTLAND: A PRACTICAL AND SPIRITUAL SURVEY. London: Routledge, 1935; rpt. London: Souvenir Press, 1977.

2596 HIGHLAND RIVER. Edinburgh: Porpoise Press, 1937; London: Hutchinson, 1974.

2597 CHOOSING A PLAY. Edinburgh: Porpoise Press, [1938].

A comedy of community drama.

2598 OFF IN A BOAT. London: Faber, 1938.

An account of a voyage with his wife from Skye to Loch Ness.

2599 OLD MUSIC. London: Nelson, [1939].

A play in one act.

2600 NET RESULTS. London: Nelson, [1939].

A play in one act.

2601 WILD GEESE OVERHEAD. London: Faber, 1939.

2602 SECOND SIGHT. London: Faber, 1940.

2603 THE SILVER DARLINGS. London: Faber, 1941; 1969.

2604 YOUNG ART AND OLD HECTOR. London: Faber, 1942; rpt. London: Souvenir Press, 1976.

2605 THE SERPENT. London: Faber, 1943; rpt. London: Souvenir Press, 1978; issued as MAN GOES ALONE, New York: Stewart, 1944.

2606 THE GREEN ISLE OF THE GREAT DEEP. London: Faber, 1944; rpt. London: Souvenir Press, 1975.

2607 THE KEY OF THE CHEST. London: Faber, 1945.

2608 THE DRINKING WELL. London: Faber, 1946; rpt. London: Souvenir Press, 1978.

2609 THE SHADOW. London: Faber, 1948.

2610 THE SILVER BOUGH. London: Faber, 1948.

2611 THE LOST CHART. London: Faber, 1949.

2612 HIGHLAND PACK. London: Faber, 1949.
     Notes on country life collected from various periodicals.

2613 THE WHITE HOUR, AND OTHER STORIES. London: Faber, 1950.

2614 THE WELL AT THE WORLD'S END. London: Faber, 1951.

2615 BLOODHUNT. London: Faber, 1952.

2616 THE OTHER LANDSCAPE. London: Faber, 1954.

2617 THE ATOM OF DELIGHT. London: Faber, 1956.
     Autobiography.

SELECTIONS

2618 STORM AND PRECIPICE, AND OTHER PIECES. London: Faber, 1942.

BIOGRAPHY AND CRITICISM

CN (Alexander Scott); CSS, pages 97-98; D; H, pages 348-73; P; TCA; TCA-1.

2619 Morrison, David, ed. ESSAYS ON NEIL M. GUNN. Thurso: Caithness Books, 1971.

2620 Scott, Alexander, and Douglas Gifford, eds. NEIL M. GUNN: THE MAN AND THE WRITER. Edinburgh: Blackwood, 1973.
     A collection of eighteen biographical and critical essays.

2621 Nakamura, Tokusaburo. "Neil Miller Gunn: A Spiritual Survey." SSL, 12 (1974-75), 79-91.

2622 Pick, John Barclay. "Memories of Neil Gunn." SSL, 14 (1979), 52–71.

BIBLIOGRAPHY

2623 Aitken, William R. "Neil M. Gunn: A Bibliography." In NEIL M. GUNN: THE MAN AND THE WRITER. Ed. Alexander Scott and Douglas Gifford. Edinburgh: Blackwood, 1973, pp. 389–97.

"Hugh MacDiarmid"
Christopher Murray Grieve (1892-1978)

The foremost Scottish poet of the century, who created a whole renaissance in Scottish life and letters. His influence is as yet incalculable.

2624 NORTHERN NUMBERS, BEING REPRESENTATIVE SELECTIONS FROM CERTAIN LIVING SCOTTISH POETS. Ed. C.M.G. 3 series. Series 1 and 2, Edinburgh: T.N. Foulis, 1920, 1921; series 3, Montrose: C.M. Grieve, 1922.

2625 ANNALS OF THE FIVE SENSES. [by C.M.G.] Montrose: C.M. Grieve, 1923; Edinburgh: Porpoise Press, 1930.

2626 SANGSCHAW. Edinburgh: Blackwood, 1925.

2627 PENNY WHEEP. Edinburgh: Blackwood, 1926.

2628 A DRUNK MAN LOOKS AT THE THISTLE. Edinburgh: Blackwood, 1926; introd. David Daiches, Glasgow: Caledonian Press, 1953; Edinburgh: Castle Wynd Printers, 1956; Edinburgh: 200 Burns Club, 1962; illus. Frans Masereel, Falkland: Duval and Hamilton, 1969.

2629 A DRUNK MAN LOOKS AT THE THISTLE. Ed. John C. Weston. Amherst: University of Massachusetts Press, 1971.

An annotated edition of MacDiarmid's key work, with the spelling standardized.

2630 CONTEMPORARY SCOTTISH STUDIES: FIRST SERIES. [by C.M.G.] London: Leonard Parsons, 1926.

Articles reprinted from the SCOTTISH EDUCATIONAL JOURNAL, June 1925–July 1926, with an introductory chapter, conclusion, and bibliography.

CONTEMPORARY SCOTTISH STUDIES. Edinburgh: Scottish Educational Journal, 1976.

A new edition published to mark both the centenary of the SCOTTISH EDUCATIONAL JOURNAL as a weekly paper and the jubilee of the first publication of these articles in book form. It reprints the complete series of articles, June 1925–February 1927, with the "furious and fascinating" correspondence they evoked. The introductory chapter, conclusion, and bibliography of the 1926 edition are not reprinted.

2631 ALBYN, OR SCOTLAND AND THE FUTURE. [by C.M.G.] London: Kegan Paul, 1927.

2632 THE LUCKY BAG. Edinburgh: Porpoise Press, 1927.

2633 TO CIRCUMJACK CENCRASTUS, OR THE CURLY SNAKE. Edinburgh: Blackwood, 1930.

2634 FIRST HYMN TO LENIN, AND OTHER POEMS. London: Unicorn Press, 1931.

2635 SCOTS UNBOUND, AND OTHER POEMS. Stirling: Eneas Mackay, 1932.

2636 SCOTTISH SCENE, OR THE INTELLIGENT MAN'S GUIDE TO ALBYN. With Lewis Grassic Gibbon. London: Jarrolds, 1934.

2637 STONY LIMITS, AND OTHER POEMS. London: Gollancz, 1934.

2638 AT THE SIGN OF THE THISTLE: A COLLECTION OF ESSAYS. London: Stanley Nott, 1934.

2639 SECOND HYMN TO LENIN, AND OTHER POEMS. London: Stanley Nott, 1935.

2640 SCOTTISH ECCENTRICS. London: Routledge, 1936; rpt. New York: Johnson Reprint Corp., 1972.

A series of biographical essays.

2641 THE ISLANDS OF SCOTLAND: HEBRIDES, ORKNEYS, AND SHETLANDS. London: Batsford, 1939.

2642 THE GOLDEN TREASURY OF SCOTTISH POETRY. London: Macmillan, 1940.

Includes MacDiarmid's translations from the Gaelic of "The Birlinn of Clanranald" and "The Praise of Ben Dorain."

2643 LUCKY POET: A SELF-STUDY IN LITERATURE AND POLITICAL IDEAS. London: Methuen, 1943; rpt., with a new "Author's Note," London: Cape, 1972.

2644 A KIST OF WHISTLES: NEW POEMS. Glasgow: Maclellan, 1947.

2645 CUNNINGHAME GRAHAM: A CENTENARY STUDY. Glasgow: Caledonian Press, 1952.

2646 FRANCIS GEORGE SCOTT: AN ESSAY ON THE OCCASION OF HIS SEVENTY-FIFTH BIRTHDAY. Edinburgh: Macdonald, 1955.

2647 IN MEMORIAM JAMES JOYCE: FROM A VISION OF WORLD LANGUAGE. Glasgow: Maclellan, 1955; rpt. with corrections, 1956.

2648 STONY LIMITS AND SCOTS UNBOUND, AND OTHER POEMS. Edinburgh: Castle Wynd Printers, 1956.

Reprints STONY LIMITS (2637) with the addition of certain poems excluded from the earlier edition and the title poem from SCOTS UNBOUND (2635).

2649 THREE HYMNS TO LENIN. Edinburgh: Castle Wynd Printers, 1957.

For the FIRST HYMN and SECOND HYMN, see 2634 and 2639. The THIRD HYMN, printed in part in LUCKY POET (2643), is here published in full for the first time in book form.

2650 THE BATTLE CONTINUES. Edinburgh: Castle Wynd Printers, 1957.

2651 BURNS TODAY AND TOMORROW. Edinburgh: Castle Wynd Printers, 1959.

2652 THE KIND OF POETRY I WANT. Edinburgh: Duval, 1961.

Parts of this poem were published in LUCKY POET (2643) and A KIST OF WHISTLES (2644).

2653 THE COMPANY I'VE KEPT. London: Hutchinson, 1966.

Autobiographical.

2654 DIREADH I, II, and III. Frenich, Foss: Duval and Hamilton, 1974.

The definitive edition of three poems, of which the first was published originally in the VOICE OF SCOTLAND in 1938, and the second and third in LUCKY POET (2643).

COLLECTIONS AND SELECTIONS

2655 SELECTED POEMS. London: Macmillan, 1934.

A selection chosen by the poet himself.

2656 SELECTED POEMS. Ed. Robert Crombie Saunders. Glasgow: Maclellan, 1944.

2657 SPEAKING FOR SCOTLAND: SELECTED POEMS. Baltimore: Contemporary Poetry, 1946.

The first American edition has an introduction by Compton Mackenzie. The selection, by the poet himself, is almost the same as the SELECTED POEMS (2655), with the addition of three poems.

2658 SELECTED POEMS. Ed. Oliver Brown. Glasgow: Maclellan, 1954; reissued as POEMS, Glasgow: Scottish Secretariat, 1955.

2659 COLLECTED POEMS. New York: Macmillan, 1962; Edinburgh: Oliver and Boyd, 1962.

2660 COLLECTED POEMS. Rev. ed., with enlarged glossary prepared by John C. Weston. New York: Macmillan; London: Collier-Macmillan, 1967.

MacDiarmid later pointed out that the COLLECTED POEMS (2659, 2660) was wrongly entitled. "The book was only a big selection of my poems." He added three supplementary collections, all published in London by MacGibbon and Kee: A LAP OF HONOUR (1967), A CLYACK-SHEAF (1969), and MORE COLLECTED POEMS (1970).

2661 THE UNCANNY SCOT: A SELECTION OF PROSE. Ed. Kenneth Buthlay. London: MacGibbon and Kee, 1968.

2662 SELECTED ESSAYS. Ed. Duncan Glen. London: Cape, 1969; Berkeley and Los Angeles: University of California Press, 1970.

2663 SELECTED POEMS. Ed. David Craig and John Manson. Harmondsworth: Penguin, 1970.

2664 THE HUGH MacDIARMID ANTHOLOGY: POEMS IN SCOTS AND ENGLISH. Ed. Michael Grieve and Alexander Scott. London: Routledge and Kegan Paul, 1972.

2665 THE SOCIALIST POEMS OF HUGH MacDIARMID. Ed. T.S. Law and Thurso Berwick. London: Routledge and Kegan Paul, 1978.

2666 COMPLETE POEMS, 1920-1976. Ed. Michael Grieve and William R. Aitken. 2 vols. London: Martin Brian and O'Keeffe, 1978.

The definitive edition.

MacDiarmid edited four important periodicals: THE SCOTTISH CHAPBOOK (1922-23), THE SCOTTISH NATION (1923), THE NORTHERN REVIEW (1924), and THE VOICE OF SCOTLAND (1938-39; 1945-49; 1955-58); he also edited selections from Burns (1926, 1949, 1962), Dunbar (1952, 1955), and Henryson (1973), a slim anthology, LIVING SCOTTISH POETS (1931), and the COLLECTED POEMS OF WILLIAM SOUTAR (1948); and he translated Harry Martinson's ANIARA (1963) and Bertolt Brecht's THE THREEPENNY OPERA (1973).

BIOGRAPHY AND CRITICISM

CA-7/8; CP (Maurice Lindsay); D; P; T; TCA; TCA-1; W.

2667 Frost, A.C. "Hugh MacDiarmid: Scotland's Vortex Maker." BOOKMAN, 86 (1934), 287-88.

2668 Shepherd, Nan. "The Poetry of Hugh MacDiarmid." ABERDEEN UNIVERSITY REVIEW, 26 (1938-39), 49-61.

2669 Southworth, James Granville. SOWING THE SPRING: STUDIES IN BRITISH POETS FROM HOPKINS TO MacNEICE. Oxford: Blackwell, 1940, pp. 92-107.

2670 Saunders, Robert Crombie. "The Thistle in the Lion's Mouth: The Poetry of Hugh MacDiarmid." LIFE AND LETTERS TODAY, 44 (1945), 147-55.

2671 Daiches, David. "Hugh MacDiarmid and Scottish Poetry." POETRY, 72 (1948), 202-18.

2672 Aitken, Mary Baird. "The Poetry of Hugh MacDiarmid." SCOTTISH ART AND LETTERS, 4 (1949), 5-25.

2673 Glicksberg, Charles I. "Hugh MacDiarmid: Marxist Messiah." PRAIRIE SCHOONER, 26 (1952), 325-35.

2674 Leslie, Arthur. THE POLITICS AND POETRY OF HUGH MacDIARMID. Glasgow: Caledonian Press, 1952.

Reprinted from the NATIONAL WEEKLY, where it appeared

serially. This pseudonymous essay is reprinted in SELECTED ES-SAYS (2662), where it is acknowledged to be "MacDiarmid on MacDiarmid."

2675 _____. "Jerqueing Every Idioticon: Some Notes on MacDiarmid's Joyce Poem." VOICE OF SCOTLAND, 6 (July 1955), 23-31.

2676 Duval, Kulgin D., and Sydney Goodsir Smith, eds. HUGH MacDIARMID: A FESTSCHRIFT. Edinburgh: Duval, 1962.

A collection of critical essays.

2677 Buthlay, Kenneth. HUGH MacDIARMID (C.M. GRIEVE). Edinburgh: Oliver and Boyd, 1964.

2678 Glen, Duncan. HUGH MacDIARMID (CHRISTOPHER MURRAY GRIEVE) AND THE SCOTTISH RENAISSANCE. Edinburgh: Chambers, 1964.

2679 "Hugh MacDiarmid and Scottish Poetry." Double issue. AGENDA, 5-6 (1967-68).

2680 Smith, Iain Crichton. "Hugh MacDiarmid: SANGSCHAW and A DRUNK MAN LOOKS AT THE THISTLE." SSL, 7 (1969-70), 169-79.

2681 AKROS, No. 13-14 (April 1970), entire issue.

Special Hugh MacDiarmid issue in two parts.

2682 Glen, Duncan, ed. HUGH MacDIARMID: A CRITICAL SURVEY. Edinburgh: Scottish Academic Press, 1972.

A collection of critical essays, some reprinted from the FESTS-CHRIFT of 1962 (2676).

2683 AKROS, No. 19 (August 1972), entire issue.

A special number for MacDiarmid's eightieth birthday.

2684 Morgan, Edwin. ESSAYS. Cheadle: Carcanet Press, 1974.

Three of the essays are on MacDiarmid: "MacDiarmid Embat-tled," pages 194-202; "Poetry and Knowledge in MacDiarmid's Later Work," pages 203-13; and "MacDiarmid at Seventy-Five," pages 214-21.

2685 Buthlay, Kenneth. "The Appreciation of the Golden Lyric: Early Scots Poems of Hugh MacDiarmid." SLJ, 2 (July 1975), 41-66; errata in SLJ, 2 (December 1975), 63-64.

2686 Watson, Roderick. HUGH MacDIARMID. Milton Keynes: Open University Press, 1976.

2687 Morgan, Edwin. HUGH MacDIARMID. London: Longman, for the British Council, 1976.

2688 AKROS, No. 34-35 (August 1977), entire issue.

A special double number to mark MacDiarmid's eighty-fifth birthday.

2689 Pacey, Philip. HUGH MacDIARMID AND DAVID JONES: CELTIC WONDER-VOYAGERS. Preston: Akros, 1977.

2690 Wright, Gordon. MacDIARMID: AN ILLUSTRATED BIOGRAPHY. Edinburgh: Gordon Wright, 1977.

2691 McQuillan, Ruth. "MacDiarmid's Other Dictionary." LINES REVIEW, No. 66 (September 1978), 5-14.

2692 LINES REVIEW, No. 67 (December 1978).

A MacDiarmid memorial number.

2693 SLJ, 5 (December 1978).

A MacDiarmid memorial number.

2694 "To the Memory of Hugh MacDiarmid." Special issue. AQUARIUS, 11 (1979), entire issue.

2695 McQuillan, Ruth, and Agnes Shearer. IN LINE WITH THE RAMNA STACKS. Edinburgh: Challister Press, 1980.

An essay on the fishing poems of Hugh MacDiarmid.

2696 Scott, Paul H., and Albert C. Davis, eds. THE AGE OF MacDIARMID: ESSAYS ON HUGH MacDIARMID AND HIS INFLUENCE ON CONTEMPORARY SCOTLAND. Edinburgh: Mainstream, 1980.

BIBLIOGRAPHY

2697 Aitken, William R. "C.M. Grieve/Hugh MacDiarmid: A First Checklist." BIBLIOTHECK, 1, No. 4 (1958), 3-23; "A Second Checklist." BIBLIOTHECK, 5 (1970), 253-63.

2698 Glen, Duncan. "Hugh MacDiarmid: A Chronological Bibliography." In HUGH MacDIARMID AND THE SCOTTISH RENAISSANCE. Edinburgh: Chambers, 1964, pp. 245-62.

2699 _____. A SMALL PRESS AND HUGH MacDIARMID. Preston: Akros, 1970.

A checklist of Akros publications, 1962-70, including a number of interesting items by and about MacDiarmid.

2700 Aitken, William R. "A Hugh MacDiarmid Bibliography." In HUGH Mac-DIARMID: A CRITICAL SURVEY. Ed. Duncan Glen. Edinburgh: Scottish Academic Press, 1972, pp. 228-41.

2701 _____. "Hugh MacDiarmid's Recent Bibliography, [1972-76]. AKROS, No. 34-35 (August 1977), 111-14.

2702 _____. "Hugh MacDiarmid's 'Unpublished' Books: A Bibliographical Exploration." In OF ONE ACCORD. Ed. Frank McAdams. Glasgow: Scottish Library Association, 1977, pp. 57-72.

2703 Glenday, Michael K. "Hugh MacDiarmid: A Bibliography of Criticism, 1924-78." BULLETIN OF BIBLIOGRAPHY, 36 (1979), 91-97.

George Blake (1893-1961)

Novelist of Glasgow and the Clyde, journalist, editor, and publisher.

2704 MINCE COLLOP CLOSE. London: Grant Richards, 1923.

A story of gang life in the Glasgow slums.

2705 THE WILD MEN. London: Grant Richards, 1925.

2706 YOUNG MALCOLM. London: Constable, 1926.

2707 PAPER MONEY. London: Constable, 1927; issued as GETTIN' IN SOCIETY. New York: Harper, 1927.

2708 THE PATH OF GLORY. London: Constable, 1929.

2709 THE SEAS BETWEEN. London: Faber, 1930.

2710 RETURNED EMPTY. London: Faber, 1931.

2711 SEA TANGLE. London: Faber, 1932.

2712 THE HEART OF SCOTLAND. London: Batsford, 1934.
Travel and description.

2713 REST AND BE THANKFUL. Edinburgh: Porpoise Press, 1934.
Essays.

2714 THE SHIPBUILDERS. London: Faber, 1935; London: Collins, 1970.
A novel of Glasgow and Clydeside during the Depression of the
1930s.

2715 DAVID AND JOANNA. London: Faber, 1936.

2716 LATE HARVEST. London: Collins, 1938.

2717 THE VALIANT HEART. London: Collins, 1940.

2718 THE CONSTANT STAR. London: Collins, 1945.

2719 THE WESTERING SUN. London: Collins, 1946.

2720 THE FIVE ARCHES. London: Collins, 1947.

2721 THE PAYING GUEST. London: Collins, 1949.

2722 MOUNTAIN AND FLOOD: THE HISTORY OF THE 52ND (LOWLAND)
DIVISION, 1939-1946. Glasgow: Jackson, 1950.

2723 THE PIPER'S TUNE. London: Collins, 1950.

2724 BARRIE AND THE KAILYARD SCHOOL. London: Arthur Barker, 1951.
An essay in literary criticism.

2725 THE FIRTH OF CLYDE. London: Collins, 1952.
A tribute to the Clyde and its steamers.

2726 THE VOYAGE HOME. London: Collins, 1952.

2727 THE INNOCENCE WITHIN. London: Collins, 1955.

2728 THE LAST FLING. London: Collins, 1957.

2729 THE PEACOCK PALACE. London: Collins, 1958.

2730 THE LOVES OF MARY GLEN. London: Collins, 1960.

BIOGRAPHY AND CRITICISM

D; P; TCA; TCA-1.

2731 Hunter, Stewart. "Waters of Change." SCOTS MAGAZINE, n.s. 94 (1970-71), 322-30.

William Jeffrey (1896-1946)

A poet of great sincerity and tenderness, whose work shows his admiration of Blake and Yeats.

2732 PROMETHEUS RETURNS, AND OTHER POEMS. London: Erskine Mac-Donald, 1921.

2733 THE WISE MEN COME TO TOWN. Glasgow: Gowans and Gray, 1923.

2734 THE NYMPH. Edinburgh: Porpoise Press, 1924.

2735 THE DOOM OF ATLAS, AND OTHER POEMS. Glasgow: Gowans and Gray, 1926.

2736 THE LAMB OF LOMOND, AND OTHER POEMS. Edinburgh: Porpoise Press, 1926.

2737 MOUNTAIN SONGS. Edinburgh: Porpoise Press, 1928.

2738 THE GOLDEN STAG. Oxford: Blackwell, 1932.

2739 EAGLE OF CORUISK: POEMS. Oxford: Blackwell, 1933.

2740 FANTASIA WRITTEN IN AN INDUSTRIAL TOWN. London: Cranley and Day, 1933.

2741 SEA GLIMMER: POEMS IN SCOTS AND ENGLISH. Glasgow: Maclellan, 1947.

SELECTIONS

2742 SELECTED POEMS. Ed. Alexander Scott. Edinburgh: Serif Books, 1951.

BIOGRAPHY AND CRITICISM

CSS, pages 43-45; P.

A[rchibald] J[oseph] Cronin (1896-1981)

A powerful, realistic, but often melodramatic novelist.

2743 HATTER'S CASTLE. London: Gollancz, 1931.

2744 THREE LOVES. London: Gollancz, 1932.

2745 GRAND CANARY. London: Gollancz, 1933.

2746 THE STARS LOOK DOWN. London: Gollancz, 1935.

2747 THE CITADEL. London: Gollancz, 1937.

2748 JUPITER LAUGHS. Boston: Little, Brown, 1940; London: Gollancz, 1941.
     A play in three acts.

2749 THE KEYS OF THE KINGDOM. Boston: Little, Brown, 1941; London: Gollancz, 1942.

2750 THE GREEN YEARS. Boston: Little, Brown, 1944; London: Gollancz, 1945.

2751 SHANNON'S WAY. London: Gollancz, 1948.

2752 THE SPANISH GARDENER. London: Gollancz, 1950.

2753 ADVENTURES IN TWO WORLDS. London: Gollancz, 1952.
     Autobiography.

2754 BEYOND THIS PLACE. London: Gollancz, 1953.

2755 CRUSADER'S TOMB. London: Gollancz, 1956; issued as A THING OF BEAUTY. Boston: Little, Brown, 1956.

2756 THE NORTHERN LIGHT. London: Gollancz, 1958.

2757 THE JUDAS TREE. London: Gollancz, 1961.

2758 A SONG OF SIXPENCE. London: Heinemann, 1964.

2759 A POCKETFUL OF RYE. London: Heinemann, 1969.

2760 THE MINSTREL BOY. London: Gollancz, 1975.

2761 DOCTOR FINLAY OF TANNOCHBRAE. London: New English Library, 1978.

2762 GRACIE LINDSAY. London: Gollancz, 1978.

BIOGRAPHY AND CRITICISM

CA-1; D; P; T; TCA; TCA-1.

2763 Davies, Horton. "Pilgrims, Not Strangers: Maugham, Cronin, Alan Paton." In his A MIRROR OF THE MINISTRY IN MODERN NOVELS. New York: OUP, 1959.

"Gordon Daviot," "Josephine Tey" Elizabeth Mackintosh (1897-1952)

A dramatist and novelist who also wrote very successful detective stories under the pseudonym, Josephine Tey.

PLAYS [BY GORDON DAVIOT] BY YEAR OF PERFORMANCE

2764 RICHARD OF BORDEAUX. [1932] London: Gollancz, 1933.

2765 THE LAUGHING WOMAN. [1934] London: Gollancz, 1934.

2766 QUEEN OF SCOTS. [1934] London: Gollancz, 1934.

2767 THE STARS BOW DOWN. [1939] London: Duckworth, 1939.

2768 LEITH SANDS. [1941]
      In 2779.

2769 THE THREE MRS. MADDERLEYS. [1944]
      In 2779.

2770 MRS. FRY HAS A VISITOR. [1944]
      In 2779.

2771 REMEMBER CAESAR. [1946]
      In 2779.

2772 THE LITTLE DRY THORN. [1947]
      In 2780 (vol. 1).

2773 VALERIUS. [1948]
      In 2780 (vol. 1).

2774 THE PEN OF MY AUNT. [1950]
      In 2780 (vol. 2).

2775 THE POMP OF MR. POMFRET. [1954]
      In 2780 (vol. 2).

2776 CORNELIA. [1955]
      In 2780 (vol. 2).

2777 DICKON. [1955]
      In 2780 (vol. 1).

2778 SWEET COZ. [1956]
      In 2780 (vol. 3).

COLLECTIONS OF PLAYS

2779 LEITH SANDS, AND OTHER SHORT PLAYS. London: Duckworth, 1946.

2780 PLAYS. 3 vols. London: Peter Davies, 1953-54.
      A number of the plays in these volumes have not been performed.

HISTORICAL BIOGRAPHY [BY GORDON DAVIOT]

2781 CLAVERHOUSE. London: Collins, 1937.

NOVELS [BY JOSEPHINE TEY, UNLESS OTHERWISE NOTED]

2782 KIF: AN UNVARNISHED HISTORY. [by G.D.] London: Benn, 1929; re-issued [by J.T.], London: Peter Davies, 1967.

2783 THE MAN IN THE QUEUE. [by G.D.] London: Methuen, 1929; reis-sued [by J.T.], London: Peter Davies, 1953.

2784 THE EXPENSIVE HALO. [by G.D.] London: Benn, 1931; reissued [by J.T.], London: Peter Davies, 1967.

2785 A SHILLING FOR CANDLES. London: Methuen, 1936.

2786 MISS PYM DISPOSES. London: Peter Davies, 1946.

2787 THE FRANCHISE AFFAIR. London: Peter Davies, 1948.

2788 BRAT FARRAR. London: Peter Davies, 1949.

2789 TO LOVE AND TO BE WISE. London: Peter Davies, 1950.

2790 THE DAUGHTER OF TIME. London: Peter Davies, 1951.

2791 THE PRIVATEER. [by G.D.] London: Peter Davies, 1952.

2792 THE SINGING SANDS. London: Peter Davies, 1952.

BIOGRAPHY AND CRITICISM

TCA-1.

2793 Gielgud, John. "Foreword." In PLAYS. By Gordon Daviot, vol. 1. London: Peter Davies, 1953.

Edward Gaitens (1897-1966)

A writer of warmth and vitality who gives a credible picture of working-class Glasgow.

2794 GROWING UP, AND OTHER STORIES. London: Cape, 1942.

> Ten short stories, six of which became chapters in his novel, below.

2795 DANCE OF THE APPRENTICES. Glasgow: Maclellan, 1948.

Naomi Mitchison (1897--)

Her early stories are tales of ancient Greece and Rome, or strange mythologies of her own making, but THE BULL CALVES is an impressive Scottish novel. She also writes vividly for children and young people.

2796 THE CONQUERED. London: Cape, 1923.

2797 WHEN THE BOUGH BREAKS, AND OTHER STORIES. London: Cape, 1924; London: Bodley Head, 1974.

2798 CLOUD CUCKOO LAND. London: Cape, 1925.

2799 THE LABURNUM BRANCH. London: Cape, 1926.

> Poems.

2800 ANNA COMNENA. London: Gerald Howe, 1928.

> Biography.

2801 BLACK SPARTA: GREEK STORIES. London: Cape, 1928.

2802 NIX-NOUGHT-NOTHING: FOUR PLAYS FOR CHILDREN. London: Cape, 1928.

2803 BARBARIAN STORIES. London: Cape, 1929.

2804 THE HOSTAGES, AND OTHER STORIES FOR BOYS AND GIRLS. London: Cape, 1930.

2805 BOYS AND GIRLS AND GODS. London: Watts, 1931.

> For young people.

2806 THE CORN KING AND THE SPRING QUEEN. London: Cape, 1931; issued as THE BARBARIAN. New York: Cameron Associates, 1961.

2807 THE PRICE OF FREEDOM. With Lewis E. Gielgud. London: Cape, 1931.

A play.

2808 THE DELICATE FIRE: SHORT STORIES AND POEMS. London: Cape, 1933.

2809 THE HOME AND A CHANGING CIVILISATION. London: John Lane, 1934.

2810 VIENNA DIARY. London: Gollancz, 1934.

2811 BEYOND THIS LIMIT. London: Cape, 1935.

2812 WE HAVE BEEN WARNED. London: Constable, 1935.

A novel.

2813 THE FOURTH PIG: STORIES AND VERSES. London: Constable, 1936.

2814 AN END AND A BEGINNING, AND OTHER PLAYS. London: Constable, 1937.

2815 SOCRATES. With Richard H.S. Crossman. London: Hogarth Press, 1937.

2816 THE MORAL BASIS OF POLITICS. London: Constable, 1938.

2817 AS IT WAS IN THE BEGINNING. With Lewis E. Gielgud. London: Cape, 1939.

A play.

2818 THE BLOOD OF THE MARTYRS. London: Constable, 1939.

2819 THE KINGDOM OF HEAVEN. London: Heinemann, 1939.

2820 THE BULL CALVES. London: Cape, 1947.

2821 NIX-NOUGHT-NOTHING AND ELFEN HILL: TWO PLAYS FOR CHILDREN. London: Cape, 1948.

2822 MEN AND HERRING: A DOCUMENTARY. With Denis Macintosh. Edinburgh: Serif Books, 1949.

2823 THE BIG HOUSE. London: Faber, 1950.

2824 SPINDRIFT. With Denis Macintosh. London: French, 1951.
   A play.

2825 LOBSTERS ON THE AGENDA. London: Gollancz, 1952.
   A novel.

2826 TRAVEL LIGHT. London: Faber, 1952.

2827 GRAEME AND THE DRAGON. London: Faber, 1954.
   ·For children.

2828 THE SWAN'S ROAD. London: Naldrett Press, 1954.
   For young people.

2829 THE LAND THE RAVENS FOUND. London: Collins, 1955.
   For young people.

2830 TO THE CHAPEL PERILOUS. London: Allen and Unwin, 1955.

2831 LITTLE BOXES. London: Faber, 1956.
   For children.

2832 BEHOLD YOUR KING. London: Muller, 1957.

2833 THE FAR HARBOUR. London: Collins, 1957.
   For young people.

2834 FIVE MEN AND A SWAN. London: Allen and Unwin, 1958.

2835 OTHER PEOPLE'S WORLDS. London: Secker and Warburg, 1958.
   On Ghana and Nigeria.

2836 JUDY AND LAKSHMI. London: Collins, 1959.
   For children.

2837 THE RIB OF THE GREEN UMBRELLA. London: Collins, 1960.
   For children.

2838 THE YOUNG ALEXANDER THE GREAT. London: Max Parrish, 1960.
For children.

2839 A FISHING VILLAGE ON THE CLYDE. With George W.L. Paterson. London: OUP, 1960.

2840 KARENSGAARD: THE STORY OF A DANISH FARM. London: Collins, 1961.
For children.

2841 PRESENTING OTHER PEOPLE'S CHILDREN. London: Paul Hamlyn, 1961.

2842 MEMOIRS OF A SPACEWOMAN. London: Gollancz, 1962.

2843 THE YOUNG ALFRED THE GREAT. London: Max Parrish, 1962.
For children.

2844 THE FAIRY WHO COULDN'T TELL A LIE. London: Collins, 1963.
For children.

2845 KETSE AND THE CHIEF. London: Nelson, 1965.
For children.

2846 WHEN WE BECOME MEN. London: Collins, 1965.

2847 FRIENDS AND ENEMIES. London: Collins, 1966.
For children.

2848 RETURN TO THE FAIRY HILL. London: Heinemann, 1966.

2849 THE BIG SURPRISE. London: Kaye and Ward, 1967.
For children.

2850 AFRICAN HEROES. London: Bodley Head, 1968.
For children.

2851 DON'T LOOK BACK. London: Kaye and Ward, 1969.
For children.

2852 THE FAMILY AT DITLABENG. London: Collins, 1969.
For children.

2853 THE AFRICANS. London: Blond, 1970.

2854 SUN AND MOON. London: Bodley Head, 1970.
For children.

2855 CLEOPATRA'S PEOPLE. London: Heinemann, 1972.

2856 THE DANISH TEAPOT. London: Kaye and Ward, 1973.
For children.

2857 SUNRISE TOMORROW: A STORY OF BOTSWANA. London: Collins, 1973.

2858 SMALL TALK . . . MEMORIES OF AN EDWARDIAN CHILDHOOD. London: Bodley Head, 1973.

2859 ALL CHANGE HERE: GIRLHOOD AND MARRIAGE. London: Bodley Head, 1975.

2860 SOLUTION THREE. London: Dobson, 1975.

2861 YOU MAY WELL ASK: A MEMOIR, 1920-1940. London: Gollancz, 1979.

A third volume of autobiography, continuing 2858 and 2859.

2862 THE CLEANSING OF THE KNIFE, AND OTHER POEMS. Edinburgh: Canongate, 1979.

BIOGRAPHY AND CRITICISM

CN (Alexander Scott); D; H, pages 182-92; P; T; TCA; TCA-1.

2863 Mitchison, Naomi. "A Self Interview." SSL, 14 (1979), 37-51.

Guy McCrone (1898--)

A Glasgow novelist who skillfully paints his picture of middle-class family life in the city in the period 1870-1901.

2864 THE STRIPED UMBRELLA. London: Constable, 1937.

2865 DUET FOR TWO MERKLANDS. London: Hodder and Stoughton, 1939.

2866 ANTIMACASSER CITY. London: Constable, 1940.

2867 WAX FRUIT: THE STORY OF THE MOORHOUSE FAMILY. London: Constable, 1947; issued as RED PLUSH. New York: Farrar, Straus, 1947.

> A trilogy. The first part, ANTIMACASSAR CITY, had been published separately in 1940; the second and third parts, THE PHILISTINES and THE PURITANS, were not published separately until reprinted in paperback in 1978.

2868 AUNT BEL. London: Constable, 1949.

2869 THE HAYBURN FAMILY. London: Constable, 1952.

2870 JAMES AND CHARLOTTE. London: Constable, 1955.

2871 AN INDEPENDENT YOUNG MAN. London: Constable, 1961.

BIOGRAPHY AND CRITICISM

TCA-1.

William Soutar (1898-1943)

Soutar was confined to his bed for the last thirteen years of his life (the result of food poisoning during his war service), but he continued to write the poems in Scots and English--particularly in Scots and for children--on which his reputation rests.

2872 GLEANINGS BY AN UNDERGRADUATE. Paisley: Gardner, 1923.

2873 CONFLICT. London: Chapman and Hall, 1931.

2874 SEEDS IN THE WIND: POEMS IN SCOTS FOR CHILDREN. Edinburgh: Grant & Murray, 1933; rev. and enl. ed., London: Dakers, 1943; illus. Colin Gibson, London: Dakers, 1948.

2875 THE SOLITARY WAY: POEMS. Edinburgh: Moray Press, 1934.

2876 BRIEF WORDS: ONE HUNDRED EPIGRAMS. Edinburgh: Moray Press, 1935.

2877 POEMS IN SCOTS. Edinburgh: Moray Press, 1935.

2878 A HANDFUL OF EARTH. Edinburgh: Moray Press, 1936.

2879 RIDDLES IN SCOTS. Edinburgh: Moray Press, 1937.

2880 IN THE TIME OF TYRANTS: POEMS, WITH AN INTRODUCTORY NOTE ON PACIFIST FAITH AND NECESSITY. Perth: Privately Printed, 1939.

2881 BUT THE EARTH ABIDETH: A VERSE SEQUENCE. London: Dakers, 1943.

2882 THE EXPECTANT SILENCE: POEMS. London: Dakers, 1944.

2883 DIARIES OF A DYING MAN. Ed. Alexander Scott. Edinburgh: Chambers, 1954.

A selection from Soutar's unpublished diaries.

2884 "William Soutar (1898-1943): A Selection of His Previously Uncollected Writings." Ed. Alexander Scott and George Bruce. SCOTTISH REVIEW, No. 10 (1978), 17-25.

The greater proportion of Soutar's prose--his diaries and journals --remains unpublished and largely unknown.

COLLECTIONS AND SELECTIONS

2885 COLLECTED POEMS. Ed. Hugh MacDiarmid. London: Dakers, 1948.

Not a complete collection.

2886 POEMS IN SCOTS AND ENGLISH. Ed. William R Aitken. Edinburgh: Oliver and Boyd, 1961; Edinburgh: Scottish Academic Press, 1975.

BIOGRAPHY AND CRITICISM

D; P.

2887 Smith, McCallum. "The Poetry of William Soutar." POETRY REVIEW, 29 (1938), 301-11.

2888 POETRY SCOTLAND, 2 (1945).

A Soutar memorial number, with contributions by Hugh MacDiarmid, William Montgomerie, and Douglas Young.

2889 Reid, Alexander. "The Life Story of William Soutar." SCOTLAND'S MAGAZINE, 50 (September 1954), 30-33.

2890 Scott, Alexander. STILL LIFE: WILLIAM SOUTAR (1898-1943). Edinburgh: Chambers, 1958.

2891 Bruce, George. WILLIAM SOUTAR (1898-1943): THE MAN AND THE POET. AN ESSAY. Edinburgh: National Library of Scotland, 1978.

2892 Scott, Alexander. "Makar/Poet: William Soutar." SCOTTISH REVIEW, No. 11 (1978), 31-37.

BIBLIOGRAPHY

2893 Aitken, William R. "William Soutar: Bibliographical Notes and a Checklist." BIBLIOTHECK, 1, No. 2 (1957), 3-14.

Eric Linklater (1899-1974)

A versatile novelist, historian, and biographer who defies classification. He has also written plays, short stories, "conversations," and books for children.

2894 POOBIE. Edinburgh: Porpoise Press, 1925.

Poems.

2895 WHITE-MAA'S SAGA. London: Cape, 1929.

2896 POET'S PUB. London: Cape, 1929.

2897 A DRAGON LAUGHED, AND OTHER POEMS. London: Cape, 1930.

2898 JUAN IN AMERICA: A NOVEL. London: Cape, 1931.

2899 BEN JONSON AND KING JAMES: A BIOGRAPHY AND A PORTRAIT. London: Cape, 1931.

2900 THE MEN OF NESS: THE SAGA OF THORLIEF COALBITER'S SONS. London: Cape, 1931.

2901 MARY QUEEN OF SCOTS. London: Peter Davies, 1933.

2902 THE CRUSADER'S KEY: A TALE. London: White Owl Press, 1933.

2903 MAGNUS MERRIMAN: A NOVEL. London: Cape, 1934.

2904 THE REVOLUTION [AND OTHER STORIES]. London: White Owl Press, 1934.

2905 ROBERT THE BRUCE. London: Peter Davies, 1934.

2906 THE DEVIL'S IN THE NEWS. London: Cape, 1934.
    A comedy to be played with occasional music.

2907 RIPENESS IS ALL: A NOVEL. London: Cape, 1935.

2908 THE LION AND THE UNICORN, OR WHAT ENGLAND HAS MEANT TO SCOTLAND. London: Routledge, 1935.

2909 GOD LIKES THEM PLAIN: SHORT STORIES. London: Cape, 1935.

2910 JUAN IN CHINA. London: Cape, 1937.

2911 THE SAILOR'S HOLIDAY. London: Cape, 1937.

2912 THE IMPREGNABLE WOMEN. London: Cape, 1938.

2913 JUDAS: A NOVEL. London: Cape, 1939.

2914 THE MAN ON MY BACK: AN AUTOBIOGRAPHY. London: Macmillan, 1941.

2915 THE CORNERSTONES: A CONVERSATION IN ELYSIUM. London: Macmillan, 1941.

2916 THE DEFENCE OF CALAIS. London: HMSO, 1941.

2917 THE NORTHERN GARRISONS. London: HMSO, 1941.

2918 THE HIGHLAND DIVISION. London: HMSO, 1942.
    These three items, 2916-18, were published in an official series, The Army at War.

2919 THE RAFT, AND SOCRATES ASKS WHY: TWO CONVERSATIONS. London: Macmillan, 1942.

2920 THE GREAT SHIP, AND RABELAIS REPLIES: TWO CONVERSATIONS. London: Macmillan, 1944.

> The five imaginary conversations (2915, 2919-20) were written for radio and broadcast, 1941-43.

2921 CRISIS IN HEAVEN: AN ELYSIAN COMEDY. London: Macmillan, 1944.

> A play.

2922 THE WIND ON THE MOON: A STORY FOR CHILDREN. London: Macmillan, 1944.

2923 PRIVATE ANGELO: A NOVEL. London: Cape, 1946.

2924 THE ART OF ADVENTURE. London: Macmillan, 1947.

> Essays.

2925 SEALSKIN TROUSERS, AND OTHER STORIES. London: Hart-Davis, 1947.

2926 THE PIRATES IN THE DEEP GREEN SEA: A STORY FOR CHILDREN. London: Macmillan, 1949.

2927 A SPELL FOR OLD BONES. London: Cape, 1949.

2928 MR. BYCULLA: A STORY. London: Hart-Davis, 1950; London: Chatto & Windus, 1970.

2929 TWO COMEDIES. London: Macmillan, 1950.

> The two plays are LOVE IN ALBANIA and TO MEET THE MAC-GREGORS.

2930 ENGLAND. London: Odhams, 1951.

2931 LAXDALE HALL: A NOVEL. London: Cape, 1951.

2932 THE CAMPAIGN IN ITALY. London: HMSO, 1951.

> A popular account of one of the campaigns of the Second World War.

2933 OUR MEN IN KOREA. London: HMSO, 1952.

2934 THE MORTIMER TOUCH. London: French, 1952.

A farcical comedy.

2935 A YEAR OF SPACE: A CHAPTER IN AUTOBIOGRAPHY. London: Macmillan, 1953.

2936 THE HOUSE OF GAIR: A NOVEL. London: Cape, 1953.

2937 THE FAITHFUL ALLY. London: Cape, 1954; issued as THE SULTAN AND THE LADY. New York: Harcourt, Brace, 1954.

2938 THE ULTIMATE VIKING. London: Macmillan, 1955.

The story of Sweyn Asleifsson set against the background of the history and saga literature of Orkney and Iceland.

2939 THE DARK OF SUMMER. London: Cape, 1956.

2940 A SOCIABLE PLOVER, AND OTHER STORIES AND CONCEITS. London: Hart-Davis, 1957.

2941 KARINA WITH LOVE. London: Macmillan, 1958.

2942 BREAKSPEAR IN GASCONY. London: Macmillan, 1958.

A play in three acts.

2943 POSITION AT NOON: A NOVEL. London: Cape, 1958; issued as MY FATHERS AND I. New York: Harcourt, Brace, 1959.

2944 THE MERRY MUSE. London: Cape, 1959.

2945 EDINBURGH. London: Newnes, 1960.

2946 ROLL OF HONOUR. London: Hart-Davis, 1961.

2947 HUSBAND OF DELILAH: A NOVEL. London: Macmillan, 1962.

2948 A MAN OVER FORTY: A NOVEL. London: Macmillan, 1963.

2949 THE PRINCE IN THE HEATHER. London: Hodder and Stoughton, 1965.

An account of the wanderings of Prince Charles Edward Stuart after Culloden.

2950 ORKNEY AND SHETLAND: AN HISTORICAL, GEOGRAPHICAL, SOCIAL AND SCENIC SURVEY. London: Robert Hale, 1965; 2nd ed. 1971.

2951 THE CONQUEST OF ENGLAND. London: Hodder and Stoughton, 1966.

2952 A TERRIBLE FREEDOM. London: Macmillan, 1966.

2953 THE SURVIVAL OF SCOTLAND: A REVIEW OF SCOTTISH HISTORY FROM ROMAN TIMES TO THE PRESENT DAY. London: Heinemann, 1968.

2954 SCOTLAND. London: Thames and Hudson, 1968.

2955 THE ROYAL HOUSE OF SCOTLAND. London: Macmillan, 1970.

2956 FANFARE FOR A TIN HAT: A THIRD ESSAY IN AUTOBIOGRAPHY. London: Macmillan, 1970.

2957 THE CORPSE ON CLAPHAM COMMON: A TALE OF SIXTY YEARS AGO. London: Macmillan, 1971.

2958 THE VOYAGE OF THE CHALLENGER. London: John Murray, 1972.

2959 THE BLACK WATCH: THE HISTORY OF THE ROYAL HIGHLAND REGI-MENT. With Andro Linklater. London: Barrie and Jenkins, 1977.

COLLECTIONS

2960 THE STORIES OF ERIC LINKLATER. London: Macmillan, 1968.

BIOGRAPHY AND CRITICISM

CAP-2; CN (J.E. Morpurgo); D; H, pages 246-72; P; T; TCA; TCA-1.

2961 Broom, John L. "A Peasant with a Pen? The Life and Work of Eric Linklater." SCOTIA REVIEW, No. 18 (Winter 1977-78), 37-51.

2962 Parnell, Michael. "Eric Linklater's Novels." SCOTTISH REVIEW, No. 12 (1978), 29-36.

BIBLIOGRAPHY

2963 Aitken, William R. "Eric Linklater: A Checklist of His Books." BIB-LIOTHECK, 5 (1967-70), 190-97.

Flora Garry (1900--)

Her poems are popularly acclaimed in the district of Buchan of which she writes in a rich Buchan dialect.

2964 BENNYGOAK AND OTHER POEMS. Preston: Akros, 1974.

BIOGRAPHY AND CRITICISM

2965 Turberville, Ruby. "Flora Garry: A Voice from Buchan." SCOTS MAGAZINE, n.s. 112 (1979-80), 180-89.

"Lewis Grassic Gibbon"
James Leslie Mitchell (1901-35)

His reputation as the outstanding Scottish novelist of the century rests on A SCOTS QUAIR, a trilogy of novels, and on the short stories and essays now collected in A SCOTS HAIRST. His other writings have their interest and should not be ignored.

2966 HANNO, OR THE FUTURE OF EXPLORATION. [by J.L.M.] London: Kegan Paul, 1928.

2967 STAINED RADIANCE: A FICTIONIST'S PRELUDE. [by J.L.M.] London: Jarrolds, 1930.

2968 THE THIRTEENTH DISCIPLE. [by J.L.M.] London: Jarrolds, 1931; ed. Douglas F. Young, Edinburgh: Paul Harris, 1980.

2969 THE CALENDS OF CAIRO. [by J.L.M.] London: Jarrolds, 1931; issued as CAIRO DAWNS. Indianapolis: Bobbs-Merrill, 1931.

2970 THREE GO BACK. [by J.L.M.] London: Jarrolds, 1932.

2971 THE LOST TRUMPET. [by J.L.M.] London: Jarrolds, 1932.

2972 SUNSET SONG. London: Jarrolds, 1932; ed. John T. Low, London: Longman, 1971.

2973 PERSIAN DAWNS, EGYPTIAN NIGHTS. [by J.L.M.] London: Jarrolds, 1932.

2974 IMAGE AND SUPERSCRIPTION: A NOVEL. [by J.L.M.] London: Jarrolds, 1933.

2975 CLOUD HOWE. London: Jarrolds, 1933.

2976 SPARTACUS. [by J.L.M.] London: Jarrolds, 1933; introd. Ian S. Munro, London: Hutchinson, 1970.

2977 NIGER: THE LIFE OF MUNGO PARK. Edinburgh: Porpoise Press, 1934.

2978 THE CONQUEST OF THE MAYA. [by J.L.M.] London: Jarrolds, 1934.

2979 GAY HUNTER. [by J.L.M.] London: Heinemann, 1934.

2980 SCOTTISH SCENE, OR THE INTELLIGENT MAN'S GUIDE TO ALBYN. With Hugh MacDiarmid. London: Jarrolds, 1934.

2981 NINE AGAINST THE UNKNOWN: A RECORD OF GEOGRAPHICAL EXPLORATION. [by J.L.M. and L.G.G.] London: Jarrolds, 1934; issued as EARTH CONQUERORS: THE LIVES AND ACHIEVEMENTS OF THE GREAT EXPLORERS [by J.L.M.]. New York: Simon and Schuster, 1934.

2982 GREY GRANITE. London: Jarrolds, 1934.

COLLECTIONS

2983 A SCOTS QUAIR, A TRILOGY OF NOVELS: SUNSET SONG, CLOUD HOWE, GREY GRANITE. London: Jarrolds, 1946; Jarrolds, 1950; Hutchinson, 1966.

2984 A SCOTS HAIRST: ESSAYS AND SHORT STORIES. Ed. Ian S. Munro. London: Hutchinson, 1967.

BIOGRAPHY AND CRITICISM

D; H, pages 229-41; P; TCA; TCA-1.

2985 Caird, James B. "Lewis Grassic Gibbon and His Contribution to the Scottish Novel." In ESSAYS IN LITERATURE. Ed. John Murray. Edinburgh: Oliver and Boyd, 1936, pp. 139-53.

2986 Montgomerie, William. "The Brown God: Lewis Grassic Gibbon's Trilogy A SCOTS QUAIR." SCOTS MAGAZINE, n.s. 44 (1945-46), 213-23.

2987 MacDiarmid, Hugh. "Lewis Grassic Gibbon: James Leslie Mitchell." SCOTTISH ART AND LETTERS, 2 (1946), 39–44; rpt. in LITTLE REVIEWS ANTHOLOGY 1946. Ed. Denys Val Baker. London: Eyre and Spottiswoode, 1946, pp. 206–13.

In the American edition of Baker's anthology, MODERN BRITISH WRITING (New York: Vanguard Press, 1947), where MacDiarmid's essay is reprinted on pages 309–19, approximately a page has been excised.

2988 Wagner, Geoffrey. "'The Greatest Since Galt': Lewis Grassic Gibbon." ESSAYS IN CRITICISM, 2 (1952), 295–310.

2989 _____. "The Other Grassic Gibbon." SALTIRE REVIEW, 5 (1955), 33–41.

2990 MacDiarmid, Hugh. "Lewis Grassic Gibbon." In SELECTED ESSAYS OF HUGH MacDIARMID. Ed. Duncan Glen. London: Cape, 1969, pp. 188–96.

The text of a talk broadcast in 1960.

2991 Macaree, David. "Myth and Allegory in Lewis Grassic Gibbon's A SCOTS QUAIR." SSL, 2 (1964–65), 45–55.

2992 Munro, Ian S. LESLIE MITCHELL: LEWIS GRASSIC GIBBON. Edinburgh: Oliver and Boyd, 1966.

2993 Young, Douglas F. BEYOND THE SUNSET: A STUDY OF JAMES LESLIE MITCHELL (LEWIS GRASSIC GIBBON). Aberdeen: Impulse Books, 1973.

2994 Campbell, Ian. "Chris Caledonia: The Search for an Identity." SLJ, 1 (December 1974), 45–57.

2995 Whittington, Graeme. "The Regionalism of Lewis Grassic Gibbon." SCOTTISH GEOGRAPHICAL MAGAZINE, 90 (1974), 75–84.

2996 Johnson, R. "Lewis Grassic Gibbon and A SCOTS QUAIR: Politics in the Novel." In THE 1930S: A CHALLENGE TO ORTHODOXY. Ed. John Lucas. Hassocks: Harvester Press, 1978, pp. 42–58.

2997 Young, Douglas F. "Lewis Grassic Gibbon." SCOTTISH REVIEW, 14 (1979), 34–40.

2998 Wilson, Patricia J. "Freedom and God: Some Implications of the Key Speech in A SCOTS QUAIR." SLJ, 7 (December 1980), 55–79.

BIBLIOGRAPHY

2999 Wagner, Geoffrey. "James Leslie Mitchell/Lewis Grassic Gibbon: A Chronological Checklist of His Writings [with Critical References]." BIBLIOTHECK, 1, No. 1 (1956), 3-21.

This basic bibliography is supplemented by the following:

Aitken, William R. "Further Notes." BIBLIOTHECK, 1, No. 2 (1957), 34-35.

Young, Douglas F. "Additions I." BIBLIOTHECK, 5 (1967-70), 169-73.

Kidd, James. "Additions II." BIBLIOTHECK, 5 (1967-70), 174-77.

Moray McLaren (1901-71)
"Michael Murray"

A novelist and miscellaneous writer of patriotic conviction.

3000 RETURN TO SCOTLAND: AN EGOIST'S JOURNEY. London: Duckworth, 1930.

3001 THE NOBLEST PROSPECT. [by Michael Murray] London: Duckworth, 1934.

A novel.

3002 A WAYFARER IN POLAND. London: Methuen, 1934.

3003 POLAND'S PROGRESS, 1919-1939. Ed. Michael Murray. London: John Murray, 1944.

3004 A DINNER WITH THE DEAD. Edinburgh: Serif Books, 1947.

Short stories.

3005 STERN AND WILD: A NEW SCOTTISH JOURNEY. London: Chapman and Hall, 1948.

3006 "BY ME . . . ": A REPORT UPON THE APPARENT DISCOVERY OF SOME WORKING NOTES OF WM. SHAKESPEARE IN A 16TH CENTURY BOOK. London: Redington, 1949.

3007 A SMALL STIR: LETTERS ON THE ENGLISH. With James Bridie. London: Hollis and Carter, 1949.

3008 THE UNPOSSESSED. London: Chapman and Hall, 1949.

A novel.

3009 THE CAPITAL OF SCOTLAND: A TWENTIETH-CENTURY CONTEMPLA-
TION. Edinburgh: Douglas and Foulis, 1950.

3010 STEVENSON AND EDINBURGH: A CENTENARY STUDY. London:
Chapman and Hall, 1950.

3011 THE SCOTS. Harmondsworth: Penguin, 1951.

3012 A SINGING REEL. London: Hollis and Carter, 1953.

The delights of angling.

3013 THE HIGHLAND JAUNT. London: Jarrolds, 1954.

A study of Boswell and Johnson upon their Highland and Hebri-
dean tour of 1773.

3014 UNDERSTANDING THE SCOTS: A GUIDE FOR SOUTH BRITONS AND
OTHER FOREIGNERS. London: Muller, 1956; Aberdeen: Impulse Books,
1972.

3015 LORD LOVAT OF THE '45: THE END OF AN OLD SONG. London:
Jarrolds, 1957.

3016 THE PURSUIT. London: Jarrolds, 1959.

A novel.

3017 THE WISDOM OF THE SCOTS: A CHOICE AND A COMMENT. London: Michael Joseph, 1961.

3018 IF FREEDOM FAIL: BANNOCKBURN, FLODDEN, THE UNION. London:
Secker and Warburg, 1964.

3019 BONNIE PRINCE CHARLIE. London: Hart-Davis, 1972.

3020 THE FISHING WATERS OF SCOTLAND. London: John Murray, 1972.

Joseph Macleod (1903--)
"Adam Drinan"

The poet, actor, producer, and historian of the theater, who was a wartime
BBC announcer.

3021 BEAUTY AND THE BEAST. London: Chatto and Windus, 1927.

3022 THE ECLIPTIC. London: Faber, 1930.

A poem.

3023 FORAY OF CENTAURS. Paris: This Quarter, 1931.

Poems.

3024 OVERTURE TO CAMBRIDGE: A SATIRICAL STORY. London: Allen and Unwin, 1936.

A novel.

3025 THE COVE: A SEQUENCE OF POEMS. [by A.D.] London: Privately Printed, 1940.

3026 THE MEN OF THE ROCKS. [by A.D.] London: Fortune Press, 1942.

Poems.

3027 THE GHOSTS OF THE STRATH. [by A.D.] London: Fortune Press, 1943.

3028 THE NEW SOVIET THEATRE. London: Allen and Unwin, 1943.

3029 WOMEN OF THE HAPPY ISLAND. [by A.D.] Glasgow: Maclellan, 1944.

Poems.

3030 ACTORS ACROSS THE VOLGA. London: Allen and Unwin, 1946.

3031 A JOB AT THE BBC. Glasgow: Maclellan, 1947.

3032 A SOVIET THEATRE SKETCH BOOK. London: Allen and Unwin, 1951.

3033 THE PASSAGE OF THE TORCH. Edinburgh: Oliver and Boyd, 1951.

A poem.

3034 SCRIPT FROM NORWAY. [by A.D.] Glasgow: Maclellan, 1953.

A poem.

3035 PEOPLE OF FLORENCE: A STUDY IN LOCALITY. London: Allen and Unwin, 1968.

3036 THE SISTERS D'ARANYI. London: Allen and Unwin, 1969.

3037 AN OLD OLIVE TREE. Loanhead: Macdonald, 1971.
   Poems.

BIOGRAPHY AND CRITICISM

CA–65/68; CP (George Bruce).

Albert D[avid] Mackie (1904--)

Poet and journalist.

3038 POEMS IN TWO TONGUES. Edinburgh: Darien Press, 1928.

3039 SING A SANG O' SCOTLAND. Glasgow: Maclellan, 1944.

3040 EDINBURGH. London: Blackie, 1951.

3041 THE BOOK OF MACNIB. Edinburgh: Castle Wynd Printers, 1956.

3042 THE HEARTS: THE STORY OF THE HEART OF MIDLOTHAN F.C. London: Stanley Paul, 1959.

3043 SCOTTISH PAGEANTRY. London: Hutchinson, 1967.

3044 DONALD'S DIVE. Loanhead: Macdonald, 1971.

3045 THE SCOTCH COMEDIANS: FROM THE MUSIC HALL TO TELEVISION. Edinburgh: Ramsay Head Press, 1973.

3046 THE SCOTCH WHISKY DRINKER'S COMPANION. Edinburgh: Ramsay Head Press, 1973.

3047 TALKING GLASGOW. Belfast: Blackstaff Press, 1978.
   On the Glasgow dialect.

BIOGRAPHY AND CRITICISM

CAP-1; CP.

William Montgomerie (1904--)

Poet, editor, and authority on the ballads and the popular poetry of Scotland.

3048 VIA: POEMS. London: Boriswood, 1933.

3049 SQUARED CIRCLE: A VISION OF THE CAIRNGORMS. London: Boriswood, 1934.

A poem.

3050 SCOTTISH NURSERY RHYMES. Ed. with Norah Montgomerie. London: Hogarth Press, 1946.

3051 SANDY CANDY AND OTHER SCOTTISH NURSERY RHYMES. Ed. with Norah Montgomerie. London: Hogarth Press, 1948.

3052 THE WELL AT THE WORLD'S END: FOLK TALES OF SCOTLAND RETOLD. With Norah Montgomerie. London: Hogarth Press, 1956; London: Bodley Head, 1975.

3053 THE HOGARTH BOOK OF SCOTTISH NURSERY RHYMES. Ed. with Norah Montgomerie. London: Hogarth Press, 1964; issued as A BOOK OF SCOTTISH NURSERY RHYMES, New York: OUP, 1965.

BIOGRAPHY AND CRITICISM

CP.

Ian Macpherson (1905-44)

An interesting but neglected novelist.

3054 SHEPHERD'S CALENDAR. London: Cape, 1931.

3055 LAND OF OUR FATHERS. London: Cape, 1933.

3056 PRIDE IN THE VALLEY. London: Cape, 1936.

3057 WILD HARBOUR. London: Methuen, 1936.

3058 LETTERS FROM A HIGHLAND TOWNSHIP. With Elizabeth Macpherson. Edinburgh: Chambers, 1939.

BIOGRAPHY AND CRITICISM

3059 Allan, John R. NORTH-EAST LOWLANDS OF SCOTLAND. London: Robert Hale, 1952; 2nd ed., 1974, pp. 180-82.

James Barke (1905-58)

His popular reputation largely rests on his series of five novels of the "life and loves" of Robert Burns, but his earlier work merits more attention.

3060 THE WORLD HIS PILLOW. London: Collins, 1933.

3061 THE WILD MACRAES. London: Collins, 1934.

3062 THE END OF THE HIGH BRIDGE. London: Collins, 1935.

3063 MAJOR OPERATION. London: Collins, 1936.

3064 THE LAND OF THE LEAL. London: Collins, 1939.

3065 THE GREEN HILLS FAR AWAY: A CHAPTER IN AUTOBIOGRAPHY. London: Collins, 1940.

3066 MAJOR OPERATION: THE PLAY OF THE NOVEL. Glasgow: Maclellan, 1943.

3067 IMMORTAL MEMORY: A NOVEL OF THE LIFE AND LOVES OF ROBERT BURNS. 5 vols. London: Collins, 1946-54.

The separate novels are THE WIND THAT SHAKES THE BARLEY (1946), THE SONG IN THE GREEN THORN TREE (1947), THE WONDER OF ALL THE GAY WORLD (1949), THE CREST OF THE BROKEN WAVE (1953), and THE WELL OF THE SILENT HARP (1954).

3068 BONNIE JEAN: A NOVEL. London: Collins, 1959.

A postscript: the story of Burns's wife and widow.

BIOGRAPHY AND CRITICISM

3069 Smith, Sydney Goodsir. "James Barke." SALTIRE REVIEW, 15 (1958), 13-15.

"Fionn MacColla"
T[homas] Douglas MacDonald (1906-75)

A novelist of distinction whose high literary reputation rests on the two novels he published, with an interval of thirteen years between them.

3070 THE ALBANNACH. London: John Heritage, 1932; rpt. with a new foreword, Edinburgh: Reprographia, 1971.

3071 AND THE COCK CREW. Glasgow: Maclellan, 1945; Glasgow: John S. Burns, 1962; rpt., London: Souvenir Press, 1977.

3072 SCOTTISH NOËL. Edinburgh: Castle Wynd Printers, 1958.

The first chapter of an unfinished novel.

3073 AT THE SIGN OF THE CLENCHED FIST. Edinburgh: Macdonald, 1967.

A study of the errors of post-Reformation Scotland. Includes "Ane Tryall of Heretiks" (pp.71-98), the second chapter of the unfinished novel of which SCOTTISH NOËL was the first.

3074 TOO LONG IN THIS CONDITION (RO FHADA MAR SO A THA MI). Thurso: Caithness Books, 1975.

Autobiography.

3075 THE MINISTERS. London: Souvenir Press, 1979.

BIOGRAPHY AND CRITICISM

H, pp. 330-31, 371-73.

3076 Morrison, David, ed. ESSAYS ON FIONN MacCOLLA. Thurso: Caithness Books, 1973.

John R[obertson] Allan (1906--)

A journalist and miscellaneous writer whose picture of his boyhood on an Aberdeenshire farm should be read along with Lewis Grassic Gibbon's SUNSET SONG.

3077 A NEW SONG TO THE LORD. Edinburgh: Porpoise Press, 1932.

3078 FARMER'S BOY. London: Methuen, 1935; Edinburgh: Serif Books, 1948; ed. Donald M. Budge, London: Longman, 1975.

3079 DOWN ON THE FARM. London: Methuen, 1937.

3080 SCOTLAND, 1938: TWENTY-FIVE IMPRESSIONS. Ed. John R. Allan. Edinburgh: Oliver and Boyd, 1938.

3081 SUMMER IN SCOTLAND. London: Methuen, 1938.

3082 ENGLAND WITHOUT END. London: Methuen, 1940.

3083 MARKET TOWN. London: OUP, 1943.

3084 NORTH-EAST LOWLANDS OF SCOTLAND. London: Robert Hale, 1952; 2nd ed., 1974.

3085 THE SEASONS RETURN: IMPRESSIONS OF FARM LIFE. London: Robert Hale, 1955.

Nancy Brysson Morrison

A novelist of distinction who writes with quiet grace and assurance.

3086 BREAKERS. London: John Murray, 1930.

3087 SOLITAIRE. London: John Murray, 1932.

3088 THE GOWK STORM. London: Collins, 1933.

3089 THE STRANGERS: A NOVEL. London: Collins, 1935.

3090 WHEN THE WIND BLOWS. London: Collins, 1937.

3091 THESE ARE MY FRIENDS. London: Geoffrey Bles, 1946.
       Verse.

3092 THE WINNOWING YEARS: A NOVEL. London: Hogarth Press, 1949.

3093 THE HIDDEN FAIRING: A NOVEL. London: Hogarth Press, 1951.

3094 THE FOLLOWING WIND: A NOVEL. London: Hogarth Press, 1954.

3095 THE OTHER TRAVELLER: A NOVEL. London: Hogarth Press, 1957.

3096 THEY NEED NO CANDLE: THE MEN WHO BUILT THE SCOTTISH KIRK. London: Epworth Press, 1957.

3097 MARY QUEEN OF SCOTS. London: Vista Books, 1960.

3098 THEA. London: Robert Hale, 1963.

3099 THE PRIVATE LIFE OF HENRY VIII. London: Robert Hale, 1964.

3100 HAWORTH HARVEST: THE LIVES OF THE BRONTËS. London: Dent, 1969.

3101 KING'S QUIVER: THE LAST THREE TUDORS. London: Dent, 1972.

3102 TRUE MINDS: THE MARRIAGE OF THOMAS AND JANE CARLYLE. London: Dent, 1974.

BIOGRAPHY AND CRITICISM

CA-15/16; D.

J[ohn] I[nnes] M[ackintosh] Stewart (1906--)
"Michael Innes"

A distinguished academic who writes literary history and criticism, and is also an urbane novelist and (as Michael Innes) a writer of stylish detective stories. These are listed separately, after the writings attributed to J.I.M. Stewart.

3103 CHARACTER AND MOTIVE IN SHAKESPEARE. London: Longmans, 1949.

3104 MARK LAMBERT'S SUPPER. London: Gollancz, 1954.

A novel.

3105 THE GUARDIANS: A NOVEL. London: Gollancz, 1955.

3106 JAMES JOYCE. London: Longmans, for the British Council, 1957.

3107 A USE OF RICHES. London: Gollancz, 1957.

A novel.

3108 THE MAN WHO WROTE DETECTIVE STORIES, AND OTHER STORIES. London: Gollancz, 1959.

277

3109 THE MAN WHO WON THE POOLS. London: Gollancz, 1961.

3110 EIGHT MODERN WRITERS. Oxford: Clarendon Press, 1963.
Volume 12 of the Oxford History of English Literature.

3111 THE LAST TRESILIANS. London: Gollancz, 1963.
A novel.

3112 THOMAS LOVE PEACOCK. London: Longmans, for the British Council, 1963.

3113 AN ACRE OF GRASS. London: Gollancz, 1965.
A novel.

3114 THE AYLWINS. London: Gollancz, 1966.
A novel.

3115 RUDYARD KIPLING. London: Gollancz, 1966.

3116 VANDERLYN'S KINGDOM. London: Gollancz, 1967.
A novel.

3117 JOSEPH CONRAD. London: Longmans, 1968.

3118 CUCUMBER SANDWICHES, AND OTHER STORIES. London: Gollancz, 1969.

3119 AVERY'S MISSION. London: Gollancz, 1971.
A novel.

3120 THOMAS HARDY. London: Longman, 1971.

3121 A PALACE OF ART. London: Gollancz, 1972.

3122 MUNGO'S DREAM. London: Gollancz, 1973.

3123 A STAIRCASE IN SURREY. 5 vols. London: Gollancz, 1974-78.
A series of five novels of Oxford university life. The separate novels are THE GAUDY (1974), YOUNG PATTULLO (1975), A MEMORIAL SERVICE (1976), THE MADONNA OF THE ASTROLABE (1977), and FULL TERM (1978).

DETECTIVE STORIES [BY MICHAEL INNES]

All published in London by Gollancz.

3124 DEATH AT THE PRESIDENT'S LODGING. 1936.

3125 HAMLET, REVENGE! 1937.

3126 LAMENT FOR A MAKAR. 1938.

An unusual detective story with a distinctly Scottish flavor.

3127 STOP PRESS. 1939; issued as THE SPIDER STRIKES, New York: Dodd, Mead, 1939.

3128 THE SECRET VANGUARD. 1940.

3129 THERE CAME BOTH MIST AND SNOW. 1940; issued as A COMEDY OF TERRORS, New York: Dodd, Mead, 1940.

3130 APPLEBY ON ARARAT. 1941.

3131 THE DAFFODIL AFFAIR. 1942.

3132 THE WEIGHT OF THE EVIDENCE. 1943.

3133 APPLEBY'S END. 1945.

3134 FROM LONDON FAR. 1946; issued as THE UNSUSPECTED CHASM, New York: Dodd, Mead, 1946.

3135 WHAT HAPPENED AT HAZELWOOD. 1946.

3136 A NIGHT OF ERRORS. 1947.

3137 THE JOURNEYING BOY. 1949; issued as THE CASE OF THE JOURNEY-ING BOY, New York: Dodd, Mead, 1949.

3138 THREE TALES OF HAMLET. By Michael Innes and Rayner Heppenstall. 1950.

Includes "The Hawk and the Handsaw" and "The Mysterious Af-fair at Elsinore" by Michael Innes.

3139 OPERATION PAX. 1951; issued as THE PAPER THUNDERBOLT, New York: Dodd, Mead, 1951.

3140 A PRIVATE VIEW. 1952; issued as ONE-MAN SHOW, New York: Dodd, Mead, 1952.

3141 CHRISTMAS AT CANDLESHOE. 1953.

3142 APPLEBY TALKING. 1954; issued as DEAD MAN'S SHOES, New York: Dodd, Mead, 1954.

    Short stories.

3143 THE MAN FROM THE SEA. 1955.

3144 APPLEBY PLAYS CHICKEN. 1956; issued as DEATH ON A QUIET DAY, New York: Dodd, Mead, 1957.

3145 APPLEBY TALKS AGAIN: EIGHTEEN DETECTIVE STORIES. 1956.

3146 OLD HALL, NEW HALL. 1956; issued as A QUESTION OF QUEENS, New York: Dodd, Mead, 1956.

3147 THE LONG FAREWELL. 1958.

3148 HARE SITTING UP. 1959.

3149 THE NEW SONIA WAYWARD. 1960; issued as THE CASE OF SONIA WAYWARD, New York: Dodd, Mead, 1960.

3150 SILENCE OBSERVED. 1961.

3151 A CONNOISSEUR'S CASE. 1962; issued as THE CRABTREE AFFAIR, New York: Dodd, Mead, 1962.

3152 MONEY FROM HOLME. 1964.

3153 THE BLOODY WOOD. 1966.

3154 A CHANGE OF HEIR. 1966.

3155 APPLEBY AT ALLINGTON. 1968.

3156 A FAMILY AFFAIR. 1969.

3157 DEATH AT THE CHASE. 1970.

3158 AN AWKWARD LIE. 1971.

3159 THE OPEN HOUSE. 1972.

3160 APPLEBY'S ANSWER. 1973.

3161 APPLEBY'S OTHER STORY. 1974.

3162 THE MYSTERIOUS COMMISSION. 1974.

3163 THE GAY PHOENIX. 1976.

3164 HONEYBATH'S HAVEN. 1977.

3165 THE AMPERSAND PAPERS. 1978.

3166 GOING IT ALONE. 1980.

BIOGRAPHY AND CRITICISM

CA-85/88; CN (H.M. Klein); D; P; TCA; TCA-1.

3167 Haycraft, Howard. MURDER FOR PLEASURE: THE LIFE AND TIMES OF THE DETECTIVE STORY. New York: Appleton, 1941.

Robert McLellan (1907--)

An important dramatist whose indomitable determination to use Scots in his plays has restricted both their performance and their publication. The plays are listed below by their year of first performance [in brackets] in the chronological sequence of his published work. Where no publication details are given for a play, it can be assumed that it has not been published.

3168 JEDDART JUSTICE: A BORDER COMEDY. [1933] Glasgow: Bone and Hulley, 1934.

3169 TARFESSOCK. [1934]

A play in three acts.

3170 THE CHANGELING: A BORDER COMEDY IN ONE ACT. [1934] In SCOTTISH ONE-ACT PLAYS. Ed. John Macnair Reid. Edinburgh: Porpoise Press, 1935. Later published separately, Edinburgh: Porpoise Press, 1938.

THE CHANGELING: A BORDER COMEDY IN ONE ACT. Revised version. In FIFTY ONE-ACT PLAYS: SECOND SERIES. London: Gollancz, 1940.

THE CHANGELING: A BORDER COMEDY IN ONE ACT. [2nd rev. version]. Glasgow: Maclellan, 1950.

3171 CIAN AND ETHLIN. [1935]

A play in three acts.

3172 TOOM BYRES: A COMEDY OF THE SCOTTISH BORDER IN THREE ACTS. [1936] Glasgow: Maclellan, 1947.

3173 JAMIE THE SAXT: A HISTORICAL COMEDY. [1937] Ed. Ian Campbell and Ronald D.S. Jack. London: Calder and Boyars, 1970.

3174 PORTRAIT OF AN ARTIST. [1939]

A play in three acts.

3175 TORWATLETIE, OR THE APOTHECARY: A COMEDY OF THE SCOTTISH BORDER IN THREE ACTS. [1946] Glasgow: Maclellan, 1950.

3176 THE CARLIN MOTH: AN ISLAND FAIRY TALE IN FOUR SCENES. [1946] In NORTH LIGHT: TEN NEW ONE-ACT PLAYS FROM THE NORTH. Ed. Winifred Bannister. Glasgow: Maclellan, 1947, pp. 148-77.

3177 THE FLOUERS O EDINBURGH. [1947]

A comedy of the eighteenth century in three acts.

3178 THE CAILLEACH: A PLAY IN ONE ACT. [1948] Glasgow: Donaldson, 1948.

3179 MARY STEWART. [1951]

A historical drama in five acts.

3180 AS ITHERS SEE US. [1954]

A radio play.

3181 THE ROAD TO THE ISLES. [1954]

A comedy in three acts.

3182 SWEET LARGIE BAY: A DRAMATIC POEM. [Broadcast 1956] In SWEET LARGIE BAY AND ARRAN BURN: TWO POEMS IN SCOTS. Preston: Akros, 1977.

3183 RAB MOSSGIEL. [1959]

A radio play.

3184 YOUNG AUCHINLECK. [1962]

A comedy in three acts.

3185 BALLOON TYTLER. [1962]

A play for radio.

3186 THE OLD BYRE AT CLASHMORE. [1965]

A radio play.

3187 ISLAND BURN. [Broadcast 1965; revised version broadcast 1966] Published as "Arran Burn" in SWEET LARGIE BAY AND ARRAN BURN: TWO POEMS IN SCOTS. Preston: Akros, 1977.

3188 THE HYPOCRITE. [1967] London: Calder and Boyars, 1970.

A comedy of the eighteenth century in five acts.

3189 THE ISLE OF ARRAN. Newton Abbot: David and Charles, 1970.

A study of the island on which the author has lived for more than forty years.

3190 SWEET LARGIE BAY AND ARRAN BURN: TWO POEMS IN SCOTS. Preston: Akros, 1977.

3191 LINMILL: SHORT STORIES IN SCOTS. Preston: Akros, 1977.

BIOGRAPHY AND CRITICISM

CA-41/44.

3192 Leach, Allan. "The High Purposes of Literature: Robert McLellan and His Work." LIBRARY REVIEW, 23 (1971-72), 3-11.

Includes an interim checklist of published and unpublished material.

3193 Cording, Alastair. "A Dramatic Life: Robert McLellan." SCOTTISH REVIEW, No. 9 (Spring 1978), 27-32.

3194 LALLANS No. 10 (Whitsunday 1978).

This number includes three articles on McLellan: Donald Campbell, "The Playwricht," pages 13-15; John T. Low, "The Story-
teller," pages 15-17; and Robert Garioch, "The Poet," pages
17-19, 26.

J[ames] K[ing] Annand (1908--)

His poems in Scots for children are in the tradition of William Soutar's bairn-
rhymes.

3195 SING IT AINCE FOR PLEISURE. Edinburgh: Macdonald, 1965.

3196 TWO VOICES. Edinburgh: Macdonald, 1968.

3197 TWICE FOR JOY. Loanhead: Macdonald, 1974.

3198 POEMS AND TRANSLATIONS. Preston: Akros, 1975.

3199 SONGS FROM CARMINA BURANA, TRANSLATED INTO SCOTS VERSE.
Loanhead: Macdonald, 1978.

3200 THRICE TO SHOW YE. Loanhead: Macdonald, 1979.

BIOGRAPHY AND CRITICISM

3201 Campbell, Janet. "The Bairyn Rhymes of J.K. Annand." AKROS, No.
26 (December 1974), 38-41.

3202 Annand, James King. "Rhyming for the Bairns." CHAPMAN, No. 18
(Spring 1977), 4-8.

Robert Kemp (1908-67)

Playwright and novelist.

3203 A TRUMP FOR JERICHO. Edinburgh: St. Giles Press, 1948.

A play.

3204 THE SATIRE OF THE THREE ESTATES. By Sir David Lindsay of the Mount.
Acting text. Edinburgh: Scots Review, 1949.

3205 THE SAXON SAINT. Edinburgh: St. Giles Press, 1950.
A play.

3206 THE KING OF SCOTS. Edinburgh: St. Giles Press, 1951.
A play.

3207 THE MALACCA CANE. London: Duckworth, 1954.
A novel.

3208 THE ASSET. London: Heinemann, 1956.
A play.

3209 THE MAESTRO. London: Duckworth, 1956.
A novel.

3210 THE HIGHLANDER. London: Duckworth, 1957.
A novel.

3211 THE OTHER DEAR CHARMER. London: Duckworth, 1957.
A play.

3212 THE CAMPAIGNS OF CAPTAIN MACGURK. London: Duckworth, 1958.
A novel.

3213 MASTER JOHN KNOX. Edinburgh: St. Andrew Press, 1960.
A play.

3214 GRETNA GREEN. Edinburgh: Chambers, 1961.
A novel.

3215 OFF A DUCK'S BACK. London: French, 1961.
A play.

BIOGRAPHY AND CRITICISM

CAP-1

George Bruce (1909--)

The background of George Bruce's poetry is the coast of his native Buchan and the lives of its people.

3216 SEA TALK. Glasgow: Maclellan, 1944.

3217 LANDSCAPES AND FIGURES: A SELECTION OF POEMS. Preston: Akros, 1967.

3218 ANNE REDPATH. Edinburgh: Edinburgh University Press, 1974.

    A study of the artist.

3219 FESTIVAL IN THE NORTH: THE STORY OF THE EDINBURGH FESTIVAL. London: Robert Hale, 1975.

3220 "The Boy on the Roof." In AS I REMEMBER. Ed. Maurice Lindsay. London: Robert Hale, 1979, pp. 23-44.

COLLECTIONS AND SELECTIONS

3221 SELECTED POEMS. Edinburgh: Oliver and Boyd, 1947.

3222 COLLECTED POEMS. Edinburgh: Edinburgh University Press, 1970.

BIOGRAPHY AND CRITICISM

CA-65/68; CP (Maurice Lindsay).

3223 Scott, Alexander. "Myth-Maker: The Poetry of George Bruce." AKROS, No. 29 (December 1975), 25-40.

"Robert Garioch"
Robert Garioch Sutherland (1909-81)

One of the most admired of the poets of the literary movement initiated by Hugh MacDiarmid. His poems have an affinity with Robert Fergusson's in the manner in which they capture the authentic Edinburgh voice.

3224 17 POEMS FOR 6D, IN GAELIC, LOWLAND SCOTS AND ENGLISH. With Somhairle MacGill-Eathain (Sorley Maclean). Edinburgh: Chalmers Press, 1940.

3225 CHUCKIES ON THE CAIRN: POEMS IN SCOTS AND ENGLISH. Edinburgh: Chalmers Press, 1949.

3226 THE MASQUE OF EDINBURGH. Edinburgh: Macdonald, 1954.

3227 GEORGE BUCHANAN: JEPHTHAH AND THE BAPTIST, TRANSLATIT FRAE LATIN IN SCOTS. Edinburgh: Oliver and Boyd, 1959.

3228 THE BIG MUSIC, AND OTHER POEMS. Thurso: Caithness Books, 1971.

3229 DOKTOR FAUST IN ROSE STREET. Loanhead: Macdonald, 1973.

3230 TWO MEN AND A BLANKET: MEMOIRS OF CAPTIVITY. Edinburgh: Southside, 1975.

> The personal reminiscences of a prisoner of war.

3231 "Early Days in Edinburgh." In AS I REMEMBER. Ed. Maurice Lindsay. London: Robert Hale, 1979, pp. 45-58.

COLLECTIONS AND SELECTIONS

3232 SELECTED POEMS. Edinburgh: Macdonald, 1966.

3233 COLLECTED POEMS. Loanhead: Macdonald, 1977.

BIOGRAPHY AND CRITICISM

CP (Edwin Morgan); D.

3234 Watson, Roderick. "The Speaker in the Gairdens: The Poetry of Robert Garioch." AKROS, No. 16 (April 1971), 69-76.

3235 Campbell, Donald. "Another Side to Robert Garioch, or a Glisk of Near-Forgotten Hell." AKROS, No. 33 (April 1977), 47-52.

Nigel Tranter (1909--)

A prolific writer who has published some seventy novels, including a dozen for children, and a number of works of nonfiction. Latterly, he has turned to fictionalized historical biography, at the ultimate end of the romantic tradition. He works on an ambitious scale, frequently developing his character or theme over a trilogy of novels. Only a selection from his output is listed here.

3236 THE FORTALICES AND EARLY MANSIONS OF SOUTHERN SCOTLAND, 1400-1650. Edinburgh: Moray Press, 1935.

3237 THE FORTIFIED HOUSE IN SCOTLAND. 5 vols. Vols. 1-4, Edinburgh: Oliver and Boyd, 1962-66; vol. 5, Edinburgh: Chambers, 1970.

NOVELS

All published in London by Hodder and Stoughton.

3238 THE MASTER OF GRAY. 1961.

3239 THE COURTESAN. 1963.

3240 PAST MASTER. 1965.
>   Completes the MASTER OF GRAY trilogy.

3241 THE STEPS TO THE EMPTY THRONE. 1969.

3242 THE PATH OF THE HERO KING. 1970.

3243 THE PRICE OF THE KING'S PEACE. 1971.
>   Completes the trilogy on ROBERT THE BRUCE.

3244 THE YOUNG MONTROSE. 1972.

3245 MONTROSE: THE CAPTAIN-GENERAL. 1973.

3246 THE WISEST FOOL: A NOVEL OF JAMES THE SIXTH AND FIRST. 1974.

3247 THE WALLACE. 1975.

3248 LORDS OF MISRULE. 1976.

3249 A FOLLY OF PRINCES. 1977.

3250 THE CAPTIVE CROWN. 1977.
>   Completes the trilogy (3248, 3249) THE RISE OF THE HOUSE OF STEWART.

3251 MACBETH THE KING. 1978.

3252 MARGARET THE QUEEN. 1979.

BIOGRAPHY AND CRITICISM

CA-11/12.

3253 Hay, Robert. "His Theme is Scotland: Nigel Tranter, Author and Patriot. " SCOTS MAGAZINE, n.s. 95 (1971), 352-59.

George Scott Moncrieff (1910-74)

The Scottish writer who coined the word "Balmorality" to describe certain Scottish Victorian attitudes he deplored. His novels earned him critical acclaim.

3254 CAFÉ BAR. London: Wishart, 1932.

A novel.

3255 TINKER'S WIND: THE SAGA OF A CHEAPJACK. London: Wishart, 1933.

A novel.

3256 SCOTTISH COUNTRY: FIFTEEN ESSAYS BY SCOTTISH AUTHORS. London: Wishart, 1935.

The fifteen essayists, each writing on his own area, include Neil Gunn on Caithness and Sutherland, Eric Linklater on Orkney, Hugh MacDiarmid on the Shetlands, and Scott Moncrieff himself on Skye.

3257 A BOOK OF UNCOMMON PRAYER. London: Methuen, 1937.

Poems.

3258 THE STONES OF SCOTLAND. London: Batsford, 1938.

3259 THE LOWLANDS OF SCOTLAND. London: Batsford, 1939.

3260 EDINBURGH. London: Batsford, 1947; 3rd ed., Edinburgh: Oliver and Boyd, 1965.

3261 DEATH'S BRIGHT SHADOW. London: Allan Wingate, 1948.

A novel.

3262 THE SCOTTISH ISLANDS. London: Batsford, 1952; 2nd ed., Edinburgh: Oliver and Boyd, 1961.

3263 FOTHERINGHAY. Edinburgh: Mercat Cross, 1953.

   A play in three acts.

3264 BURKE STREET. Edinburgh: Richard Paterson, 1956.

   Stories.

3265 THIS DAY. London: Hollis and Carter, 1959.

   Essays.

3266 THE MIRROR AND THE CROSS: SCOTLAND AND THE CATHOLIC FAITH. London: Burns and Oates, 1960.

3267 "The Scottish 'Renaissance' of the 1930s." In MEMOIRS OF A MODERN SCOTLAND. Ed. Karl Miller. London: Faber, 1970, pp. 70-82.

3268 THE CASEBOOK OF A VICTORIAN DETECTIVE. By James McLevy. Ed. G.S.M. Edinburgh: Canongate, 1975.

George Friel (1910-75)

A novelist who writes of Glasgow with realism and style.

3269 THE BANK OF TIME. London: Hutchinson, 1959.

3270 THE BOY WHO WANTED PEACE. London: John Calder, 1964.

3271 GRACE AND MISS PARTRIDGE. London: Calder and Boyars, 1969.

3272 MR. ALFRED, M.A. London: Calder and Boyars, 1972.

3273 AN EMPTY HOUSE. London: Calder and Boyars, 1974.

BIOGRAPHY AND CRITICISM

3274 Gifford, Douglas. "Modern Scottish Fiction." SSL, 13 (1978), 266-67.

Jane Duncan (1910-76)
"Janet Sandison"

Francis Russell Hart's critical enthusiasm has directed attention to the deeper values inherent in Jane Duncan's long series of interconnected novels, popularly read as "old-fashioned Scottish 'character' fiction." All her books are published in London by Macmillan and in New York by St. Martin's Press.

3275 MY FRIENDS THE MISS BOYDS. 1959.

3276 MY FRIEND MURIEL. 1959.

3277 MY FRIEND MONICA. 1960.

3278 MY FRIEND ANNIE. 1961.

3279 MY FRIEND SANDY. 1961.

3280 MY FRIEND MARTHA'S AUNT. 1962.

3281 MY FRIEND FLORA. 1962.

3282 MY FRIEND MADAME ZORA. 1963.

3283 MY FRIEND ROSE. 1964.

3284 MY FRIEND COUSIN EMMIE. 1964.

3285 MY FRIENDS THE MRS. MILLERS. 1965.

3286 MY FRIENDS FROM CAIRNTON. 1966.

3287 MY FRIEND MY FATHER. 1966.

3288 MY FRIENDS THE MACLEANS. 1967.

3289 MY FRIENDS THE HUNGRY GENERATION. 1968.

3290 MY FRIEND THE SWALLOW. 1970.

3291 MY FRIEND SASHIE. 1972.

3292 MY FRIENDS THE MISSES KINDNESS. 1974.

3293 MY FRIENDS GEORGE AND TOM. 1976.

Novels supposedly written by the central character of the "Friend" novels, Janet Sandison.

3294 JEAN IN THE MORNING. 1969.

3295 JEAN AT NOON. 1971.

3296 JEAN IN THE TWILIGHT. 1972.

3297 JEAN TOWARDS ANOTHER DAY. 1975.

AUTOBIOGRAPHY

3298 LETTER FROM REACHFAR. 1975.

FOR YOUNG PEOPLE

3299 CAMERONS ON THE TRAIL. 1963.

3300 CAMERONS ON THE HILLS. 1963.

3301 CAMERONS AT THE CASTLE. 1964.

3302 CAMERONS CALLING. 1966.

3303 CAMERONS AHOY! 1968.

BIOGRAPHY AND CRITICISM

CA-3; H, pages 385-93.

3304 Hart, Francis R. "Jane Duncan's Friends and the Reachfar Story." SSL, 6 (1968-69), 156-74.

Revised and updated in H, above.

Norman MacCaig (1910--)

According to Hugh MacDiarmid, "The best Scottish poet writing in English today."

3305 FAR CRY. London: Routledge, 1943.

3306 THE INWARD EYE. London: Routledge, 1946.

3307 RIDING LIGHTS. London: Hogarth Press, 1955.

3308 THE SINAI SORT. London: Hogarth Press, 1957.

3309 A COMMON GRACE. London: Hogarth Press, 1960.

3310 A ROUND OF APPLAUSE. London: Hogarth Press, 1962.

3311 MEASURES. London: Hogarth Press, 1965.

3312 SURROUNDINGS. London: Hogarth Press, 1966.

3313 RINGS ON A TREE. London: Hogarth Press, 1968.

3314 A MAN IN MY POSITION. London: Hogarth Press, 1970.

3315 THE WHITE BIRD. London: Hogarth Press, 1973.

3316 THE WORLD'S ROOM. London: Hogarth Press, 1974.

3317 TREE OF STRINGS. London: Hogarth Press, 1977.

3317a "My Way of It." In AS I REMEMBER. Ed. Maurice Lindsay. London: Robert Hale, 1979, pp. 79-88.

3318 THE EQUAL SKIES. London: Hogarth Press, 1980.

COLLECTIONS AND SELECTIONS

3319 SELECTED POEMS. London: Hogarth Press, 1971.

3320 [SELECTION]. In PENGUIN MODERN POETS, 21. Harmondsworth: Penguin, 1972, pp. 83-133.

3321 OLD MAPS AND NEW: SELECTED POEMS. London: Hogarth Press, 1978.

BIOGRAPHY AND CRITICISM

CA-9/10; CP (Bernard Bergonzi); D; P; T; WA-50.

3322 Smith, Iain Crichton. "The Poetry of Norman MacCaig." SALTIRE RE-
VIEW, No. 19 (Autumn 1958), 20-23.

3323 AKROS, No. 7 (March 1968), entire issue.
> A Norman MacCaig issue, with contributions by Hugh MacDiar-
> mid, R. Crombie Saunders, Alexander Scott, and G.S. Fraser.

3324 Fulton, Robin. "Ishmael Among the Phenomena: The Poetry of Norman
MacCaig." SCOTTISH INTERNATIONAL, October 1972, pp. 22-27.

3325 Scott, Mary Jane W. "Neoclassical MacCaig." SSL, 10 (1972-73), 135-44.

3326 Porter, W.S. "The Poetry of Norman MacCaig." AKROS, No. 32
(December 1976), 37-53.

3327 Frykman, Erik. "UNEMPHATIC MARVELS": A STUDY OF NORMAN
MacCAIG'S POETRY. Gothenburgh: University of Gothenburg, 1977.

Robert Nicolson

His short novels of contemporary Glasgow are well written, his characters closely
observed and sympathetically presented.

3328 MRS. ROSS. London: Constable, 1961; issued as THE WHISPERERS,
Harmondsworth: Penguin, 1966.

3329 A FLIGHT OF STEPS. London: Constable, 1966.
> A sequel to MRS. ROSS.

Hannah Aitken (1911-77)

A quiet thoughtful novelist who writes with a strangely moving quality.

3330 IN A SHAFT OF SUNLIGHT. London: Hodder and Stoughton, 1947.

3331 WHITTANS. London: Hodder and Stoughton, 1951.

3332 SEVEN NAPIER PLACE. London: Hodder and Stoughton, 1952.

3333 MUSIC FOR THE JOURNEY. London: Hodder and Stoughton, 1957.

3334 A FORGOTTEN HERITAGE: ORIGINAL FOLK TALES OF LOWLAND SCOTLAND. Edinburgh: Scottish Academic Press, 1973.

Sorley Maclean (1911--)

A Scottish Gaelic poet whose most ambitious work, AN CUILITHIONN [The Cuillin], portrays the history and struggles of the Skye crofters against a background of world history. It has been published as yet only in parts, in LINES REVIEW, No. 7 (January 1955) and in FOUR POINTS OF A SALTIRE (3338).

3335 17 POEMS FOR 6D, IN GAELIC, LOWLAND SCOTS AND ENGLISH. With Robert Garioch. Edinburgh: Chalmers, 1940.

3336 DAIN DO EIMHIR AGUS DAIN EILE. Glasgow: Maclellan, 1943.

3337 DAIN DO EIMHIR AGUS DAIN EILE/POEMS TO EIMHIR. Trans. Iain Crichton Smith. London: Gollancz, 1971.

3338 FOUR POINTS OF A SALTIRE: THE POETRY OF SORLEY MACLEAN, GEORGE CAMPBELL HAY, WILLIAM NEILL, STUART MACGREGOR. Edinburgh: Reprographia, 1970.

3339 REOTHAIRT IS CONTRAIGH: TAGHADH DE DHAIN 1932-72 [SPRING TIDE AND NEAP TIDE: SELECTED POEMS 1932-72]. Edinburgh: Canongate, 1977.

> The poems are presented in the original Gaelic with facing English line-by-line translations by the poet himself.

BIOGRAPHY AND CRITICISM

D; P.

3340 Smith, Iain Crichton. "The Poetry of Sorley Maclean." GLASGOW REVIEW, 4, No. 3 (1973), 38-41.

3341 Herdman, John. "The Poetry of Sorley Maclean: A Non-Gael's View." LINES REVIEW, No. 61 (1977), 25-36.

3342 Nicolson, Angus. "An Interview with Sorley Maclean." SSL, 14 (1979), 23-36.

J[ames] F[indlay] Hendry (1912--)

With G.S. Fraser and Henry Treece, J.F. Hendry was one of the leaders of the "Apocalypse" movement, with which Norman MacCaig was also briefly connected. Three Apocalypse anthologies were issued, in all of which Hendry was involved as editor or coeditor.

3343 THE BOMBED HAPPINESS. London: Routledge, 1942.

Poems.

3344 THE ORCHESTRAL MOUNTAIN: A SYMPHONIC ELEGY. London: Routledge, 1943.

3345 THE BLACKBIRD OF OSPO: STORIES OF JUGOSLAVIA. Glasgow: Maclellan, 1945.

3346 FERNIE BRAE: A SCOTTISH CHILDHOOD. Glasgow: Maclellan, 1947.

A novel.

3347 VERLON AND THE NEW IMAGE. Harlow, 1965.

3348 MARIMARUSA. Thurso: Caithness Books, 1978.

Poems.

BIOGRAPHY AND CRITICISM

CA-29/32; D.

Robin Jenkins (1912--)

An important novelist.

3349 SO GAILY SINGS THE LARK. Glasgow: Maclellan, 1950.

3350 HAPPY FOR THE CHILD. London: John Lehmann, 1953.

3351 THE THISTLE AND THE GRAIL. London: Macdonald, 1954.

3352 THE CONE GATHERERS. London: Macdonald, 1955; rpt., Edinburgh: Paul Harris, 1980.

3353 GUESTS OF WAR. London: Macdonald, 1956.

3354 THE MISSIONARIES. London: Macdonald, 1957.

3355 THE CHANGELING. London: Macdonald, 1958.

3356 LOVE IS A FERVENT FIRE. London: Macdonald, 1959.

3357 SOME KIND OF GRACE. London: Macdonald, 1960.

3358 DUST ON THE PAW. London: Macdonald, 1961.

3359 THE TIGER OF GOLD. London: Macdonald, 1962.

3360 A LOVE OF INNOCENCE. London: Cape, 1963.

3361 THE SARDANA DANCERS. London: Cape, 1964.

3362 A VERY SCOTCH AFFAIR. London: Gollancz, 1968.

3363 THE HOLY TREE. London: Gollancz, 1969.

3364 THE EXPATRIATES. London: Gollancz, 1971.

3365 A TOAST TO THE LORD. London: Gollancz, 1972.

3366 A FAR CRY FROM BOWMORE, AND OTHER STORIES. London: Gollancz, 1973.

3367 A FIGURE OF FUN. London: Gollancz, 1974.

3368 A WOULD-BE SAINT. London: Gollancz, 1978.

3369 FERGUS LAMONT. Edinburgh: Canongate, 1979.

BIOGRAPHY AND CRITICISM

CA-4; CN (Alexander Scott); H, pages 272-86; WA-50.

3370 Thompson, Alastair R. "Faith and Love: An Examination of Some Themes in the Novels of Robin Jenkins." NEW SALTIRE, No. 3 (Spring 1962), 57-64.

3371 Morgan, Edwin. "The Novels of Robin Jenkins." LISTENER, 12 July 1973; rpt. in his ESSAYS. Cheadle: Carcanet Press, 1974, pp. 242-45.

Sydney Tremayne (1912--)

Tremayne was born in Ayr and became a journalist in London, but he found himself in writing poetry of a distinctive but unobtrusive kind. His work has not yet been given the attention it deserves.

3372 FOR WHOM THERE IS NO SPRING. London: Pendulum Press, 1946.

3373 TIME AND THE WIND. London: Collins, 1948.

3374 THE HARDEST FREEDOM. London: Collins, 1951.

3375 THE ROCK AND THE BIRD. London: Allen and Unwin, 1955.

3376 THE SWANS OF BERWICK. London: Chatto and Windus, 1962.

3377 THE TURNING SKY. London: Hart-Davis, 1969.

3378 "Hard Times and High Times." In AS I REMEMBER. Ed. Maurice Lindsay. London: Robert Hale, 1979, pp. 141-56.

COLLECTIONS AND SELECTIONS

3379 SELECTED AND NEW POEMS. London: Chatto and Windus, 1973.

BIOGRAPHY AND CRITICISM

CA-7/8; CP (George Bruce).

3380 Bruce, George. "The Poetry of Sydney Tremayne." AKROS, No. 38 (August 1978), 32-45.

Fred Urquhart (1912--)

Novelist, short-story writer, and editor.

3381 TIME WILL KNIT. London: Duckworth, 1938.

3382 I FELL FOR A SAILOR, AND OTHER STORIES. London: Duckworth, 1940.

3383 THE CLOUDS ARE BIG WITH MERCY. Glasgow: Maclellan, 1946.
Short stories.

3384 THE LAST G.I. BRIDE WORE TARTAN. Edinburgh: Serif Books, 1948.
Short stories.

3385 THE FERRET WAS ABRAHAM'S DAUGHTER. London: Methuen, 1949.

3386 THE YEAR OF THE SHORT CORN, AND OTHER STORIES. London:
Methuen, 1949.

3387 THE LAST SISTER, AND OTHER STORIES. London: Methuen, 1950.

3388 JEZEBEL'S DUST. London: Methuen, 1951.
A sequel to THE FERRET WAS ABRAHAM'S DAUGHTER.

3389 THE LAUNDRY GIRL AND THE POLE. London: Arco, 1954.
Short stories.

3390 SCOTLAND IN COLOUR. London: Batsford, 1961.

3391 THE DYING STALLION. London: Hart-Davis, 1967.
A collection of short stories.

3392 THE PLOUGHING MATCH. London: Hart-Davis, 1968.
A further collection of short stories.

3393 PALACE OF GREEN DAYS. London: Quartet, 1979.

3394 "My Many Splendoured Pavilion." In AS I REMEMBER. Ed. Maurice
Lindsay. London: Robert Hale, 1979, pp. 157-74.

3395 PROUD LADY IN A CAGE. Edinburgh: Paul Harris, 1980.

3396 A DIVER IN CHINA SEAS. London: Quartet, 1980.

BIOGRAPHY AND CRITICISM

CA-11/12; CN (Naomi Mitchison).

Douglas Young (1913-73)

Poet, scholar, and man of letters.

3397 AUNTRAN BLADS: AN OUTWALE O VERSES. Glasgow: Maclellan, 1943.

3398 A BRAIRD O THRISTLES: SCOTS POEMS. Glasgow: Maclellan, 1947.

Includes "The Kirkyaird by the Sea," a Scots version of Valery's "Le Cimetière Marin."

3399 "PLASTIC SCOTS" AND THE SCOTTISH LITERARY TRADITION: AN AUTHORITATIVE INTRODUCTION TO A CONTROVERSY. Glasgow: Maclellan, 1947.

3400 CHASING AN ANCIENT GREEK. London: Hollis and Carter, 1950.

Discursive reminiscences of a European journey.

3401 ROMANISATION IN SCOTLAND: AN ESSAY IN PERSPECTIVE. Tayport: The Author, 1956.

3402 SCOTLAND'S STORY. Edinburgh: Scotland's Magazine, 1957.

3403 THE PUDDOCKS: A VERSE PLAY IN SCOTS FRAE THE AULD GREEK O ARISTOPHANES. Tayport: The Author, 1957.

3404 THE BURDIES: A COMEDY IN SCOTS VERSE BY ARISTOPHANES AND DOUGLAS YOUNG. Tayport: The Author, 1959.

3405 EDINBURGH IN THE AGE OF SIR WALTER SCOTT. Norman: University of Oklahoma Press, 1965.

3406 SCOTS BURDS AND EDINBURGH REVIEWERS. Edinburgh: Macdonald, 1966.

3407 ST. ANDREWS: TOWN AND GOWN. London: Cassell, 1969.

3408 SCOTLAND. London: Cassell, 1971.

COLLECTIONS AND SELECTIONS

3409 SELECTED POEMS. Edinburgh: Oliver and Boyd, 1950.

3410 A CLEAR VOICE: DOUGLAS YOUNG, POET AND POLYMATH. Ed. Clara Young and David Murison. Loanhead: Macdonald, 1977.

A selection from his writings, with a memoir and a bibliography.

BIOGRAPHY AND CRITICISM

CAP-1; CP (Edwin Morgan); D; P.

See also 3410.

BIBLIOGRAPHY

See 3410.

Gavin Maxwell (1914-69)

A naturalist who brought a remarkable imaginative quality to his writing about otters.

3411 HARPOON AT A VENTURE. London: Hart-Davis, 1952; issued as HARPOON VENTURE, New York: Viking, 1952.

3412 GOD PROTECT ME FROM MY FRIENDS. London: Longmans, Green, 1956; issued as BANDIT, New York: Dutton, 1956.

3413 A REED SHAKEN BY THE WIND. London: Longmans, Green, 1957; issued as PEOPLE OF THE REEDS, New York: Harper, 1957.

3414 THE TEN PAINS OF DEATH. London: Longmans, 1959.

3415 RING OF BRIGHT WATER. London: Longmans, 1960.

3416 THE OTTER'S TALE. London: Longmans, 1962.

For young people.

3417 THE ROCKS REMAIN. London: Longmans, 1963.

3418 THE HOUSE OF ELRIG. London: Longmans, 1965.

Autobiography.

3419 LORDS OF THE ATLAS. London: Longmans, 1966.

3420 RAVEN SEEK THY BROTHER. London: Longmans, 1968.

BIOGRAPHY AND CRITICISM

CA-7/8; WA-50.

3421 Frere, Richard. MAXWELL'S GHOST: AN EPILOGUE TO GAVIN MAX-
WELL'S CAMUSFEARNA. London: Gollancz, 1976.

Ruthven Todd (1914-78)

Poet, novelist, and art critic.

3422 THE LAUGHING MULATTO: THE STORY OF ALEXANDRE DUMAS. London: Rich and Cowan, 1939.

3423 OVER THE MOUNTAIN. London: Harrap, 1939.
   A novel.

3424 TEN POEMS. Edinburgh: Privately Printed, 1940.

3425 UNTIL NOW. London: Fortune Press, 1942.
   Poems.

3426 THE LOST TRAVELLER. London: Grey Walls Press, 1943.
   A novel.

3427 THE ACREAGE OF THE HEART. Glasgow: Maclellan, 1944.
   Poems.

3428 THE PLANET IN MY HAND. London: Grey Walls Press, 1946.
   Poems.

3429 TRACKS IN THE SNOW: STUDIES IN ENGLISH SCIENCE AND ART.
London: Grey Walls Press, 1946.

3430 LOSER'S CHOICE. New York: Hermitage House, 1953.
   A novel.

3431 A MANTELPIECE OF SHELLS. New York: Bonacio and Saul, 1955.

3432 GARLAND FOR THE WINTER SOLSTICE: SELECTED POEMS. London: Dent, 1961.

BIOGRAPHY AND CRITICISM

CA-81/84; CP (Alexander Scott); T; TCA-1.

3433 Stanford, Derek. "Ruthven Todd." In his THE FREEDOM OF POETRY; STUDIES IN CONTEMPORARY VERSE. London: Falcon Press, 1947, pp. 224-43.

3434 Symons, Julian. "Ruthven Todd, 1914-1978: Some Details for a Portrait." LONDON MAGAZINE, 19 (April-May 1979), 62-80.

Alexander Reid (1914--)

It was Alexander Reid, dramatist and critic, who said "Bridie had put a think-ing head on the shoulders of the new theatre. It was McLellan's great service to put a Scots tongue in the Scots head." Reid's own plays used Scots effective-ly, but they were Anglicized for publication.

3435 STEPS TO A VIEWPOINT. London: Dakers, 1947.

Poems.

3436 ZOO-ILLOGICAL RHYMES. Edinburgh: Heriot Press, 1947; London: Hutchinson, 1960.

For children.

3437 THE YOUNG TRAVELLER IN FRANCE. London: Phoenix House, 1952.

3438 THE LASS WI' THE MUCKLE MOU', OR ONCE UPON A RHYME: A COMEDY. London: Collins, 1958.

3439 THE WORLD'S WONDER. A PHANTASY. London: Collins, 1958.

3440 TWO SCOTS PLAYS. London: Collins, 1958.

The two plays listed above, bound together with a foreword by the author. They are Anglicized versions of plays originally written in Braid Scots, and successfully presented.

Sydney Goodsir Smith (1915-75)

A writer of incredibly diverse talents and solid achievement: poet, translator, literary critic, art critic, dramatist, and editor.

3441 SKAIL WIND: POEMS. Edinburgh: Chalmers Press, 1941.

3442 THE WANDERER, AND OTHER POEMS. Edinburgh: Oliver and Boyd, 1943.

3443 THE DEEVIL'S WALTZ. Glasgow: Maclellan, 1946.

3444 CAROTID CORNUCOPIUS, CAIRD OF THE CANNON GAIT AND VOY-EUR OF THE OUTLOOK TOUER. 1947; rev. and extended, Edinburgh: Macdonald, 1964.

A Rabelaisian-cum-Joycean extravanganza.

3445 UNDER THE EILDON TREE: A POEM IN XXIV ELEGIES. Edinburgh: Serif Books, 1948; 1954.

3446 THE AIPPLE AND THE HAZEL. Glasgow: Caledonian Press, 1951.

3447 SO LATE INTO THE NIGHT: FIFTY LYRICS, 1944-1948. London: Peter Russell, 1952.

3448 COKKILS. Edinburgh: Macdonald, 1953.

3449 ORPHEUS AND EURYDICE: A DRAMATIC POEM. Edinburgh: Macdonald, 1955.

3450 OMENS: NINE POEMS. Edinburgh: Macdonald, 1955.

3451 FIGS AND THISTLES. Edinburgh: Oliver and Boyd, 1959.

3452 THE VISION OF THE PRODIGAL SON. Edinburgh: Macdonald, 1960.

3453 THE WALLACE: A TRIUMPH IN FIVE ACTS. Edinburgh: Oliver and Boyd, 1960.

3454 KYND KITTOCK'S LAND. Edinburgh: Macdonald, 1965.

3455 FIFTEEN POEMS AND A PLAY. Edinburgh: Southside, 1969.

The play of the title is THE STICK-UP, OR FULL CIRCLE.

3456 GOWDSPINK IN REEKIE. Loanhead: Macdonald, 1974.

COLLECTIONS AND SELECTIONS

3457 SELECTED POEMS. Edinburgh: Oliver and Boyd, 1947.

3458 COLLECTED POEMS, 1941-1975. London: John Calder, 1975.

BIOGRAPHY AND CRITICISM

CP (Maurice Lindsay); D; P; T; WA-50.

3459 Scott, Alexander. "Daylight and the Dark: Edinburgh in the Poetry of Robert Fergusson and Sydney Goodsir Smith." LINES, No. 3 (1953), 9-13.

3460 MacCaig, Norman. "The Poetry of Sydney Goodsir Smith." SALTIRE RE-VIEW, No. 1 (1954), 14-19.

3461 MacDiarmid, Hugh. "Sydney Goodsir Smith." [1963] In his THE UN-CANNY SCOT. London: MacGibbon and Kee, 1968, pp. 164-68.

3462 AKROS, No. 10 (May 1969), entire issue.

A Sydney Goodsir Smith issue, with contributions by Hugh Mac-Diarmid, Alexander Scott, and Robert Garioch.

3463 Crawford, Thomas. "The Poetry of Sydney Goodsir Smith." SSL, 7 (1969-70), 40-59.

See also the rejoinder by Alexander Scott in SSL, 8 (1970-71), 65.

3464 Gold, Eric. SYDNEY GOODSIR SMITH'S "UNDER THE EILDON TREE." Preston: Akros, 1975.

3465 SCOTIA REVIEW, 9 (1975), entire issue.

A Sydney Goodsir Smith memorial issue, with contributions from Hugh MacDiarmid, Tom Scott, Duncan Glen, and Alan Bold.

3466 FOR SYDNEY GOODSIR SMITH. Loanhead: Macdonald, 1975.

A memorial volume.

3467 Crawford, Thomas. "Goodsir Smith: The Auk of the Mandrake Hert." SCOTTISH REVIEW, No. 2 (1976), 17-22.

3468 Buthlay, Kenneth. "Sydney Goodsir Smith: Makar Macironical." AKROS, No. 31 (1976), 46–56.

BIBLIOGRAPHY

3469 Aitken, William R. "Sydney Goodsir Smith, 1915–75: A Checklist of His Books and Pamphlets." In FOR SYDNEY GOODSIR SMITH. Loanhead: Macdonald, 1975, pp. 85–91.

G[eorge] S[utherland] Fraser (1915-80)

A gentle and restrained lyric poet and a perceptive critic.

3470 THE FATAL LANDSCAPE, AND OTHER POEMS. London: Editions Poetry London, 1943.

3471 HOME TOWN ELEGY. London: Editions Poetry London, 1944.

3472 VISION OF SCOTLAND. London: Paul Elek, 1948.

The poet's view of his native country.

3473 THE TRAVELLER HAS REGRETS, AND OTHER POEMS. London: Harvill Press and Editions Poetry London, 1948.

3474 NEWS FROM SOUTH AMERICA. London: Harvill Press, 1949.

Travel.

3475 THE MODERN WRITER AND HIS WORLD. London: Verschoyle, 1953; new ed. Deutsch, 1955; 3rd ed. Deutsch, 1964.

3476 W.B. YEATS. London: Longmans, Green, for the British Council, 1954.

3477 DYLAN THOMAS. London: Longmans, Green, for the British Council, 1957.

3478 VISION AND RHETORIC: STUDIES IN MODERN POETRY. London: Faber, 1959.

3479 EZRA POUND. Edinburgh: Oliver and Boyd, 1960.

3480 LAWRENCE DURRELL: A STUDY. London: Faber, 1968.

3481 CONDITIONS. Nottingham: Byron Press, 1969.
Poems.

3482 METRE, RHYME AND FREE VERSE. London: Methuen, 1970.

3483 LAWRENCE DURRELL. London: Longmans, for the British Council, 1970.

BIOGRAPHY AND CRITICISM

CA-85/88; CP (Maurice Lindsay); D; P; T; WA-50.

George Campbell Hay (1915--)

A poet who writes both in Gaelic and in Scots, and a versatile linguist.

3484 FUARAN SLEIBH. RAINN GHAIDHLIG. Glasgow: Maclellan, 1948.
With English translations.

3485 WIND ON LOCH FYNE. Edinburgh: Oliver and Boyd, 1948.

3486 O NA CEITHIR AIRDEAN. Edinburgh: Oliver and Boyd, 1952.
Poems, including translations, with English prose versions of most
of the original poems.

3487 FOUR POINTS OF A SALTIRE: THE POETRY OF SORLEY MACLEAN,
GEORGE CAMPBELL HAY, WILLIAM NEILL, STUART MACGREGOR.
Edinburgh: Reprographia, 1970.

BIOGRAPHY AND CRITICISM

CP (Derick Thomson); P.

3488 Neill, William. "The Poetry of George Campbell Hay." SCOTIA RE-
VIEW, No. 8 (1974), 50-56.

Elspeth Davie

A writer of careful distinction.

3489 PROVIDINGS. London: John Calder, 1965.

3490 THE SPARK, AND OTHER STORIES. London: Calder and Boyars, 1968.

3491 CREATING A SCENE: A NOVEL. London: Calder and Boyars, 1971.

3492 THE HIGH TIDE TALKER, AND OTHER STORIES. London: Hamish Hamilton, 1976.

3493 CLIMBERS ON A STAIR. London: Hamish Hamilton, 1978.

BIOGRAPHY AND CRITICISM

H, pages 319-20.

3494 Gifford, Douglas. "Modern Scottish Fiction." SSL, 13 (1978), 272.

J[ohn] D[ick] Scott (1917--)

A novelist who has also written on industrial administration and the histories of two firms. These other writings are not listed here.

3495 THE CELLAR. London: Pilot Press. 1947; issued as BUY IT FOR A SONG, New York: Pellegrini and Cudahy, 1948.

3496 THE MARGIN. London: Pilot Press, 1949.

3497 THE WAY TO GLORY. London: Eyre and Spottiswoode, 1952.

3498 THE END OF AN OLD SONG. London: Eyre and Spottiswoode, 1954.

3499 LIFE IN BRITAIN. London: Eyre and Spottiswoode, 1956.
    A study.

3500 THE PRETTY PENNY: AN ADVENTURE STORY. London: Eyre and Spottiswoode, 1963.

BIOGRAPHY AND CRITICISM

CN (John Lucas); D.

Jessie Kesson

A realistic novelist whose realism is illumined by sympathetic imagination.

3501 THE WHITE BIRD PASSES. London: Chatto and Windus, 1958; Edinburgh: Paul Harris, 1980.

3502 GLITTER OF MICA. London: Chatto and Windus, 1963.

3503 "Where the Apple Ripens." In NEW WRITING AND WRITERS, 15. London: John Calder, 1978, pp. 129-87.

W[illiam] S[ydney] Graham (1918--)

David Daiches has said of Graham that he is a poet who writes "profoundly Scottish poems in English."

3504 CAGE WITHOUT GRIEVANCE. Glasgow: Parton Press, 1942.

3505 THE SEVEN JOURNEYS. Glasgow: Maclellan, 1944.

3506 SECOND POEMS. London: Editions Poetry London, 1945.

3507 THE WHITE THRESHOLD. London: Faber, 1949.

3508 THE NIGHTFISHING. London: Faber, 1955.

3509 MALCOLM MOONEY'S LAND. London: Faber, 1970.

3510 IMPLEMENTS IN THEIR PLACES. London: Faber, 1977.

COLLECTIONS AND SELECTIONS

3511 [SELECTION]. In PENGUIN MODERN POETS, 17. Harmondsworth: Penguin, 1970, pp. 75-127.

3512 COLLECTED POEMS, 1942-1977. London: Faber, 1979.

BIOGRAPHY AND CRITICISM

CA-73/76; CP (Edwin Morgan); D; T.

3513 Bedient, Calvin. "W.S. Graham." In his EIGHT CONTEMPORARY POETS. London: OUP, 1974.

3514 Duxbury, Robert. "The Poetry of W.S. Graham." AKROS, No. 38 (1978), 62-71.

3515 Kessler, J. "Coming Down." PARNASSUS, 6 (1978), 205-12.

Maurice Lindsay (1918--)

Journalist, poet, critic, literary historian, and indefatigable editor.

3516 THE ADVANCING DAY. Privately Printed, 1940.

Poems.

3517 PERHAPS TOMORROW. Oxford: Blackwell, 1941.

Poems.

3518 PREDICAMENTS: THIRTEEN POEMS. Oxford: Alden Press, 1942.

3519 NO CROWN FOR LAUGHTER: POEMS. London: Fortune Press, 1943.

3520 HURLYGUSH: POEMS IN SCOTS. Edinburgh: Serif Books, 1948.

3521 AT THE WOOD'S EDGE. Edinburgh: Serif Books, 1950.

Poems.

3522 ODE FOR ST. ANDREW'S NIGHT, AND OTHER POEMS. Edinburgh: New Alliance, 1951.

3523 THE LOWLANDS OF SCOTLAND: GLASGOW AND THE NORTH. London: Robert Hale, 1953; 2nd ed., 1973.

3524 ROBERT BURNS: THE MAN, HIS WORK, THE LEGEND. London: Macgibbon and Kee, 1954; 2nd ed., 1968; rpt., London: Robert Hale, 1979.

3525 THE LOWLANDS OF SCOTLAND: EDINBURGH AND THE SOUTH. London: Robert Hale, 1956; rev. ed., 1977.

3526 CLYDE WATERS: VARIATIONS AND DIVERSIONS ON A THEME OF PLEASURE. London: Robert Hale, 1958.

3527 THE BURNS ENCYCLOPAEDIA. London: Hutchinson, 1959; rev. ed., 1970; 3rd ed., London: Robert Hale, 1980.

3528 BY YON BONNIE BANKS: A GALLIMAUFRY. London: Hutchinson, 1961.

3529 SNOW WARNING. Arundel: Linden Press, 1962.

Poems.

3530 THE DISCOVERY OF SCOTLAND. London: Robert Hale, 1964.

3531 ONE LATER DAY. London: Brookside Press, 1964.

Poems.

3532 THIS BUSINESS OF LIVING. Preston: Akros, 1969.

Poems.

3533 THE EYE IS DELIGHTED: SOME ROMANTIC TRAVELLERS IN SCOTLAND. London: Muller, 1971.

3534 COMINGS AND GOINGS: POEMS. Preston: Akros, 1971.

3535 PORTRAIT OF GLASGOW. London: Robert Hale, 1972.

3536 SCOTLAND: AN ANTHOLOGY. London: Robert Hale, 1974.

3537 HISTORY OF SCOTTISH LITERATURE. London: Robert Hale, 1977.

3538 WALKING WITHOUT AN OVERCOAT: POEMS, 1972-76. London: Robert Hale, 1977.

3539 AS I REMEMBER: TEN SCOTTISH AUTHORS RECALL HOW WRITING BEGAN FOR THEM. Ed. Maurice Lindsay. London: Robert Hale, 1979.

Lindsay himself is one of the ten authors. His contribution is "I Belong to Glasgow," pages 59-77.

3540 LOWLAND SCOTTISH VILLAGES. London: Robert Hale, 1980.

3541 FRANCIS GEORGE SCOTT AND THE SCOTTISH RENAISSANCE. Edinburgh: Paul Harris, 1980.

COLLECTIONS AND SELECTIONS

3542 THE ENEMIES OF LOVE: POEMS, 1941-45. Glasgow: Maclellan, 1946.

3543 SELECTED POEMS. Edinburgh: Oliver and Boyd, 1947.

3544 THE EXILED HEART: POEMS, 1941-56. London: Robert Hale, 1957.

3545 SELECTED POEMS, 1942-1972. London: Robert Hale, 1973.

3546 THE RUN FROM LIFE: MORE POEMS, 1942-1972. Burford: Cygnet Press, 1975.

3547 COLLECTED POEMS. Edinburgh: Paul Harris, 1979.

BIOGRAPHY AND CRITICISM

CA-9/10; CP (Robert Nye); D; P.

3548 Macintyre, Lorn M. "The Poetry of Maurice Lindsay." AKROS, No. 42 (December 1979), 44-53.

Tom Scott (1918--)

A robust poet, an industrious editor, and a formidable critic.

3549 SEEVEN POEMS O MAISTER FRANCIS VILLON MADE OWRE INTIL SCOTS. London: Peter Russell, 1953.

3550 AN ODE TIL NEW JERUSALEM. Edinburgh: Macdonald, 1956.

3551 THE SHIP, AND ITHER POEMS. London: OUP, 1963.

3552 DUNBAR: A CRITICAL EXPOSITION OF THE POEMS. Edinburgh: Oliver and Boyd, 1966.

3553 AT THE SHRINE O THE UNKENT SODGER: A POEM FOR RECITATION. Preston: Akros, 1968.

3554 TALES OF KING ROBERT THE BRUCE: FREELY ADAPTED FROM THE BRUS OF JOHN BARBOUR. Oxford: Pergamon, 1969; rpt. Edinburgh: Reprographia, 1975.

3555 TRUE THOMAS. With Heather Scott. London: OUP, 1971.

3556 BRAND THE BUILDER. London: Ember Press, 1975.

3557 THE TREE: AN ANIMAL FABLE. Dunfermline: Borderline Press, 1977.

BIOGRAPHY AND CRITICISM

CA-9/10; CP (William Cookson); D.

3558 Herdman, John. "Towards New Jerusalem: The Poetry of Tom Scott." AKROS, No. 16 (April 1971), 43-49.

3559 Crawford, Thomas. "Tom Scott: From Apocalypse to Brand." AKROS, No. 31 (August 1976), 57-69.

3560 SCOTIA REVIEW, No. 13-14 (August-November 1976), entire issue.

This was a double number devoted to Tom Scott, with articles by Alan Bold and John Herdman, among others, and autobiographical notes by the poet.

3561 McClure, J.D. "The Versification of Tom Scott's THE TREE." SLJ, suppl. 10 (1979), 17-32.

Muriel Spark (1918--)

Although Muriel Spark was born in Edinburgh, her novels are "sparse in identifiably Scottish elements," according to Francis Russell Hart, yet her Scottish connections are there.

3562 CHILD OF LIGHT: A REASSESSMENT OF MARY SHELLEY. London: Tower Bridge, 1951.

3563 THE FANFARLO. Aldington: Hand and Flower Press, 1952.

3564 EMILY BRONTË: HER LIFE AND WORK. With Derek Stanford. London: Peter Owen, 1953.

3565 JOHN MASEFIELD. London: Peter Nevill, 1953.

3566 THE COMFORTERS. London: Macmillan, 1957.

A novel.

3567 THE GO-AWAY BIRD, AND OTHER STORIES. London: Macmillan, 1958.

3568 ROBINSON. London: Macmillan, 1958.

3569 MEMENTO MORI. London: Macmillan, 1959.

3570 THE BALLAD OF PECKHAM RYE. London: Macmillan, 1960.

3571 THE BACHELORS. London: Macmillan, 1960.

3572 VOICES AT PLAY. London: Macmillan, 1961.
Short stories and plays.

3573 THE PRIME OF MISS JEAN BRODIE. London: Macmillan, 1961.

3574 DOCTORS OF PHILOSOPHY. London: Macmillan, 1963.
A play.

3575 THE GIRLS OF SLENDER MEANS. London: Macmillan, 1963.

3576 THE MANDELBAUM GATE. London: Macmillan, 1965.

3577 THE PUBLIC IMAGE. London: Macmillan, 1968.

3578 THE VERY FINE CLOCK. London: Macmillan, 1969.
For children.

3579 THE DRIVER'S SEAT. London: Macmillan, 1970.

3580 THE FRENCH WINDOW. London: Macmillan, 1970.
For children.

3581 NOT TO DISTURB. London: Macmillan, 1971.

3582 THE HOT-HOUSE BY THE EAST RIVER. London: Macmillan, 1973.

3583 THE ABBESS OF CREWE. London: Macmillan, 1974.

3584 THE TAKEOVER. London: Macmillan, 1976.

3585 TERRITORIAL RIGHTS. London: Macmillan, 1979.

COLLECTIONS

3586 COLLECTED POEMS. Vol. 1. London: Macmillan, 1967.

3587 COLLECTED STORIES. Vol. 1. London: Macmillan, 1967.

BIOGRAPHY AND CRITICISM

CA-7/8; CN (Derek Stanford); CP (Burton Kendle); H, pages 294-310; P; T; W; WA-50.

3588 Stanford, Derek. MURIEL SPARK. Fontwell: Centaur Press, 1963.

3589 Hoyt, Charles Alva. "Muriel Spark: The Surrealist Jane Austen." In CONTEMPORARY BRITISH NOVELISTS. Ed. Charles Shapiro. Carbondale: Southern Illinois University Press, 1965.

3590 Malkoff, Karl. MURIEL SPARK. New York: Columbia University Press, 1968.

3591 Bradbury, Malcolm. "Muriel Spark's Fingernails." CRITICAL QUARTERLY, 14 (1972), 241-50; rpt. in his POSSIBILITIES: ESSAYS ON THE STATE OF THE NOVEL, London: OUP, 1973, pp. 247-55.

3592 Kemp, Peter. MURIEL SPARK. London: Paul Elek, 1974.

3593 Keyser, Barbara. "The Transfiguration of Edinburgh in THE PRIME OF MISS JEAN BRODIE." SSL, 12 (1974-75), 181-89.

3594 Ray, Philip E. "Jean Brodie and Edinburgh: Personality and Place in Muriel Spark's THE PRIME OF MISS JEAN BRODIE." SSL, 13 (1978), 24-31.

3595 Massie, Allan. MURIEL SPARK. Edinburgh: Ramsay Head Press, 1979.

3596 Whittaker, R. "'Angels Dining at the Ritz'; The Faith and Fiction of Muriel Spark." STRATFORD-UPON-AVON STUDIES, 18 (1979), 157-79.

BIBLIOGRAPHY

3597 Tominaga, Thomas, and Wilma Schneidermeyer. IRIS MURDOCH AND MURIEL SPARK: A BIBLIOGRAPHY. Metuchen, N.J.: Scarecrow Press, 1976.

Hamish Henderson (1919--)

A poet and an authority on the oral literature of the traveling folk of Scotland.

3598 BALLADS OF WORLD WAR II. Glasgow: Privately Printed, 1947.

3599 ELEGIES FOR THE DEAD IN CYRENAICA. London: John Lehmann, 1948; Edinburgh: EUSPB, 1977.

BIOGRAPHY AND CRITICISM

CP (Edward Lucie-Smith).

3600 [INTERVIEW]. In THE POET SPEAKS. Ed. Peter Orr. London: Routledge and Kegan Paul, 1966, pp. 75-81.

3601 Mitchell, J. "Hamish Henderson and the Scottish Tradition." CALGACUS, 3 (1976), 26-31.

James Allan Ford (1920--)

An interesting novelist who emerged in the 1960s.

3602 THE BRAVE WHITE FLAG. London: Hodder and Stoughton, 1961.

3603 SEASON OF ESCAPE. London: Hodder and Stoughton, 1963.

3604 A STATUE FOR A PUBLIC PLACE. London: Hodder and Stoughton, 1965.

3605 A JUDGE OF MEN. London: Hodder and Stoughton, 1968.

3606 THE MOUTH OF TRUTH. London: Gollancz, 1972.

BIOGRAPHY AND CRITICISM

CAP-1; H, page 315.

3607 Gifford, Douglas. "Modern Scottish Fiction." SSL, 13 (1978), 265-66.

Edwin Morgan (1920--)

A versatile and urbane poet and critic who is also a linguist and a writer of experimental and "concrete" poetry. (The term is defined as the attempt to turn poetry into a graphic art, where the poem is a visual experience rather than a communication of meaning.)

3608 THE VISION OF CATHKIN BRAES. Glasgow: Maclellan, 1952.

3609 THE CAPE OF GOOD HOPE. London: Peter Russell, 1955.

3610 THE SECOND LIFE: SELECTED POEMS. Edinburgh: Edinburgh University Press, 1968.

3611 GNOMES. Preston: Akros, 1968.

3612 TWELVE SONGS. West Linton: Castlelaw Press, 1970.

3613 THE HORSEMAN'S WORD: A SEQUENCE OF CONCRETE POEMS. Preston: Akros, 1970.

3614 GLASGOW SONNETS. West Linton: Castlelaw Press, 1972.

3615 INSTAMATIC POEMS. London: Ian McKelvie, 1972.

3616 WI THE HAILL VOICE: 25 POEMS BY MAYAKOVSKY TRANSLATED INTO SCOTS. Oxford: Carcanet Press, 1972.

3617 THE WHITTRICK: A POEM IN EIGHT DIALOGUES. Preston: Akros, 1973.

3618 FROM GLASGOW TO SATURN. Cheadle: Carcanet Press, 1973.

3619 ESSAYS. Cheadle: Carcanet Press, 1974.

3620 RITES OF PASSAGE: SELECTED TRANSLATIONS. Cheadle: Carcanet Press, 1976.

3621 HUGH MacDIARMID. London: Longman, for the British Council, 1976.

3622 THE NEW DIVAN. Manchester: Carcanet Press, 1977.

SELECTIONS

3623 [SELECTION]. In PENGUIN MODERN POETS, 15. Harmondsworth: Penguin, 1969, pp. 125-75.

BIOGRAPHY AND CRITICISM

CA-7/8; CP (Maurice Lindsay); WA-70.

3624 Walker, Marshall. "Edwin Morgan: An Interview." AKROS, No. 32 (December 1976), 3-23.

Alexander Scott (1920--)

Poet, dramatist, critic, and editor, and head of the department of Scottish literature in the University of Glasgow.

3625 PROMETHEUS 48. Aberdeen: S.R.C., 1948.

    A play.

3626 THE LATEST IN ELEGIES. Glasgow: Caledonian Press, 1949.

3627 UNTRUE THOMAS. Glasgow: Caledonian Press, 1952.

    A play.

3628 MOUTH MUSIC: POEMS AND DIVERSIONS. Edinburgh: Macdonald, 1954.

3629 SHETLAND YARN. London: Evans Brothers, 1954.

    A play.

3630 STILL LIFE: WILLIAM SOUTAR (1898-1943). Edinburgh: Chambers, 1958.

3631 CANTRIPS. Preston: Akros, 1968.

3632 GREEK FIRE: A SEQUENCE OF POEMS. Preston: Akros, 1971.

3633 DOUBLE AGENT: POEMS IN ENGLISH AND SCOTS. Preston: Akros, 1972.

3634 THE MacDIARMID MAKARS, 1923-1972. Preston: Akros, 1972.

3635 "Growing Up with Granite." In AS I REMEMBER. Ed. Maurice Lindsay. London: Robert Hale, 1979, pp. 89-105.

COLLECTIONS AND SELECTIONS

3636 SELECTED POEMS. Edinburgh: Oliver and Boyd, 1950.

3637 SELECTED POEMS, 1943-1974. Preston: Akros, 1975.

BIOGRAPHY AND CRITICISM

CP (Norman MacCaig); D.

3638 MacCaig, Norman. [Review of CANTRIPS]. AKROS, No. 9 (January 1969), 67-69.

3639 Annand, James King. "Alexander Scott: An Introduction." AKROS, No. 16 (April 1971), 43-49.

3640 Bruce, George. "The Poetry of Alexander Scott." AKROS, No. 19 (August 1972), 30-33.

3641 Mason, Leonard. TWO NORTH-EAST MAKARS: ALEXANDER SCOTT AND ALASTAIR MACKIE. A STUDY OF THEIR SCOTS POETRY. Preston: Akros, 1975.

3642 Buchan, David. "New Dimensions." LIBRARY REVIEW, 25 (1975-76), 85-86.

A review of Scott's SELECTED POEMS (3637).

3643 Lennox, Ruth. "The Poetry of Alexander Scott." AKROS, No. 33 (April 1977), 60-68.

George Mackay Brown (1921--)

A poet, novelist, and short-story writer who lives in his native Orkney and draws his material from its people, history, and landscape.

3644 THE STORM, AND OTHER POEMS. Kirkwall: Orkney Press, 1954.

3645 LOAVES AND FISHES. London: Hogarth Press, 1959.

Poems.

3646 THE YEAR OF THE WHALE. London: Hogarth Press, 1965.

Poems.

3647 A CALENDAR OF LOVE, AND OTHER STORIES. London: Hogarth Press, 1967.

3648 A TIME TO KEEP, AND OTHER STORIES. London: Hogarth Press, 1969.

3649 AN ORKNEY TAPESTRY. London: Gollancz, 1969.

A miscellany about the islands.

3650 A SPELL FOR GREEN CORN. London: Hogarth Press, 1970.

A play.

3651 FISHERMEN WITH PLOUGHS: A POEM CYCLE. London: Hogarth Press, 1971.

3652 GREENVOE: A NOVEL. London: Hogarth Press, 1972; ed. Donald M. Budge, London: Longman, 1977.

3653 MAGNUS: A NOVEL. London: Hogarth Press, 1973.

3654 HAWKFALL, AND OTHER STORIES. London: Hogarth Press, 1974.

3655 THE TWO FIDDLERS: TALES FROM ORKNEY. London: Hogarth Press, 1974.

3656 LETTERS FROM HAMNAVOE. Edinburgh: Gordon Wright, 1975.

Essays.

3657 WINTERFOLD. London: Hogarth Press, 1976.

Poems.

3658 THE SUN'S NET: STORIES. London: Hogarth Press, 1976.

3659 PICTURES IN THE CAVE. London: Hogarth Press, 1977.

Stories.

3660 UNDER BRINKIE'S BRAE. Edinburgh: Gordon Wright, 1979.

Essays.

3661 "An Autobiographical Essay." In AS I REMEMBER. Ed. Maurice Lindsay. London: Robert Hale, 1979, pp. 9-21.

COLLECTIONS AND SELECTIONS

3662 POEMS NEW AND SELECTED. London: Hogarth Press, 1971.

3663 [SELECTION]. In PENGUIN MODERN POETS, 21. Harmondsworth: Penguin, 1972, pp. 139-206.

3664 SELECTED POEMS. London: Hogarth Press, 1977.

3665 WITCH, AND OTHER STORIES. With commentary and notes by Donald M. Budge. London: Longman, 1977.

BIOGRAPHY AND CRITICISM

CA-21/24; CN (Alexander Scott); CP (Alexander Scott); WA-70.

3666 Roberts, N. "George Mackay Brown." CAMBRIDGE QUARTERLY, 6 (1973), 181-89.

3667 Dunn, Douglas. "'Finished Fragrance': The Poems of George Mackay Brown." POETRY NATION, 2 (1974), 80-92.

3668 Pacey, Philip. "The Fire of Images: The Poetry of George Mackay Brown." AKROS, No. 32 (December 1976), 61-71.

3669 Bold, Alan. GEORGE MACKAY BROWN. Edinburgh: Oliver and Boyd, 1978.

Clifford Hanley (1922--)
"Henry Calvin"

A novelist with a fine blend of comic vigor and shrewd understanding.

3670 DANCING IN THE STREETS. London: Hutchinson, 1958.

　　Autobiographical.

3671 LOVE FROM EVERYBODY. London: Hutchinson, 1959.

3672 THE TASTE OF TOO MUCH. London: Hutchinson, 1960.

3673 NOTHING BUT THE BEST. London: Hutchinson, 1964; issued as SECOND TIME ROUND. Boston: Houghton Mifflin, 1964.

3674 A SKINFUL OF SCOTCH. London: Hutchinson, 1965.

3675 THE HOT MONTH. London: Hutchinson, 1967.

3676 THE RED-HAIRED BITCH. London: Hutchinson, 1969.

3677 THE UNSPEAKABLE SCOT. Edinburgh: Blackwood, 1977.

An essay.

3678 PRISSY. London: Collins, 1978.

3679 THE SCOTS. Newton Abbot: David and Charles, 1980.

THRILLERS [BY HENRY CALVIN]

All published in London by Hutchinson.

3680 THE SYSTEM. 1962.

3681 IT'S DIFFERENT ABROAD. 1963.

3682 THE ITALIAN GADGET. 1966.

3683 A NICE FRIENDLY TOWN. 1967.

3684 THE D.N.A. BUSINESS. 1967.

3685 MIRANDA MUST DIE. 1968; issued as BOKA LIVES, New York: Harper, 1969.

3686 THE CHOSEN INSTRUMENT. 1969.

3687 THE POISON CHASERS. 1970.

3688 TAKE TWO POPES. 1972.

BIOGRAPHY AND CRITICISM

CA-9/10; CN (Alexander Scott); H, pages 317-18.

Dorothy Dunnett (1923--)

Dorothy Dunnett, the author of a number of light comedy thrillers under her maiden name of Dorothy Halliday, uses her married name for an ambitious series of six novels, an ingenious development of historical romance on the grand scale. All are published in London by Cassell and in New York by Putnam.

3689 THE GAME OF KINGS. 1961.

3690 QUEEN'S PLAY. 1964.

3691 THE DISORDERLY KNIGHTS. 1966.

3692 PAWN IN FRANKINCENSE. 1969.

3693 THE RINGED CASTLE. 1971.

3694 CHECKMATE. 1975.

BIOGRAPHY AND CRITICISM

CA-1/4; H, pages 193-97.

Ian Hamilton Finlay (1925--)

Finlay is Scotland's most notable "concrete" poet (see p. 316). Over the last twenty years he has published many booklets and broadsheets from his Wild Hawthorn Press, of which there is a comprehensive bibliography in Duncan Glen's BIBLIOGRAPHY OF SCOTTISH POETS (Preston: Akros, 1974), pages 46-49.

3695 THE SEA-BED, AND OTHER STORIES. Edinburgh: Castle Wynd Printers, 1960.

3696 POEMS TO SEE AND HEAR. London: Collier-Macmillan, 1971.

BIOGRAPHY AND CRITICISM

CA-81/84; CP (Edwin Morgan); WA-50.

3697 MacDiarmid, Hugh. THE UGLY BIRDS WITHOUT WINGS. Edinburgh: Allan Donaldson, 1962.

A reply to the attacks of Ian Hamilton Finlay and others and a criticism of the position they adopted in a poetry broadsheet, POOR. OLD. TIRED. HORSE., which Finlay was editing at the time.

3698 Tait, Robert. "The Wild Hawthorn Press." SCOTTISH INTERNATIONAL, No. 5 (January 1969), 64-66.

3699 Scobie, Stephen. "The Side-Road to Dunsyre: Some Comments on Hugh MacDiarmid and Ian Hamilton Finlay." AKROS, No. 15 (August 1970), 51-61.

Alastair Mackie (1925--)

An Aberdeenshire poet with complete command of his vigorous native Scots.

3700 SOUNDINGS. Preston: Akros, 1966.

3701 CLYTACH: POEMS. Preston: Akros, 1972.

3702 AT THE HEICH KIRKYAIRD: A HIELANT SEQUENCE. Preston: Akros, 1974.

BIOGRAPHY AND CRITICISM

CA-19/20; CP (George Bruce).

3703 Mason, Leonard. TWO NORTH-EAST MAKARS: ALEXANDER SCOTT AND ALASTAIR MACKIE. A STUDY OF THEIR SCOTS POETRY. Preston: Akros, 1975.

3704 Bruce, George. "The Poetry of Alastair Mackie, or Feet on the Grun." AKROS, No. 33 (April 1977), 76-86.

Alastair Reid (1926--)

Poet, essayist, and translator.

3705 TO LIGHTEN MY HOUSE. Scarsdale, N.Y.: Morgan and Morgan, 1953.

3706 FAIR-WATER. Boston: Houghton Mifflin, 1957.

3707 ALLTH. Boston: Houghton Mifflin, 1958.

3708 I WILL TELL YOU OF A TOWN. London: Hutchinson, 1959.

3709 ODDMENTS, INKLINGS, OMENS, MOMENTS. London: Dent, 1960.

3710 OUNCE, DICE, TRICE. London: Dent, 1960.
     For children.

3711 SUPPOSING. Boston: Little, Brown, 1960.

3712 A BALLOON FOR A BLUNDERBUSS. New York: Harper, 1961.

3713 PASSWORDS: PLACES, POEMS, PREOCCUPATIONS. London: Weidenfeld and Nicolson, 1964.

3714 UNCLE TIMOTHY'S TRAVIATA. New York: Delacorte, 1967.

BIOGRAPHY AND CRITICISM

CA-7/8; CP (George Bruce); WA-50.

[James] Burns Singer (1928-64)

A poet whose work may have been overestimated at the time of his early death
can now be seen in better perspective.

3715 STILL AND ALL. London: Secker and Warburg, 1957.

Poems.

3716 LIVING SILVER: AN IMPRESSION OF THE BRITISH FISHING INDUSTRY.
London: Secker and Warburg, 1957.

COLLECTIONS AND SELECTIONS

3717 COLLECTED POEMS. Ed. Walter A.S. Keir. London: Secker and Warburg, 1970.

3718 SELECTED POEMS. Ed. Anne Cluysenaar. Manchester: Carcanet Press,
1977.

BIOGRAPHY AND CRITICISM

CP (Robert Nye); WA-50.

3719 MacDiarmid, Hugh. THE COMPANY I'VE KEPT. London: Hutchinson,
1966, pp. 217-18.

3720 Schmidt, Michael. "Burns Singer." POETRY NATION, 5 (1975), 94-99.

James Kennaway (1928-68)

A novelist of great promise and achievement, tragically killed in an accident.

3721 TUNES OF GLORY. London: Putnam, 1956; Edinburgh: Mainstream, 1980.

3722 HOUSEHOLD GHOSTS. London: Longmans, 1961; Edinburgh: Mainstream, 1980.

3723 THE MIND BENDERS. London: Heinemann, 1963.

3724 THE BELLS OF SHOREDITCH. London: Longmans, 1963.

3725 SOME GORGEOUS ACCIDENT. London: Longmans, 1967; Edinburgh: Mainstream, 1980.

3726 THE COST OF LIVING LIKE THIS. London: Longmans, 1969; Edinburgh: Mainstream, 1980.

3727 SILENCE. London: Cape, 1972.

3728 THE KENNAWAY PAPERS. Ed. Susan Kennaway. London: Cape, 1981.

BIOGRAPHY AND CRITICISM

H, pages 287-94; WA-50.

3729 Mackay, Hugh. "The Novels of James Kennaway." LIBRARY REVIEW, 23 (1971-72), 230-32.

3730 McAra, Duncan. "James Kennaway." LONDON MAGAZINE, 17 (February 1978), 37-55.

Iain Crichton Smith (1928--)

A poet and novelist writing both in Gaelic and in English. His Gaelic work is not listed here.

3731 THE LONG RIVER. Edinburgh: Macdonald, 1955.

Poems.

3732 THISTLES AND ROSES. London: Eyre and Spottiswoode, 1961.

Poems.

3733 THE LAW AND THE GRACE. London: Eyre and Spottiswoode, 1965.
Poems.

3734 THE GOLDEN LYRIC: AN ESSAY ON THE POETRY OF HUGH MacDIAR-
MID. Preston: Akros, 1967.

3735 CONSIDER THE LILIES. London: Gollancz, 1968; Oxford: Pergamon,
1970; issued as THE ALIEN LIGHT, Boston: Houghton Mifflin, 1969.
A novel.

3736 FROM BOURGEOIS LAND. London: Gollancz, 1969.
Poems.

3737 THE LAST SUMMER. London: Gollancz, 1969.
A novel.

3738 BEN DORAIN. Preston: Akros, 1969.
Translated from the Gaelic of Duncan Ban MacIntyre.

3739 SURVIVAL WITHOUT ERROR. London: Gollancz, 1970.
Short stories.

3740 MY LAST DUCHESS. London: Gollancz, 1971.
A novel.

3741 POEMS TO EIMHIR. London: Gollancz, 1971.
Poems from DAIN DO EIMHIR by Sorley Maclean, translated
from the Gaelic.

3742 LOVE POEMS AND ELEGIES. London: Gollancz, 1972.

3743 HAMLET IN AUTUMN. Loanhead: Macdonald, 1972.
Poems.

3744 THE BLACK AND THE RED, AND OTHER STORIES. London: Gollancz,
1973.

3745 GOODBYE, MR. DIXON. London: Gollancz, 1974.
A novel.

3746 ORPHEUS, AND OTHER POEMS. Preston: Akros, 1974.

3747 THE NOTEBOOKS OF ROBINSON CRUSOE. London: Gollancz, 1975.
Poems.

3748 THE PERMANENT ISLAND. Loanhead: Macdonald, 1975.
Gaelic poems translated by the author.

3749 THE VILLAGE. Inverness: Club Leabhar, 1976.
A novel.

3750 THE HERMIT, AND OTHER STORIES. London: Gollancz, 1977.

3751 IN THE MIDDLE. London: Gollancz, 1977.
Poems.

3752 "The Highland Element in My English Work." SLJ, 4 (May 1977), 47-60.

3753 RIVER, RIVER: POEMS FOR CHILDREN. Loanhead: Macdonald, 1978.

3754 AN END TO AUTUMN. London: Gollancz, 1978.
A novel.

3755 ON THE ISLAND. London: Gollancz, 1979.
A novel.

3756 "Between Sea and Moor." In AS I REMEMBER. Ed. Maurice Lindsay.
London: Robert Hale, 1979, pp. 107-22.

COLLECTIONS AND SELECTIONS

3757 SELECTED POEMS. London: Gollancz, 1970.

3758 [SELECTION]. In PENGUIN MODERN POETS, 21. Harmondsworth:
Penguin, 1972, pp. 13-79.

BIOGRAPHY AND CRITICISM

CA-23/24; CN (Derick Thomson); CP (Derick Thomson); H, pages 319-21,
327-34; P; W; WA-70.

3759 Morgan, Edwin. "The Raging and the Grace: Some Notes on the Poetry of Iain Crichton Smith." LINES REVIEW, No. 21 (Summer 1965); rpt. in his ESSAYS, Cheadle: Carcanet Press, 1974, pp. 222-31.

3760 LINES REVIEW, No. 29 (June 1969), entire issue.

A special issue devoted to new work by Iain Crichton Smith, with reviews (pp. 46-49), and a select bibliography (pp.50-52).

3761 Macintyre, Lorn. "Poet in Bourgeois Land: Interview with Iain Crichton Smith." SCOTTISH INTERNATIONAL (September 1971), 22-27.

3762 Fulton, Robin. "The Poetry of Iain Crichton Smith." LINES REVIEW, No. 42-43 (1972), 92-116.

3763 Tait, Bob. "Love and Death in Space." SCOTTISH INTERNATIONAL, 5 (October 1972), 28-29.

3764 Lindsay, Frederic. "Disputed Angels: The Poetry of Iain Crichton Smith." AKROS, No. 36 (December 1977), 15-26.

William Watson (1931--)

An interesting writer whose two novels are in striking contrast.

3765 BETTER THAN ONE. London: Barrie and Rockliff, 1969.

3766 SAWNEY BEAN. With Robert Nye. London: Calder and Boyars, 1970.
A play.

3767 BELTRAN IN EXILE. London: Chatto and Windus, 1979.

George Macbeth (1932--)

Poet and editor of a number of anthologies, including three Penguin books of verse. In the list which follows, a score of small pamphlets are omitted.

3768 A FORM OF WORDS. Oxford: Fantasy Press, 1954.

3769 THE BROKEN PLACES. Lowestoft: Scorpion Press, 1963.

3770 A DOOMSDAY BOOK: POEMS AND POEM GAMES. Lowestoft: Scorpion Press, 1965.

3771 NOAH'S JOURNEY. London: Macmillan, 1966.

3772 THE COLOUR OF BLOOD: POEMS. London: Macmillan, 1967.

3773 THE NIGHT OF STONES: POEMS. London: Macmillan, 1968.

3774 A WAR QUARTET. London: Macmillan, 1969.

3775 THE BURNING CONE. London: Macmillan, 1970.

3776 THE ORLANDO POEMS. London: Macmillan, 1971.

3777 SHRAPNEL. London: Macmillan, 1973.

3778 A POET'S YEAR. London: Gollancz, 1973.

3779 MY SCOTLAND: FRAGMENTS OF A STATE OF MIND. London: Macmillan, 1973.
   A book of prose poems.

3780 THE TRANSFORMATION. London: Gollancz, 1975.

3781 IN THE HOURS WAITING FOR THE BLOOD TO COME. London: Gollancz, 1975.

3782 THE SAMURAI. London: Quartet, 1976.

3783 THE SURVIVOR. London: Quartet, 1977.

3784 THE SEVEN WITCHES. London: W.H. Allen, 1978.

COLLECTIONS AND SELECTIONS

3785 [SELECTION]. In PENGUIN MODERN POETS, 6. Harmondsworth: Penguin, 1964, pp. 87-121.

3786 COLLECTED POEMS, 1958-1970. London: Macmillan, 1971.

BIOGRAPHY AND CRITICISM

CA-25/28; CP (Peter Porter); WA-50.

3787 [INTERVIEW]. In THE POET SPEAKS. Ed. Peter Orr. London: Routledge and Kegan Paul, 1966, pp. 131-36.

3788 Black, David M. "The Poetry of George Macbeth." SCOTTISH INTERNATIONAL, No. 3 (August 1968), 40-47.

Duncan Glen (1933--)
"Ronald Eadie Munro"

Poet, editor, and publisher. The literary periodical, AKROS, which he has edited since he launched it in 1965, and the publishing enterprise associated with it, have been most influential.

3789 HUGH MacDIARMID (CHRISTOPHER MURRAY GRIEVE) AND THE SCOTTISH RENAISSANCE. Edinburgh: Chambers, 1964.

3790 STANES: A TWALSOME O POEMS. Privately Printed, 1966.

3791 SCOTTISH POETRY NOW. Preston: Akros, 1966.

3792 KYTHINGS, AND OTHER POEMS. [by Ronald Eadie Munro] Thurso: Caithness Books, 1969.

3793 SUNNY SUMMER SUNDAY AFTERNOON IN THE PARK? Preston: Akros, 1969.

3794 A SMALL PRESS AND HUGH MacDIARMID. Preston: Akros, 1970.

A checklist of Akros publications, 1962-70.

3795 THE MacDIARMIDS: A CONSERVATION WITH HUGH MacDIARMID. Preston: Akros, 1970.

3796 IN APPEARANCES. Preston: Akros, 1971.

3797 CLYDESDALE: A SEQUENCE O POEMS. Preston: Akros, 1971.

3798 THE INDIVIDUAL AND THE 20TH CENTURY SCOTTISH LITERARY TRADITION. Preston: Akros, 1971.

3799 FERES: POEMS. Preston: Akros, 1971.

3800 A JOURNEY PAST: A SEQUENCE O POEMS. Preston: Glen, 1972.

3801 A CLED SCORE: POEMS. Preston: Akros, 1974.

3802 MR. & MRS. J.L. STODDART AT HOME. Preston: Akros, 1975.
A poem.

3803 BUITS AND WELLIES: A SEQUENCE O POEMS. Preston: Akros, 1976.

3804 FOLLOW! FOLLOW! FOLLOW! AND OTHER POEMS. Preston: Akros, 1976.

3805 SPOILED FOR CHOICE: POEMS. Preston: Akros, 1976.

3806 GAITHERINGS: POEMS IN SCOTS. Preston: Akros, 1977.

3807 IN PLACE OF WORK: A SEQUENCE IN THIRTY PAIRTS. Preston: Akros, 1977.

3808 OF PHILOSOPHERS AND TINKS: A SEQUENCE OF POEMS. Preston: Akros, 1977.

BIOGRAPHY AND CRITICISM

CA-21/22; CP (George Bruce)

3809 Mason, Leonard. TWO YOUNGER POETS: DUNCAN GLEN AND DONALD CAMPBELL. A STUDY OF THEIR SCOTS POETRY. Preston: Akros, 1976.

3810 Watson, Roderick. "The Soul as Goalie." SLJ, suppl. 3 (1976), 50-52.
A review-article on four recent collections of Glen's poetry.

3811 Pacey, Philip. "The Poetry of Duncan Glen, or Lallans and Heich Places." AKROS, No. 33 (April 1977), 91-102.

BIBLIOGRAPHY

3812 Glen, Duncan. FORWARD FROM HUGH MacDIARMID: OR MOSTLY OUT OF SCOTLAND, BEING FIFTEEN YEARS OF DUNCAN GLEN/AKROS PUBLICATIONS, 1962-1977. Preston: Akros, 1977.

With a checklist of publications, 1962-77, including about a score of slim books of verse by Glen.

Joan Lingard

Novelist and writer of books for children.

3813 LIAM'S DAUGHTER. London: Hodder and Stoughton, 1963.

3814 THE PREVAILING WIND. London: Hodder and Stoughton, 1964; Edinburgh: Paul Harris, 1978.

3815 THE TIDE COMES IN. London: Hodder and Stoughton, 1966.

3816 THE HEADMASTER. London: Hodder and Stoughton, 1967.

3817 A SORT OF FREEDOM. London: Hodder and Stoughton, 1969.

3818 THE LORD ON OUR SIDE. London: Hodder and Stoughton, 1970.

3819 THE TWELFTH DAY OF JULY. London: Hamish Hamilton, 1970.

3820 ACROSS THE BARRICADES. London: Hamish Hamilton, 1972.

3821 INTO EXILE. London: Hamish Hamilton, 1973.

3822 FRYING AS USUAL. London: Hamish Hamilton, 1973.

3823 THE CLEARANCE. London: Hamish Hamilton, 1974.

3824 THE RESETTLING. London: Hamish Hamilton, 1975.

3825 A PROPER PLACE. London: Hamish Hamilton, 1975.

3826 THE PILGRIMAGE. London: Hamish Hamilton, 1976.

3827 HOSTAGES TO FORTUNE. London: Hamish Hamilton, 1976.

3828 SNAKE AMONG THE SUNFLOWERS. London: Hamish Hamilton, 1977.

3829 THE REUNION. London: Hamish Hamilton, 1977.

3830 THE GOOSEBERRY. London: Hamish Hamilton, 1978.

3831 THE SECOND FLOWERING OF EMILY MOUNTJOY. Edinburgh: Paul
Harris, 1979.

BIOGRAPHY AND CRITICISM

CA-41/44.

Alan Sharp (1934--)

Alan Sharp is a novelist who captures character, scene, and atmosphere with
great skill.

3832 A GREEN TREE IN GEDDE. London: Michael Joseph, 1965.

3833 THE WIND SHIFTS. London: Michael Joseph, 1967.
A sequel to A GREEN TREE IN GEDDE. The third part of the
trilogy has not yet appeared.

3834 THE HIRED MAN. London: Corgi, 1971.

3835 NIGHT MOVES. London: Corgi, 1975.

BIOGRAPHY AND CRITICISM

CA-15/16; H, pages 311-12.

3836 Smith, William Gordon, and John Herdman. "Alan Sharp's Journey."
SCOTTISH INTERNATIONAL, 5 (January 1972), 20-28.
This feature is in three parts: W. Gordon Smith, "Two-Thirds
of Alan Sharp," pages 21-22; "On Films and Filming," Alan
Sharp interviewed by W. Gordon Smith, pages 23-26; and John
Herdman, "Sharp's Trilogy So Far," pages 27-28.

3837 Gifford, Douglas. "Modern Scottish Fiction." SSL, 13 (1978), 257-58.

Gordon M[aclean] Williams (1934--)

Williams was born in Paisley, Renfrewshire, and became a journalist. He writes
realistic novels of considerable power, describing forceful and violent action in
a vivid style.

3838 THE LAST DAY OF LINCOLN CHARLES. London: Secker and Warburg,
1965.

3839 THE CAMP. London: Secker and Warburg, 1966.

3840 THE MAN WHO HAD POWER OVER WOMEN. London: Secker and Warburg, 1967.

3841 FROM SCENES LIKE THESE. London: Secker and Warburg, 1968.

3842 THE SIEGE OF TRENCHER'S FARM. London: Secker and Warburg, 1969.

3843 THE UPPER PLEASURE GARDEN. London: Secker and Warburg, 1970.

3844 THEY USED TO PLAY ON GRASS. With Terry Venables. London: Hodder and Stoughton, 1971.

3845 WALK, DON'T WALK: A SCOTS BURGH BOY'S DREAM OF AMERICA. London: Hodder and Stoughton, 1972.

3846 BIG MORNING BLUES. London: Hodder and Stoughton, 1974.

3847 THE DUELLISTS. London: Collins, 1977.

BIOGRAPHY AND CRITICISM

H, pages 316-18.

3848 Lloyd, John, and Douglas Eadie. "A Novelist in the Mirror." SCOTTISH INTERNATIONAL (August 1971), 22-30.

> This feature is in two parts: Gordon Williams interviewed by John Lloyd, pages 22-28; and Douglas Eadie, "Survival and Gordon Williams," pages 29-30.

3849 Gifford, Douglas. "Modern Scottish Fiction." SSL, 13 (1978), 269.

Stewart Conn (1936--)

A poet and dramatist who skillfully adapted several of Neil Gunn's novels for radio, a medium of singular impermanence in which he has done valuable work.

3850 THUNDER IN THE AIR: POEMS. Preston: Akros, 1967.

3851 THE CHINESE TOWER: A POEM SEQUENCE. Edinburgh: Macdonald, 1967.

3852 STOATS IN THE SUNLIGHT: POEMS. London: Hutchinson, 1968.

3853 THE KING. In NEW ENGLISH DRAMATISTS, 14. Harmondsworth: Penguin, 1970, pp. 157-83.

3854 AN EAR TO THE GROUND. London: Hutchinson, 1972.

Poems.

3855 THE BURNING: A PLAY. London: Calder and Boyars, 1973.

3856 THE AQUARIUM; THE MAN IN THE GREEN MUFFLER; I DIDN'T ALWAYS LIVE HERE. London: John Calder, 1976.

Three plays.

3857 UNDER THE ICE. London: Hutchinson, 1978.

Poems.

BIOGRAPHY AND CRITICISM

CD; CP (George Bruce).

3858 Bruce, George. "'Bound by Necessity': The Poetry of Stewart Conn." AKROS, No. 40 (April 1979), 58-70.

William McIlvanney (1936--)

An important novelist.

3859 REMEDY IS NONE. London: Eyre and Spottiswoode, 1966.

3860 A GIFT FROM NESSUS. London: Eyre and Spottiswoode, 1968.

3861 THE LONGSHIPS IN HARBOUR: POEMS. London: Eyre and Spottiswoode, 1970.

3862 DOCHERTY. London: Allen and Unwin, 1975.

3863 LAIDLAW. London: Hodder and Stoughton, 1977.

A thriller which also works on a deeper level.

BIOGRAPHY AND CRITICISM

CA-25/28; H, pages 313-14.

3864 Gifford, Douglas. "Modern Scottish Fiction." SSL, 13 (1978), 260-61.

3865 _____. "Scottish Fiction 1975-1977." SSL, 14 (1979), 211-12.

Donald Campbell (1940--)

Poet, dramatist, and critic.

3866 RHYMES N' REASONS. Edinburgh: Reprographia, 1972.
Poems.

3867 THE JESUIT: A PLAY. Edinburgh: Paul Harris, 1976.
See also Campbell's "Bless You, John Ogilvie: A Sinner's Account of his Acquaintance with a Saint." SCOTTISH REVIEW, No. 4 (1976), 8-11.

3868 "Four Figures in a Personal Landscape." In JOCK TAMSON'S BAIRNS: ESSAYS ON A SCOTS CHILDHOOD. Ed. Trevor Royle. London: Hamish Hamilton, 1977, pp. 99-111.

3869 SOMERVILLE THE SOLDIER. Edinburgh: Paul Harris, 1978.
A play.

3870 BLETHER: A COLLECTION OF POEMS. Nottingham: Akros, 1979.

3871 THE WIDOWS OF CLYTH: A PLAY. Edinburgh: Paul Harris, 1979.

BIOGRAPHY AND CRITICISM

CA-69/72; CP (Alexander Scott).

3871a Mason, Leonard. TWO YOUNGER POETS: DUNCAN GLEN AND DONALD CAMPBELL. A STUDY OF THEIR SCOTS POETRY. Preston: Akros, 1976.

Bill Bryden (1942--)

Dramatist and producer.

3872 WILLIE ROUGH: A PLAY. Edinburgh: Southside, 1972.

3873 BENNY LYNCH: SCENES FROM A SHORT LIFE. A PLAY. Edinburgh: Southside, 1975.

3874 OLD MOVIES: A PLAY. London: Heinemann, for the National Theatre, 1977.

3875 "'Member 'At." In JOCK TAMSON'S BAIRNS: ESSAYS ON A SCOTS CHILDHOOD. Ed. Trevor Royle. London: Hamish Hamilton, 1977, pp. 78-87.

BIOGRAPHY AND CRITICISM

3876 Bold, Alan. "Bryden Meets Bold." SCOTIA REVIEW, No. 8 (1974), 9-16.

Section 6

POPULAR AND FOLK LITERATURE

This section deals with the popular and folk literature of Scotland. This literature is also treated separately in the ANNUAL BIBLIOGRAPHY OF SCOTTISH
LITERATURE and in the critical surveys provided by THE YEAR'S WORK IN
SCOTTISH LITERARY AND LINGUISTIC STUDIES (for details of these publications, see 11 and 12).

Popular literature is concerned mainly with chapbooks and broadsides. For a
definition of folk literature, see Professor David Buchan's note in SCOTTISH
LITERARY NEWS, 2 (1971-72), 116, where he comments on the four main
divisions by which that literature is normally classified: folk song, folk narrative, folk drama, and folk say. These are the headings adopted here.

Under each heading or subheading the works are arranged in chronological order.

A. POPULAR LITERATURE

Texts and Studies

3877 Fraser, John. THE HUMOROUS CHAP-BOOKS OF SCOTLAND. New York: H.L. Hinton, 1873.

3878 JOHN CHEAP, THE CHAPMAN'S LIBRARY: THE SCOTTISH CHAP LITERATURE OF THE LAST CENTURY. 3 vols. Glasgow, 1877-78; rpt., Detroit: Singing Tree Press, Gale Research Co., 1968.

3879 Graham, Dougal. THE COLLECTED WRITINGS OF DOUGAL GRAHAM, THE SKELLAT BELLMAN OF GLASGOW. Ed. George MacGregor. 2 vols. Glasgow, 1883; rpt. Detroit: Gale Research Co., 1968.

3880 Harvey, William. SCOTTISH CHAPBOOK LITERATURE. Paisley: Gardner, 1903; rpt. New York: Burt Franklin, 1971.

3881 Pinto, Vivian de Sola, and Allan Edwin Rodway, eds. THE COMMON MUSE: AN ANTHOLOGY OF POPULAR BRITISH BALLAD POETRY, 15TH-20TH CENTURY. London: Chatto and Windus, 1957; Harmondsworth: Penguin, 1965.

3882 Shepard, Leslie. THE BROADSIDE BALLAD: A STUDY IN ORIGINS AND MEANING. London: Jenkins, 1962.

3883 Parsons, Coleman O. "Chapbook Versions of the Waverley Novels." SSL, 3 (1965-66), 189-220.

3884 Collison, Robert. THE STORY OF STREET LITERATURE: FORERUNNER OF THE POPULAR PRESS. London: Dent, 1973.

3885 Shepard, Leslie. THE HISTORY OF STREET LITERATURE. Newton Abbot: David and Charles, 1973.

3886 Roy, G. Ross. "Some Notes on Scottish Chapbooks." SLJ, 1 (July 1974), 50-60.

3887 Holloway, John, and Joan Black, eds. LATER ENGLISH BROADSIDE BALLADS. London: Routledge and Kegan Paul, 1975.

3888 Preston, M.J., et al. "The Peace Egg Chapbooks in Scotland: An Analytic Approach to the Study of Chapbooks." BIBLIOTHECK, 8 (1976-77), 71-90.

3889 Neuberg, Victor E. POPULAR LITERATURE: A HISTORY AND A GUIDE. Harmondsworth: Penguin, 1977.

> A first-rate introduction to the subject. See also Neuberg's earlier books, THE PENNY HISTORIES (London: OUP, 1968), a study of chapbooks as children's literature, and POPULAR EDUCATION IN EIGHTEENTH-CENTURY ENGLAND (London: Woburn Press, 1971).

Bibliography

3890 Corson, James C. "Scott's Boyhood Collection of Chapbooks." BIBLIO-THECK, 3 (1960-62), 202-18.

3891 Ratcliffe, F.W. "Chapbooks with Scottish Imprints in the Robert White Collection, the University Library, Newcastle upon Tyne." BIBLIO-THECK, 4 (1963-66), 88-174.

3892 THE EUING COLLECTION OF ENGLISH BROADSIDE BALLADS IN THE LIBRARY OF THE UNIVERSITY OF GLASGOW. Introd. John Holloway. Glasgow: University of Glasgow, 1971.

3893 Thompson, Alastair R. "Chapbook Printers." BIBLIOTHECK, 6 (1971-73), 76-83.

3894 Neuberg, Victor E. CHAPBOOKS: A GUIDE TO REFERENCE MATERIAL ON ENGLISH, SCOTTISH AND AMERICAN CHAPBOOK LITERATURE OF THE EIGHTEENTH AND NINETEENTH CENTURIES. 2nd ed. London: Woburn Press, 1972.

B. FOLK LITERATURE

General Collections and Studies

3895 Chambers, Robert. POPULAR RHYMES OF SCOTLAND. Edinburgh, 1826; new ed., Edinburgh: Chambers, 1870; rpt. Detroit: Singing Tree Press, Gale Research Co., 1969.

3896 Henderson, William. NOTES ON THE FOLK-LORE OF THE NORTHERN COUNTIES OF ENGLAND AND THE BORDERS. London: Folk-Lore Society, 1879; rpt. New York: Kraus, 1967.

> Much Scottish material is included.

3897 Gregor, Walter. NOTES ON THE FOLK-LORE OF THE NORTHEAST OF SCOTLAND. London: Folk-Lore Society, 1881; rpt. New York: Kraus, 1967.

Popular and Folk Literature

3898 Black, George F. COUNTY FOLK-LORE III. THE ORKNEY AND SHET-
LAND ISLANDS. London: Folk-Lore Society, 1901; rpt. New York:
Kraus, 1967.

3899 Rymour Club, Edinburgh. MISCELLANEA. 2 vols. Edinburgh: Privately
Printed. Vol. 1, 1906-11; vol. 2, 1912-19. Vol. 3, published as
TRANSACTIONS. Edinburgh: Privately Printed, 1928.

All three volumes reprinted as a set, Norwood, Pa.: Norwood
Editions, 1973.

3900 Simpkins, John Ewart. COUNTY FOLK-LORE VII. FIFE, CLACKMAN-
NAN AND KINROSS-SHIRE. London: Folk-Lore Society, 1912; rpt.
New York: Kraus, 1967.

3901 Briggs, Katherine M. A DICTIONARY OF BRITISH FOLK-TALES. 4
vols. London: Routledge and Kegan Paul, 1970-71.

An encyclopedic work of reference.

3902 TOCHER. Edinburgh: University of Edinburgh, School of Scottish Studies,
1971-- . Quarterly.

This journal prints tales, music, and songs from the school's
archives. The school's older periodical, SCOTTISH STUDIES,
continues to print articles and texts that deserve and are given
more extensive commentary.

3903 Marwick, Ernest W. THE FOLKLORE OF ORKNEY AND SHETLAND.
London: Batsford, 1975.

3904 Fenton, Alexander. SCOTTISH COUNTRY LIFE. Edinburgh: John Donald, 1976.

3905 Kirk, Robert. THE SECRET COMMONWEALTH, AND A SHORT TREATISE
OF CHARMS AND SPELS. Ed. Stewart F. Sanderson. Cambridge: Brewer,
for the Folk-Lore Society, 1976.

A critical edition of the account written by the minister of Aber-
foyle at the end of the seventeenth century, and first published
in 1815.

Folk Song (Including the Ballads)

COLLECTIONS

3906 [Herd, David]. ANCIENT AND MODERN SCOTTISH SONGS. 2 vols.
Edinburgh, 1776; Glasgow: Kerr and Richardson, 1869; rpt. Edinburgh:
Scottish Academic Press, 1973.

3907 Scott, Sir Walter. MINSTRELSY OF THE SCOTTISH BORDER. 2 vols.
Kelso, 1802; vol. 3, Edinburgh, 1803. Ed. Thomas F. Henderson. 4
vols. Edinburgh: Blackwood, 1902. Ed. Thomas Henderson. London:
Harrap, 1931.

Among critical studies of the MINSTRELSY the following may be noted:

3908 Dobie, Marryat Ross. "The Development of Scott's MINSTRELSY: An
Attempt at a Reconstruction." TRANSACTIONS OF THE EDINBURGH
BIBLIOGRAPHICAL SOCIETY, 2 (1946), 65-87.

3909 Wood, Harriet Harvey. "Scott and Jamieson: The Relationship between
Two Ballad Collectors." SSL, 9 (1971-72), 71-96.

3910 Zug, Charles G., III. "The Ballad Editor as Antiquary: Scott and the
MINSTRELSY." JOURNAL OF THE FOLKLORE INSTITUTE, 13 (1976),
57-73.

3911 Stevenson, Thomas G. CHOICE OLD SCOTTISH BALLADS. Edinburgh:
Stevenson, 1868; rpt. Wakefield: E.P., 1976.

A collected edition of four earlier collections: Charles Kirk-
patrick Sharpe's A BALLAD BOOK (1823), James Maidment's A
NORTH COUNTRIE GARLAND (1824), George Ritchie Kinloch's
THE BALLAD BOOK (1827), and James Maidment's A NEW
BOOK OF BALLADS (1844).

3912 Crawfurd, Andrew. ANDREW CRAWFURD'S COLLECTION OF BALLADS
AND SONGS. Ed. Emily B. Lyle. Edinburgh: STS, 1975-- .

Andrew Crawford (1786-1854) was an antiquary who left a considerable amount of manuscript material.

3913 Child, Francis J. THE ENGLISH AND SCOTTISH POPULAR BALLADS.
5 vols. 1882-98; rpt. [in 2 vols.] New York: Folklore Press, 1957;
rpt. [in 5 vols.] New York: Cooper Square, 1965.

The definitive collection. There is a convenient one-volume
edition by H.C. Sargent and G.L. Kittredge (1904), with a
long introduction.

3914 Greig, Gavin. FOLK-SONG OF THE NORTH-EAST. Aberdeen, 1907-
11; rpt. Hatboro, Pa.: Folklore Associates, 1963.

3915 _____ . LAST LEAVES OF TRADITIONAL BALLADS AND BALLAD AIRS.
Ed. Alexander Keith. Aberdeen: Buchan Club, 1925.

3916 Ord, John. THE BOTHY SONGS AND BALLADS OF ABERDEEN, BANFF AND MORAY, ANGUS AND THE MEARNS. Paisley: Gardner, 1930; rpt. Edinburgh: John Donald, 1973.

3917 Beattie, William. BORDER BALLADS. Harmondsworth: Penguin, 1952.

An excellent introductory selection.

3918 Leach, MacEdward. THE BALLAD BOOK. New York: Barnes; London: Yoseloff, 1955.

3919 Friedman, Albert B. THE VIKING BOOK OF FOLK BALLADS OF THE ENGLISH-SPEAKING WORLD. New York: Viking Press, 1956; issued as THE PENGUIN BOOK OF FOLK BALLADS OF THE ENGLISH-SPEAK-ING WORLD, Harmondsworth: Penguin, 1978.

With the musical airs.

3920 Bronson, Bertrand H. THE TRADITIONAL TUNES OF THE CHILD BAL-LADS, WITH THEIR TEXTS. 4 vols. Princeton: Princeton University Press, 1959-72

3921 Hodgart, Matthew J.C. THE FABER BOOK OF BALLADS. London: Faber, 1965.

3922 Buchan, David. A SCOTTISH BALLAD BOOK. London: Routledge and Kegan Paul, 1973.

3923 Buchan, Norman, and Peter Hall. THE SCOTTISH FOLKSINGER: 118 MODERN AND TRADITIONAL FOLKSONGS. London: Collins, 1973.

A collection of songs, mainly texts recorded this century, includ-ing "great ballads, moving love songs and the cheeky derisory songs of the streets."

STUDIES

3924 Entwistle, William J. EUROPEAN BALLADRY. Oxford: Clarendon Press, 1939; 2nd impression corrected, 1951.

3925 Hodgart, Matthew J.C. THE BALLADS. London: Hutchinson, 1950; rev. ed., 1962

3926 Leach, MacEdward, and Tristram P. Coffin, eds. THE CRITICS AND THE BALLAD. Carbondale: Southern Illinois University Press, 1961.

3927 Muir, Willa. LIVING WITH BALLADS. London: Hogarth Press, 1965.

3928 Collinson, Francis. THE TRADITIONAL AND NATIONAL MUSIC OF SCOTLAND. London: Routledge and Kegan Paul, 1966.

3929 Buchan, David. THE BALLAD AND THE FOLK. London: Routledge and Kegan Paul, 1972.

3930 Lyle, Emily B., ed. BALLAD STUDIES. Cambridge: Brewer, for the Folklore Society, 1976.

3931 Cameron, David Kerr. THE BALLAD AND THE PLOUGH: A PORTRAIT OF THE LIFE OF THE OLD SCOTTISH FARMTOUNS. London: Gollancz, 1978.

3932 Murison, David D. "The Language of the Ballads." SLJ, suppl. 6 (1978), 54-64.

Folk Narrative

3933 Chambers, Robert. POPULAR RHYMES OF SCOTLAND. Edinburgh, 1826; new ed., Edinburgh: Chambers, 1870; rpt. Detroit: Singing Tree Press, Gale Research Co., 1969.

3934 Douglas, Sir George. SCOTTISH FAIRY AND FOLK TALES. London: Walter Scott, 1893; rpt. Wakefield: E.P., 1977.

The stories are well chosen, but unfortunately rewritten in Victorian-English prose.

3935 Buchan, Peter. ANCIENT SCOTTISH TALES: AN UNPUBLISHED COLLECTION. Peterhead: Buchan Field Club, 1908; rpt. Darby, Pa.: Norwood Editions, 1973.

3936 TOCHER. Edinburgh: University of Edinburgh, School of Scottish Studies, 1971-- . Quarterly.

This journal prints tales from the school's archives.

3937 Aitken, Hannah. A FORGOTTEN HERITAGE: ORIGINAL FOLK TALES OF LOWLAND SCOTLAND. Edinburgh: Scottish Academic Press, 1973.

3938 Lewis, Mary Ellen. "Burns' 'Tale o' Truth,' a Legend in Literature." JOURNAL OF THE FOLKLORE INSTITUTE, 13 (1976), 241-62.

Folk Drama and Play

3939 Mill, Anna J. MEDIAEVAL PLAYS IN SCOTLAND. Edinburgh: Blackwood, 1927.

A pioneer work that still holds its place after more than fifty years.

3940 Banks, Mary Macleod. BRITISH CALENDAR CUSTOMS: SCOTLAND. 3 vols. London: Folk-Lore Society, 1937–41; rpt. New York: Kraus, 1967.

Includes local and seasonal festivals and games.

3941 _____. BRITISH CALENDAR CUSTOMS: ORKNEY AND SHETLAND. London: Folk-Lore Society, 1946; rpt. New York: Kraus, 1967.

3942 Opie, Iona, and Peter Opie. THE LORE AND LANGUAGE OF SCHOOL CHILDREN. Oxford: Clarendon Press, 1959.

Includes some Scottish material.

3943 Ritchie, James T.R. THE SINGING STREET. Edinburgh: Oliver and Boyd, 1964.

3944 Opie, Iona, and Peter Opie. CHILDREN'S GAMES IN STREET AND PLAYGROUND. Oxford: Clarendon Press, 1969.

Includes Scottish material from Langholm to Whalsay.

3945 Mill, Anna J. "The Records of Scots Medieval Plays: Interpretations and Misinterpretations." In BARDS AND MAKARS: SCOTTISH LANGUAGE AND LITERATURE, MEDIEVAL AND RENAISSANCE. Ed. Adam Jack Aitken et al. Glasgow: University of Glasgow Press, 1977, pp. 136–42.

Folk Say: Proverbs

COLLECTIONS

3946 Fergusson, David. FERGUSSON'S SCOTTISH PROVERBS. Ed. Erskine Beveridge. Edinburgh: STS, 1924.

A collection made in the second half of the sixteenth century, and first printed in 1641.

3947 Carmichaell, James. THE JAMES CARMICHAELL COLLECTION OF PROVERBS IN SCOTS. Ed. Mark L. Anderson. Edinburgh: Edinburgh University Press, 1957.

A collection made before 1628, previously unpublished.

3948 Kelly, James. A COMPLETE COLLECTION OF SCOTTISH PROVERBS. London, 1721; rpt. Folcroft, Pa.: Folcroft Library Editions, 1976.

3949 Ramsay, Allan. A COLLECTION OF SCOTS PROVERBS. Edinburgh, 1737.

> Included in THE WORKS OF ALLAN RAMSAY, vol. 5, ed. Alexander M. Kinghorn and Alexander Law (Edinburgh: STS, 1972).

3950 Henderson, Andrew. SCOTTISH PROVERBS. Edinburgh, 1832; ed. James Donald, Glasgow: Morison, 1881; rpt. Detroit: Gale Research Co., 1969.

3951 Hislop, Alexander. THE PROVERBS OF SCOTLAND. Glasgow, 1862; 3rd ed. rev., Edinburgh: Hislop, 1868; rpt. Detroit: Gale Research Co., 1968.

3952 Cheviot, Andrew. PROVERBS, PROVERBIAL EXPRESSIONS AND POPU-LAR RHYMES OF SCOTLAND. Paisley: Gardner, 1896; rpt. Detroit: Gale Research Co., 1969.

3953 Fenton, Alexander. "Proverbs and Sayings from the Auchterless Area of Aberdeenshire." SCOTTISH STUDIES, 3 (1959), 39-71.

3954 Sanderson, Stewart F., and Calum I. Maclean. "A Collection of Riddles from Shetland." SCOTTISH STUDIES, 4 (1960), 150-86.

STUDIES

3955 Murison, David D. "The Scots Tongue: The Folk Speech." FOLKLORE, 75 (1964), 37-47.

3956 Parsons, Coleman O. "Scottish Proverb Books." SSL, 8 (1970-71), 194-205.

AUTHOR INDEX

This index includes all authors, editors, compilers, translators, and other contributors to works cited in the text. Secondary authors <u>only</u> are included; for <u>main</u> <u>authors</u> refer to the Subject Index. References are to entry numbers (unless preceded by a "p.") and alphabetization is letter by letter.

A

Abbott, Claude Colleer 699
Aberdein, Jennie W. 1104
Aird, Thomas 1327
Aitken, Adam Jack 86, 87, 95, 103, 183, 185, 189, 272, 292, 302, 316, 402, 411, 3945
Aitken, George A. 502
Aitken, Hannah 3937
Aitken, James M. 334
Aitken, William R. 162, 780, 1876, 2623, 2666, 2697, 2700-2702, 2886, 2893, 2963, 2999, 3469
Alaya, Flavia 1684
Aldington, Richard 2129
Aldis, Harry G. 223, 471
Aldrich, Ruth I. 1114
Alexander, John Huston 1018
Alexander, Patrick P. 1487
Alison, James N. 68
Allan, John R. 3059, 3080
Allardyce, Alexander 448, 1128
Altick, Richard D. 1265
Amours, François Joseph 200, 241
Anderson, James 997
Anderson, James Maitland 335
Anderson, Mark L. 3947
Anderson, William Eric Kinloch 790, 973, 1028, 1651, 1817, 1854
Angellier, Auguste 748

B

Annand, James King 1901, 3202, 3639
Archer, Charles 1699
Armstrong, Richard 1231
Asquith, Cynthia 1848
Auden, Wystan Hugh 1188, 1421

Backscheider, Paula R. 629
Bailey, Margery 680
Baker, Denys Val 2987
Balfour, Graham 1623
Balfour-Melville, Evan W.M. 246
Banks, Mary Macleod 3940-41
Bannister, Winifred 1930, 2166, 2578, 3176
Baring-Gould, William Stuart 1756, 1764
Barke, James 443
Barker, Gerard A. 712
Barnes, Robert J. 1225
Barrie, James Matthew 790
Barrow, Geoffrey W.S. 218, 235, 400
Bateson, Frederick W. 4
Batho, Edith C. 903
Batty, Archibald 2574
Bawcutt, Priscilla 1, 291, 298, 301
Baxter, John Walker 285
Bayne, Peter 1338, 1341
Beasley, Jerry C. 613

349

Author Index

Beattie, Lester M. 503
Beattie, William 1052
Beattie, William (librarian) 740, 3917
Bedient, Calvin 3513
Bell, Alan 13, 1012, 1110, 1125-26, 1139
Bellenden, John 198
Benger, Elizabeth O. 861
Bennett, Charles H. 683
Besterman, Theodore 824, 1669
Beveridge, Erskine 3946
Binding, Paul 1619
Bingham, Madeleine 217
Birdie, James 3007
Birkin, Andrew 1855
Black, David M. 1901, 3788
Black, George F. 14, 3898
Black, Joan 3887
Blackie, Agnes A.C. 819
Blake, George 790, 1650, 1794, 1816, 1847, 1891, 2094-95, 2143
Blake, William 518
Blessington, Lady 1192
Bliss, Trudy 1288-89
Bloomfield, Barry C. 1966, 1972
Bloomfield, Paul 2040
Boege, Fred W. 595
Boece, Hector 318
Bold, Alan 1926, 3465, 3560, 3669, 3876
Booth, Bradford A. 1119
Boston, Richard 420
Boucé, Paul-Gabriel 605-07
Boyd, Elizabeth F. 1201
Bradbury, Malcolm 3591
Bradlaugh, Charles p. 149
Bradley, Philip 1029
Brand, Jack 1946
Brander, Laurence 739
Brend, Gavin 1761
Bridie, James 3007
Brie, Friedrich 179
Briggs, Asa 854, 1362
Briggs, Katherine M. 3901
Brisbane, Thomas 1489
Bronson, Bertrand H. 3920
Brooks, Alfred Russell 693, 695
Broom, John L. 1894, 2961
Brown, David 1019
Brown, George Douglas 790
Brown, George Mackay 2517
Brown, Gordon 1944

Brown, Ian 251
Brown, James 174
Brown, Jennifer M. 186, 221
Brown, Oliver 2658
Brown, Peter Hume 129, 327, 331, 340
Brown, Thomas 1042
Browning, David C. 114
Bruce, Donald 600
Bruce, George 1896, 1922, 2511, 2884, 2891, 3380, 3640, 3704, 3858
Brunton, Alexander 1058
Buchan, David 696, 1116, 3642, 3922, 3929
Buchan, John 60, 426, 981, 2093
Buchan, Norman 3923
Buchan, Peter 3935
Buchan, Susan 2236, 2238
Buchanan, David 696
Buchanan-Brown, John 21
Budge, Donald M. 3078, 3665
Bulloch, James 139-41
Bulloch, John Malcolm 1429
Burgess, Moira 781, 1879
Burleigh, John H.S. 138
Burns, Robert 442-43
Burton, John Hill 615
Bushnell, George Herbert 1558
Bushnell, Nelson S. 544, 992-93, 1138
Butcher, S.H. 1543
Buthlay, Kenneth 411, 2661, 2677, 2685, 3468
Butter, Peter H. 2510, 2512, 2514
Buxton, John 1216

C

Caird, James B. 38, 1129, 1896, 2985
Calder, Angus 928, 1000
Calder, Grace J. 1301
Calder, Jenni 1000, 1618, 1638
Caldwell, Elsie N. 1628
Calvert, William J. 1197
Cameron, David Kerr 3931
Cameron, James Kerr 339
Cammell, Charles Richard 1939, 2057
Campbell, Donald 3194, 3235
Campbell, Hilbert H. 541
Campbell, Ian 790, 796, 911, 1020, 1116, 1253, 1273, 1312, 1317, 1428, 1479, 1509, 1637, 1651, 1817, 1854, 2146-47, 2994, 3173

Telfer, John 720
Temple, Ruth Z. 1864, p. 192
Tennyson, George B. 1277, 1308
Thin, James 836
Thompson, Alastair R. 808, 3370, 3893
Thompson, Alexander Hamilton 1162
Thompson, Harold W. 707, 710
Thomson, Derick S. 674-75
Thomson, George p. 80
Thomson, Thomas 106, 352
Thornton, Robert D. 762, 1900
Thorslev, Peter L. 1212
Tillyard, Eustace M.W. 261
Timothy, Hamilton B. 1113
Tinker, Chauncey Brewster 686, 689
Tobin, Terence 430-32, 496
Todd, William Burton 461, 565, 571, 634
Tominaga, Thomas 3597
Tomlinson, Henry Major 2127
Tonge, John 154
Tough, William 406
Townsend, James B. 1725
Traill, Henry D. 1275
Tredrey, Frank D. 821
Trelawny, Edward J. 1193
Trueblood, Paul G. 1202
Tschiffely, Aimé Felix 2039, 2044
Tucker, Martin 1864, p. 192
Tunney, Hubert J. 618
Turberville, Ruby 2965
Turnbull, Andrew 1722
Turner, Arthur C. 2239

U

Ungar, Frederick 1869, 1900
Urquhart, Fred 72, 1932, 1936
Usborne, Richard 2240

V

Valdimir, John 560
Van Arsdel, Rosemary T. 840
Vann, J. Don 840
VaValley, Albert J. 1309
Veitch, James 2144
Venables, Terry 3844

Vickers, Brian 701
Vinson, James 1865-67, p. 192
Visiak, E.H. 2326
Von Hendy, Andrew 250
Vulliamy, Colwyn Edward 690

W

Wagner, Geoffrey 2988-89, 2999
Waingrow, Marshall 1622
Wakeman, John 118-19, 1870, 2053-54, p. 192
Walker, Hugh 1483
Walker, Ian C. 232, 482
Walker, Imogene B. 1507
Walker, John 2041, 2053-54
Walker, Marshall 3624
Walker, Ralph S. 337, 660-61
Wallace, William 736, 744
Waller, Alfred R. 39
Ward, Adolphus W. 39
Warrack, Alexander 100
Warrender, Margaret 1360
Waterston, Elizabeth 1087
Watson, George 1, 79
Watson, James 439
Watson, John Richard 800
Watson, Roderick 2686, 3234, 3810
Watson, William J. 96
Watt, Donald E.R. 109
Watt, Lauchlan Maclean 299, 1484
Wattie, Margaret 517
Watts, Cedric 2049, 2052
Webb, Keith 1945
Webster, Adam Blyth 1577
Webster, Bruce 219
Wedgwood, C.V. 427
Weinstein, Mark A. 969, 1381
Weir, John Lowe 425, 727
Welsh, Alexander 991
West, Herbert Faulkner 2043, 2051
Weston, John C. 171, 2629, 2660
Whatley, Christopher A. 1117
White, James H. 1910, 1966
Whittaker, R. 3596
Whittington, Graeme 2995
Wiles, A.G.D. 388
Wilkins, William Henry 728
Willcock, John 422
Williams, Ioan 966

TITLE INDEX

This index includes titles of books and journals cited in the text. In some cases titles have been shortened. References are to entry numbers (unless preceded by a "p.") and alphabetization is letter by letter.

A

Abbess of Crewe, The 3583
Abbot, The 937
Aberdeen University Press, 1840-1963 816
Aberdeen University Review 1955
About the Theatre 1688
Above Your Heads 2282
Abstracts of English Studies 8
Accessions of Scottish Literary Manuscripts, National Library of Scotland 13
Account of Corsica, The Journal of a Tour to That Island and Memoirs of Pascal Paoli, The 678
Achievement of Walter Scott, The 1001
Acreage of the Heart, The 3427
Acre of Grass, An 3113
Across the Barricades 3820
Across the Plains with Other Memories and Essays 1604
Actis and Deidis of the Illustere and Vailzeand Campioun Schir William Wallace, Knight of Ellerslie, The 273
Actors across the Volga 3030
Adam and Charles Black, 1807-1957 818

Adam Smith: A System of Social Science 642
Adam Smith and the Scotland of His Day 639
Admirable Crichton, The 1827
Admirable Urquhart, The 420
Admiral Guinea 1605
Adonis, Attis, Osiris 1652
Advancing Day, The 3516
Adventures among Books 1570
Adventures in Two Worlds 2753
Adventures of an Aide-de-Camp 1383
Adventures of Frederick, Count Fathom, The 577-78
Adventures of Gerard 1742
Adventures of Monsieur de Mailly 2322
Adventures of Peregrine Pickle, The 575-76
Adventures of Roderick Random, The 573-74
Adventures of Sherlock Holmes, The 1732
Adversary, The 2452
Aegean Memories 2406
African Heroes 2850
Africans, The 2853
Aftermath 1665
Afterwards, and Other Stories 1646

Title Index

Mirror of the Ministry in Modern
Novels, A 2763
Miscellanea of the Rymour Club 3899
Miscellaneous Plays 865
Miscellaneous Prose Works 959
Miscellanies in Prose and Verse 501
Missionaries, The 3354
Miss Marjoribanks 1464-65
Miss Oona McQuarrie 1486
Miss Pym Disposes 2786
MLA International Bibliography 7
Modern Conquistador, A 2043
Modern Fantasy 1426
Modern Scot, The 1966
Modern Scots Verse, 1922-1977 1928
Modern Scottish Literature 1887
Modern Scottish Literature: A
Popular Guide-Book Catalogue
1874
Modern Scottish Poetry: An Anthol-
ogy of the Scottish Renaissance
1916, 1920, 1927
Modern Scottish Short Stories 1936
Modern Scottish Theatre, The 1902
Modern Scottish Writers 1697, 1723,
1774, 1842, 2140
Modern Writer and His World, The
3475
Mogreb-el-Acksa 2011
Moment's Monuments, The 2255
Monarchick Tragedies, The 381
Monarch of the Glen, The 2409
Monarchs and the Muse 209
Monastery, The 936
Money from Holme 3152
Monk of Fife, A 1559
Montrose 426, 2212
Montrose: For Covenant and King
428
Montrose: The Captain-General
3245
Moon Endureth, The 2194
Moral Basis of Politics, The 2816
Moral Plays 2576
Mordaunt 649-50
More Collected Poems (Cruickshank)
2480
More Collected Poems (MacDiarmid)
2660
More Poetic Gems 1491

More Songs of Angus and Others
2068
Morning Tide 2590
Mortimer Touch, The 2934
Moss Troopers, The 1814
Mountain and Flood 2722
Mountain Bard, The 877
Mountain Lovers, The 1671
Mountain Meadow 2233
Mountain Songs 2737
Mouth Music 3628
Mouth of Truth, The 3606
Mr. Alfred, M.A. 3272
Mr. & Mrs. J.L. Stoddart at Home
3802
Mr. Bolfry 2558-60
Mr. Bridie's Alphabet for Little
Glasgow Highbrows 2539
Mr. Buchan, Writer 2239
Mr. Byculla 2928
Mr. Carlyle: My Patient 1302
Mr. Gillie 2571
Mr. Roosevelt 2413
Mrs. Barry 2305
Mrs. Fry Has a Visitor 2770,
2779
Mrs. Grundy in Scotland 2585
Mrs. Ritchie 2584
Mrs. Ross 3328
Mr. Standfast 2201
Mungo's Dream 3122
Murder for Pleasure 3167
Muriel Spark (Kemp) 3592
Muriel Spark (Malkoff) 3590
Muriel Spark (Massie) 3595
Muriel Spark (Stanford) 3588
Musical Chair, A 2405
Music and Society in Lowland Scot-
land in the Eighteenth Century
458
Music for the Journey 3333
My Dear Holmes 1761
My Friend Annie 3278
My Friend Cousin Emmie 3284
My Friend Flora 3281
My Friend Madame Zora 3282
My Friend Martha's Aunt 3280
My Friend Monica 3277
My Friend Muriel 3276
My Friend My Father 3287

O

Title Index

Works (Fowler) 368
Works (Galt) 1100
Works (Home) 626
Works (Mackenzie) 491
Works (Mure) 406
Works (North) 1155
Works (Ramsay) 510
Works (Smollett) 589
Works (Stevenson) 1613-15
Works (Urquhart) 418
Works of Allan Ramsay, The 3949
Works of Ossian, The 669
Works of Robert Burns, with an Account of His Life and a Criticism on His Writings, The 733
Works of Sir David Lindsay of the Mount, The 304
World Authors: 1950-1970 118, 1870, p. 192
World Authors: 1970-1975 119, 1870, p. 192
World His Pillow, The 3060
World of Ice, The 1435
World's Desire, The 1557
World's Room, The 3316
World's Wonder, The 3439
Worship of Nature, The 1659
Wotton Reinfred 1274
Would-Be Saint, A 3368
Wrecker, The 1606
Writing of PAST AND PRESENT, The 1301
Writings of Fiona Macleod, The 1682
Writ in Sand 2035
Wrong Box, The 1603

Y

Yale Editions of the Private Papers of James Boswell, The 688
Year of Space, A 2935
Year of the Short Corn, and Other Stories, The 3386
Year of the Whale, The 3646
Year's Work in English Studies, The 5
Year's Work in Scottish Literary and Linguistic Studies, The 12
Yellow Frigate, or the Three Sisters, The 1387
You May Well Ask 2861
Young Alexander the Great, The 2838
Young Alfred the Great, The 2843
Young Art and Old Hector 2604
Young Auchinleck 3184
Young Barbarians 1647
Young Boswell 689
Young Fur Traders, The 1431
Young Malcolm 2706
Young Montrose, The 3244
Young Pattullo 3123
Young Traveller in France, The 3437
Youth's Encounter 2364

Z

Zeluco 646
Zoo-Illogical Rhymes 3436

SUBJECT INDEX

In addition to topics, this index includes all names of <u>main authors</u> cited in the text. Alphabetization is letter by letter and references are to entry number (unless preceded by "p."). Main areas within a subject have been underlined.

A

Aberdeen University Press 816
Aitken, Hannah 3330-34
Akros (publishers), checklist of publications from 2699
Alexander, Sir William (1567?-1640)
   biography and criticism of 386-88
   writings by 380-85
Alexander, William (1826-94)
   biography and criticism of 1450
   writings by 1446-49
Allan, John Robertson 3077-85
Allegory
   Lindsay's use of 2331
   Gibbon's use of 2991
   Alexander Montgomerie's use of 358
   Thomson's use of 532-33
Andrew of Wyntoun 241
Angus, Marion
   biography and criticism of 2110
   writings by 2103-09
Annand, James King
   biography and criticism of 3201-02
   writings by 3195-3200
Arbuthnot, John
   biography and criticism of 503
   writings by 501-02
Archer, William
   biography and criticism 1697-1700
   writings by 1686-96
Association for Scottish Literary
     Studies 167

Ayton, Sir Robert
   biography and criticism of
     391-392
   writings by 389-90
Aytoun, William Edmondstoune
   biography and criticism of
     1379-81
   writings by 1369-78

B

Baillie, Joanna
   biography and criticism of 871-72
   writings by 862-70
Ballads. See Songs (including folk
     songs and ballads)
Ballantyne, Robert Michael
   bibliography on 1445
   biography and criticism of
     1443-44
   writings by 1430-42
Barbour, John
   bibliography on 236
   biography and criticism of
     231-35
   writings by 227-30
Barke, James
   biography and criticism of 3069
   writings by 3060-68
Barnard, Lady Anne 727-29
Barrie, Sir James Matthew 790
   bibliography on 1856-58
   biography and criticism of 1842-55

writings by 1818-41
Baxter, Charles, correspondence with
Stevenson 1622
Beattie, James
bibliography on 664
biography and criticism of 662-63
writings by 656-61
Bellenden, John
biography and criticism of 318-19
writings by 317-18
Black, Adam and Charles (publishers)
817-18
Black, William
biography and criticism of 1541
writings by 1526-40
Blackie and Son (publishers) 819
Blackwood (publishers) 820-22
Blair, Robert
biography and criticism of 520-22
writings by 518-19
Blake, George
biography and criticism of 2731
writings by 2704-30
Blank verse, of Blair 518
Blind Harry. See Harry the Minstrel
Boswell, James
bibliography on 697-99
biography and criticism of 689-96
writings by 677-88
Brandane, John
biography and criticism of 2166
writings by 2149-65
Bridie, James
biography and criticism of 2577-81
writings by 2523-76
Broadsides. See Songs (including folk
songs and ballads)
Brown (booksellers) 823
Brown, George Douglas
biography and criticism of
2136, 2138-48
writings by 2135-37
Brown, George Mackay
biography and criticism of 3666-69
writings by 3644-65
Browning, Robert, correspondence with
Carlyle 1287
Bruce, George
biography and criticism of 3223
writings by 3216-22

Bruce, Michael
biography and criticism of 715
writings by 713-14
Brunton, Mary 1056-58
Bryden, Bill
biography and criticism of 3876
writings by 3872-75
Buchan, Anna. See Douglas, O.
Buchan, John
bibliography on 2245
biography and criticism of 2238-44
writings by 2184-2237
Buchanan, George
bibliography on 335-36
biography and criticism 331-34
writings by 327-30
Buchanan, Robert Williams
biography and criticism on 1524-25
writings by 1510-23
BUIK OF ALEXANDER, THE 237
Burns, Robert
bibliography and reference works on
769-73
biography and criticism of 29,
436, 747-68, 897, 2651
writings by 442-43, 730-46
Byron, George Gordon
bibliography and reference works on
1224-29
biography and criticism of 1191-
1223
writings by 1159-90

C

Cadell and Davies (publishers) 824
Calvin, Henry. See Hanley, Clifford
Campbell, Donald
biography and criticism of 3871a
writings by 3866-71
Campbell, Thomas
biography and criticism of 1052-55
writings by 1045-51
Carlyle, Alexander 615-16
Carlyle, Jane Welsh
biography of 1304
correspondence of 1279, 1283-84,
1286, 1288-89, 1291
Carlyle, Thomas
bibliography on 1318-20

Glen, Duncan
  bibliography on 3812
  biography and criticism of 3809-11
  writings by 3789-3808
Goethe, Johann Wolfgang von, cor-
    respondence with Carlyle
    1282
Graham, Dougal 3879
Graham, James, Marquis of Montrose
  biography and criticism of 426-28
  writings by 425
Graham, Robert Bontine Cunning-
    hame
  bibliography on 2050-54
  biography and criticism of 2043-49
  writings by 2009-42
Graham, William Sydney
  biography and criticism of 3513-15
  writings by 3504-12
Grahame, Kenneth
  biography and criticism of 1774-78
  writings by 1768-73
Grammar. See Language and linguis-
    tics (dialect, grammar,
    etc.)
Grant, James
  biography and criticism of 1395-96
  writings by 1382-94
Gray, Sir Alexander
  biography and criticism of 2360
  writings by 2349-59
Grieve, Christopher Murray. See
    MacDiarmid, Hugh
GUDE AND GODLIE BALLATIS, THE
    324-25
  criticism of 326
Guiccioli, Teresa, relationship with
    Byron 1203
Gunn, Neil Miller
  bibliography on 2623
  biography and criticism of 2619-22
  writings by 2588-618

H

Haliburton, Hugh. See Robertson,
    James Logie
Hamilton, Elizabeth
  biography and criticism of 861
  writings by 860

Hamilton, William
  biography and criticism of 544
  writings by 542-43
Hanley, Clifford 3670-88
Harry the Minstrel
  bibliography on 277
  biography and criticism of 232,
    275-76
  writings by 273-74
Hay, George Campbell
  biography and criticism of 3488
  writings by 3484-87
Hay, John MacDougall
  biography and criticism of 2346-48
  writings by 2343-45
Henderson, Hamish
  biography and criticism of 3600-3601
  writings by 3598-99
Hendry, James Findlay 3343-48
Henryson, Robert
  bibliography on 170
  biography and criticism of 260-72
  writings by 254-59
Herd, David 446
Heroes, of Byron 1212
Hogg, James
  bibliography on 903
  biography and criticism of 902-12
  writings by 876-901
Home, John
  bibliography on 630
  biography and criticism of 627-29
  writings by 617-26
Hume, Alexander
  biography and criticism of 366-67
  writings by 365
Hume, David
  bibliography on 570-72
  biography and criticism of 563-69
  writings by 545-62

I

Imagery, Dunbar's use of 291
Innes, Michael. See Stewart, John
    Innes Mackintosh
Italy, influence on Scottish literature
    184, 369-70

J

Jacob, Violet 2058-75